THE REVOLUTIONARY WRITINGS OF

John Adams

Selected and with a Foreword by C. Bradley Thompson

LIBERTY FUND

INDIANAPOLIS

This book is published by Liberty Fund, Inc., a foundation established to encourage study of the ideal of a society of free and responsible individuals.

 ⬚⬚⬚

The cuneiform inscription that serves as our logo and as the design motif for our endpapers is the earliest-known written appearance of the word "freedom" (*amagi*), or "liberty." It is taken from a clay document written about 2300 B.C. in the Sumerian city-state of Lagash.

© 2000 Liberty Fund, Inc. All rights reserved.
Frontispiece from Corbis-Bettmann.

Printed in the United States of America

C 10 9 8 7 6 5 4 3
P 10 9 8 7 6 5 4

Library of Congress Cataloging-in-Publication Data

Adams, John, 1735–1826.
    The revolutionary writings of John Adams/selected and with a foreword by
    C. Bradley Thompson.
       p.   cm.
    Includes bibliographical references and index.
    ISBN 0-86597-284-2 (alk. paper)—ISBN 0-86597-285-0 (pbk.: alk. paper)
    1. United States—Politics and government—1775–1783. 2. Massachusetts—
Politics and government—1775–1783. I. Thompson, C. Bradley. II. Title.
E302.A262 2000
973.4′4′092—dc21   99-046495

Liberty Fund, Inc.
8335 Allison Pointe Trail, Suite 300
Indianapolis, Indiana 46250-1684

Fiat Justitia ruat Coelum

[Let justice be done though the heavens should fall]

John Adams to Elbridge Gerry
December 6, 1777

To Henry, Samuel, and Islay

Contents

Contents

FOREWORD

Modern scholars of the American Revolution have published countless books on Thomas Jefferson, James Madison, Alexander Hamilton, Benjamin Franklin, and George Washington. Surprisingly, John Adams has not fared so well. On the whole, historians have neglected Adams's Revolutionary thought, and a one-volume collection of his political writings has not been available for several decades. This anomaly in the scholarly literature is curious because Adams is often regarded as the most learned and penetrating thinker of the founding generation, and his central role in the American Revolution is universally recognized. Benjamin Rush thought there was a consensus among the generation of 1776 that Adams possessed "more learning probably, both ancient and modern, than any man who subscribed the Declaration of Independence." Another contemporary is reported to have said that "The man to whom the country is most indebted for the great measure of independence is Mr. John Adams. . . . I call him the Atlas of American independence."[1]

John Adams witnessed the American Revolution from beginning to end: he assisted James Otis in the Writs of Assistance case in 1761, and he participated in negotiating the peace treaty with Britain in 1783. As a Revolutionary statesman, he will always be remembered as an important leader of the radical political movement in Boston and as one of the earliest and most principled voices for independence in the Continental Congress. Likewise, as a public intellectual, Adams wrote some of the most important and influential essays, constitutions, and treatises of the Revolutionary period. If Samuel Adams and Patrick Henry represent the spirit of the independence movement, John Adams exemplifies the mind of the American Revolution.

Despite his extraordinary achievements, Adams has always posed a genuine problem for historians. From the moment he entered public life, he always seemed to travel the road not taken. Americans have rarely seen a political leader of such fierce independence and unyielding integrity. In de-

---

1. Benjamin Rush quoted in Joseph J. Ellis, *The Passionate Sage: The Character and Legacy of John Adams* (New York: W. W. Norton, 1994), 29; Richard Stockton quoted in *The Works of John Adams, Second President of the United States,* ed. Charles Francis Adams, 10 vols. (Boston: Little, Brown and Co., 1850–56), 3:56.

ix

bate he was intrepid to the verge of temerity, and his political writings reveal an utter contempt for the art of dissimulation. Unable to meet falsehoods halfway and unwilling to stop short of the truth, Adams was in constant battle with the accepted, the conventional, the fashionable, and the popular. He would compromise neither with Governor Thomas Hutchinson nor with the Boston mob. From his defense of English soldiers at the Boston Massacre trial to his treaty with the French in 1800, he had a way of shocking both his most ardent supporters and his most partisan opponents. To some, however, the complexity of the man and his thought are the very reasons why he is worth studying.

John Adams was born on October 19, 1735, in Braintree, Massachusetts. His father, Deacon John Adams, was a fifth-generation Massachusetts farmer, and his mother, the former Susanna Boylston, descended from another old New England family. The young man's sense of life and moral virtues were shaped early by the manners and mores of a Puritan culture that honored sobriety, industry, thrift, simplicity, and diligence.

After graduating from Harvard College, Adams taught school for three years and began reading for a career in the law. To that end, he adopted a strict daily regimen of hard work and Spartan-like austerity. In his diary, he implored himself to "Let no trifling Diversion or amuzement or Company decoy you from your Books, i.e., let no Girl, no Gun, no cards, no flutes, no Violins, no Dress, no Tobacco, no Laziness, decoy from your Books." He was always demanding of himself that he return to his study to tackle the great treatises and casebooks of the law.

> Labour to get Ideas of Law, Right, Wrong, Justice, Equity. Search for them in your own mind, in Roman, grecian, french, English Treatises of natural, civil, common, Statute Law. Aim at an exact Knowledge of the Nature, End, and Means of Government. Compare the different forms of it with each other and each of them with their Effects on Public and private Happiness. Study Seneca, Cicero, and all other good moral Writers. Study Montesque, Bolingbroke [Vinnius?], &c. and all other good, civil Writers, &c.[2]

Adams was admitted to the Boston bar in 1758 and soon settled into a successful career in the law. In 1764 he married Abigail Smith to whom he was devoted for fifty-four years. Despite many years of separation because of

---

2. *The Diary and Autobiography of John Adams,* ed. L. H. Butterfield et al. 4 vols. (Cambridge, Mass.: The Belknap Press of Harvard University Press, 1961), 1:72–73.

his duties to the American cause at home and abroad, theirs was a love story of almost fictional quality. Together they had five children.

The passage of the Stamp Act in 1765 thrust Adams into the public affairs of colony and empire. In that year, he published his first major political essay, *A Dissertation on the Canon and Feudal Law,* and he also composed the influential "Braintree Instructions." Both pieces attacked the Stamp Act for depriving the American colonists of two basic rights guaranteed to all Englishmen by Magna Carta: the rights to be taxed only by consent and to be tried only by a jury of one's peers.

Adams's understanding of the Patriot cause is revealed in two decisions that he made during the early years of the imperial crisis. In 1768 he refused a request from Governor Bernard to accept the post of advocate general of the court of admiralty. Despite the lucrative salary and "Royal Favour and promotion" associated with the position, he declined to accept on the grounds that he could not lay himself "under any restraints, or Obligations of Gratitude to the Government for any of their favours." Nor would he sanction a government that persisted "in a System, wholly inconsistent with all my Ideas of Right, Justice and Policy." Two years later, Adams risked falling out of favor with the Patriot movement by accepting the legal defense of Captain Preston in the Boston Massacre trial. He took the case in order to defend the rule of law and because "Council ought to be the very last thing that an accused Person should want in a *free* Country." Every lawyer, he wrote, must be "responsible not only to his Country, but to the highest and most infallible of all Trybunals."[3] In word and deed, Adams always chose to act in ways that he thought right and just, regardless of reward or punishment.

Between 1765 and 1776, Adams's involvement in radical politics ran apace with the escalation of events. In 1770, he was elected to the Massachusetts House of Representatives, and he later served as chief legal counsel to the Patriot faction and wrote several important resolutions for the lower house in its running battle with Governor Thomas Hutchinson. He also wrote a penetrating essay on the need for an independent judiciary, and his Novanglus letters are generally regarded as the best expression of the American case against parliamentary sovereignty. By the mid-1770s, Adams had distinguished himself as one of America's foremost constitutional scholars.

The year 1774 was critical in British-American relations, and it proved to be a momentous year for John Adams. With Parliament's passage of the Coercive Acts, Adams realized that the time had come for the Americans to

---

3. Ibid., 3:287, 292.

invoke what he called "revolution-principles."[4] Later that year he was elected to the first Continental Congress. Over the course of the next two years no man worked as hard or played as important a role in the movement for independence. His first great contribution to the American cause was to draft, in October 1774, the principal clause of the Declaration of Rights and Grievances. Adams also chaired the committee that drafted the Declaration of Independence, he drafted America's first Model Treaty, and, working eighteen-hour days, he served as a one-man department of war and ordnance. In the end, he worked tirelessly on some thirty committees. "Every member of Congress," Benjamin Rush would later write, "acknowledged him to be the first man in the House."[5]

Shortly after the battles at Lexington and Concord, Adams began to argue that the time had come for the colonies to declare independence and to constitutionalize the powers, rights, and responsibilities of self-government. In May 1776, in large measure due to Adams's labors, Congress passed a resolution recommending that the various colonial assemblies draft constitutions and construct new governments. At the request of several colleagues, Adams wrote his own constitutional blueprint. Published as *Thoughts on Government*, the pamphlet circulated widely and constitution makers in at least four states used its design as a working model.

Adams's greatest moment in Congress came in the summer of 1776. On June 10, Congress appointed a committee to prepare a declaration that would implement the following resolution: "That these United Colonies are, and of right ought to be free and independent states; that they are absolved, from all Allegiance to the British Crown; and that all political connection between them and the State of Great Britain, is and ought to be totally dissolved." On July 1, Congress considered final arguments on the question of independence. John Dickinson argued forcefully against independence. When no one responded to Dickinson, Adams rose and delivered a passionate but reasoned speech that moved the assembly to vote in favor of independence. Years later, Thomas Jefferson recalled that so powerful in "thought & expression" was Adams's speech, that it "moved us from our seats." Adams was, Jefferson said, "our Colossus on the floor."[6]

---

4. Adams, "Letters of Novanglus," in *Papers of John Adams,* ed. Robert Taylor et al. (Cambridge, Mass.: The Belknap Press of Harvard University Press, 1977–), 2:230.

5. *The Autobiography of Benjamin Rush: His "Travels Through Life" Together with His Commonplace Book for 1789–1813,* ed. George W. Corner (Princeton: Princeton University Press, 1948), 140.

6. "Notes on a Conversation with Thomas Jefferson," in *The Papers of Daniel Webster: Cor-*

In the fall of 1779, Adams was asked to draft a constitution for Massachusetts. Subsequently adopted by the people of the Bay State, the Massachusetts Constitution of 1780 was the most systematic and detailed constitution produced during the Revolutionary era. It was copied by other states in later years, and it was an influential model for the framers of the Federal Constitution of 1787.

Adams spent much of the 1780s in Europe as a diplomat and propagandist for the American Revolution. He succeeded in convincing the Dutch Republic to recognize American independence and he negotiated four critical loans with Amsterdam bankers. In 1783, he joined Benjamin Franklin and John Jay in Paris and played an important role in negotiating the Treaty of Peace with England. Adams completed his European tour of duty as America's first minister to Great Britain.

It was during his time in London that Adams wrote his great treatise in political philosophy, the three-volume *A Defence of the Constitutions of Government of the United States of America* (1787–88). Written as a guidebook for American and European constitution makers, the *Defence* is a sprawling historical survey and analysis of republican government and its philosophic foundations. The *Defence* represents a unique attempt in the history of political philosophy to synthesize the classical notion of mixed government with the modern teaching of separation of powers. We know that the book was influential at the Constitutional Convention in 1787 and that it was used by French constitution makers in 1789 and again in 1795.

After his return to America in 1788, Adams was twice elected vice president of the United States. The eight years that he served as Washington's second in command were the most frustrating of his life. He played virtually no role in the decision-making processes of the administration and he was forced daily to quietly preside over the Senate. In fact, Adams's most notable accomplishment during this period was the publication in 1790–91 of his philosophical *Discourses on Davila*. His purpose in these essays was to lampoon the initial phase of the French Revolution and the influence that its principles were then having in America.

Adams's elevation to the presidency in 1796 was the culmination of a long public career dedicated to the American cause. Unfortunately, the new president inherited two intractable problems from George Washington: an intense ideological party conflict between Federalists and Republicans, and hostile relations with an increasingly belligerent French Republic. This last,

---

respondence, ed. Charles M. Wiltse (Hanover, N.H.: The University Press of New England, 1974), 1:375.

known as the Quasi-War, became the central focus of his administration. Consistent with his views on American foreign policy dating back to 1776, Adams's guiding principle was "that we should make no treaties of alliance with any European power; that we should consent to none but treaties of commerce; that we should separate ourselves as far as possible and as long as possible from all European politics and war." However, in order to protect American rights, Adams was forced to walk a hostile gauntlet between pro-French Republicans and pro-English Federalists.

Adams angered Republicans first by proposing a series of recommendations for strengthening the American navy and for a provisional army in response to France's insulting treatment of American diplomats and its depredations of her commerce. He then delivered a stinging rebuke to the high Federalists of his own party by announcing the appointment of an American commissioner to negotiate a new peace treaty with France. The crowning achievement of his presidency was the ensuing peace convention of 1800 that reestablished American neutrality and commercial freedom. When Adams left office and returned to Quincy in 1801, he could proudly say that America was stronger and freer than the day he took office.

The bitterness of his electoral loss to Thomas Jefferson in 1800 soon faded as Adams spent the next twenty-five years enjoying the scenes of domestic bliss and a newfound philosophic solitude. During his last quarter century he read widely in philosophy, history, and theology, and in 1812 he reconciled with Jefferson and resumed with his friend at Monticello a correspondence that is unquestionably the most impressive in the history of American letters. In his final decade Adams experienced both tragedy and triumph. On October 28, 1818, his beloved Abigail died, a loss from which he would never quite recover. His only consolation during his last years—indeed, it was a moment of great pride—was the election in 1824 of his son, John Quincy, to the highest office in the land.

As the fiftieth anniversary of the Declaration of Independence approached, the ninety-one-year-old Adams was asked to provide a toast for the upcoming celebration in Quincy. He offered as his final public utterance this solemn toast: "INDEPENDENCE FOREVER." These last words stand as a signature for his life and principles. John Adams died on July 4, 1826, fifty years to the day after the signing of the Declaration of Independence.

A great many books have been published in this century on the causes of the American Revolution. The important question that most attempt to address is why the colonists acted as they did. What drove this remarkably free and prosperous people to react so passionately and violently to the seemingly benign if not well-intended actions of English imperial officials? One obvious place to look for answers to these questions is in the major speeches and pamphlets of the Revolutionary era. But abstruse arguments derived from natural and constitutional law are no longer thought to have determined the outcome of the Revolution one way or the other. John Adams thought otherwise. During his retirement years, he was fond of saying that the War for Independence was a consequence of the American Revolution. The *real* revolution, he declared, had taken place in the minds and hearts of the colonists in the fifteen years prior to 1776. According to Adams, the American Revolution was first and foremost an intellectual revolution.

To assist us in recovering this forgotten world of John Adams, we might begin by considering several questions: Why did Adams think there was a conspiracy by British officials to enslave America? What evidence did he produce to demonstrate a British design against American liberties? Was Adams an irrational revolutionary ideologue, or did his political thought represent a reasoned response to a real threat? How did he understand the constitutional relationship between colonies and Parliament? Was Adams a conservative defender of traditional colonial liberties or was he a revolutionary republican advancing Enlightenment theories of natural law? What principles of liberty and equality, justice and virtue, did he think worth defending?

Central to Adams's political philosophy is the distinction that he drew between "principles of liberty" and "principles of political architecture." The first relates to questions of political right and the second to constitutional design. The chronology of Adams's writings during the Revolutionary period mirrors this distinction. In the years before 1776, he debated with American Loyalists and English imperial officials over the principles of justice and the nature of rights. In the years after Independence, he turned to the task of designing and constructing constitutions. Because he wrote so much over the course of sixty years and because it is important that his writings be read unabridged, the selections in this volume have been limited to those essays and reports written during the imperial crisis and the war for independence.

John Adams had an enormous influence on the outcome of the American Revolution. He dedicated his life, his property, and his sacred honor to the cause of liberty and to the construction of republican government in America. The force of his reasoning, the depth of his political vision, and the integrity of his moral character are undeniable. From the beginning of his public career until the very end he always acted on principle and from a profound love of country. In his later years, though, Adams lamented that "Mausoleums, statues, monuments will never be erected to me. . . . Panegyrical romances will never be written, nor flattering orations spoken, to transmit me to posterity in brilliant colors."[7] The present volume erects no statues to Adams nor does it portray his life in brilliant colors. Readers must judge for themselves whether he is deserving of such accolades. We can say with confidence, however, that no study of the American Revolution would be complete without confronting the political ideas of John Adams. He was, after all, the "Atlas of American independence."

C. BRADLEY THOMPSON
Department of History and Political Science
Ashland University

7. John Adams to Benjamin Rush, March 23, 1809, in *The Spur of Fame: Dialogues of John Adams and Benjamin Rush, 1805–1813,* ed. John Schutz and Douglass Adair (San Marino, Calif.: The Huntington Library, 1966), 139.

ACKNOWLEDGMENTS

Joseph J. Ellis, Peter S. Onuf, Richard A. Ryerson, and Gordon S. Wood have, each in his own way, provided helpful advice on this project. I am particularly thankful to Joe Ellis for so graciously abdicating his own project to edit a volume of Adams's writings so that I might proceed with the present volume.

My greatest thanks go to my family. It was not until Henry, Samuel, and Islay came along that I could fully understand what John Adams meant by the "spirit of liberty." They show me every day what this spirit is and they inspire me to nurture and protect it. And it is their mother who steels me every day to pursue *justitiam ruat coelum.*

Editor's Note

With a few minor exceptions, this volume includes all of John Adams's Revolutionary and pre-Revolutionary political writings. All documents are reproduced in their entirety and, with one exception, have been taken from volumes 3 and 4 of Charles Francis Adams's ten-volume collection of *The Works of John Adams* (Boston, 1850–56). In turn, the Charles Francis Adams documents were reproduced from original newspaper publications. "Two Replies of the Massachusetts House of Representatives to Governor Hutchinson" was taken from the original Journal of the House of Representatives of Massachusetts.

In the spirit of introducing modern readers to documents reproduced in exactly the same form in which they were read by eighteenth-century readers, I have decided against annotating any of these documents. In order to recapture the distant past we must first appreciate its strangeness and differentness from the present. My intention is to permit Adams to speak for himself and to challenge the modern reader to further study the philosophic and political contexts in which Adams wrote. Nor, for the most part, have I attempted to modernize the text. The definitive annotated edition of Adams's Revolutionary writings will be found in the ongoing publication of the *Papers of John Adams* (Boston, 1977–). I have also removed all footnotes and annotation used by Charles Francis Adams.

THE REVOLUTIONARY WRITINGS OF
John Adams

ESSAYS AND

CONTROVERSIAL

PAPERS

OF THE

REVOLUTION

In 1763, a twenty-eight-year-old John Adams was settling into a promising law career when Boston became engulfed in an acrimonious political dispute. At its core, this intramural quarrel pitted the faction of James Otis, Jr., against that of Governor Francis Bernard and Lieutenant Governor Thomas Hutchinson. At issue were matters both personal and constitutional. The squabble began when Bernard appointed Hutchinson to the position of chief justice of the Massachusetts Supreme Court. Otis was offended because Bernard's predecessor had promised the postition to his father and then doubly so because Hutchinson was not trained in the law. Otis also accused Hutchinson of violating the principle of separation of powers through the accumulation of political offices. Over the course of the next several years, Massachusetts politics was rife with dispute between the two factions that resulted more than once in fisticuffs and lawsuits.

It was within this larger context that Adams penned his first public essays. More immediately, he was provoked to write in response to a series of essays published by his friend Jonathan Sewell under the pseudonym "J." Sewell ridiculed the Otises and defended the Bernard-Hutchinson administration. Writing as "U," Adams refused to support either faction. He called instead for disinterested magnanimity.

We see in these earlist essays Adam's philosophic turn of mind. They are important for their elucidation of ideas that he would more fully develop several decades later in his *Defence of the Constitutions of Government of the United States of America* and the *Discourses on Davila*.

I

ESSAYS AND
CONTROVERSIAL PAPERS
OF THE REVOLUTION

On Private Revenge

1 August, 1763

No. 1

MAN IS DISTINGUISHED from other animals, his fellow inhabitants of this planet, by a capacity of acquiring knowledge and civility, more than by any excellency, corporeal, or mental, with which mere nature has furnished his species. His erect figure and sublime countenance would give him but little elevation above the bear or the tiger; nay, notwithstanding those advantages, he would hold an inferior rank in the scale of being, and would have a worse prospect of happiness than those creatures, were it not for the capacity of uniting with others, and availing himself of arts and inventions in social life. As he comes originally from the hands of his Creator, self-love or self-preservation is the only spring that moves within him; he might crop the leaves or berries with which his Creator had surrounded him, to satisfy his hunger; he might sip at the lake or rivulet to slake his thirst; he might screen himself behind a rock or mountain from the bleakest of the winds; or he might fly from the jaws of voracious beasts to preserve himself from immediate destruction. But would such an existence be worth preserving? Would not the first precipice or the first beast of prey that could put a period to the wants, the frights, and horrors of such a wretched being, be a friendly object and a real blessing?

When we take one remove from this forlorn condition, and find the species propagated, the banks of clams and oysters discovered, the bow and arrow invented, and the skins of beasts or the bark of trees employed for covering, although the human creature has a little less anxiety and misery than before, yet each individual is independent of all others. There is no intercourse of friendship; no communication of food or clothing; no conversation or connection, unless the conjunction of sexes, prompted by instinct, like that of hares and foxes, may be called so. The ties of parent, son, and brother, are of little obligation. The relations of master and servant, the distinction of magistrate and subject, are totally unknown. Each individual is his own sovereign, accountable to no other upon earth, and punishable by none. In this savage state, courage, hardiness, activity, and strength, the virtues of their brother brutes, are the only excellencies to which men can aspire. The man who can run with the most celerity, or send the arrow with the greatest force, is the best qualified to procure a subsistence. Hence, to chase a deer over the most rugged mountain, or to pierce him at the greatest distance, will be held, of all accomplishments, in the highest estimation. Emulations and competitions for superiority in such qualities, will soon commence; and any action which may be taken for an insult, will be considered as a pretension to such superiority; it will raise resentment in proportion, and shame and grief will prompt the savage to claim satisfaction or to take revenge. To request the interposition of a third person to arbitrate between the contending parties, would be considered as an implicit acknowledgment of deficiency in those qualifications, without which, none in such a barbarous condition would choose to live. Each one, then, must be his own avenger. The offended parties must fall to fighting. Their teeth, their nails, their feet, or fists, or, perhaps, the first club or stone that can be grasped, must decide the contest, by finishing the life of one. The father, the brother, or the friend, begins then to espouse the cause of the deceased; not, indeed, so much from any love he bore him living, or from any grief he suffers for him dead, as from a principle of bravery and honor, to show himself able and willing to encounter the man who had just before vanquished another. Hence arises the idea of an avenger of blood, and thus the notions of revenge, and the appetite for it grow apace. Every one must avenge his own wrongs when living, or else lose his reputation, and his near relation must avenge them for him after he is dead, or forfeit his. Indeed, nature has implanted in the human heart a disposition to resent an injury when offered; and this disposition is so strong, that even the horse treading by accident on a gouty toe, or a brickbat falling on the shoulders, in the first twinges of pain, seems to excite the angry passions, and we feel an inclination to kill the horse and to break the brickbat. Consideration, however, that the horse and brick were without design, will cool us; whereas the thought that any mischief has been done on purpose to abuse, raises revenge in all its strength and terrors; and the man feels the sweetest, highest gratification, when he inflicts the punishment himself. From this source arises the ardent desire in men to judge for themselves, when, and to what degree they are injured, and to carve out their own remedies for themselves. From the same source arises that obstinate disposition in barbarous nations to continue barbarous, and the extreme difficulty of introducing civility and Christianity among them. For the great distinction between savage nations and polite ones, lies in this,—that among the former every individual is his own judge and his own executioner; but among the latter all pretensions to judgment and punishment are resigned to tribunals erected by the public; a resignation which savages are not, without infinite difficulty, persuaded to make, as it is of a right and privilege extremely dear and tender to an uncultivated nature.

To exterminate from among mankind such revengeful sentiments and tempers, is one of the highest and most important strains of civil and humane policy. Yet the qualities which contribute most to inspire and support them may, under certain regulations, be indulged and encouraged. Wrestling, running, leaping, lifting, and other exercises of strength, hardiness, courage, and activity, may be promoted among private soldiers, common sailors, laborers, manufacturers, and husbandmen, among whom they are most wanted, provided sufficient precautions are taken that no romantic, cavalier-like principles of honor intermix with them, and render a resignation of the right of judging, and the power of executing, to the public, shameful. But whenever such notions spread so inimical to the peace of society, that boxing, clubs, swords, or firearms, are resorted to for deciding every quarrel, about a girl, a game at cards, or any little accident that wine or folly or jealousy may suspect to be an affront,—the whole power of the government should be exerted to suppress them.

If a time should ever come when such notions shall prevail in this Province to a degree, that no privileges shall be able to exempt men from indignities and personal attacks, not the privilege of a counsellor, nor the privilege of a House of Representatives of "speaking freely in that assembly, without impeachment or question in any court or place," out of the General Court—when whole armed mobs shall assault a member of the House, when violent attacks shall be made upon counsellors, when no place shall be sacred, not the very walls of legislation, when no personages shall overawe, not the whole General Court added to all the other gentlemen on 'Change, when the broad noon-day shall be chosen to display before the world such high, heroic sentiments of gallantry and spirit, when such assailants shall live unexpelled from the legislature, when slight censures and no punishments shall be inflicted,—

there will really be danger of our becoming universally ferocious, barbarous, and brutal, worse than our Gothic ancestors before the Christian era.

The doctrine, that the person assaulted "should act with spirit," "should defend himself by drawing his sword and killing, or by wringing noses, and boxing it out with the offender," is the tenet of a coxcomb and the sentiment of a brute. The fowl upon the dunghill, to be sure, feels a most gallant and heroic spirit at the crowing of another, and instantly spreads his cloak, and prepares for combat. The bull's wrath enkindles into a noble rage, and the stallion's immortal spirit can never forgive the pawings, neighings, and defiances of his rival. But are cocks and bulls and horses the proper exemplars for the imitation of men, especially of men of sense, and even of the highest personages in the government!

Such ideas of gallantry have been said to be derived from the army. But it was injuriously said, because not truly. For every gentleman, every man of sense and breeding in the army, has a more delicate and manly way of thinking, and from his heart despises all such little, narrow, sordid notions. It is true that a competition, and a mutual affectation of contempt, is apt to arise among the lower, more ignorant, and despicable, of every rank and order in society. This sort of men, (and some few such there are in every profession,) among divines, lawyers, physicians, as well as husbandmen, manufacturers, and laborers, are prone, from a certain littleness of mind, to imagine that their labors alone are of any consequence to the world, and to affect a contempt for all others. It is not unlikely, then, that the lowest and most despised sort of soldiers may have expressed a contempt for all other orders of mankind, may have indulged a disrespect to every personage in a civil character, and have acted upon such principles of revenge, rusticity, barbarity, and brutality, as have been above described. And, indeed, it has been observed by the great Montesquieu, that "From a manner of thinking that prevails among mankind," (the most ignorant and despicable of mankind, he means,) "they set a higher value upon courage than timorousness, on activity than prudence, on strength than counsel. Hence, the army will ever despise a senate, and respect their own officers; they will naturally slight the orders sent them by a body of men whom they look upon as cowards, and therefore unworthy to command them." This respect to their own officers, which produces a contempt of senates and councils, and of all laws, orders, and constitutions, but those of the army and their superior officers, though it may have prevailed among some soldiers of the illiberal character above described, is far from being universal. It is not found in one gentleman of sense and breeding in the whole service. All of this character know that the common law of England is superior to all other laws, martial or common, in every English government, and has often asserted triumphantly its own preëminence against the insults and encroachments of a giddy and unruly soldiery. They know, too, that civil officers in England hold a great superiority to military officers, and that a frightful despotism would be the speedy consequence of the least alteration in these particulars. And, knowing this, these gentlemen, who have so often exposed their lives in defence of the religion, the liberties, and rights of men and Englishmen, would feel the utmost indignation at the doctrine which should make the civil power give place to the military, which should make a respect to their superior officers destroy or diminish their obedience to civil magistrates, or which should give any man a right in conscience, honor, or even in punctilio and delicacy, to neglect the institutions of the public, and seek his own remedy for wrongs and injuries of any kind.

On Self-Delusion

29 August, 1768

No. II

TO THE PRINTERS

MY WORTHY AND INGENIOUS FRIEND, Mr. J., having strutted his hour upon the stage, and acquired as well as deserved a good reputation, as a man of sense and learning, some time since made his exit, and now is heard no more.

Soon after Mr. J.'s departure, your present correspondent made his appearance, but has not yet executed his intended plan. Mr. J. enlisted himself under the banners of a faction, and employed his agreeable pen in the propagation of the principles and prejudices of a party, and for this purpose he found himself obliged to exalt some characters, and depress others, equally beyond the truth. The greatest and best of all mankind deserve less admiration, and even the worst and vilest deserve more candor, than the world in general is willing to allow them. The favorites of parties, although they have always some virtues, have always many imperfections. Many of the ablest tongues and pens have, in every age, been employed in the foolish, deluded, and pernicious flattery of one set of partisans, and in furious, prostitute invectives against another; but such kinds of oratory never had any charms for me; and if I must do one or the other, I would quarrel with both parties and with every individual of each, before I would subjugate my understanding, or prostitute my tongue or pen to either.

To divert men's minds from subjects of vain curiosity, or unprofitable science, to the useful, as well as entertaining speculations of agriculture; to eradicate the Gothic and pernicious principles of private revenge that have been lately spread among my countrymen, to the debasement of their character, and to the frequent violation of the public peace, and to recommend a careful attention to political measures, and a candid manner of reasoning about them, instead of abusive insolence or uncharitable imputations upon men and characters, has, since I first undertook the employment of entertaining the public, been my constant and invariable view. The difficulty or impracticability of succeeding in my enterprise, has often been objected to me by my friends; but even this has not wholly disheartened me. I own it would be easier to depopulate a province, or subvert a monarchy, to transplant a nation, or enkindle a new war; and that I should have a fairer prospect of success in such designs as those. But my consolation is this,—that if I am unable by my writings to effect any good purpose, I never will subserve a bad one. If engagements to a party are necessary to make a fortune, I had rather make none at all; and spend the remainder of my days like my favorite author, that ancient and immortal husbandman, philosopher, politician, and general, Xenophon, in his retreat, considering kings and princes as shepherds, and their people and subjects like flocks and herds, or as mere objects of contemplation and parts of a curious machine in which I had no interest, than to wound my own mind by engaging in any party, and spreading prejudices, vices, or follies. Notwithstanding this, I remember the monkish maxim,—*fac officium taliter qualiter, sed sta bene cum priore;* and it is impossible to stand well with the abbot without fighting for his cause through *fas* and *nefas.*

Please to insert the foregoing and following, which is the last deviation I purpose to make from my principal and favorite views of writing on husbandry and mechanic arts.

U.

THERE IS NOTHING in the science of human nature more curious, or that deserves a critical attention from every order of men so much, as that principle which moral writers have distinguished by the name of self-deceit. This principle is the spurious offspring of self-love; and is, perhaps, the source of far the greatest and worst part of the vices and calamities among mankind.

The most abandoned minds are ingenious in contriving excuses for their crimes, from constraint, necessity, the strength or suddenness of temptation, or the violence of passion, which serve to soften the remordings of their own consciences, and to render them by degrees insensible equally to the charms of virtue and the turpitude of vice. What multitudes in older countries discover, even while they are suffering deservedly the most infamous and terrible of civil punishments, a tranquillity and even a magnanimity like that which we may suppose in a real patriot dying to preserve his country! Happy would it be for the world if the fruits of this pernicious principle were confined to such profligates. But, if we look abroad, shall we not see the most modest, sensible, and virtuous of the common people, almost every hour of their lives, warped and blinded by the same disposition to flatter and deceive themselves? When they think themselves injured by any foible or vice in others, is not this injury always seen through the magnifying end of the perspective? When reminded of any such imperfection in themselves, by which their neighbors or fellow-citizens are sufferers, is not the perspective instantly reversed? Insensible of the beams in our own eyes, are we not quick in discerning motes in those of others? Nay, however melancholy it may be, and how humbling soever to the pride of the human heart, even the few favorites of nature, who have received from her clearer understandings and more happy tempers than other men, who seem designed, under Providence, to be the great conductors of the art and science, the war and peace, the laws and religion of this lower world, are often snared by this unhappy disposition in their minds, to their own destruction, and the injury, nay, often to the utter desolation of millions of their fellow-men. Since truth and virtue, as the means of present and future happiness, are confessed to be the only objects that deserve to be pursued, to what imperfection in our nature, or unaccountable folly in our conduct, excepting this of which we have been speaking, can mankind impute the multiplied diversity of opinions, customs, laws, and religions that have prevailed, and are still triumphant, in direct opposition to both? From what other source can such fierce disputations arise concerning the two things which seem the most consonant to the entire frame of human nature?

Indeed, it must be confessed, and it ought to be with much contrition lamented, that those eyes, which have been given us to see, are willingly suffered by us to be obscured, and those consciences, which by the commission of God Almighty have a rightful authority over us, to be deposed by prejudices, appetites, and passions, which ought to hold a much inferior rank in the intellectual and moral system. Such swarms of passions, avarice and ambition, servility and adulation, hopes, fears, jealousies, envy, revenge, malice, and cruelty, are continually buzzing in the world, and we are so extremely prone to mistake the impulses of these for the dictates of our consciences,—

that the greatest genius, united to the best disposition, will find it hard to hearken to the voice of reason, or even to be certain of the purity of his own intentions.

From this true, but deplorable condition of mankind, it happens that no improvements in science or literature, no reformation in religion or morals, nor any rectification of mistaken measures in government, can be made without opposition from numbers, who, flattering themselves that their own intentions are pure, (how sinister soever they may be in fact) will reproach impure designs to others, or, fearing a detriment to their interest or a mortification to their passions from the innovation, will even think it lawful directly and knowingly to falsify the motives and characters of the innocent.

Vain ambition and other vicious motives were charged by the sacred congregation upon Galileo, as the causes of his hypothesis concerning the motion of the earth, and charged so often and with so many terms, as to render the old man at last suspicious, if not satisfied, that the charge was true, though he had been led to this hypothesis by the light of a great genius and deep researches into astronomy. Sedition, rebellion, pedantry, desire of fame, turbulence, and malice, were always reproached to the great reformers, who delivered us from the worst chains that were ever forged by monks or devils for the human mind. Zosimus and Julian could easily discover or invent anecdotes to dishonor the conversion of Constantine, and his establishment of Christianity in the empire.

For these reasons we can never be secure in a resignation of our understandings, or in confiding enormous power either to the bramble or the cedar; no, nor to any mortal, however great or good; and for the same reasons we should always be upon our guard against the epithets and reflections of writers and declaimers, whose constant art it is to falsify and blacken the characters and measures they are determined to discredit.

These reflections have been occasioned by the late controversies in our newspapers about certain measures in the political world. Controversies that have this in common with others of much greater figure and importance, and, indeed, with all others, (in which numbers have been concerned,) from the first invention of letters to the present hour; that more pains have been employed in charging desire of popularity, restless turbulence of spirit, ambitious views, envy, revenge, malice, and jealousy on one side; and servility, adulation, tyranny, principles of arbitrary power, lust of dominion, avarice, desires of civil or military commissions on the other; or, in fewer words, in attempts to blacken and discredit the motives of the disputants on both sides, than in rational inquiries into the merits of the cause, the truth, and rectitude of the measures contested.

Let not writers nor statesmen deceive themselves. The springs of their own conduct and opinions are not always so clear and pure, nor are those of their antagonists in politics always so polluted and corrupted, as they believe, and would have the world believe too. Mere readers and private persons can see virtues and talents on each side; and to their sorrow they have not yet seen any side altogether free from atrocious vices, extreme ignorance, and most lamentable folly. Nor will mere readers and private persons be less excusable if they should suffer themselves to be imposed on by others, who first impose upon themselves. Every step in the public administration of government concerns us nearly. Life and fortune, our own and those of our posterity, are not trifles to be neglected or totally entrusted to other hands; and these, in the vicissitudes of human things, may be rendered in a few years either totally uncertain, or as secure as fixed laws and the British constitution well administered can make them, in consequence of measures that seem at present but trifles, and to many scarcely worth attention. Let us not be bubbled then out of our reverence and obedience to government on one hand; nor out of our right to think and act for ourselves in our own department on the other. The steady management of a good government is the most anxious, arduous, and hazardous vocation on this side the grave. Let us not encumber those, therefore, who have spirit enough to embark in such an enterprise, with any kind of opposition that the preservation or perfection of our mild, our happy, our most excellent constitution, does not soberly demand.

But, on the other hand, as we know that ignorance, vanity, excessive ambition and venality, will, in spite of all human precautions, creep into government, and will ever be aspiring at extravagant and unconstitutional emoluments to individuals, let us never relax our attention, or our resolution, to keep these unhappy imperfections in human nature, out of which material, frail as it is, all our rulers must be compounded, under a strict inspection and a just control. We electors have an important constitutional power placed in our hands; we have a check upon two branches of the legislature, as each branch has upon the other two; the power I mean of electing, at stated periods, one branch, which branch has the power of electing another. It becomes necessary to every subject then, to be in some degree a statesman, and to examine and judge for himself of the tendency of political principles and measures. Let us examine, then, with a sober, a manly, a British, and a Christian spirit; let us neglect all party virulence and advert to facts; let us believe no man to be infallible or impeccable in government, any more than in religion; take no man's word against evidence, nor implicitly adopt the sentiments of others, who may be deceived themselves, or may be interested in deceiving us.

U.

On Private Revenge

5 September, 1768

No. III

Impiger, iracundus, inexorabilis, acer,
Jura neget sibi nata, nihil non arroget armis.

HOR.

Rebuke the spearmen, and the troops
Of bulls that mighty be.

NOVANG.

TO THE PRINTERS

IT SEEMS TO BE NECESSARY FOR ME, (notwithstanding the declaration in my last) once more to digress from the road of agriculture and mechanic arts, and to enter the list of disputation with a brace of writers in the Evening Post, one of whom has subscribed himself X, and the other W. I shall agree with the first of these gentlemen, that "to preach up non-resistance with the zeal of a fanatic," would be as extraordinary as to employ a bastile in support of the freedom of speech or the press, or an inquisition in favor of liberty of conscience; but if he will leave his own imagination, and recur to what I have written, he will not find a syllable against resistance. Resistance to sudden violence, for the preservation not only of my person, my limbs and life, but of my property, is an indisputable right of nature which I never surrendered to the public by the compact of society, and which, perhaps, I could not surrender if I would. Nor is there any thing in the common law of England, (for which Mr. X supposes I have so great a fondness,) inconsistent with that right. On the contrary, the dogmas of Plato, the maxims of the law, and the precepts of Christianity, are precisely coincident in relation to this subject.

Plato taught that revenge was unlawful, although he allowed of self-defence. The divine Author of our religion has taught us that trivial provocations are to be overlooked; and that if a man should offer you an insult, by boxing one ear, rather than indulge a furious passion and return blow for blow, you ought even to turn the other also. This expression, however, though it inculcates strongly the duty of moderation and self-government upon sudden provocations, imports nothing against the right of resistance or of self-defence. The sense of it seems to be no more than this: that little injuries and insults ought to be borne patiently for the present, rather than run the risk of violent consequences by retaliation.

Now, the common law seems to me to be founded on the same great principle of philosophy and religion. It will allow of nothing as a justification of blows, but blows; nor will it justify a furious beating, bruising, and wounding, upon the provocation of a fillip of the finger, or a kick upon the shins; but if I am assaulted, I can justify nothing but laying my hands lightly upon the aggressor for my own defence; nothing but what was absolutely necessary for my preservation. I may parry or ward off any blow; but a blow received is no sufficient provocation for fifty times so severe a blow in return. When life, which is one of the three favorites of the law, comes into consideration, we find a wise and humane provision is made for its preservation. If I am assaulted by another, sword in hand, and if I am even certain of his intention to murder me, the common law will not suffer me to defend myself, by killing him, if I can avoid it. Nay, my behavior must absolutely be what would be called cowardice, perhaps, by Mr. X and W, though it would be thought the truest bravery, not only by the greatest philosophers and legislators, but by the best generals of the world; I must run away from such an assailant, and avoid him if I have room, rather than stand my ground and defend myself; but if I have no room to escape, or if I run and am pursued to the wall or into a corner where I cannot elude his fury, and have no other way to preserve my own life from his violence, but by taking his there, I have an indisputable right to do it, and should be justified in wading through the blood of a whole army, if I had power to shed it and had no other way to make my escape.

What is said by Mr. W, that "if a gentleman should be hurried by his passions so far as to take the life of another, the common law will not adjudge it murder or manslaughter, but justifiable homicide only," — by which he must mean, if in truth he had any meaning at all, that killing upon a sudden provocation is justifiable homicide, — is a position in comparison of which the observations of the grave-digger upon the death of the young lady, in Shakspeare's Hamlet, ought to be ranked among the *responsa prudentium*.

Every catechumen in law, nay, every common man, and even every porter upon the dock, that ever attended a trial for murder, knows that a sudden provocation raising a violent passion, where there is no precedent malice, is, in consideration of human frailty, allowed to soften killing from murder down to manslaughter; but manslaughter is a heinous crime, and subjected to heavy punishments.

Such is the wisdom and humanity of English law; upon so thorough a knowledge of human nature is it founded, and so well is it calculated to preserve the lives and limbs of men and the interior tranquillity of societies! I shall not dispute with Mr. X my affection for this law, in preference to all other systems of law that have ever appeared in the world. I have no connection with parishioners, nor patients, nor clients, nor any dependence upon either for business or bread; I study law as I do divinity and physic; and all of them as I do husbandry and mechanic arts, or the motions and revolutions of the heavenly bodies; or as I do magistracy and legislation; namely, as means and instruments of human happiness. It has been my amusement for many years past, as far as I have had leisure, to examine the systems of all the legislators, ancient and modern, fantastical and real, and to trace their effects in history upon the felicity of mankind; and the result of this long examination is a settled opinion that the liberty, the unalienable, indefeasible rights of men, the honor and dignity of human nature, the grandeur and glory of the public, and the universal happiness of individuals, were never so skilfully and successfully consulted as in that most excellent monument of human art, the common law of England; a law that maintains a great superiority, not only to every other system of laws, martial or canon, or civil and military, even to majesty itself; it has a never-sleeping jealousy of the canon law, which in many countries, Spain in particular, has subjected all officers and orders, civil and military, to the avarice and ambition, the caprice and cruelty of a clergy; and it is not less watchful over the martial law, which in many cases and in many countries, France in particular, is able to rescue men from the justice of the municipal laws of the kingdom; and I will own, that to revive in the minds of my countrymen a reverence for this law, and to prevent the growth of sentiments that seemed to me to be in their tendency destructive of it, especially to revive a jealousy of martial laws and cavalier-like tempers, was the turn which I designed to serve for myself and my friends in that piece which has given offence to X and W.

A certain set of sentiments have been lately so fashionable, that you could go into few companies without hearing such smart sayings as these,—"If a man should insult me, by kicking my shins, and I had a sword by my side I would make the sun shine through him;"—"if any man, let him be as big as Goliah, should take me by the nose, I would let his bowels out with my sword, if I had one, and if I had none, I would beat his brains out with the first club I could find." And such tempers have been animated by some inadvertent expressions that have fallen from persons of higher rank and better sentiments. Some of these have been heard to say, that "should a man offer a sudden insult to them, they could not answer for themselves, but they should lay him prostrate at their feet in his own blood." Such expressions as these, which are to be supposed but modest expressions of the speaker's diffidence of his own presence of mind, and government of his passions, when suddenly assaulted, have been taken for a justification of such returns to an insult, and a determination to practice them upon occasion. But such persons as are watching the lips of others for wise speeches, in order to utter them afterwards as their own sentiments, have generally as little of understanding as they have of spirit, and most miserably spoil, in reporting, a good reflection. Now, what I have written upon this subject was intended to show the inhumanity of taking away the life of a man, only for pulling my nose or boxing my ear; and the folly of it too, because I should be guilty of a high crime, that of manslaughter at least, and forfeit all my goods, besides receiving a brand of infamy.

But I have not yet finished my history of sentiments. It has been said by others that "no man ought to receive a blow without returning it;" "a man ought to be despised that receives a cuff without giving another in return." This I have heard declared for a sober opinion by some men of figure and office and importance. But I beg leave to repeat it,—this is the tenet of a coxcomb and the sentiment of a brute; and the horse, the bull, and the cock, that I mentioned before, daily discover precisely the same temper and the same sense of honor and decency. If, in walking the streets of this town, I should be met by a negro, and that negro should lay me over the head with his cudgel, should I think myself bound in honor or regard to reputation to return the blow with another cudgel? to put myself on a level with that negro, and join with him in a competition which was most expert and skilful at cudgels? If a mad dog should meet me and bite me, should I think myself bound in honor, (I mean before the poison had worked upon me enough to make me as mad as the dog himself,) to fall upon that dog and bite him again? It is not possible for me to express that depth of contempt that I feel for such sentiments, and for every mortal that entertains them; and I should choose to be "the butt, the jest, and contempt" of all companies that entertain such opinions, rather than to be in their admiration or esteem. I would take some other way to preserve myself and other men from such insolence and violence for the future; but I would never place myself upon a level with such an animal for the present.

Far from aiming at a reputation for such qualities and accomplishments as those of boxing or cuffing, a man of sense would hold even the true martial qualities, courage, strength, and skill in war, in a much lower estimation than the attributes of wisdom and virtue, skill in arts and sciences, and a true taste to what is right, what is fit, what is true, generous, manly, and noble, in civil life. The competition between Ajax and Ulysses is well known.

"Tu vires sine mente geris, mihi cura futuri,
Tu pugnare potes:
                    Tu tantum corpore prodes,
Nos animo;
Pectora sunt potiora manu. Vigor omnis in illis."

And we know in whose favor the prize was decreed.

I shall not be at the pains of remarking upon all the rodomontade in the two pieces under consideration, and Mr. X and Mr. W, and the whole alphabet of writers may scribble as many volumes as the twenty-four letters are capable of variations, without the least further notice from me, unless more reasoning and merit appear in proportion to the quantity of lines than is to be found in those two pieces. But since I have made some remarks upon them, it will, perhaps, before I conclude, be worth my while to mention one thing more in each. Mr. X tells us "that cases frequently occur where a man's person or reputation suffer to the greatest degree, and yet it is impossible for the law to make him any satisfaction."

This is not strictly true; such cases but seldom occur, though it must be confessed they sometimes do; but it seldom happens, very seldom indeed, where you know the man who has done you the injury, that you can get no satisfaction by law; and if such a case should happen, nothing can be clearer than that you ought to sit down and bear it; and for this plain reason, because it is necessary, and you cannot get satisfaction in any way. The law, by the supposition, cannot redress you; and you cannot, if you consider it, by any means redress yourself. A flagellation in the dark would be no reparation of the injury, no example to others, nor have any tendency to reform the subject of it, but rather a provocation to him to contrive some other way to injure you again; and of consequence would be no satisfaction at all to a man even of that false honor and delicacy of which I have been speaking, unless he will avow an appetite for mere revenge, which is not only worse than brutal, but the attribute of devils; and to take satisfaction by a flagellation in public would be only, in other words, taking a severe revenge upon yourself; for this would be a trespass and a violation of the peace, for which you would expose yourself to the resentment of the magistrate and the action of the party, and would be like running your sword through your own body to revenge yourself on another for boxing your ears; or like the behavior of the rattle-snake that will snap and leap and bite at every stick that you put near him, and at last when provoked beyond all honorable bearing, will fix his sharp and poisonous teeth into his own body.

I have nothing more to add, excepting one word of advice to Mr. W and all his readers, to have a care how they believe or practise his rule about "passion and killing," lest the halter and the gibbet should become their portion; for a killing that should happen by the hurry of passion would be much more likely to be adjudged murder than justifiable homicide only. Let me conclude, by advising all men to look into their own hearts, which they will find to be deceitful above all things and desperately wicked. Let them consider how extremely addicted they are to magnify and exaggerate the injuries that are offered to themselves, and to diminish and extenuate the wrongs that they offer to others. They ought, therefore, to be too modest and diffident of their own judgment, when their own passions and prejudices and interests are concerned, to desire to judge for themselves in their own causes, and to take their own satisfactions for wrongs and injuries of any kind.

U.

A Dissertation
on the Canon
and Feudal
Law

Early in 1765 John Adams began writing an essay on the history of ecclesiastical and civil despotism for the Sodality, a private club of Boston lawyers. His purpose was to contrast the tyranny of the canon and feudal law against New England's heroic struggle for freedom. He soon decided to expand and publish his "Dissertation on the Canon and Feudal Law" when he learned of Parliament's approval of the Stamp Act in March 1765. In his diary, Adams described the Stamp Act as an "enormous Engine, fabricated by the british Parliament, for battering down all the Rights and Liberties of America."

The "Dissertation" is an essay in political education. Its larger purpose was to raise an alarm against an impending threat and to rouse the people in defense of their rights. Adams saw in the Stamp Act an early-warning signal indicating the direction of British colonial policy. It violated in two important ways the most fundamental principle of the English constitution: the principle of consent. The Stamp Act denied the rights guaranteed by Magna Carta that no citizen shall be deprived of his property or taxed without his consent, and it extended juryless courts of admiralty into the American colonies. When combined with the recently passed Sugar Act, the Stamp Act permitted the transfer of revenue enforcement from regular common-law courts to the newly empowered admiralty courts. In Adams's eyes, this meant that unconstitutional courts would now enforce unconstitutional taxes. He concludes rather ominously by suggesting that there was "a direct and formal design on foot, to enslave all America."

2

A Dissertation on
the Canon and
Feudal Law

"Ignorance and inconsideration are the two great causes of the ruin of mankind." This is an observation of Dr. Tillotson, with relation to the interest of his fellow men in a future and immortal state. But it is of equal truth and importance if applied to the happiness of men in society, on this side the grave. In the earliest ages of the world, absolute monarchy seems to have been the universal form of government. Kings, and a few of their great counsellors and captains, exercised a cruel tyranny over the people, who held a rank in the scale of intelligence, in those days, but little higher than the camels and elephants that carried them and their engines to war.

By what causes it was brought to pass, that the people in the middle ages became more intelligent in general, would not, perhaps, be possible in these days to discover. But the fact is certain; and wherever a general knowledge and sensibility have prevailed among the people, arbitrary government and every kind of oppression have lessened and disappeared in proportion. Man has certainly an exalted soul; and the same principle in human nature,—that aspiring, noble principle founded in benevolence, and cherished by knowledge; I mean the love of power, which has been so often the cause of slavery,—has, whenever freedom has existed, been the cause of freedom. If it is this principle that has always prompted the princes and nobles of the earth, by every species of fraud and violence to shake off all the limitations of their power, it is the same that has always stimulated the common people to aspire at independency, and to endeavor at confining the power of the great within the limits of equity and reason.

The poor people, it is true, have been much less successful than the great. They have seldom found either leisure or opportunity to form a union and exert their strength; ignorant as they were of arts and letters, they have seldom been able to frame and support a regular opposition. This, however, has been known by the great to be the temper of mankind; and they have accordingly labored, in all ages, to wrest from the populace, as they are contemptuously called, the knowledge of their rights and wrongs, and the power to assert the former or redress the latter. I say RIGHTS, for such they have, undoubtedly, antecedent to all earthly government,—*Rights,* that cannot be repealed or restrained by human laws—*Rights,* derived from the great Legislator of the universe.

Since the promulgation of Christianity, the two greatest systems of tyranny that have sprung from this original, are the canon and the feudal law. The desire of dominion, that great principle by which we have attempted to account for so much good and so much evil, is, when properly restrained, a very useful and noble movement in the human mind. But when such restraints are taken off, it becomes an encroaching, grasping, restless, and ungovernable power. Numberless have been the systems of iniquity contrived by the great for the gratification of this passion in themselves; but in none of them were they ever more successful than in the invention and establishment of the canon and the feudal law.

By the former of these, the most refined, sublime, extensive, and astonishing constitution of policy that ever was conceived by the mind of man was framed by the Romish clergy for the aggrandisement of their own order. All the epithets I have here given to the Romish policy are just, and will be allowed to be so when it is considered, that they even persuaded mankind to believe, faithfully and undoubtingly, that God Almighty had entrusted them with the keys of heaven, whose gates they might open and close at pleasure; with a power of dispensation over all the rules and obligations of morality; with authority to license all sorts of sins and crimes; with a power of deposing princes and absolving subjects from allegiance; with a power of procuring or withholding the rain of heaven and the beams of the sun; with the management of earthquakes, pestilence, and famine; nay, with the mysterious, awful, incomprehensible power of creating out of bread and wine the flesh and blood of God himself. All these opinions they were enabled to spread and rivet among the people by reducing their minds to a state of sordid ignorance and staring timidity, and by infusing into them a religious horror of letters and knowledge. Thus was human nature chained fast for ages in a cruel, shameful, and deplorable servitude to him, and his subordinate tyrants, who, it was foretold, would exalt himself above all that was called God, and that was worshipped.

In the latter we find another system, similar in many respects to the former; which, although it was originally formed, perhaps, for the necessary defence of a barbarous people against the inroads and invasions of her neighboring nations, yet for the same purposes of tyranny, cruelty, and lust, which had dictated the canon law, it was soon adopted by almost all the princes of Europe, and wrought into the constitutions of their government. It was originally a code of laws for a vast army in a perpetual encampment. The general was invested with the sovereign propriety of all the lands within the territory. Of him, as his servants and vassals, the first rank of his great officers held the lands; and in the same manner the other subordinate officers held of them; and all ranks and degrees held their lands by a variety of duties and services, all tending to bind the chains the faster on every order of mankind. In this manner the common people were held together in herds and clans in a state of servile dependence on their lords, bound, even by the tenure of their lands, to follow them, whenever they commanded, to their wars, and in a state of total ignorance of every thing divine and human, excepting the use of arms and the culture of their lands.

But another event still more calamitous to human liberty, was a wicked confederacy between the two systems of tyranny above described. It seems to have been even stipulated between them, that the temporal grandees should contribute every thing in their power to maintain the ascendency of the priesthood, and that the spiritual grandees in their turn, should employ their ascendency over the consciences of the people, in impressing on their minds a blind, implicit obedience to civil magistracy.

Thus, as long as this confederacy lasted, and the people were held in ignorance, liberty, and with her, knowledge and virtue too, seem to have deserted the earth, and one age of darkness succeeded another, till God in his benign providence raised up the champions who began and conducted the Reformation. From the time of the Reformation to the first settlement of America, knowledge gradually spread in Europe, but especially in England; and in proportion as that increased and spread among the people, ecclesiastical and civil tyranny, which I use as synonymous expressions for the canon and feudal laws, seem to have lost their strength and weight. The people grew more and more sensible of the wrong that was done them by these systems, more and more impatient under it, and determined at all hazards to rid themselves of it; till at last, under the execrable race of the Stuarts, the struggle between the people and the confederacy aforesaid of temporal and spiritual tyranny, became formidable, violent, and bloody.

It was this great struggle that peopled America. It was not religion alone, as is commonly supposed; but it was a love of universal liberty, and a hatred, a dread, a horror, of the infernal confederacy before described, that projected, conducted, and accomplished the settlement of America.

It was a resolution formed by a sensible people,—I mean the Puritans,—

almost in despair. They had become intelligent in general, and many of them learned. For this fact, I have the testimony of Archbishop King himself, who observed of that people, that they were more intelligent and better read than even the members of the church, whom he censures warmly for that reason. This people had been so vexed and tortured by the powers of those days, for no other crime than their knowledge and their freedom of inquiry and examination, and they had so much reason to despair of deliverance from those miseries on that side the ocean, that they at last resolved to fly to the wilderness for refuge from the temporal and spiritual principalities and powers, and plagues and scourges of their native country.

After their arrival here, they began their settlement, and formed their plan, both of ecclesiastical and civil government, in direct opposition to the canon and the feudal systems. The leading men among them, both of the clergy and the laity, were men of sense and learning. To many of them the historians, orators, poets, and philosophers of Greece and Rome were quite familiar; and some of them have left libraries that are still in being, consisting chiefly of volumes in which the wisdom of the most enlightened ages and nations is deposited,—written, however, in languages which their great-grandsons, though educated in European universities, can scarcely read.

Thus accomplished were many of the first planters in these colonies. It may be thought polite and fashionable by many modern fine gentlemen, perhaps, to deride the characters of these persons, as enthusiastical, superstitious, and republican. But such ridicule is founded in nothing but foppery and affectation, and is grossly injurious and false. Religious to some degree of enthusiasm it may be admitted they were; but this can be no peculiar derogation from their character; because it was at that time almost the universal character not only of England, but of Christendom. Had this, however, been otherwise, their enthusiasm, considering the principles on which it was founded and the ends to which it was directed, far from being a reproach to them, was greatly to their honor; for I believe it will be found universally true, that no great enterprise for the honor or happiness of mankind was ever achieved without a large mixture of that noble infirmity. Whatever imperfections may be justly ascribed to them, which, however, are as few as any mortals have discovered, their judgment in framing their policy was founded in wise, humane, and benevolent principles. It was founded in revelation and in reason too. It was consistent with the principles of the best and greatest and wisest legislators of antiquity. Tyranny in every form, shape, and appearance was their disdain and abhorrence; no fear of punishment, nor even of death itself in exquisite tortures, had been sufficient to conquer that steady, manly, pertinacious spirit with which they had opposed the tyrants of those days in church and state. They were very far from being enemies to monarchy; and they knew as well as any men, the just regard and honor that is due to the character of a dispenser of the mysteries of the gospel of grace. But they saw clearly, that popular powers must be placed as a guard, a control, a balance, to the powers of the monarch and the priest, in every government, or else it would soon become the man of sin, the whore of Babylon, the mystery of iniquity, a great and detestable system of fraud, violence, and usurpation. Their greatest concern seems to have been to establish a government of the church more consistent with the Scriptures, and a government of the state more agreeable to the dignity of human nature, than any they had seen in Europe, and to transmit such a government down to their posterity, with the means of securing and preserving it forever. To render the popular power in their new government as great and wise as their principles of theory, that is, as human nature and the Christian religion require it should be, they endeavored to remove from it as many of the feudal inequalities and dependencies as could be spared, consistently with the preservation of a mild limited monarchy. And in this they discovered the depth of their wisdom and the warmth of their friendship to human nature. But the first place is due to religion. They saw clearly, that of all the nonsense and delusion which had ever passed through the mind of man, none had ever been more extravagant than the notions of absolutions, indelible characters, uninterrupted successions, and the rest of those fantastical ideas, derived from the canon law, which had thrown such a glare of mystery, sanctity, reverence, and right reverend eminence and holiness, around the idea of a priest, as no mortal could deserve, and as always must, from the constitution of human nature, be dangerous in society. For this reason, they demolished the whole system of diocesan episcopacy; and, deriding, as all reasonable and impartial men must do, the ridiculous fancies of sanctified effluvia from episcopal fingers, they established sacerdotal ordination on the foundation of the Bible and common sense. This conduct at once imposed an obligation on the whole body of the clergy to industry, virtue, piety, and learning, and rendered that whole body infinitely more independent on the civil powers, in all respects, than they could be where they were formed into a scale of subordination, from a pope down to priests and friars and confessors,—necessarily and essentially a sordid, stupid, and wretched herd,—or than they could be in any other country, where an archbishop held the place of a universal bishop, and the vicars and curates that of the ignorant, dependent, miserable rabble aforesaid,—and infinitely more sensible and learned than they could be in either. This subject has been seen in the same light by many illustrious patriots, who have lived in America since the days of our forefathers, and who have adored their memory for the same reason. And methinks there has not appeared in New England a stronger veneration for their memory, a more penetrating insight into the grounds and principles and spirit of their policy, nor a more earnest desire of perpetuating the blessings of it to posterity, than that fine institution of the late Chief Justice Dudley, of a lecture against popery, and on the validity of presbyterian ordination. This was certainly intended by that wise and excellent man, as an eternal memento of the wisdom and goodness of the very principles that settled America. But I must again return to the feudal law. The adventurers so often mentioned, had an utter contempt of all that dark ribaldry of hereditary, indefeasible right,— the Lord's anointed,—and the divine, miraculous original of government, with which the priesthood had enveloped the feudal monarch in clouds and mysteries, and from whence they had deduced the most mischievous of all doctrines, that of passive obedience and non-resistance. They knew that government was a plain, simple, intelligible thing, founded in nature and reason, and quite comprehensible by common sense. They detested all the base services and servile dependencies of the feudal system. They knew that no such unworthy dependencies took place in the ancient seats of liberty, the republics of Greece and Rome; and they thought all such slavish subordinations were equally inconsistent with the constitution of human nature and that religious liberty with which Jesus had made them free. This was certainly the opinion they had formed; and they were far from being singular or extravagant in thinking so. Many celebrated modern writers in Europe have espoused the same sentiments. Lord Kames, a Scottish writer of great reputation, whose authority in this case ought to have the more weight as his countrymen have not the most worthy ideas of liberty, speaking of the feudal law, says,—"A constitution so contradictory to all the principles which govern mankind can never be brought about, one should imagine, but by foreign conquest or native usurpations."* Rousseau, speaking of the same system, calls it,—"That most iniquitous and absurd form of government by which human nature was so shamefully degraded."† It would be easy to multiply authorities, but it must be needless; because, as the original of this form of government was among savages, as the spirit of it is military and despotic, every writer who would allow the people to have any right to life or property or freedom more than the beasts of the field, and who was not hired or enlisted under arbitrary, lawless power, has been always willing to admit the feudal system to be inconsistent with liberty and the rights of mankind.

* Brit. Ant. p. 2.
† Social Compact, page 164.

To have holden their lands allodially, or for every man to have been the sovereign lord and proprietor of the ground he occupied, would have constituted a government too nearly like a commonwealth. They were contented, therefore, to hold their lands of their king, as their sovereign lord; and to him they were willing to render homage, but to no mesne or subordinate lords; nor were they willing to submit to any of the baser services. In all this they were so strenuous, that they have even transmitted to their posterity a very general contempt and detestation of holdings by quitrents, as they have also a hereditary ardor for liberty and thirst for knowledge.

They were convinced, by their knowledge of human nature, derived from history and their own experience, that nothing could preserve their posterity from the encroachments of the two systems of tyranny, in opposition to which, as has been observed already, they erected their government in church and state, but knowledge diffused generally through the whole body of the people. Their civil and religious principles, therefore, conspired to prompt them to use every measure and take every precaution in their power to propagate and perpetuate knowledge. For this purpose they laid very early the foundations of colleges, and invested them with ample privileges and emoluments; and it is remarkable that they have left among their posterity so universal an affection and veneration for those seminaries, and for liberal education, that the meanest of the people contribute cheerfully to the support and maintenance of them every year, and that nothing is more generally popular than projections for the honor, reputation, and advantage of those seats of learning. But the wisdom and benevolence of our fathers rested not here. They made an early provision by law, that every town consisting of so many families, should be always furnished with a grammar school. They made it a crime for such a town to be destitute of a grammar schoolmaster for a few months, and subjected it to a heavy penalty. So that the education of all ranks of people was made the care and expense of the public, in a manner that I believe has been unknown to any other people ancient or modern.

The consequences of these establishments we see and feel every day. A native of America who cannot read and write is as rare an appearance as a Jacobite or a Roman Catholic, that is, as rare as a comet or an earthquake. It has been observed, that we are all of us lawyers, divines, politicians, and philosophers. And I have good authorities to say, that all candid foreigners who have passed through this country, and conversed freely with all sorts of people here, will allow, that they have never seen so much knowledge and civility among the common people in any part of the world. It is true, there has been among us a party for some years, consisting chiefly not of the descendants of the first settlers of this country, but of high churchmen and high statesmen imported since, who affect to censure this provision for the education of our youth as a needless expense, and an imposition upon the rich in favor of the poor, and as an institution productive of idleness and vain speculation among the people, whose time and attention, it is said, ought to be devoted to labor, and not to public affairs, or to examination into the conduct of their superiors. And certain officers of the crown, and certain other missionaries of ignorance, foppery, servility, and slavery, have been most inclined to countenance and increase the same party. Be it remembered, however, that liberty must at all hazards be supported. We have a right to it, derived from our Maker. But if we had not, our fathers have earned and bought it for us, at the expense of their ease, their estates, their pleasure, and their blood. And liberty cannot be preserved without a general knowledge among the people, who have a right, from the frame of their nature, to knowledge, as their great Creator, who does nothing in vain, has given them understandings, and a desire to know; but besides this, they have a right, an indisputable, unalienable, indefeasible, divine right to that most dreaded and envied kind of knowledge, I mean, of the characters and conduct of their rulers. Rulers are no more than attorneys, agents, and trustees, for the people; and if the cause, the interest and trust, is insidiously betrayed, or wantonly trifled away, the people have a right to revoke the authority that they themselves have deputed, and to constitute abler and better agents, attorneys, and trustees. And the preservation of the means of knowledge among the lowest ranks, is of more importance to the public than all the property of all the rich men in the country. It is even of more consequence to the rich themselves, and to their posterity. The only question is, whether it is a public emolument; and if it is, the rich ought undoubtedly to contribute, in the same proportion as to all other public burdens,—that is, in proportion to their wealth, which is secured by public expenses. But none of the means of information are more sacred, or have been cherished with more tenderness and care by the settlers of America, than the press. Care has been taken that the art of printing should be encouraged, and that it should be easy and cheap and safe for any person to communicate his thoughts to the public. And you, Messieurs printers, whatever the tyrants of the earth may say of your paper, have done important service to your country by your readiness and freedom in publishing the speculations of the curious. The stale, impudent insinuations of slander and sedition, with which the gormandizers of power have endeavored to discredit your paper, are so much the more to your honor; for the jaws of power are always opened to devour, and her arm is always stretched out, if possible, to destroy the freedom of thinking, speaking, and writing. And if the public interest, liberty, and happiness have been in danger from the ambition or avarice of any great man, whatever may be his politeness, address, learning, ingenuity, and, in other respects, integrity and humanity, you have done yourselves honor and your country service by publishing and pointing out that avarice and ambition. These vices are so much the more dangerous and pernicious for the virtues with which they may be accompanied in the same character, and with so much the more watchful jealousy to be guarded against.

"Curse on such virtues, they've undone their country."

Be not intimidated, therefore, by any terrors, from publishing with the utmost freedom, whatever can be warranted by the laws of your country; nor suffer yourselves to be wheedled out of your liberty by any pretences of politeness, delicacy, or decency. These, as they are often used, are but three different names for hypocrisy, chicanery, and cowardice. Much less, I presume, will you be discouraged by any pretences that malignants on this side the water will represent your paper as factious and seditious, or that the great on the other side the water will take offence at them. This dread of representation has had for a long time, in this province, effects very similar to what the physicians call a hydropho, or dread of water. It has made us delirious; and we have rushed headlong into the water, till we are almost drowned, out of simple or phrensical fear of it. Believe me, the character of this country has suffered more in Britain by the pusillanimity with which we have borne many insults and indignities from the creatures of power at home and the creatures of those creatures here, than it ever did or ever will by the freedom and spirit that has been or will be discovered in writing or action. Believe me, my countrymen, they have imbibed an opinion on the other side the water, that we are an ignorant, a timid, and a stupid people; nay, their tools on this side have often the impudence to dispute your bravery. But I hope in God the time is near at hand when they will be fully convinced of your understanding, integrity, and courage. But can any thing be more ridiculous, were it not too provoking to be laughed at, than to pretend that offence should be taken at home for writings here? Pray, let them look at home. Is not the human understanding exhausted there? Are not reason, imagination, wit, passion, senses, and all, tortured to find out satire and invective against the characters of the vile and futile fellows who sometimes get into place and power? The most exceptionable paper that ever I saw here is perfect prudence and modesty in comparison of multitudes of their applauded writings. Yet the high regard they have for the freedom of the press, indulges all. I must and will repeat it, your paper deserves the patronage of every friend to his country. And whether the defamers of it are arrayed in robes of scarlet or sable, whether they lurk and skulk in an insurance office, whether they assume the venerable character of a priest, the sly one of a scrivener, or the dirty, infamous, abandoned one of an informer, they are all the creatures and tools of the lust of domination.

The true source of our sufferings has been our timidity.

We have been afraid to think. We have felt a reluctance to examining into the grounds of our privileges, and the extent in which we have an indisputable right to demand them, against all the power and authority on earth. And many who have not scrupled to examine for themselves, have yet for certain prudent reasons been cautious and diffident of declaring the result of their inquiries.

The cause of this timidity is perhaps hereditary, and to be traced back in history as far as the cruel treatment the first settlers of this country received, before their embarkation for America, from the government at home. Everybody knows how dangerous it was to speak or write in favor of any thing, in those days, but the triumphant system of religion and politics. And our fathers were particularly the objects of the persecutions and proscriptions of the times. It is not unlikely, therefore, that although they were inflexibly steady in refusing their positive assent to any thing against their principles, they might have contracted habits of reserve, and a cautious diffidence of asserting their opinions publicly. These habits they probably brought with them to America, and have transmitted down to us. Or we may possibly account for this appearance by the great affection and veneration Americans have always entertained for the country from whence they sprang; or by the quiet temper for which they have been remarkable, no country having been less disposed to discontent than this; or by a sense they have that it is their duty to acquiesce under the administration of government, even when in many smaller matters grievous to them, and until the essentials of the great compact are destroyed or invaded. These peculiar causes might operate upon them; but without these, we all know that human nature itself, from indolence, modesty, humanity, or fear, has always too much reluctance to a manly assertion of its rights. Hence, perhaps, it has happened, that nine tenths of the species are groaning and gasping in misery and servitude.

But whatever the cause has been, the fact is certain, we have been excessively cautious of giving offence by complaining of grievances. And it is as certain, that American governors, and their friends, and all the crown officers, have availed themselves of this disposition in the people. They have prevailed on us to consent to many things which were grossly injurious to us, and to surrender many others, with voluntary tameness, to which we had the clearest right. Have we not been treated, formerly, with abominable insolence, by officers of the navy? I mean no insinuation against any gentleman now on this station, having heard no complaint of any one of them to his dishonor. Have not some generals from England treated us like servants, nay, more like slaves than like Britons? Have we not been under the most ignominious contribution, the most abject submission, the most supercilious insults, of some custom-house officers? Have we not been trifled with, browbeaten, and trampled on, by former governors, in a manner which no king of England since James the Second has dared to indulge towards his subjects? Have we not raised up one family, in them placed an unlimited confidence, and been soothed and flattered and intimidated by their influence, into a great part of this infamous tameness and submission? "These are serious and alarming questions, and deserve a dispassionate consideration."

This disposition has been the great wheel and the mainspring in the American machine of court politics. We have been told that "the word *rights* is an offensive expression;" "that the king, his ministry, and parliament, will not endure to hear Americans talk of their *rights;*" "that Britain is the mother and we the children, that a filial duty and submission is due from us to her," and that "we ought to doubt our own judgment, and presume that she is right, even when she seems to us to shake the foundations of government;" that "Britain is immensely rich and great and powerful, has fleets and armies at her command which have been the dread and terror of the universe, and that she will force her own judgment into execution, right or wrong." But let me entreat you, sir, to pause. Do you consider yourself as a missionary of loyalty or of rebellion? Are you not representing your king, his ministry, and parliament, as tyrants,—imperious, unrelenting tyrants,—by such reasoning as this? Is not this representing your most gracious sovereign as endeavoring to destroy the foundations of his own throne? Are you not representing every member of parliament as renouncing the transactions at Runing Mede, (the meadow, near Windsor, where Magna Charta was signed;) and as repealing in effect the bill of rights, when the Lords and Commons asserted and vindicated the rights of the people and their own rights, and insisted on the king's assent to that assertion and vindication? Do you not represent them as forgetting that the prince of Orange was created King William, by the people, on purpose that their rights might be eternal and inviolable? Is there not something extremely fallacious in the common-place images of mother country and children colonies? Are we the children of Great Britain any more than the cities of London, Exeter, and Bath? Are we not brethren and fellow subjects with those in Britain, only under a somewhat different method of legislation, and a totally different method of taxation? But admitting we are children, have not children a right to complain when their parents are attempting to break their limbs, to administer poison, or to sell them to enemies for slaves? Let me entreat you to consider, will the mother be pleased when you represent her as deaf to the cries of her children,—when you compare her to the infamous miscreant who lately stood on the gallows for starving her child,—when you resemble her to Lady Macbeth in Shakspeare, (I cannot think of it without horror,) who

> "Had given suck, and knew
> How tender 't was to love the babe that milked her,"

but yet, who could

> "Even while 't was smiling in her face,
> Have plucked her nipple from the boneless gums,
> And dashed the brains out."

Let us banish for ever from our minds, my countrymen, all such unworthy ideas of the king, his ministry, and parliament. Let us not suppose that all are become luxurious, effeminate, and unreasonable, on the other side the water, as many designing persons would insinuate. Let us presume, what is in fact true, that the spirit of liberty is as ardent as ever among the body of the nation, though a few individuals may be corrupted. Let us take it for granted, that the same great spirit which once gave Caesar so warm a reception, which denounced hostilities against John till Magna Charta was signed, which severed the head of Charles the First from his body, and drove James the Second from his kingdom, the same great spirit (may heaven preserve it till the earth shall be no more) which first seated the great grandfather of his present most gracious majesty on the throne of Britain,—is still alive and active and warm in England; and that the same spirit in America, instead of provoking the inhabitants of that country, will endear us to them for ever, and secure their good-will.

This spirit, however, without knowledge, would be little better than a brutal rage. Let us tenderly and kindly cherish, therefore, the means of knowledge. Let us dare to read, think, speak, and write. Let every order and degree among the people rouse their attention and animate their resolution. Let them all become attentive to the grounds and principles of government, ecclesiastical and civil. Let us study the law of nature; search into the spirit of the British constitution; read the histories of ancient ages; contemplate the great examples of Greece and Rome; set before us the conduct of our own British ancestors, who have defended for us the inherent rights of mankind against foreign and domestic tyrants and usurpers, against arbitrary kings and cruel priests, in short, against the gates of earth and hell. Let us read and recollect and impress upon our souls the views and ends of our own more immediate forefathers, in exchanging their native country for a dreary, inhospitable wilderness. Let us examine into the nature of that power, and the cruelty of that oppression, which drove them from their homes. Recollect their amazing fortitude, their bitter sufferings,—the hunger, the nakedness, the cold, which they patiently endured,—the severe labors of clearing their grounds, building their houses, raising their provisions, amidst dangers from wild beasts and savage men, before they had time or money or materials for commerce. Recollect the civil and religious principles and hopes and expectations which constantly supported and carried them through all hardships with patience and resignation. Let us recollect it was liberty, the hope of liberty for themselves and us and ours, which conquered all discouragements, dangers, and trials. In such researches as these, let us all in our several departments cheerfully engage,—but especially the proper patrons and supporters of law, learning, and religion!

Let the pulpit resound with the doctrines and sentiments of religious liberty. Let us hear the danger of thraldom to our consciences from ignorance, extreme poverty, and dependence, in short, from civil and political slavery. Let us see delineated before us the true map of man. Let us hear the dignity of his nature, and the noble rank he holds among the works of God,—that consenting to slavery is a sacrilegious breach of trust, as offensive in the sight of God as it is derogatory from our own honor or interest or happiness,— and that God Almighty has promulgated from heaven, liberty, peace, and good-will to man!

Let the bar proclaim, "the laws, the rights, the generous plan of power" delivered down from remote antiquity,—inform the world of the mighty struggles and numberless sacrifices made by our ancestors in defence of freedom. Let it be known, that British liberties are not the grants of princes or parliaments, but original rights, conditions of original contracts, coequal with prerogative, and coeval with government; that many of our rights are inherent and essential, agreed on as maxims, and established as preliminaries, even before a parliament existed. Let them search for the foundations of British laws and government in the frame of human nature, in the constitution of the intellectual and moral world. There let us see that truth, liberty, justice, and benevolence, are its everlasting basis; and if these could be removed, the superstructure is overthrown of course.

Let the colleges join their harmony in the same delightful concert. Let every declamation turn upon the beauty of liberty and virtue, and the deformity, turpitude, and malignity, of slavery and vice. Let the public disputations become researches into the grounds and nature and ends of government, and the means of preserving the good and demolishing the evil. Let the dialogues, and all the exercises, become the instruments of impressing on the tender mind, and of spreading and distributing far and wide, the ideas of right and the sensations of freedom.

In a word, let every sluice of knowledge be opened and set a-flowing. The encroachments upon liberty in the reigns of the first James and the first Charles, by turning the general attention of learned men to government, are said to have produced the greatest number of consummate statesmen which has ever been seen in any age or nation. The Brookes, Hampdens, Vanes, Seldens, Miltons, Nedhams, Harringtons, Nevilles, Sidneys, Lockes, are all said to have owed their eminence in political knowledge to the tyrannies of those reigns. The prospect now before us in America, ought in the same manner to engage the attention of every man of learning, to matters of power and of right, that we may be neither led nor driven blindfolded to irretrievable destruction. Nothing less than this seems to have been meditated for us, by somebody or other in Great Britain. There seems to be a direct and formal design on foot, to enslave all America. This, however, must be done by degrees. The first step that is intended, seems to be an entire subversion of the whole system of our fathers, by the introduction of the canon and feudal law into America. The canon and feudal systems, though greatly mutilated in England, are not yet destroyed. Like the temples and palaces in which the great contrivers of them once worshipped and inhabited, they exist in ruins; and much of the domineering spirit of them still remains. The designs and labors of a certain society, to introduce the former of them into America, have been well exposed to the public by a writer of great abilities;* and the further attempts to the same purpose, that may be made by that society, or by the ministry or parliament, I leave to the conjectures of the thoughtful. But it seems very manifest from the Stamp Act itself, that a design is formed to strip us in a great measure of the means of knowledge, by loading the press, the colleges, and even an almanack and a newspaper, with restraints and duties; and to introduce the inequalities and dependencies of the feudal system, by taking from the poorer sort of people all their little subsistence, and conferring it on a set of stamp officers, distributors, and their deputies. But I must proceed no further at present. The sequel, whenever I shall find

* The late Rev. Dr. Mayhew.

health and leisure to pursue it, will be a "disquisition of the policy of the stamp act." In the mean time, however, let me add,—These are not the vapors of a melancholy mind, nor the effusions of envy, disappointed ambition, nor of a spirit of opposition to government, but the emanations of a heart that burns for its country's welfare. No one of any feeling, born and educated in this once happy country, can consider the numerous distresses, the gross indignities, the barbarous ignorance, the haughty usurpations, that we have reason to fear are meditating for ourselves, our children, our neighbors, in short, for all our countrymen and all their posterity, without the utmost agonies of heart and many tears.

Instructions of the Town of Braintree to Their Representative

In September 1765, John Adams called for a town meeting in order to instruct its representative to the General Court on how the colony should respond to Parliament and the Stamp Act. A committee of five, including Adams, was chosen by the townspeople to compose a set of instructions. The committee slightly revised Adams's prepared draft and sent it to the town meeting where it was unanimously accepted.

The Braintree Instructions are a succinct and forthright defense of colonial rights and liberties. They argue against the Stamp Act on two general counts. First, that it is objectionable because unwise. The tax on stamped paper and other goods would necessarily inflict economic hardship in Massachusetts that would ultimately redound to England. Second, and most important, the Stamp Act is unconstitutional and therefore void because it deprives Americans of their traditional English rights to taxation by consent and trial by jury. In fact, it was the extension of the power of juryless courts of admiralty into America that most alarmed Adams. Undercutting the authority of colonial common law courts, admiralty court justices were to sit during the pleasure of the king and they would be granted commissions on all confiscated goods. In other words, they would have a pecuniary incentive to convict.

The Braintree Instructions are unique in the Revolutionary literature because they argue very early in the controversy that, though unwritten, the "essential fundamental principles of the British constitution" retain the status of a higher law impervious to Parliamentary legislation.

3

Instructions of the Town of Braintree to Their Representative, 1765

Boston, 14 October

To Ebenezer Thayer, Esq.

Sir, —In all the calamities which have ever befallen this country, we have never felt so great a concern, or such alarming apprehensions, as on this occasion. Such is our loyalty to the King, our veneration for both houses of Parliament, and our affection for all our fellow-subjects in Britain, that measures which discover any unkindness in that country towards us are the more sensibly and intimately felt. And we can no longer forbear complaining, that many of the measures of the late ministry, and some of the late acts of Parliament, have a tendency, in our apprehension, to divest us of our most essential rights and liberties. We shall confine ourselves, however, chiefly to the act of Parliament, commonly called the Stamp Act, by which a very burthensome, and, in our opinion, unconstitutional tax, is to be laid upon us all; and we subjected to numerous and enormous penalties, to be prosecuted, sued for, and recovered, at the option of an informer, in a court of admiralty, without a jury.

We have called this a burthensome tax, because the duties are so numerous and so high, and the embarrassments to business in this infant, sparsely-settled country so great, that it would be totally impossible for the people to subsist under it, if we had no controversy at all about the right and authority of imposing it. Considering the present scarcity of money, we have reason to think, the execution of that act for a short space of time would drain the country of its cash, strip multitudes of all their property, and reduce them to absolute beggary. And what the consequence would be to the peace of the province, from so sudden a shock and such a convulsive change in the whole course of our business and subsistence, we tremble to consider. We further apprehend this tax to be unconstitutional. We have always understood it to be a grand and fundamental principle of the constitution, that no freeman should be subject to any tax to which he has not given his own consent, in person or by proxy. And the maxims of the law, as we have constantly received them, are to the same effect, that no freeman can be separated from his property but by his own act or fault. We take it clearly, therefore, to be inconsistent with the spirit of the common law, and of the essential fundamental principles of the British constitution, that we should be subject to any tax imposed by the British Parliament; because we are not represented in that assembly in any sense, unless it be by a fiction of law, as insensible in theory as it would be injurious in practice, if such a taxation should be grounded on it.

But the most grievous innovation of all, is the alarming extension of the power of courts of admiralty. In these courts, one judge presides alone! No juries have any concern there! The law and the fact are both to be decided by the same single judge, whose commission is only during pleasure, and with whom, as we are told, the most mischievous of all customs has become established, that of taking commissions on all condemnations; so that he is under a pecuniary temptation always against the subject. Now, if the wisdom of the mother country has thought the independency of the judges so essential to an impartial administration of justice, as to render them independent of every power on earth,—independent of the King, the Lords, the Commons, the people, nay, independent in hope and expectation of the heir-apparent, by continuing their commissions after a demise of the crown, what justice and impartiality are we, at three thousand miles distance from the fountain, to expect from such a judge of admiralty? We have all along thought the acts of trade in this respect a grievance; but the Stamp Act has opened a vast number of sources of new crimes, which may be committed by any man, and cannot but be committed by multitudes, and prodigious penalties are annexed, and all these are to be tried by such a judge of such a court! What can be wanting, after this, but a weak or wicked man for a judge, to render us the most sordid and forlorn of slaves?—we mean the slaves of a slave of the servants of a minister of state. We cannot help asserting, therefore, that this part of the act will make an essential change in the constitution of juries, and it is directly repugnant to the Great Charter itself; for, by that charter, "no amerciament shall be assessed, but by the oath of honest and lawful men of the vicinage;" and, "no freeman shall be taken, or imprisoned, or disseized of his freehold, or liberties of free customs, nor passed upon, nor condemned, but by lawful judgment of his peers, or by the law of the land." So that this act will "make such a distinction, and create such a difference between" the subjects in Great Britain and those in America, as we could not have expected from the guardians of liberty in "both."

As these, sir, are our sentiments of this act, we, the freeholders and other inhabitants, legally assembled for this purpose, must enjoin it upon you, to comply with no measures or proposals for countenancing the same, or assisting in the execution of it, but by all lawful means, consistent with our allegiance to the King, and relation to Great Britain, to oppose the execution of it, till we can hear the success of the cries and petitions of America for relief.

We further recommend the most clear and explicit assertion and vindication of our rights and liberties to be entered on the public records, that the world may know, in the present and all future generations, that we have a clear knowledge and a just sense of them, and, with submission to Divine Providence, that we never can be slaves.

Nor can we think it advisable to agree to any steps for the protection of stamped papers or stamp-officers. Good and wholesome laws we have already for the preservation of the peace; and we apprehend there is no further danger of tumult and disorder, to which we have a well-grounded aversion; and that any extraordinary and expensive exertions would tend to exasperate the people and endanger the public tranquillity, rather than the contrary. Indeed, we cannot too often inculcate upon you our desires, that all extraordinary grants and expensive measures may, upon all occasions, as much as possible, be avoided. The public money of this country is the toil and labor of the people, who are under many uncommon difficulties and distresses at this time, so that all reasonable frugality ought to be observed. And we would recommend particularly, the strictest care and the utmost firmness to prevent all unconstitutional draughts upon the public treasury.

The Earl

of Clarendon

to William Pym

IN 1765, A LONDON NEWSPAPER PRINTED FOUR LETTERS on the Stamp Act crisis by an author writing under the pseudonym of William Pym. (The writer had actually mistaken John Pym's first name for William.) Pym's second letter was subsequently reprinted in a Boston newspaper. Adams, writing as the Earl of Clarendon, responded to Pym in three installments between January 13 and 27, 1766.

The historical John Pym and the Earl of Clarendon (Edward Hyde) were two of the most respected statesmen of seventeenth-century England. Pym the parliamentarian and Clarendon the royal advisor were rival advocates of mixed government and of drawing the English monarchy into a constitutional balance with Parliament. Among the many arguments advanced by the new Pym in defense of the Stamp Act, the most provocative was his claim that the British Parliament had the authority and power to abrogate the colonial charters whenever it chose to do so.

Adams's response ranks among the most elegant and moving pieces that he ever wrote. He clearly enjoyed the fiction of writing an other-worldly debate between these two great statesmen of the English Civil War. His prose crackles with sarcasm as he mocks Pym for his apostasy from the principles of revolutionary republicanism. The theme of Clarendon's first letter is the unconstitutionality of juryless courts and taxation without consent. The second letter is a stirring defense of the spiritedness of American liberty and virtue against the doctrine of passive obedience. The third letter, one of the most literary pieces that Adams ever wrote, is a systematic explication of the "essentials and fundamentals" of the British constitution.

4

The Earl of Clarendon
to William Pym

13 January, 1766

No. 1

Sir,—The revolution which one century has produced in your opinions and principles is not quite so surprising to me as it seems to be to many others. You know very well, I had always a jealousy that your humanity was counterfeited, your ardor for liberty cankered with simulation, and your integrity problematical at least.

I must confess, however, that such a sudden transition from licentiousness to despotism, so entire a transformation from a fiery, furious declaimer against power, to an abject hireling of corruption, though it furnishes a clue to the labyrinth of your politics in 1641, gives me many painful reflections on the frailty, inconstancy, and depravity of the human race. These reflections, nevertheless, are greatly mollified, by the satisfaction I feel in finding your old friend and coadjutor, Mr. Hampden, unaltered and unalterable in the glorious cause of liberty and law. His inflexibility has confirmed the great esteem my Lord Falkland and I always had of his wisdom, magnanimity, and virtue; and we are both of us at present as well convinced of his excellency, as a subject and citizen, as we were formerly of his amiable accomplishments in private life. But your apostasy has confirmed our belief of what was formerly suspected, namely,—your subornation of witnesses, your perjuries, briberies, and cruelties; and that though your cunning was exquisite enough to conceal your crimes from the public scrutiny, your heart was desperately wicked and depraved.

Can any thing less abominable have prompted you to commence an enemy to liberty,—an enemy to human nature? Can you recollect the complaints and clamors, which were sounded with such industry, and supported by such a profusion of learning in law and history, and such invincible reasoning, by yourself and your friends, against the Star-Chamber and High Commission, and yet remain an advocate for the newly-formed courts of

45

admiralty in America? Can you recall to your memory the everlasting changes which were rung, by yourself and your party, against ship-money, and the other projects of that disgraceful reign, and on the consent of the subject as indispensably necessary to all taxations, aids, reliefs, talliages, subsidies, duties, &c., and yet contend for a taxation of more than five million subjects, not only without their consent, expressed or implied, but directly against their most explicit and determined declarations and remonstrances?

You, of all mankind, should have been the last to be hired by a minister to defend or excuse such taxes and such courts,—taxes more injurious and ruinous than Danegeld of old, which our countryman Speed says, "emptied the land of all the coin, the kingdom of her glory, the commons of their content, and the sovereign of his wonted respects and observance;"—courts which seem to have been framed in imitation of an ancient jurisdiction, at the bare mention of which I have often seen your eyes lighten, I mean the court of the masters of the king's forfeitures. I cannot omit so fair an opportunity of repeating the history and unfolding the powers of that court, as it seems to have been the very antitype of the new courts of admiralty in America, and to have been created and erected with the same powers and for the same purposes. It was in the reign of King Henry VII. that a British Parliament was found to be so timid, or ignorant, or corrupt, as to pass an act, that justices of assize, as well as justices of peace, without any finding or presentment of twelve men, upon a bare information for the king, should have full power and authority to hear and determine, by their discretions, all offences against the form, ordinance, and effect of certain penal statutes. This unconstitutional act was passed in the eleventh year of that reign; and thus the commons were found to sacrifice that sacred pillar, that fundamental law, that everlasting monument of liberty, the Great Charter, in complaisance to the ravenous avarice of that monarch. In pursuance of this act, Sir Richard Empson and Edmund Dudley were made justices throughout England, and "masters of the king's forfeitures." The old sage, Coke, says, that act was against and in the face of that fundamental law, Magna Charta, and that it is incredible what oppressions and exactions were committed by Empson and Dudley upon this unjust and injurious act, shaking that fundamental law. "And that, in the first year of the reign of King Henry VIII. the Parliament recited that unconstitutional act, and declared it void." And those two vile oppressors fell a sacrifice to the righteous indignation of an injured and exasperated nation. And he closes with an admonition, that the fearful end of these two oppressors should deter others from committing the like, and admonish parliaments that, instead of this ordinary and precious trial, *per pares et per legem terrae,* they bring not in absolute and partial trials by discretion.

46

Give me leave, now, to ask you, Mr. Pym, what are the powers of the new courts of admiralty in America? Are the trials in these courts *per pares* or *per legem terrae?* Is there any grand jury there to find presentments or indictments? Is there any petit jury to try the fact, guilty or not? Is the trial *per legem terrae,* or by the institutes, digests, and codes and novels of the Roman law? Is there not a judge appointed, or to be appointed, over all America? Is not this a much more extensive jurisdiction than that of Empson and Dudley, as justices over all England? Will you say, that no Empsons and Dudleys will be sent to America? Perhaps not; but are not the jurisdiction and power given to the judges greater than that to those oppressors? Besides, how can you prove that no Empsons will be sent there? Pray, let me know, are not the forfeitures to be shared by the governors and the informers? Are we not to prophesy the future by the experience of the past? And have not many governors been seen in America whose avarice was at least as ravenous as that of Henry VII.? Have not many of their tools been as hungry, restless, insolent, and unrelenting as Empson and Dudley, in proportion to their power? Besides, are not the Americans at such a distance from their king, and the august council of the mother country, and, at the same time, so poor, as to render all redress of such insolence and rapacity impracticable?

If you consider the nature of these new American taxations, the temper and manners of the people in that country, their religious and civil principles; and if you recollect the real constitution of Great Britain, and the nature of the new courts of admiralty, you will not wonder at the spirit that has appeared in that country. Their resistance is founded in much better principles, and aims at much better ends, than I fear yours did in Charles's reign; though I own you were much nearer the truth and right of the cause then than now. And you know, if you had lived in America, and had not been much changed, you would have been the first to have taken arms against such a law, if no other kind of opposition would do. You would have torn up the foundations, and demolished the whole fabric of the government, rather than have submitted; and would have suffered democracy, aristocracy, monarchy, anarchy, any thing or nothing, to have arisen in its place.

You may, perhaps, wonder to hear such language as the foregoing from me, as I was always in an opposite faction to yours while we lived on earth. I will confess to you, that I am in many respects altered since my departure from the body; my principles in government were always the same, founded in law, liberty, justice, goodness, and truth; but in the application of those principles, I must confess, my veneration for certain churchmen, and my aspiring, ambitious temper, sometimes deceived me and led me astray. This was a source of remorse, at times, through my life; and, since my separation, and the sublimation of my faculties, and the purification of my temper, the detestation of some parts of my conduct has been greatly increased. But as these are subjects of very great importance, I shall make them the materials of a correspondence with you for some time to come.

CLARENDON

THE EARL OF CLARENDON
TO WILLIAM PYM

20 January, 1766

No. II

SIR,—You and I have changed sides. As I told you in my last, I can account for your tergiversation, only on the supposition of the insincerity, baseness, and depravity of your heart. For my own part, as the change in me is not so great, neither is it so unaccountable. My education was in the law, the grounds of which were so riveted in me that no temptation could induce me, knowingly, to swerve from them. The sentiments, however, which I had imbibed in the course of my education from the sages of the law, were greatly confirmed in me by an accident that happened to me in my youth. This is an anecdote relative to my father and me which I presume you must have heard. A scene which will remain with indelible impressions on my soul throughout my duration. I was upon that circuit which led me down to my native county, and on a visit to my aged father, who gave me an invitation to take a walk with him in the field. I see the good old gentleman, even at this distance of time, and in his venerable countenance that parental affection to me, that zeal for the law, that fervent love of his country, that exalted piety to God and good-will to all mankind, which constituted his real character. "My son," said he, "I am very old, and this will probably be the last time I shall ever see your face; your welfare is near my heart; the reputation you have in your profession for learning, probity, skill, and eloquence, will, in all probability, call you to manage the great concerns of this nation in parliament, and to counsel your king in some of the greatest offices of state; let me warn you against that ambition which I have often observed in men of your profession, which will sacrifice all to their own advancement; and I charge you, on a father's blessing, never to forget this nation, nor to suffer

48

the hope of honors or profits, nor the fear of menaces or punishments from the crown, to seduce you from the law, the constitution, and the real welfare and freedom of this people." And these words were scarcely pronounced, before his zeal and concern were too great for his strength, and he fell upon the ground before me, never to rise more! His words sunk deep into my heart, and no temptation, no bias or prejudice, could ever obliterate them. And you, Mr. Pym, are one witness for me, that, although I was always of the royal party, and for avoiding violence and confusion, I never defended what could be proved to be real infringements on the constitution. While I sat in parliament with you, I was as heartily for rectifying those abuses, and for procuring still further security of freedom, as any of you; and after the restoration, when the nations were rushing into a delirium with loyalty, I was obliged, in order to preserve even the appearance of the constitution, to make a stand; and, afterwards, in the reign of my infamous and detestable, though royal son-in-law, James II., I chose to go into banishment, rather than renounce the religion and liberties of my country.

I have made these observations to excuse my conduct in those reigns, in some degree, though I must confess there were many parts of it which admit of no excuse at all. I suffered myself to be blindly attached to the king and some of his spiritual and temporal minions, particularly Laud and Strafford, in some instances, and to connive at their villanous projects, against my principles in religion and government, and against the dying precepts of my father. Besides, my intimacy with that sort of company had gradually wrought into me too great a reverence for kingly and priestly power, and too much contempt of the body of the people, as well as too much virulence against many worthy patriots of your side of the question, with whom, if I had coöperated instead of assisting the court, perhaps all the confusions and bloodshed which followed might have been prevented, and all the nation's grievances redressed.

These reflections were a source of remorse at times, through my life; and since my departure from the earth I have revolved these things so often, and seen my errors so clearly, that were I to write a history of your opposition now, I should not entitle it a rebellion; nay, I should scarcely call the protectorate of Cromwell a usurpation.

With such principles as these, and divested as I am of all views and motives of ambition, as well as attachment to any party, you may depend upon it, the conduct of Barbadoes has given me great uneasiness. That island was settled in the Oliverian times by certain fugitives of the royal party, who were zealous advocates for passive obedience; and I suppose a remnant of the servile spirit of their ancestors and of that ruinous doctrine has prevailed on them to submit. I own it is a severe mortification to me to reflect that I ever acted in concert with a people with such sentiments, a people who were capable of so mean and meaching a desertion of the cause both of liberty and humanity.* But the gallant struggle in St. Christopher's and on the continent of North America, is founded in principles so indisputable in the moral law, in the revealed law of God, in the true constitution of Britain, and in the most apparent welfare of the British nation, as well as of the whole body of the people in America, that it rejoices my very soul. When I see that worthy people, even in the reign of a wise and good king fettered, chained, and sacrificed by a few abandoned villains, whose lust of gain and power would, at any time, fasten them in the interest of France or Rome or hell, my resentment and indignation are unutterable.

If ever an infant country deserved to be cherished it is America. If ever any people merited honor and happiness they are her inhabitants. They are a people whom no character can flatter or transmit in any expressions equal to their merit and virtue; with the high sentiments of Romans, in the most prosperous and virtuous times of that commonwealth, they have the tender feelings of humanity and the noble benevolence of Christians; they have the most habitual, radical sense of liberty, and the highest reverence for virtue; they are descended from a race of heroes, who, placing their confidence in Providence alone, set the seas and skies, monsters and savages, tyrants and devils, at defiance for the sake of religion and liberty.

And the present generation have shown themselves worthy of their ancestors. Those cruel engines, fabricated by a British minister, for battering down all their rights and privileges, instead of breaking their courage and causing despondency, as might have been expected in their situation, have raised and spread through the whole continent a spirit that will be recorded to their honor with all future ages. In every colony, from Georgia to New Hampshire inclusively, the executioners of their condemnation have been compelled by the unconquerable and irresistible vengeance of the people to renounce their offices. Such and so universal has been the resentment, that every man who has dared to speak in favor of them, or to soften the detestation in which they are held, how great soever his character had been before, or whatever had been his fortune, connections, and influence, has been seen to sink into universal contempt and ignominy. The people, even to the lowest ranks, have become more attentive to their liberties, more inquisitive about them, and more determined to defend them, than they were ever before

---

* Nova Scotia, Quebec, Pensacola, &c., are more excusable on account of their weakness and other peculiar circumstances.

known or had occasion to be; innumerable have been the monuments of wit, humor, sense, learning, spirit, patriotism, and heroism, erected in the several provinces in the course of this year. Their counties, towns, and even private clubs and sodalities have voted and determined; their merchants have agreed to sacrifice even their bread to the cause of liberty; their legislatures have resolved; the united colonies have remonstrated; the presses have everywhere groaned; and the pulpits have thundered; and such of the crown officers as have wished to see them enslaved, have everywhere trembled, and all their little tools and creatures been afraid to speak and ashamed to be seen. Yet this is the people, Mr. Pym, on whom you are contributing, for paltry hire, to rivet and confirm everlasting oppression.

CLARENDON

THE EARL OF CLARENDON
TO WILLIAM PYM

27 January, 1766

No. III

SIR,—You are pleased to charge the colonists with ignorance of the British constitution; but let me tell you there is not ever a son of liberty among them who has not manifested a deeper knowledge of it, and a warmer attachment to it, than appears in any of your late writings; they know the true constitution and all the resources of liberty in it, as well as in the law of nature, which is one principal foundation of it, and in the temper and character of the people much better than you, if we judge by your late impudent pieces, or than your patron and master, if we judge by his late conduct.

The people in America have discovered the most accurate judgment about the real constitution, I say, by their whole behavior, excepting the excesses of a few, who took advantage of the general enthusiasm to perpetrate their ill designs; though there has been great inquiry and some apparent puzzle among them about a formal, logical, technical definition of it. Some have defined it to be the practice of parliament; others, the judgments and precedents of the king's courts; but either of these definitions would make it a constitution of wind and weather, because the parliaments have sometimes voted the king absolute, and the judges have sometimes adjudged him to be so. Some have called it custom, but this is as fluctuating and variable as the other. Some have called it the most perfect combination of human powers in society which finite wisdom has yet contrived and reduced to practice for the preservation of liberty and the production of happiness. This is rather a character of the constitution and a just observation concerning it, than a regular definition of it, and leaves us still to dispute what it is. Some have said that the whole body of the laws, others that king, lords, and commons, make the constitution. There has also been much inquiry and dispute about the essentials and fundamentals of the constitution, and many definitions and descriptions have been attempted; but there seems to be nothing satisfactory to a rational mind in any of these definitions; yet I cannot say that I am at a loss about any man's meaning when he speaks of the British constitution or the essentials and fundamentals of it.

What do we mean when we talk of the constitution of the human body? what by a strong and robust, or a weak and feeble constitution? Do we not mean certain contextures of the nerves, fibres, and muscles, or certain qualities of the blood and juices, as sizy or watery, phlegmatic or fiery, acid or alkaline? We can never judge of any constitution without considering the end of it; and no judgment can be formed of the human constitution without considering it as productive of life or health or strength. The physician shall tell one man that certain kinds of exercise or diet or medicine are not adapted to his constitution, that is, not compatible with his health, which he would readily agree are the most productive of health in another. The patient's habit abounds with acid and acrimonious juices. Will the doctor order vinegar, lemon juice, barberries, and cranberries, to work a cure? These would be unconstitutional remedies, calculated to increase the evil which arose from the want of a balance between the acid and alkaline ingredients in his composition. If the patient's nerves are overbraced, will the doctor advise to jesuits'-bark? There is a certain quantity of exercise, diet, and medicine, best adapted to every man's constitution, which will keep him in the best health and spirits, and contribute the most to the prolongation of his life. These determinate quantities are not perhaps known to him or any other person; but here lies the proper province of the physician, to study his constitution and give him the best advice what and how much he may eat and drink; when and how long he shall sleep; how far he may walk or ride in a day; what air and weather he may improve for this purpose; when he shall take physic, and of what sort it shall be, in order to preserve and perfect his health and prolong his life.

But there are certain other parts of the body which the physician can, in no case, have any authority to destroy or deprave; which may properly be called *stamina vitae,* or essentials and fundamentals of the constitution; parts, without which, life itself cannot be preserved a moment. Annihilate the heart, lungs, brain, animal spirits, blood, any one of these, and life will depart at once. These may be strictly called fundamentals of the human constitution. Though the limbs may be all amputated, the eyes put out, and many other mutilations practised to impair the strength, activity, and other attributes of the man, and yet the essentials of life may remain unimpaired many years.

Similar observations may be made, with equal propriety, concerning every kind of machinery. A clock has also a constitution, that is a certain combination of weights, wheels, and levers, calculated for a certain use and end, the mensuration of time. Now, the constitution of a clock does not imply such a perfect constructure of movement as shall never go too fast or too slow, as shall never gain nor lose a second of time in a year or century. This is the proper business of Quare, Tomlinson, and Graham, to execute the workmanship like artists, and come as near to perfection, that is, as near to a perfect mensuration of time, as the human eye and finger will allow. But yet there are certain parts of a clock, without which it will not go at all, and you can have from it no better account of the time of day than from the ore of gold, silver, brass, and iron, out of which it was wrought. These parts, therefore, are the essentials and fundamentals of a clock. Let us now inquire whether the same reasoning is not applicable in all its parts to government. For government is a frame, a scheme, a system, a combination of powers for a certain end, namely,—the good of the whole community. The public good, the *salus populi,* is the professed end of all government, the most despotic as well as the most free. I shall enter into no examination which kind of government, whether either of the forms of the schools, or any mixture of them, is best calculated for this end. This is the proper inquiry of the founders of empires. I shall take for granted, what I am sure no Briton will controvert, namely,—that liberty is essential to the public good, the *salus populi.* And here lies the difference between the British constitution and other forms of government, namely, that liberty is its end, its use, its designation, drift, and scope, as much as grinding corn is the use of a mill, the transportation of burdens the end of a ship, the mensuration of time the scope of a watch, or life and health the designation of the human body.

Were I to define the British constitution, therefore, I should say, it is a limited monarchy, or a mixture of the three forms of government commonly known in the schools, reserving as much of the monarchical splendor, the aristocratical independency, and the democratical freedom, as are necessary that each of these powers may have a control, both in legislation and execution, over the other two, for the preservation of the subject's liberty.

According to this definition, the first grand division of constitutional powers is into those of legislation and those of execution. In the power of legislation, the king, lords, commons, and people are to be considered as essential and fundamental parts of the constitution. I distinguish between the house of commons and the people who depute them; because there is in nature and fact a real difference, and these last have as important a depart-ment in the constitution as the former—I mean the power of election. The constitution is not grounded on "the enormous faith of millions made for one." It stands not on the supposition, that kings are the favorites of heaven, that their power is more divine than the power of the people, and unlimited but by their own will and discretion. It is not built on the doctrine, that a few nobles or rich commons have a right to inherit the earth, and all the blessings and pleasures of it; and that the multitude, the million, the popu-lace, the vulgar, the mob, the herd, and the rabble, as the great always delight to call them, have no rights at all, and were made only for their use, to be robbed and butchered at their pleasure. No, it stands upon this principle, that the meanest and lowest of the people are by the unalterable, indefeasible laws of God and nature, as well entitled to the benefit of the air to breathe, light to see, food to eat, and clothes to wear, as the nobles or the king. All men are born equal; and the drift of the British constitution is to preserve as much of this equality as is compatible with the people's security against foreign invasions and domestic usurpation. It is upon these fundamental principles that popular power was placed, as essential, in the constitution of the legislature; and the constitution would be as complete without a kingly as without a popular power. This popular power, however, when the numbers grew large, became impracticable to be exercised by the universal and im-mediate suffrage of the people; and this impracticability has introduced from the feudal system an expedient which we call representation. This expedient is only an equivalent for the suffrage of the whole people in the common management of public concerns. It is in reality nothing more than this, the people choose attorneys to vote for them in the great council of the nation, reserving always the fundamentals of the government, reserving also a right to give their attorneys instructions how to vote, and a right at certain, stated intervals, of choosing a-new; discarding an old attorney, and choosing a wiser and better. And it is this reservation of fundamentals, of the right of giving instructions, and of new elections, which creates a popular check upon the whole government which alone secures the constitution from becoming an aristocracy, or a mixture of monarchy and aristocracy only.

The other grand division of power is that of execution. And here the king is, by the constitution, supreme executor of the laws, and is always present, in person or by his judges, in his courts, distributing justice among the people. But the executive branch of the constitution, as far as respects the administration of justice, has in it a mixture of popular power too. The judges answer to questions of fact as well as law; being few, they might be easily corrupted; being commonly rich and great, they might learn to despise the common people, and forget the feelings of humanity, and then the subject's liberty and security would be lost. But by the British constitution, *ad quaestionem facti respondent juratores,*—the jurors answer to the question of fact. In this manner, the subject is guarded in the execution of the laws. The people choose a grand jury, to make inquiry and presentment of crimes. Twelve of these must agree in finding the bill. And the petit jury must try the same fact over again, and find the person guilty, before he can be punished. Innocence, therefore, is so well protected in this wise constitution, that no man can be punished till twenty-four of his neighbors have said upon oath that he is guilty. So it is also in the trial of causes between party and party. No man's property or liberty can be taken from him till twelve men in his neighborhood have said upon oath, that by laws of his own making it ought to be taken away, that is, that the facts are such as to fall within such laws.

Thus, it seems to appear, that two branches of popular power, voting for members of the house of commons, and trials by juries, the one in the legislative and the other in the executive part of the constitution, are as essential and fundamental to the great end of it, the preservation of the subject's liberty, to preserve the balance and mixture of the government, and to prevent its running into an oligarchy or aristocracy, as the lords and commons are to prevent its becoming an absolute monarchy. These two popular powers, therefore, are the heart and lungs, the mainspring and the centre wheel, and without them the body must die, the watch must run down, the government must become arbitrary, and this our law books have settled to be the death of the laws and constitution. In these two powers consist wholly the liberty and security of the people. They have no other fortification against wanton, cruel power; no other indemnification against being ridden like horses, fleeced like sheep, worked like cattle, and fed and clothed like swine and hounds; no other defence against fines, imprisonments, whipping-posts, gibbets, bastinadoes, and racks. This is that constitution which has prevailed in Britain from an immense antiquity. It prevailed, and the house of commons and trials by jury made a part of it, in Saxon times, as may be abundantly proved by many monuments still remaining in the Saxon language. That constitution which has been for so long a time the envy and admiration of surrounding nations; which has been no less than five and fifty times since the Norman conquest, attacked in parliament, and attempted to be altered, but without success; which has been so often defended by the people of England, at the expense of oceans of their blood; and which, coöperating with the invincible spirit of liberty inspired by it into the people, has never failed to work the ruin of the authors of all settled attempts to destroy it.

What a fine reflection and consolation is it for a man, that he can be subjected to no laws which he does not make himself, or constitute some of his friends to make for him,—his father, brother, neighbor, friend, a man of his own rank, nearly of his own education, fortune, habits, passions, prejudices, one whose life and fortune and liberty are to be affected, like those of his constituents, by the laws he shall consent to for himself and them! What a satisfaction is it to reflect, that he can lie under the imputation of no guilt, be subjected to no punishment, lose none of his property, or the necessaries, conveniences, or ornaments of life, which indulgent Providence has showered around him, but by the judgment of his peers, his equals, his neighbors, men who know him and to whom he is known, who have no end to serve by punishing him, who wish to find him innocent, if charged with a crime, and are indifferent on which side the truth lies, if he disputes with his neighbor!

Your writings, Mr. Pym, have lately furnished abundant proofs that the infernal regions have taken from you all your shame, sense, conscience, and humanity; otherwise I would appeal to them, who has discovered the most ignorance of the British constitution,—you who are for exploding the whole system of popular power with regard to the Americans, or they who are determined to stand by it, in both its branches, with their lives and fortunes.

CLARENDON

Governor Winthrop to Governor Bradford

IN THE WINTER OF 1766–77, Adams's old friend, Jonathan Sewell, published a series of articles under the pseudonym Philanthrop. Sewell wrote to defend Governor Bernard from recent attacks alleging, among other things, that Bernard had violated the rights of the Massachusetts House of Representatives to judge the qualifications of its members by refusing to administer the oath to two newly elected representatives from Newbury.

In his "Govenor Winthrop to Governor Bradford" essays, Adams once again returned to a favorite literary device: a fictional correspondence between two great statesmen of the seventeenth century. Invoking the memory of New England's two founding fathers—John Winthrop of Massachusetts Bay and William Bradford of Plymouth—Adams devotes these letters to examining the authority of the Governor to interfere with the privileges of the House and to drawing a parallel between the tyrannical actions of James I and the political principles of Philanthrop.

More importantly, Adams wrote these letters to counteract what he saw as a political and moral lethargy descending upon the people of Massachusetts in the months after the repeal of the Stamp Act. In a diary entry at the time, Adams feared that the people of Massachusetts had fallen as "quiet and submissive to Government, as any People under the sun." By calling to life these venerable statesmen, Adams hoped to remind his fellow citizens that the price of liberty is eternal vigilance. In doing so, he hoped also to resurrect the ancient "spirit of liberty" that had inspired Winthrop and Bradford a century before and which had more recently animated the colonies in their fight against parliamentary taxation.

5

GOVERNOR WINTHROP TO GOVERNOR BRADFORD

26 January, 1767

No. 1

WE HAVE OFTEN CONGRATULATED EACH OTHER, with high satisfaction, on the glory we secured in both worlds by our favorite enterprise of planting America. We were Englishmen; we were citizens of the world; we were Christians. The history of nations and of mankind was familiar to us; and we considered the species chiefly in relation to the system of great nature and her all-perfect Author. In consequence of such contemplations as these, it was the unwearied endeavor of our lives to establish a society on English, humane, and Christian principles. This, (although we are never unwilling to acknowledge that the age in which we lived, the education we received, and the scorn and persecution we endured, had tinctured our minds with prejudices unworthy of our general principles and real designs,) we are conscious, was our noble aim. We succeeded to the astonishment of all mankind; and our posterity, in spite of all the terrors and temptations which have from first to last surrounded them, and endangered their very being, have been supremely happy. But what shall we say to the principles, maxims, and schemes, which have been adopted, warmly defended, and zealously propagated in America, since our departure out of it,—adopted, I say, and propagated, more by the descendants of some of our worthiest friends than by any others? You and I have been happier, in this respect, than most of our contemporaries. If our posterity have not without interruption maintained the principal ascendency in public affairs, they have always been virtuous and worthy, and have never departed from the principles of the Englishman, the citizen of the world, and the Christian. You very well remember the grief we felt, for many years together, at the gradual growth and prevalence of principles opposite to ours; nor have you forgotten our mutual joy at the very unexpected resurrection of a spirit which contributed so much to the restoration of that temper and those maxims which we have all along wished and prayed might

59

be established in America. Calamities are the caustics and cathartics of the body politic. They arouse the soul. They restore original virtues. They reduce a constitution back to its first principles. And, to all appearance, the iron sceptre of tyranny, which was so lately extended over all America, and which threatened to exterminate all for which it was worth while to exist upon earth, terrified the inhabitants into a resolution and an ardor for the noble foundations of their ancestors.

But how soon is this ardor extinguished! In the course of a few months they have cooled down into such a tame, torpid state of indolence and inattention, that the missionaries of slavery are suffered to preach their abominable doctrines, not only with impunity, but without indignation and without contempt. What will be the consequence if that (I will not say contemptible but abominable) writer, Philanthrop, is allowed to continue his wicked labors? I say allowed, though I would not have him restrained by any thing but the cool contempt and dispassionate abhorrence of his countrymen; because the country whose interior character is so depraved as to be endangered from within by such a writer, is abandoned and lost. We are fully persuaded, that New England is in no danger from him, unless his endeavors should excite her enemies abroad, of whom she has many, and extremely inveterate and malicious, and enable them, in concert with others within her own bosom, whose rancor is no less malignant and venomous, to do her a mischief. With pleasure I see that gentlemen are taking measures to administer the antidote with the poison.

As the sober principles of civil and ecclesiastical tyranny are so gravely inculcated by this writer, as his artifices are so insidious, and his misaffirmations so numerous and egregious, you will excuse me if I should again trouble you with a letter upon these subjects from your assured and immutable friend,

WINTHROP

Governor Winthrop to Governor Bradford

9 and 16 February 1767

No. 11

That the Hypocrite reign not, lest the People be ensnared.

Job.

Sir,—You have my promise of another letter, concerning the maxims, arts, and positions of Philanthrop; whose performances of the last week I shall proceed to consider, without any formal apology for departing from the plan I proposed at first.

The art employed by this writer, in the introduction to his account of the Concord anecdote, is worth observation, before we undertake an examination of the account itself, and his reasonings upon it. God forbid that I should trifle with religion, or blame any man for professing it publicly. But there is a decency to be observed in this. True religion is too modest and reserved to seek out the market-places and corners of the streets, party newspapers and political pamphlets, to exhibit her prayers and devotions. Besides, there is so much in the temper of times and manners of ages, that ostentation of this kind may be more excusable in one century than another. The age in which you and I lived was religious to enthusiasm. Yet we may safely say, that canting and hypocrisy were never carried to so shameless a pitch, even by a Sir Henry Vane, an Oliver St. John, an Oliver Cromwell or a Hugh Peters, as Philanthrop in his last Monday's paper has carried them. True religion, my friend Bradford, was the grand motive, with you and me, to undertake our arduous and hazardous enterprise, and to plant a religion in the world, on the large and generous principles of the Bible, without teaching for doctrines the commandments of men, or any mixture of those pompous rituals, and theatrical ceremonies, which had been so successfully employed to delude and terrify men out of all their knowledge, virtue, liberty, piety, and happiness. A religion that should never be made subservient to the pride, ambition, avarice, or lust, of an assuming priesthood, or a cruel and usurping magistracy, was our incessant aim, and unwearied endeavor. And we have now the happiness to reflect on our success; for at least we have approached nearer to such an institution than any others have done since the primitive ages of Christianity. And although stiffness, formality, solemnity, grimace, and cant, very common in our times, have worn off, in a great measure, from New England; yet true religion, on the plan of freedom, popular power, and private judgment, remains and prospers. This, we are fully persuaded, is truth, though the deluded Philanthrop seems to be so far given up to blindness of mind, as to think that his quotations from Scripture, his affected meekness, charity, benevolence, and piety, his formal stiffness, and hypocritical grimace, will divest his countrymen of their senses, and screen him from their jealousy, while he is tearing up, by his principles and practices, conversation and writings, the foundations of their constitution, both in church and state.

But it is not only by attempting to throw around himself the rays of religion, that this writer has attempted to deceive his countrymen; he has labored to possess their minds with principles in government utterly subversive of all freedom, tending to lull them into an indolent security and inattention. In one of his late papers he has a paragraph to this purpose,—"A brave and free people, who are not through luxury enervated and sunk to that degree of effeminate indolence, which renders them insensible to the difference between freedom and slavery, can never fail to perceive the approaches of arbitrary power. The constitution of all free governments, especially that of the English, is of such a nature, the principles of it are so familiar, and so interwoven with the human mind, and the rulers are so circumscribed with positive laws, for the directing and controlling their power, that they can never impose chains and shackles on the people, nor even attempt it, without being discovered. In such a government, and among such a people, the very first act in pursuance of a design to enslave or distress the subjects in general, must be so obvious, as to render all false coloring totally unnecessary to arouse the public attention; a simple narration of facts, supported by evidence, which can never be wanting in such a case, will be sufficient, and will be the surest means to convince the people of their danger."

What conclusion shall a candid reader draw by a fair interpretation from this wordy, cloudy passage? Would he not conclude that a free government, especially the English, was a kind of machine, calculated for perpetual motion and duration; that no dangers attended it; and that it may easily preserve and defend itself, without the anxiety or attention of the people?

The truth is precisely the reverse of this. Though a few individuals may perceive the approaches of arbitrary power, and may truly publish their perceptions to the people, yet it is well known, the people are not persuaded without the utmost difficulty to attend to facts and evidence. Those who covet such power, always have recourse to secrecy and the blackness of darkness to cover their wicked views, and have always their parties and instruments and minions at hand, to disguise their first approaches, and to vilify and abuse,—as turbulent destroyers of the public peace, as factious, envious, malicious pretenders to patriotism, as sowers and stirrers of sedition,—all those who perceive such approaches, and endeavor to inform and undeceive their neighbors. Liberty, instead of resting within the intrenchment of any free constitution of government ever yet invented and reduced to practice, has always been surrounded with dangers, exposed to perils by water and by fire. The world, the flesh, and the devil, have always maintained a confederacy against her, from the fall of Adam to this hour, and will, probably, continue so till the fall of Antichrist. Consider the commonwealths of Greece. Were not the wisest of them so sensible of it as to establish a security of liberty, I mean the ostracism, even against the virtues of their own citizens,—that no individual, even by his valor, public spirit, humanity, and munificence, might endear himself so much to his fellow citizens as to be able to deceive them and engross too much of their confidence and power? In Rome, how often were the people cheated out of their liberties, by kings, decemvirs, triumvirs, and conspirators of other denominations! In the times when Roman valor, simplicity, public spirit, and frugality, were at the highest, tyranny, in spite of all the endeavors of her enemies, was sometimes well-nigh established, and even a Tarquin could not be expelled but by civil war. In the history of the English nation, which Philanthrop is pleased to distinguish from all others, how many arbitrary reigns do we find since the conquest! Sometimes, for almost a whole century together, notwithstanding all the murmur, clamor, speeches in the senate, writings from the press, and discourses from the pulpit, of those whom Philanthrop calls turbulent destroyers of the public peace, but you and I think the guardian angels of their country's liberties, the English nation has trembled and groaned under tyranny.

For reasons like these, the spirit of liberty is and ought to be a jealous, a watchful spirit. *Obsta principiis* is her motto and maxim, knowing that her enemies are secret and cunning, making the earliest advances slowly, silently, and softly, and that, according to her unerring oracle, Tacitus, "the first advances of tyranny are steep and perilous, but, when once you are entered, parties and instruments are ready to espouse you." It is one of these early advances, these first approaches of arbitrary power, which are the most dangerous of all, and, if not prevented but suffered to steal into precedents, will leave no hope of a remedy without recourse to nature, violence, and war, that I now propose to consider.

And, in the first place, let us see how far the court writer and his opponents are agreed in the facts. They seem to agree that two gentlemen, chosen and returned as members of the house, were expressly excepted by the Governor in the *dedimus,* or power of administering the usual oaths to the members of the house; that the house, that is, the gentlemen returned from the other towns besides Newbury, would not receive the *dedimus* with this exception, that is, refused themselves to be sworn by virtue of it. I say, by the way, that Philanthrop agrees to this fact, though he seems to endeavor, by the obscurity of his expression, to disguise it; because the house itself must have considered the exception as an infraction of their right, though Philanthrop only says it was so considered by some among them; otherwise the house would not have chosen a committee to remonstrate against the exception. That the Governor erased the exception, or gave a new *dedimus,* upon the remonstrance of the committee; that the Governor, however, gave it up only for that time, expressly reserving the claim of right to except members out of the commission, and told the committee he should represent the case home for further instructions concerning it. This being the acknowledged state of facts, trifling with the instance in the reign of king James the First, is as good a proof of Philanthrop's knowledge in history and the constitution as his shrewd suggestion, that Cassius and B. B. are the same person, is of his sagacity. It is with real sorrow that I now observe and propose hereafter to demonstrate, that both Philanthrop and his idol are too much enamored with the fine example of the Jemmys and Charleys, and too much addicted to an awkward imitation of their conduct. One example of such an imitation is this of the *dedimus* at Concord, this memorable attempt to garble the house of representatives, which bears so exact a resemblance to the conduct of that self-sufficient innovator, that pedantical tyrant, that I own it seems more probable to me to have been copied designedly from it than to have happened by accident. For the gentleman whose conduct and character Philanthrop defends, cannot be denied to be well read in the reigns of the Stuarts, and therefore cannot be supposed to have been ignorant of James's conduct. That a solid judgment may be formed of the nature of the privilege for which I contend, and whether it has been invaded or not, I shall produce a short sketch of the history of that transaction, and will then produce the opinion of writers quite impartial, or to be sure not partial in my favor, concerning it.

If we go back so far as the reign of Elizabeth, we find her, on one occasion, infringing on this privilege of the commons, of judging solely of their own elections and returns. This attempt was, however, so warmly resented by the commons that they instantly voted,—"That it was a most perilous precedent, when two knights of a county were duly elected, if any new writ should issue out, for a second election, without order of the house itself. That the discussing and adjudging of this and such like differences belonged only to the house; and that there should be no message sent to the Lord Chancellor, not so much as to inquire what he had done in the matter; because it was conceived to be a matter derogatory to the power and privilege of the house." After this vote, which had in it something of the spirit of liberty and independency, we hear of no more disputes upon that subject till we come to the reign of James the First, whose whole life was employed in endeavoring to demolish every popular power in the constitution, and to establish the awful and absolute sovereignty of kingship, that, as he expressed himself to the convocation, Jack and Tom and Dick and Will might not meet and censure him and his council. And in order to accomplish the important purpose of his reign, he thought that nothing could be more useful than to wrest from the commons into his own hands, or those of his creature, the chancellor, the adjudication of their elections and returns. Outlaws, whether for misdemeanors or debts, had been declared by the judges, in the reign of Henry the Sixth, incapable by law of a seat in the house, where they themselves must be lawgivers. Sir Francis Goodwin was now chosen for the county of Bucks; and his return was made as usual into chancery. The chancellor decreed him an outlaw, vacated his seat, and issued writs for a new election. Sir John Fortescue was chosen in his room. But the first act of the house was to reverse the decree of the chancellor, and restore Goodwin to his seat. At James's instigation, the lords desired a conference on this subject, but were absolutely refused by the commons, as the question regarded entirely their own privileges. They agreed, however, to make a remonstrance to the king, by their speaker; where they maintained that though the returns were by form made into chancery, yet the sole right of *judging* with regard to elections belonged to the house itself. James was not satisfied, and ordered a conference between the house and the judges. The commons were in some perplexity. Their eyes were now opened; and they saw the consequences of that power which had been assumed, and to which their predecessors had in some instances blindly submitted. This produced many free speeches in the house. "By this course," said one member, "the free election of the counties is taken away; and none shall be chosen but such as shall please the king and council. Let us therefore with fortitude, understanding, and sincerity, seek to maintain our privileges. This cannot be construed any contempt in us, but merely a maintenance of our common rights, which our ancestors have left us, and which is just and fit for us to transmit to our posterity." Another said,—"This may be called a *quo warranto,* to seize all our liberties." "A chancellor," added a third, "by this course may call a parliament consisting of what persons he pleases. Any suggestion, by any person, may be the cause of sending a new writ. It is come to this plain question, whether the chancery or parliament ought to have authority." The commons, however, notwithstanding this watchful spirit of liberty, appointed a committee to confer with the judges before the king and council. There the question began to appear a little more doubtful than the king had imagined; and, to bring himself off, he proposed that Goodwin and Fortescue should both be set aside, and a writ be issued by the house for a new election. Goodwin consented; and the commons embraced this expedient, but in such a manner that, while they showed their regard for the king, they secured for the future the free possession of their seats, and the right which they claimed of judging solely of their own elections and returns. Hume, who will not be suspected of prejudice against the Stuarts, and very nearly in whose words this story is related, remarks at the conclusion,—"A power like this, so essential to the exercise of all their other powers, themselves so essential to public liberty, cannot fairly be deemed an encroachment in the commons, but must be regarded as an inherent privilege, happily rescued from that ambiguity which the negligence of former parliaments had thrown upon it." Smollett concludes his account of this affair with this reflection,—"Thus the commons secured to themselves the right of judging solely in their own elections and returns." And my Lord Bolingbroke, whose knowledge of the constitution will not be disputed, whatever may be justly said of his religion and his morals, remarks upon this transaction of James thus,—"Whether the will of the prince becomes a law independently of parliament, or whether it is made so upon every occasion by the concurrence of parliament, arbitrary power is alike established. The only difference lies here. Every degree of this power which is obtained without parliament, is obtained against the forms, as well as against the spirit of the constitution, and must, therefore, be obtained with difficulty, and possessed with danger. Whereas, in the other method of obtaining and exercising this power, by and with parliament, if it can be obtained at all, the progress is easy and short, and the possession of it so far from being dangerous, that liberty is disarmed as well as oppressed by this method; that part of the constitution, (namely, the house of commons,) which was instituted to oppose the encroachments of the crown, the maladministration of men in power, and every other grievance, being influenced to abet these encroachments, to support this maladministration, and even to concur in imposing the grievances."

Now, if we compare the attempt of King James with the attempt of the governor, who can discern a difference between them? James would have vacated the seat of Sir Francis Goodwin, because his election was against law; that is, because Sir Francis was an outlaw. The governor would have vacated the seats of Colonel Gerrish and Captain Little, because their election was against law, that is, because they were both chosen and returned by a town which by law was to choose and return but one. The king in one case, the governor in the other, made himself judge of the legality of an election, and usurped authority to vacate the seats of members. I consider the power of the chancellor here, which the king contended for, as the power of the king; because there is no great difference in such cases, as has been very well known from the time of James to this day, between the power of the creator and that of the creature. And I say, vacate the seats, because an exception from the *dedimus* is an absolute annihilation of a gentleman's seat; because by charter no man can vote or act as a representative till he has taken the oaths. It is as entire an exclusion from the house as an expulsion would be.

We will now, if you please, throw together a few reflections upon the soothing, amazing, melting solution of this arduous difficulty with which Philanthrop has entertained the public.

He begins with an instruction to the governor from his majesty not to consent to the division of towns. There has often been conversation during the administration of several late governors, concerning such a royal instruction, which, for any thing I know, may be a good one; but let it be good or evil, or whether there is any such or not, it has been found in experience, that when the division of a town would make way for the election of a friend, this instruction has been no impediment; and I need not go further than Concord and Newbury for two examples of this. Though I must go as far as the celebrated Berkshire for an instance of another member and favorite, chosen and returned as expressly against the instruction and law of the province, and knowingly suffered by the governor to be sworn, without any exception in the *dedimus,* and to vote for the council; and finally left to the house, without any exception, caveat, message, or hint, to judge of their privilege, and vacate his seat. But to return to the instruction, is it a command to the governor to take upon himself to judge of the legality or illegality of the choice, returns, or qualifications of the members of the house? No man will pretend this, or dare throw such an infamous affront upon his majesty or his ministers, who perfectly know that even his majesty himself has no right or authority whatever to judge in this matter; and that for the king himself to attempt to judge of the elections, returns, or qualifications of the members of the house of commons, or of the house of representatives, would be an invasion of their privilege as really, as for them to coin money, or issue commissions in the militia, would be an encroachment on the royal prerogative. If Newbury had sent ten, and Boston forty, members, has the common law, or any act of parliament, or any law of the province, or this, his majesty's instruction, made the governor the judge, that those towns have not a right by law to send so many? The only question is, who shall judge? Is it the purport of that instruction, that the governor should except the forty and the ten out of the *dedimus?* Would it not be as much as the king would expect of the governor, if he should give the *dedimus* in the usual form, that is, to swear all the members, and leave it to the house to judge who the members were? And if the governor really supposed, as Philanthrop says he did, that the house would be jealous of the honor of their own laws, why should he have taken that jealousy away from them? Why did he not leave it to them to vindicate their own cause? If he had known any facts in this case, of which the house was not apprized, it would have been friendly and constitutional in him to have hinted it privately to some member of the house, that he might have moved it there. But there was no pretence of this, the case of Newbury being as well known to the house as to the governor. Or if he must have inserted himself in the business publicly, he might have sent the necessary information to the house in a message, recommending it to their consideration, not giving his own opinion, for this would have been an infraction of their privilege, because they are the sole judges in the matter, and ought not to be under the influence even of a message from his *Excellency,* expressing his opinion, in deciding so very delicate a point as elections and returns, a point on which all the people's liberties depend. Five members chosen and returned by Boston would be an illegal election; but how should the governor come by his knowledge, that Boston had chosen and returned five? How should the precepts and returns come into his hands? It is no part of his excellency's duty to examine the returns which are made to the sheriff, and lodged in the secretary's office. There can be no objection to his looking over them to satisfy his curiosity; but to judge of them belongs wholly to another department. Suppose him to have inspected them, and found five returned for Boston; would not this be as manifestly against the spirit of the instruction, and the standing law of the province, as the case of Newbury? And what pretence would he have to judge of this illegal election, any more than of any other? Suppose, for instance, it was proved to his excellency, that twenty members returned were chosen by corruption, that is, had purchased the votes of the electors by bribery; or let it be proved that any members had taken Rhode Island or New Hampshire bills, were outlaws, or chosen by a few inhabitants of their towns without any legal meeting, these would be equally illegal elections, equally against the instructions and the law of the land; but shall the governor judge of these things, and vacate all such seats, by refusing them their oaths? Let it be suggested that a member is an infant, an idiot, a woman in man's clothing, a leper, a *petit-maître,* an enemy to government, a friend to the governor's enemies, a turbulent destroyer of the public peace, an envious, malicious pretender to patriotism, any one of these or a thousand other pretences, if the governor is once allowed to judge of the legality or illegality of elections and returns, or of the qualifications or disqualifications of members, may soon be made sufficient to exclude any or all whom the governor dislikes. The supposition that Boston should send forty, and all the other towns ten, is possible; but it is not less improbable than that the governor, and all others in authority, should be suddenly seized with a delirium, negative every counsellor chosen, dissolve the house, call another, dissolve that, command all the militia to muster and march to the frontiers, and a thousand other raving facts; and all that can be said is, that when such cases shall happen, the government will be dissolved, and individuals must scramble as well as they can for themselves, there being no resource in the positive constitution for such wild cases. But surely, a negative, a right of exception in the *dedimus,* would be of no service to him in such a case. So that no justification or excuse for the governor's apprehensions or conduct, can be drawn from such supposed cases.

How the governor's conduct in signing the bill for dividing Newbury came to be considered as so very friendly and highly obliging, is not easily comprehended, unless every act of the governor is to be considered in that light. If he signed the bill to oblige any particular friend, or in order that a friend's friend might get into the house, it was friendly and obliging no doubt to such friends; but if he signed it because he thought it for the general good, as I suppose he did, it was a part of his general duty, as governor, and no more obliging than any other act of equal importance. I suppose here, that such conduct was not inconsistent with what he knew to be the intention of his instructions; for surely no man will call it friendly and obliging wilfully to break his instructions for so small a benefit to the province as dividing a town. So that he can't be imagined to have run any risk in this case, any more than in any other instance of his duty.

It is asserted that the governor had been misinformed concerning the custom of the house. How far this is true, I know not. But had he been informed that they had a custom to let the governor judge of their elections and returns; a custom to let him pick out whom he would to be sworn, and whom he would to send home? Unless he had been informed of such a custom, I cannot see that any other misinformation can defend or even palliate his taking that part upon himself. But surely, he had opportunity enough to have had the truest information. There were gentlemen enough of both houses ready to acquaint him with the customs, nay, the journals of the house would have informed him that the returns were all read over the first day before they proceeded to the choice of counsellors. And he ought, one would think, to have been very sure he was right before he made so direct on onset on so fundamental a privilege. Besides, it has been, and is very credibly reported, and I believe it to be true, that he gave out, more than a week before that election, what he would do and did, and that some of his friends, fearing the consequences, waited on him, on purpose to dissuade him from such an attempt, but without success. So that it was no sudden thought, nor inadvertency, nor rashness of passion. I report this, as I have before some other things, from credible information and real belief, without calling on witnesses by name; as such evidence has lately come in fashion and is thought alone sufficient to support narratives and depositions, sent to the boards at home, charging the blackest crimes on the country and some of the most respectable characters in it. But admitting he was misinformed of the custom, I can't see that this is of any weight at all in the dispute. Whether the house examined any returns at all the first day, or not, he could have no pretence to interpose. If he thought the custom was to examine no returns till the second day, and that such a custom was wrong, and ought to be altered, he might, for aught I know unexceptionably, have sent a message recommending this matter to the consideration of the house, not dictating to them how they should decide; much less should he have decided himself without consulting them; much less should he have taken from them the opportunity of judging at all, as, by excepting the gentlemen out of the *dedimus,* in fact he did.

Philanthrop makes it a problematical point, whether his excellency's apprehensions or the custom of the house be most consonant to reason and our constitution. I confess myself at a loss to know, from his account, what his excellency's apprehensions were. If he means, that his excellency apprehended that the house ought to change their custom, and decide upon all elections and returns before they proceed to the choice of counsellors, I agree with him that such a point is immaterial to the present dispute; but if he means, that his excellency apprehended he had a right to except such members out of the *dedimus* as he pleased, or any members at all, he begs the question, and assumes that it is problematical whether he is or is not the sole judge of elections, has or has not the same cathartic negative to administer, when he thinks proper, to the house, as he has to the board; which, according to all the authorities I have cited before, and according to common sense, is to make it problematical whether the governor has or has not plenary possession of arbitrary power.

It is asserted by our writer that the two gentlemen were sworn, and voted, or might have voted. As to their being sworn, there could not possibly any harm accrue from any gentleman's taking the oaths of allegiance, subscribing the declaration, &c. and if the committee had been pleased to swear the whole country on that occasion, no damage would have been done; and from whence the governor's dread of administering the oaths of allegiance to those gentlemen could arise, I can't conceive. From scruples of conscience it could not be, because he has often taken those oaths himself. As to the gentlemen's voting, I believe Philanthrop is mistaken; because I have been strongly assured they did not, but that they stood by till the elections were over, as it was expected by the other members that they should. However, I do not affirm this. The gentlemen themselves can easily determine this matter.

Philanthrop is often complaining of "skulking, dark insinuations," &c.; but I know of no man who deals in them so much as he. Witness, among a thousand others, his base insinuations about the senate and Gazette, in his first piece, and what he says in his last about such a thing "being given out from a certain quarter, from what principle he will not say," a very dark, unintelligible insinuation of nobody knows what, against nobody knows whom, which leaves everybody at liberty to fix what he will on whom he will, and tends only to amuse and mislead. And nearly of the same character is a curious expression somewhere in the piece, calling the exception of the two gentlemen out of the *dedimus,* a "*caveat* to the house;" which is about as sensible as it would be to cut off a man's legs and chain him fast to a tree, and then give him a caution, a *caveat,* not to run away.

That the governor did not succeed in his attempt is no proof that he did not make it. Our thanks are not due to him, but to the house, that this *dedimus* was not received, all the members sworn by virtue of it, and itself lodged on file, as a precedent, to silence all envious and revengeful declaimers, both for himself and all his successors. It is equally true, that King James did not succeed in his attempt, but gave it up. Yet all historians have recorded that attempt, as a direct and formidable attack on the freedom of elections, and as one proof that he aimed at demolishing the constitution, at stretching prerogative beyond its just bounds, and at abridging the constitutional rights and liberties of the nation. What should hinder, but that a governor's attempt should be recorded too? I doubt not a Bacon quibbling and canting his adulation to that monarch, in order to procure the place of attorney-general or lord chancellor, might celebrate his majesty's friendly, modest, obliging behavior in that affair; yet even the mighty genius of Bacon could never rescue his sordid soul from contempt for that very adulation, with any succeeding age.

WINTHROP

THE INDEPENDENCE

OF THE

JUDICIARY

In the summer of 1772, Massachusetts Governor Thomas Hutchinson announced that he and all superior court judges would no longer need or accept the payment of their salaries from the Massachusetts legislature because the Crown would henceforth assume payment drawn from customs revenues. The following December, spurred on by Boston radicals, the town of Cambridge condemned the attempt to make the judges' salaries payable by the royal exchequer as a violation of their ancient liberties and practices. At the Cambridge meeting, however, General William Brattle defended the crown's assumption of the judges' salaries and issued a challenge to all patriots and, more particularly, to John Adams by name, to debate him on the subject. In brief, Brattle argued that Massachusetts judges were de facto appointed for life, and therefore the assumption of their salaries by the Crown would little threaten their independence.

In a dazzling and relentless display of historical and legal research, Adams demonstrated in seven essays that the so-called "independence" of English judges was an eighteenth-century innovation that did not extend to the colonies. The tenure of colonial judges was, Adams argued, dependent on the pleasure of the Crown. The implications for Massachusetts were massive. A judiciary dependent on the Crown for appointment and salary would be entirely beholden to its patron. Adams wrote therefore to alert the people of Massachusetts to the danger of Brattle's myth and to the need for truly independent judiciary.

6

The Independence of the Judiciary;

A Controversy Between William Brattle and John Adams

11 January, 1773

To the Printers

General Brattle, by his rank, station, and character, is entitled to politeness and respect even when he condescends to harangue in town meeting or to write in a newspaper; but the same causes require that his sentiments, when erroneous and of dangerous tendency, should be considered with entire freedom, and the examination be made as public as the error. He cannot, therefore, take offence at any gentleman for offering his thoughts to the public with decency and candor, though they may differ from his own.

In this confidence I have presumed to publish a few observations which have occurred to me upon reading his narration of the proceedings of the late town meeting at Cambridge. It is not my intention to remark upon all things in that publication which I think exceptionable, but only on a few which I think the most so.

The General is pleased to say, "That no man in the province could say whether the salaries granted to the judges were *durante beneplacito,* or *quamdiu bene se gesserint,* as the judges of England have their salaries granted them. I supposed the latter, though these words are not expressed, but necessarily implied." This is said upon the supposition that salaries are granted by the crown to the judges.

Now it is not easy to conceive how the General or any man in the province could be at a loss to say, upon supposition that salaries are granted, whether they are granted in the one way or the other. If salaries are granted by the crown, they must be granted in such a manner as the crown has power to grant them. Now it is utterly denied that the crown has power to grant them in any other manner than *durante beneplacito.*

The power of the crown to grant salaries to any judges in America is derived solely from the late act of parliament, and that gives no power to grant salaries for life or during good behavior. But not to enlarge upon this at present.

The General proceeds,—"I was very far from thinking there was any necessity of having *quamdiu bene se gesserint* in their commissions; for they have their commissions now by that tenure as truly as if said words were in."

It is the wish of almost all good men that this was good law. This country would be forever obliged to any gentleman who would prove this point from good authorities to the conviction of all concerned in the administration of government here and at home. But I must confess that my veneration for General Brattle's authority by no means prevails with me to give credit to this doctrine; nor do his reasons in support of it weigh with me even so much as his authority. He says, "What right, what estate vests in them, (that is, the judges,) in consequence of their nomination and appointment, the common law of England, the birthright of every man here as well as at home, determines, and that is an estate for life, provided they behave well." I must confess I read these words with surprise and grief; and the more I have reflected upon them, the more these sentiments have increased in my mind.

The common law of England is so far from determining that the judges have an estate for life in their offices, that it has determined the direct contrary; the proofs of this are innumerable and irresistible. My Lord Coke, in his fourth Institute, 74, says, "Before the reign of Edward I. the chief justice of this court was created by letters-patent, and the form thereof (taking one example for all) was in these words:—

"Rex, &c., archiepiscopis, episcopis, abbatibus, prioribus, comitibus, baronibus, vice-comitibus, forestariis, et omnibus aliis fidelibus regni Angliae, salutem. Cum pro conservatione nostrâ, et tranquillitatis regni nostri, et ad justitiam universis et singulis de regno nostro exhibendam constituerimus dilectum et fidelem nostrum Philippum Basset justiciarium Angliae *quamdiu nobis placuerit* capitalem, &c." And my Lord Coke says afterwards in the same page,—"King Edward I. being a wise and prudent prince, knowing that, cui plus licet quam par est, plus vult quam licet, (as most of these summi justiciarii did) made three alterations. 1. By limitation of his authority. 2. By changing summus justiciarius to capitalis justiciarius. 3. By a new kind of creation, namely, by writ, lest, if he had continued his former manner of creation, he might have had a desire of his former authority; which three do expressly appear by the writ yet in use, namely,—Rex, &c. E. C. militi salutem. Sciatis quod constituimus vos justiciarium nostrum capitalem ad placita coram nobis tenenda, *durante beneplacito nostro.* Teste, &c." Afterwards, in the same page, Lord Coke observes, "It is a rule in law, that ancient offices must be granted in such forms and in such manner as they have used to be, unless the alteration were by authority of parliament. And continual experience approveth, that for many successions of ages without intermission, they have been, and yet are called by the said writ." His lordship informs us also in the same page that "the rest of the judges of the king's bench have their offices by letters-patent in these words,—Rex omnibus ad quos presentes literae pervenerint salutem. Sciatis quod constituimus dilectum et fidelem Johannem Doderidge militem unum justiciariorum ad placita coram nobis tenenda *durante beneplacito nostro.* Teste, &c."

His lordship says, indeed, that these judges are called *perpetui* by Bracton, because "they ought not to be removed without just cause." But the question is not what the crown ought to do, but what it had legal power to do.

The next reason given by the General, in support of his opinion, is that "these points of law have been settled and determined by the greatest sages of the law, formerly and more lately." This is so entirely without foundation, that the General might, both with safety and decency, be challenged to produce the name of any one sage of the law, ancient or modern, by whom it has been so settled and determined, and the book in which such determination appears. The General adds, "It is so notorious that it becomes the common learning of the law." I believe he may decently and safely be challenged again to produce one lawyer in this country who ever before entertained such an opinion or heard such a doctrine. I would not be misunderstood. There are respectable lawyers who maintain that the judges here hold their offices during good behavior; but it is upon other principles, not upon the common law of England. "My Lord Chief Justice Holt settled it so, not long before the statute of William and Mary, that enacts that the words *quamdiu bene se gesserint* shall be in the judges' commissions;" and afterwards he says, that the commissions, as he apprehends, were without these words inserted in them during the reigns of King William, Queen Mary, and Queen Anne.

This, I presume, must have been conjectured from a few words of Lord Holt, in the case of Harcourt against Fox, which I think are these. I repeat them from memory, having not the book before me at present. "Our places as judges are so settled, determinable only upon misbehavior."

Now from these words I should draw an opposite conclusion from the General, and should think that the influence of that interest in the nation, which brought King William to the throne, prevailed upon him to grant the commissions to the judges expressly during good behavior. I say this is the most natural construction, because it is certain their places were not at that time, namely, 5 William and Mary, determined, by an act of parliament, to be determinable only upon misbehavior; and it is as certain, from Lord Coke and from all history, that they were not so settled by the common law of England.

However, we need not rest upon this reasoning because we happen to be furnished with the most explicit and decisive evidence that my conclusion is just, from my Lord Raymond. In the beginning of his second volume of Reports, his lordship has given us a list of the chief officers in the law at the time of the death of King William III., 8 March, 1701–2. And he says in these words, that "Sir John Holt, Knight, chief justice of the king's bench, holding his office by writ, though it was *quamdiu se bene gesserit,* held it to be determined by the demise of the king, notwithstanding the act of 12 and 13 William III. And, therefore, the queen in council gave orders that he should have a new writ, which he received accordingly, and was sworn before the lord keeper of the great seal the Saturday following, namely, the 14th of March, chief justice of king's bench." From this several things appear: 1. That General Brattle is mistaken in apprehending that the judges' commissions were without the clause, *quamdiu bene se gesserint,* in the reign of King William and Queen Mary, and most probably also in the reign of Queen Anne; because it is not likely that Lord Holt would have accepted a commission from the queen during pleasure, when he had before had one from King William during good behavior; and because if Queen Anne had made such an alteration in the commission, it is most likely Lord Raymond would have taken notice of it. 2. That Lord Holt's opinion was, that by common law he had not an estate for life in his office; for, if he had, it could not expire on the demise of the king. 3. That Lord Holt did not think the clause in the statute of 12 and 13 William III. to be a declaration of what was common law before, nor in affirmance of what was law before, but a new law, and a total alteration of the tenure of the judges' commissions established by parliament, and not to take place till after the death of the Princess Anne. 4. That in Lord Holt's opinion it was not in the power of the crown to alter the tenure of the judges' commissions, and make them a tenure for life, determinable only upon misbehavior, even by inserting that express clause in them, *quamdiu se bene gesserint.*

I have many more things to say upon this subject, which may possibly appear some other time.

Meanwhile, I am, Messrs. Printers,
  Your humble servant,

            JOHN ADAMS

18 January, 1773

To the printers

It has been said already that the common law of England has not determined the judges to have an estate for life in their offices, provided they behaved well. The authorities of Lord Coke and Lord Holt have been produced relative to the judges of the king's bench; and, indeed, authorities still more ancient than Coke might have been adduced. For example, the learned Chancellor Fortescue, in his book in praise of the laws of England, chap. 51, says, "When any one judge of the king's bench dies, resigns, or is superseded, the king, with the advice of his council, makes choice of one of the sergeants-at-law, whom he constitutes a judge by his letters-patents in the room of the judge so deceased, resigning, or superseded." And afterwards he says, "It is no degree in law, but only an office and a branch of magistracy determinable on the king's good pleasure." I have quoted a translation in this place, as I choose to do whenever I can obtain one; but I do not venture to translate passages myself, lest I should be charged with doing it unfairly. The original words of Fortescue are unusual and emphatical: "Ad regis nutum duratura."

The judges of the court of common pleas held their offices by a tenure as precarious. "The chief justice of the common pleas is created by letters-patents,—Rex, &c. Sciatis quod constituimus dilectum et fidelem E. C. militem, capitalem justiciarium de communi banco. *Habendum quamdiu nobis placuerit,* cum vadiis et feodis ab antiquo debitis et consuetis. In cujus rei testimonium has literas nostras fieri fecimus patentes. Teste, &c. And each of the justices of this court hath letters-patents. Sciatis quod constituimus dilectum et fidelem P. W., militem, unum justiciariorum nostrorum de communi banco,"* &c.; and this &c. implies the *habendum quamdiu nobis placuerit,* as in the patent of the chief justice.

It is true that in the same *Fourth Institute,* 117, we read, that "the chief baron" (that is, of the exchequer) "is created by letters-patents, and the office is granted to him *quamdiu se bene gesserit,* wherein he hath a more fixed estate (it being an estate for life) than the justices of either bench, who have their offices but at will. And *quamdiu se bene gesserit* must be intended in matters concerning his office, and is no more than the law would have implied if the office had been granted for life. And in like manner are the rest of the barons of the exchequer constituted; and the patents of the attorney-general and solicitor are also *quamdiu se bene gesserit.*"

---

* 4 Inst. 100.

It is also true, that by the law of this province a superior court of judicature, court of assize, and general jail delivery is constituted over this whole province, to be held and "kept by one chief justice and four other justices to be appointed and commissionated for the same; who shall have cognizance of all pleas, real, personal, or mixed, as well all pleas of the crown, &c.; and generally of all other matters, as fully and amply to all intents and purposes whatsoever, as the courts of king's bench, common pleas, and exchequer, within his majesty's kingdom of England, have, or ought to have," &c.

Will it be said that this law, giving our judges cognizance of all matters of which the court of exchequer has cognizance, gives them the same estate in their offices which the barons of exchequer had? or will it be said that by "the judges," General Brattle meant the barons of the exchequer?

The passages already cited will afford us great light in considering the case of Harcourt and Fox. Sir Thomas Powis, who was of counsel in that case for the plaintiff, indeed says, "I take it, by the common law and the ancient constitution of the kingdom, all officers of courts of justice, and immediately relating to the execution of justice, were in for their lives, only removable for misbehavior in their offices. Not only my lords the judges of the courts in Westminster Hall were anciently as they now are, since the revolution, *quamdiu se bene gesserint,* but all the officers of note in the several courts under them were so, and most of them continue so to this day, as the clerks of the crown in this court, and in the chancery, the chief clerk on the civil side in this court, the prothonotaries in the common pleas, the master of the office of pleas in the exchequer, and many others. I think, speaking generally, they were all in for their lives by the common law, and are so still to this day."

"And in this particular the wisdom of the law is very great; for it was an encouragement to men to fit and prepare themselves for the execution and performance of those offices, that when by such a capacity they had obtained them, they might act in them safely, without fear or dependence upon favor. And when they had served in them faithfully and honestly, and done their duty, they should not be removable at pleasure. And on the other side, the people were safe; for injustice, corruption, or other misdemeanors in an office were sufficient causes for removal and displacing the offender."

And Sergeant Levinz says, "If any judicial or ministerial office be granted to any man to hold, so long as he behaves himself well in the office, that is an estate for life, unless he lose it for misbehavior. So was Sir John Waller's case, as to the office of chief baron of the exchequer; and so was Justice Archer's case in the time of King Charles the Second. He was made a judge of the common pleas *quamdiu se bene gesserit;* and though he was displaced

80

as far as they could, yet he continued judge of that court to the time of his death; and his name was used in all the fines, and other records of the court; and so it is in all cases of grants from the king, or from any other person." And afterwards,—"It is a grievance that runs through the whole common law, as to ministerial offices; for all the offices in this court, in the chancery, in the exchequer, in the common pleas, and generally all over the kingdom, relating to the administration of justice, and even the judges themselves, are officers for life; and why there should be more of a grievance in this case than in theirs, I do not see. In general, they are all for life, though some few particular ones may be excepted indeed."

I have repeated at length these sayings of Sir Thomas Powis and Sergeant Levinz, because they are music in my ears; and I sincerely wish they were well supported; and because I suspect that General Brattle derived much of his learning relative to the judges' offices from them.

But, alas! so far as they make for his purpose, the whole stream of law and history is against them. And, indeed, Mr. Hawles, who was of counsel for Mr. Fox, seems to have given a true and sufficient answer to them in these words:—"Whatsoever the common law was as to offices that were so ancient, is no rule in this matter; though it is we know, that, as our books tell us, some offices were for life. And the office of chancellor of England, my Lord Coke says, could not be granted to any one for life. And why? Because it never was so granted. *Custom and nothing else prevails, and governs in all those cases;* of those offices that were usually granted for life, a grant of such an office for life was good, and of those that were not usually granted for life, a grant of such an office for life was void."

The judges, indeed, did not expressly deny any of those sayings of Sir Thomas Powis, or of Sergeant Levinz, who spoke after him on the same side; but the reason of this is plain; because it was quite unnecessary, in that case, to determine what was common law; for both the office of *custos rotulorum,* and that of clerk of the peace, were created by statute, not erected by common law, as was clearly agreed both on the bench and at the bar.

Nevertheless, my Lord Holt seems to have expressed his opinion when he said, "I compare it to the case which my Lord Chief Justice Hobart puts of himself in his book, 153, Colt and Glover's case. Saith he, 'I cannot grant the offices of my gift as chief justice for less time than for life;' and he puts the case there of a man's assigning a rent for dower out of the lands dowable, that it must be for no less estate than life; for the estate was by custom, and it cannot be granted for a lesser estate *than what the custom appoints;* and in that case of the chief justice, in granting offices in his gift, all that he had to do was *to point out the person that should have the office, the custom settled his estate in it.*"

Thus, we see that the sentiments of Lord Coke and of Lord Holt concur with those of Mr. Hawles, that the custom was the criterion, and that alone. So that, if the king should constitute a baron of the exchequer during pleasure, he would have an estate for life in his office, or the grant would be void. Why? Because the custom had so settled it. If the king should constitute a judge of the king's bench, or common bench, during good behavior, he would have only an estate at will of the grantor. Why? Because the custom hath determined it so. And that custom could not be annulled or altered but by act of parliament.

But I go on with my delightful work of quotation. "In order to maintain both the dignity and independency of the judges in the superior courts, it is enacted by the stat. 13 W. III. c. 2, that their commissions shall be made, not, as formerly, *durante beneplacito,* but *quamdiu se bene gesserint,* and their salaries ascertained and established; but that it may be lawful to remove them on the address of both houses of parliament. And now, by the noble improvements of that law in the statute of 1 G. III. c. 23, enacted at the earnest recommendation of the king himself from the throne, the judges are continued in their offices during their good behavior, notwithstanding any demise of the crown, which was formerly held (see Lord Raym. 747) immediately to vacate their seats; and their full salaries are absolutely secured to them during the continuance of their commissions,—his majesty having been pleased to declare, that he looked upon the independence and uprightness of the judges as essential to the impartial administration of justice; as one of the best securities of the rights and liberties of his subjects; and as most conducive to the honor of the crown."*

It would be endless to run over all the passages in English history relating to this subject, and the examples of judges displaced by kings. It may not be amiss to turn our attention to a very few, however. The oracle himself was silenced by this power in the crown. "Upon the 18th November, this term, Sir Henry Montague was made chief justice of the king's bench, in the place of Sir Edward Coke, the late chief justice, who, being in the king's displeasure, was removed from his place by a writ from the king, reciting that whereas he had appointed him by writ to that place, that he had now amoved him, and appointed him to desist from the further execution thereof. And now this day, Egerton, lord chancellor, came into the king's bench; and Sir Henry Montague, one of the king's sergeants, being accompanied with Sergeant

---

* 1 Blackstone's Comm. 267–8.

Hutten and Sergeant Francis Moore, came to the middle of the bar; and then the lord chancellor delivered unto him the king's pleasure, to make choice of him to that place."*

There is a passage in Hume's History of England which I cannot forbear transcribing. "The Queen's (Elizabeth's) menace," says he, "of trying and punishing Hayward for treason, could easily have been executed, let his book have been ever so innocent. While so many terrors hung over the people, no jury durst have acquitted a man when the court was resolved to have him condemned. And, indeed, there scarcely occurs an instance during all these reigns, that the sovereign or the ministers were ever disappointed in the issue of a prosecution. Timid juries, and judges who held their offices during pleasure, never failed to second all the views of the crown."

Sergeant Levinz, in the argument of Harcourt against Fox, speaking of the first parliament under King William, says,—"The parliament might observe, that some years before there had been great changing of offices that usually were for life into offices *quamdiu placuerit.* This is very well known in Westminster Hall; and I did know some of them myself, particularly the judges of the courts of common law; for I myself (among others) lost my judge's place by it," &c.

Mr. Hume, in the reign of James the Second, says,—"The people had entertained such violent prepossessions against the use which James here made of his prerogative, that he was obliged, before he brought on Hales's cause, to displace four of the judges, Jones, Montague, Charlton, and Nevil."

There is not in history a more terrible example of judges perishing at the royal nod than this, nor a stronger evidence that the power and prerogative of removing judges at pleasure were allowed to be, by law, in the crown. It was loudly complained of as a grievance, no doubt, and an arbitrary exertion of prerogative; but it was allowed to be a legal prerogative still. And it cannot be doubted, that the legality of it would have been denied everywhere, if the sense of the nation, as well as the body of the law, had not been otherwise, when the circumstances of that case of Sir Edward Hales are considered. And they ought to be remembered, and well considered by every well-wisher to the public; because they show the tendency of a precarious, dependent tenure of the judges' offices. Sir Edward Hales was a papist; yet the king gave him a commission as a colonel of foot; and he refused to receive the sacrament, and to take the oaths and test, within the time prescribed by an act of parliament, 25 Car. II. c. 2, by which refusal, and that statute, he forfeited five hundred pounds. By concert between King James and Sir Ed-

* Croke, Jac. 407.

ward, his coachman was employed to bring an action against him upon that statute, for the penalty. Sir Edward appears, and pleads a dispensation under the broad seal, to act *non obstante* that statute. To this the plaintiff demurs. When this action was to be brought to trial, the judges were secretly closeted by the king, and asked their opinions. Such as had scruples about judging as the court directed, were plainly told by the king himself, that he would have twelve judges of his own opinion, and turned out of their offices. The judges mentioned by Hume were thus displaced, to their lasting honor; and one of them, Jones, had the fortitude and integrity to tell the king to his face, that he might possibly make twelve judges, but *he would scarcely find twelve lawyers of his opinion.* Bedingfield, Atkins, Lutwyche, and Heath, to their disgrace and infamy, were created judges. And Westminster Hall thus garbled became the sanctuary of despotism and injustice. All the judges excepting one gave their opinions for the king, and made it a general rule in law,—"1. That the laws of England are the king's laws. 2. That, therefore, it is an incident, inseparable prerogative of the kings of England, as of all other sovereign princes, to dispense with all penal laws in particular cases, and upon particular, necessary reasons. 3. That of these reasons and necessities the king is the sole judge. Consequently, 4. That this is not a trust invested in and granted to the king, but the ancient remains of the sovereign power of the kings of England, which never was yet taken from them, nor can be." In consequence of this decision, the papists, with the king's permission, set up everywhere in the kingdom in the free and open exercise of their religion. To enumerate all the struggles of the people, the petitions and addresses to kings, praying that the judges' commissions might be granted during good behavior, the bills which were actually brought into one or the other house of parliament for that purpose, which failed of success until the final establishment in the 12 & 13 William III., would be too tedious;* and, indeed, I anxiously fear I have been so already.

I also fear the proofs that the common law of England has not determined the judges to have estates for life in their offices, appear to be very numerous, and quite irresistible. I very heartily wish General Brattle success in his researches after evidence of the contrary position; and while he is thus engaged, if I should find neither business more profitable nor amusement more inviting, I shall be preparing for your press a few other observations on his first publication.

John Adams

---

* See Rapin, Burnet, Skinner, Comberbach, State Trials, and Sir Edward Herbert's Vindication of Himself.

25 January, 1773

TO THE PRINTERS

ANOTHER OBSERVATION which occurred to me upon reading General Brattle's first publication was upon these words: — "That by the charter and common law of England, there is no necessity of having any commission at all; a nomination and appointment recorded is enough; *nomination and appointment* are the words of the charter, a commission for them not so much as mentioned in it. Their commission is only declarative of their nomination and appointment." Two questions arise upon this paragraph; and the first is, what provision is made by our charter? and the next is, what was necessary to the creation of a judge at common law?

As to our charter. The king thereby grants and ordains, — "That it shall and may be lawful for the said governor, with the advice and consent of the council or assistants, from time to time to nominate and appoint judges, commissioners of oyer and terminer, sheriffs, provosts, marshals, justices of the peace, and other officers to our council and courts of justice belonging."

It is obvious from this, that there is no superior court of judicature, court of assize and general jail delivery, nor any inferior court of common pleas, or any court of exchequer, expressly erected by the charter. Commissioners of oyer and terminer, the governor, with the advice and consent of the council, is empowered to nominate and appoint; but it will not follow from hence that a nomination and appointment will alone constitute and empower commissioners of oyer and terminer. For the judges, whom the governor with the advice of council is empowered to nominate and appoint, are not vested with any powers at all by the charter; but by another clause in it, the great and general court or assembly "shall forever have full power and authority to erect and constitute judicatories and courts of record, or other courts, to be held in the name of us, our heirs and successors, for the hearing, trying, and determining of all manner of crimes, offences, pleas, processes, plaints, actions, matters, causes, and things, whatsoever, arising or happening within our said province or territory, or between persons inhabiting and residing there, whether the same be criminal or civil, and whether the said crimes be capital or not capital, and whether the said pleas be real, personal, or mixt, and for the awarding and making out execution thereupon."

In pursuance of this authority, our legislature, in 1699, by a law, 2 William III. c. 3, have established "a superior court of judicature, court of assize, and general jail delivery within this province, to be held by one chief justice and four other justices, to be appointed and commissionated for the same," &c.

Is not General Brattle, then, greatly mistaken when he says, that "a nomination and appointment recorded is enough?" Enough for what? Enough to constitute judges of our superior court, for they alone can be meant by the General, because the General himself determines his own meaning to be, "they who have the same powers with the king's bench, common bench, and exchequer;" and no other judges have those powers but the judges of our superior court, &c., and they have them, not by charter, but by the law of the province. If the governor should nominate and appoint, with advice and consent, &c. A to be a judge, or A, B, and C to be judges, in the words of the charter, what powers would this nomination and appointment convey? None at all. It would be nugatory and void; for, according to Lord Coke,* a "new court cannot be erected but by act of parliament. And when a new court is erected, it is necessary that the jurisdiction and authority of the court be certainly set down. And that the court can have no other jurisdiction than is expressed in the erection." And he there mentions the case of a letter-patent granted by Edward IV. in these words: "We will and ordain that Richard Beauchampe, &c., should have it (that is, the office of the chancellor of the garter) for his life, and after his decease, that his successors should have it forever"; and "it was resolved unanimously that this grant was void; for that a new office was erected, and it was not defined what jurisdiction or authority the officer should have; and, therefore, for the uncertainty, it was void."

Let us next inquire whether, by the common law of England, there is or is not a necessity of the judges having any commissions at all. The authorities cited before seem to show very plainly that the judges, either of the king's bench, common bench, or exchequer, can be created only by writ, or by letters-patent; and although these may be said not to be commissions, yet they are surely something more than nomination and appointment. However, writs and letters-patent are commissions, I presume; and should never have doubted it, if I had never read a newspaper. But if I had doubted, I might easily have resolved the doubt; for we read† that "all judges must derive their authority from the crown by some commission warranted by law. The judges of Westminster are (all except the chief justice of the king's bench, who is created by writ) appointed by patent, and formerly held their places only during the king's pleasure, &c."‡

---

* 4 Inst. 200.

† 1 Bacon's Abr. 555.

‡ 4 Inst. 75. "Where, in 5 E. 4. it is holden by all the chief justices in the exchequer chamber that a man cannot be justice by writ, but by patent or commission, it is to be understood of

And Lord Coke observes, that "the creation of the office of chief justice was first by writ, and afterwards by letters-patents." "As all judges must derive their authority from the crown by some commission warranted by law, they must also exercise it in a legal manner."*

In order to see whether writs and letters-patent are not commissions, let us look into any common dictionary or interpreter of law terms. "Commission, *commissio*," (says Cowell, and after him, in the same words, Cunningham,) "is for the most part, in the understanding of the law, as much as *delegatio* with the civilians,† and is taken for the warrant, or letters-patent, that all men exercising jurisdiction, either ordinary or extraordinary, have for their power to hear or determine any cause or action."

Thus it seems to be very clear that, by the common law of England, a commission was absolutely necessary for all the judges known at common law; and as to others, erected by statute, let the statute speak. By 27 H. 8, c. 24, it is enacted: "That no person or persons, of what estate, degree, or condition soever they be, shall have any power or authority to make any justices of eyre, justices of assize, justices of peace, or justices of jail delivery; but that all such officers and ministers shall be made by letters-patent, under the king's great seal, in the name and by the authority of the king's highness, in all shires, counties palatine, Wales, &c., or any other his dominions, &c., any grants, usages, allowance, or act of parliament to the contrary notwithstanding."

I shall add no more upon this point but this. We find in Jenkin's Centuries, 123, this question determined by all the judges of England in the exchequer chamber: "A writ of *admittas* in association is directed to the justices of assize; A. shows this writ of *admittas* in association to them, but does not show the patent by which he is made justice. In this case, both ought to be shown to the justices of assize.

By all the Judges in the Exchequer Chamber.

The judges of the king's bench and common pleas, and the barons of the exchequer are made by patent, in which the word *constituimus* is used. The chief justice of the king's bench is constituted only by writ."

JOHN ADAMS

---

all the judges, saving the chief justice of this court (that is, the king's bench); but both the chief justice and the rest of the judges may be discharged by writ under the great seal."

* Bacon's Abr. 555.

† See Brooke and Lit. Commission.

1 February, 1773

One thing at one time. —

De Witt

To the printers

THE QUESTION IS, in the present state of the controversy, according to my apprehension of it, whether, by the common law of England, the judges of the king's bench and common bench had estates for life in their offices, determinable on misbehavior, and determinable also on the demise of the crown. General Brattle still thinks they had; I cannot yet find reason to think so. And as whether they had or had not is the true question between us, I will endeavor to confine myself to it without wandering.

Now, in order to pursue my inquiry regularly, it is necessary to determine with some degree of precision what is to be understood by the terms "common law." Out of the Mercian laws, the laws of the West Saxons, and the Danish law, King Edward the Confessor extracted one uniform digest of laws, to be observed throughout the whole kingdom, which seems to have been no more than a fresh promulgation of Alfred's code, or Dome Book, with such improvements as the experience of a century and a half had suggested, which is now unhappily lost. This collection is of higher antiquity than memory or history can reach; they have been used time out of mind, or for a time whereof the memory of man runneth not to the contrary. General customs, which are the universal rule of the whole kingdom, form the common law in its stricter and more usual signification. This is that law which determines that there shall be four superior courts of record, the chancery, the king's bench, the common pleas, and the exchequer, among a multitude of other doctrines, that are not set down in any written statute or ordinance, but depend merely upon immemorial usage, that is, upon common law, for their support. Judicial decisions are the principal and most authoritative evidence that can be given of the existence of such a custom as shall form a part of the common law. The law and the opinion of the judge are not always convertible terms; though it is a general rule, that the decisions of courts of justice are the evidence of what is common law.*

I have endeavored to ascertain what is meant by the common law of England, and the method of determining all questions concerning it, from Blackstone. Let us now see what is said upon the same subject, by Justice Fortescue Aland, in the preface to his Reports. "Our judges," says he, "do

---

* See 1 Blackst. Comm. 65–73.

not determine according to their princes, or their own arbitrary will and pleasure; but according to the settled and established rules and ancient customs of the nation, approved for many successions of ages. . . . . . . King Alfred, who began his reign in 871, *magnus juris Anglicani conditor,* the great founder of the laws of England, with the advice of his wise men, collected out of the laws of Ina, Offa, and Aethelbert, such as were the best, and made them to extend equally to the whole nation, and therefore very properly called them the common law of England, because those laws were now first of all made common to the whole English nation. This *jus commune, jus publicum,* or folcright, that is, the people's right, set down in one code, was probably the same with the Doom-Book, or *liber judicialis,* which is referred to in all the subsequent laws of the Saxon kings, and was the book that they determined causes by. And in the next reign, that of Edward the elder, the king commands all his judges to give judgment to all the people of England according to the Doom-Book. And it is from this origin that our common law judges fetch that excellent usage of determining causes, according to the settled and established rules of law, and that they have acted up to this rule for above eight hundred years together, and continue to do so to this very day. Edward the Confessor was afterwards but the restorer of the common law founded by Alfred, and William the Conqueror confirms and proclaims these to be the laws of England, to be kept and observed under grievous penalties, and took an oath to keep them inviolable himself. King Henry I. promised to observe them; King Stephen, King Henry II., and Richard I. confirmed them; King John swore to restore them; King Henry III. confirmed them; *Magna Charta* was founded on them, and King Edward I. in parliament, confirmed them."

Now I apprehend General Brattle's opinion to be, that the common law of England, the birthright of every subject, or, in the language of the Saxons, the folkright, determines the judges of the king's bench and common pleas to have estates for life in their offices, determinable only on misbehavior, or the demise of the crown. And this, I suppose, was the meaning of Sir Thomas Powis, when he said, "I take it, *by the common law* and the *ancient constitution of the kingdom,* all officers of courts of justice, &c., were in for their lives, &c.; not only my lords the judges of the courts in Westminster Hall were anciently, as they now are since this revolution, *quamdiu se bene gesserint.*"

I have never expressed any disrespect to the character of Sir Thomas Powis, and I have no disposition to harbor any; it is enough for me to say, that these expressions were used by him when arguing a cause for his client at the bar, not when he was determining a cause as a judge; that they were entirely unnecessary for the support of his cause, which was a very good one, let these expressions be true or otherwise,—that is, whether the judges were anciently in for their lives, or only at pleasure; that they depend wholly upon his affirmation, or rather his opinion, without the color or pretence of an authority to support them; and that I really believe them to be untrue. And I must add, it appears to me extraordinary, that a gentleman educated under that great Gamaliel, Mr. Read, should ever adduce the simple dictum of a counsel at the bar, uttered *arguendo,* and as an ornament to his discourse too, rather than any pertinent branch of his reasoning, as evidence of a point "settled and determined by the greatest sages of the law formerly and more lately." Does Sir Thomas Powis produce the Dome-Book itself in support of his doctrine? That was irrecoverably lost for ages before he had a being. Does he produce any judicial decision, ancient or modern, to prove this opinion? No such thing pretended. Does he produce any legal authority, a Hengham, Britton, Fleta, Fortescue, Coke; or any antiquarian, Matthew Paris, Dugdale, Lambard, or any other; or even the single opinion of one historian, to give a color to his doctrine? No such matter. Nay, I must inquire further, can General Brattle draw from any of these sources a single iota to support this opinion? But, in order to show, for the present, the improbability that any such authority will be found, let us look a little into history. Mr. Rapin, in his Dissertation on the Government of the Anglo-Saxons, says, "One of the most considerable of the king's prerogatives was the power of appointing the earls, viscounts, *judges,* and other officers, as well civil as military. *Very probably it was in the king's power to change these officers, according to his pleasure,* of which we meet with several instances in history." By this it appears to have been Mr. Rapin's opinion, that very probably the kings, under the ancient Saxon constitution, had power to change the judges according to their pleasure. I would not be understood, however, to lay any great stress on the opinions of historians and compilers of antiquities, because it must be confessed that the Saxon constitution is involved in much obscurity, and that the monarchical and democratic factions in England, by their opposite endeavors to make the Saxon constitutions swear for their respective systems, have much increased the difficulty of determining, to the satisfaction of the world, what that constitution, in many important particulars, was. Yet Mr. Rapin certainly was not of that monarchical faction; his bias, if he had any, was the other way; and therefore his concession makes the more in my favor.

Mr. Hume, in his Feudal and Anglo-Norman Government and Manners,* says: "The business of the court was wholly managed by the chief justiciary and the law-barons, who were men appointed by the king, *and*

* History of England, vol. i. Appendix II.

wholly at his disposal." And since I am now upon Hume, it may be proper to mention the case of Hubert de Burgh, who, "while he enjoyed his authority, had an entire ascendant over Henry III., and was loaded with honors and favors beyond any other subject, . . . and, by *an unusual concession,* was made chief justiciary of England for life."* Upon this I reason thus: If his being made justiciary for life was an "unusual concession," it could not be by the immemorial, uninterrupted usage and custom, which is the criterion of common law. And the very next words of Hume show how valid and effectual this grant of the office for life was then esteemed. "Yet Henry, in a sudden caprice, *threw off* this faithful minister;" which implies that he was discarded and displaced in both his capacities, because the *summus justiciarius* or chief justiciary, was in those reigns supreme regent of the kingdom, and first minister of state, as well as of the law; and this seems to show that the grant for life was void, and not binding on the king, in the sense of those times, ancient as they were (1231). This *summus justiciarius* is the officer whose original commission I gave the public from Lord Coke, in my first paper, which was expressly during pleasure. And my Lord Coke's account of the change of the chief justice's commission and authority may receive some additional light from Lord Gilbert's Historical View of the Court of Exchequer. Towards the latter end of the Norman period, the power of the justiciar was broken, so that the *aula regis,* which was before one great court, only distinguished by several offices, and all ambulatory with the king before *Magna Charta,* was divided into four distinct courts,—chancery, exchequer, king's bench, and common pleas. The justiciary was laid aside, lest he should get into the throne, as Capet and Pepin, who were justiciars in France, had done there.† Now, from the exorbitant powers and authority of these justiciaries arises a proof, from the frame of the government and the balance of the estates, that the office in those ages was always considered as dependent on the pleasure of the king, because the jealousy between the kings and nobles, or between the monarchical and aristocratical factions, during the whole Norman period, was incessant and unremitted; and therefore it may be depended on, that kings never would have come into the method of granting such an office usually for life. For such a grant, if it had been made, and been valid, must have cost the grantor his throne, as it made the justiciar independent of the king, and a much more powerful man than himself. And if, during the whole Norman period, and quite down to the death of Sir Edward Coke, a course of almost six hundred years, the offices of

---

* 2 Hume, 162.

† See also Gilbert's *History and Practice of the High Court of Chancery.*

judges were held during pleasure, what becomes of the title to them for life, which General Brattle sets up, by immemorial, uninterrupted usage, or common law?

Sir Thomas Powis, however, has not determined whether, by the *ancient* constitution of the kingdom, he meant under the Norman or the Saxon period; and in order to show the improbability that the judges held their offices during good behavior, in either of those periods, I must beg the pardon of your readers if I lead them into ages, manners, and government more ancient and barbarous than any mentioned before. Our Saxon ancestors were one of those enterprising northern nations, who made inroads upon the provinces of the Roman empire, and carried with them, wherever they went, the customs, maxims, and manners of the feudal system; and although, when they intermingled with the ancient Britons, they shook off some part of the feudal fetters, yet they never disengaged themselves from the whole. They retained a vast variety of the *regalia principis* of the feudal system, from whence most branches of the present prerogatives of our kings are derived; and, among other *regalia,* the creation and annihilation of judges was an important branch. For evidence of this, we must look into the feudal law. It was in consequence of this prerogative that the courts were usually held in the *aula regis,* and often in the king's presence, who often heard and determined causes in person; and in those ages the justiciary was only a substitute or deputy to the king, whose authority ceased entirely in the king's presence. This part of the prerogative has a long time ago been divested from the crown, and it has been determined that the king has delegated all his authority to his judges. The power of the king in the Saxon period was absolute enough, however, and he sometimes treated them with very little ceremony. Alfred himself is said, in the Mirror of Justices, to have hanged up forty-four of his judges in one year for misdemeanors.

To some of these facts and principles Bracton is a witness. "Dictum est," (says he,) "de ordinaria jurisdictione, quae pertinet ad regem, consequenter dicendum est de jurisdictione delegata, ubi quis ex se ipso nullam habet auctoritatem, sed ab alio sibi commissam, cum ipse qui delegat non sufficiat per se omnes causas sive jurisdictiones terminare. Et si ipse dominus rex ad singulas causas terminandas non sufficiat, ut levior sit illi labor, in plures personas partito onere, eligere debet de regno suo viros sapientes et timentes Deum . . . Item justiciariorum, quidam sunt capitales, generales, perpetui et majores a latere regis residentes, qui omnium aliorum corrigere tenentur injurias et errores. Sunt etiam alii perpetui, certo loco residentes, sicut in banco, . . . qui omnes jurisdictionem habere incipiunt praestito sacramento . . . Et quamvis quidam eorum perpetui sunt, ut videtur, finitur tamen eorum jurisdictio multis modis, s. mortuo eo qui delegavit, &c. *Item cum delegans revocaverit jurisdictionem,*" &c. Bracton, chap. 10, lib. 3.

Sergeant Levinz says, "If any judicial or ministerial office be granted to any man to hold, so long as he behaves himself well in the office, that is an estate for life, unless he lose it for misbehavior. So was Sir John Waller's case, as to the office of chief baron of the exchequer." To all this I agree, provided it is an office that by custom, that is, immemorial usage, or common law, (as that of the chief baron of the exchequer was,) or by an express act of parliament, (as that of clerk of the peace, in the case of Harcourt against Fox, was,) has been granted in that manner, but not otherwise; and therefore these words have no operation at all against me. But the Sergeant goes on: "And so was Justice Archer's case, in the time of King Charles II. He was made a judge of the common pleas *quamdiu se bene gesserit;* and though he was displaced as far as they could, yet he continued judge of that court to the time of his death; and his name was used in all the fines and other records of the court." General Brattle thinks these words are full in his favor; and he cannot reconcile this patent to Judge Archer with the history of Charles II.'s reign, &c. We shall presently see if a way to reconcile it cannot be discovered: but before I come to this attempt, as it is my desire to lay before the public every thing I know of, which favors General Brattle's hypothesis, and to assist his argument to the utmost of my power, I will help him to some other authorities, which seem to corroborate Sergeant Levinz's saying; and the first is Justice Fortescue Aland:* "Justice Archer was removed from the common pleas; but his patent being *quamdiu se bene gesserit,* he refused to surrender his patent without a *scire facias,* and continued justice, though prohibited to sit there; and in his place Sir William Ellis was sworn." The next is Sir Thomas Raymond, 217: "This last vacation, Justice Archer was amoved from sitting in the court of common pleas, *pro quibusdam causis mihi incognitis;* but the judge having his patent to be judge *quamdiu se bene gesserit,* refused to surrender his patent without a *scire facias,* and continued justice of that court, though prohibited to sit there; and in his place Sir William Ellis, Knight, was sworn."

But will any man from these authorities conclude that King Charles II. had power by the common law to grant Judge Archer an estate for life in his office? If he had, how could he be prohibited to sit? how came Justice Ellis to be sworn in his stead? Was not the admission of Ellis by his brother judges an acknowledgment of the king's authority? Will any man conclude from these authorities that it had before been the custom, time out of mind, for

---

* Reports, 394, known as Lord Fortescue's.

kings to grant patents to the judges, *quamdiu se bene gesserint?* If we look into Rushworth, 1366, we shall find some part of this mystery unriddled: "After the passing of these votes against the judges, and transmitting of them unto the house of peers, and their concurring with the house of commons therein, an address was made unto the king shortly after, that his majesty for the future would not make any judge by patent during pleasure, but that they may hold their places hereafter *quamdiu se bene gesserint,* and his majesty did readily grant the same, and in his speech to both houses of parliament, at the time of giving his royal assent to two bills, one to take away the high commission court, and the other the court of star-chamber, and regulating the power of the council table, he hath this passage,—'If you consider what I have done this parliament, discontents will not sit in your hearts; for I hope you remember that I have granted that the judges hereafter shall hold their places, *quamdiu se bene gesserint.*' And likewise his gracious majesty, King Charles II. observed the same rule and method in granting patents to judges, *quamdiu se bene gesserint,* as appears upon record in the rolls, namely,—to Sergeant Hyde, to be lord chief justice of the king's bench, Sir Orlando Bridgeman to be lord chief baron, and afterwards lord chief justice of the common pleas, to Sir Robert Foster, and others. Mr. Sergeant Archer, now living, (notwithstanding his removal,) still enjoys his patent, being *quamdiu se bene gesserit,* and receives a share in the profits of that court, as to fines and other proceedings, by virtue of his said patent, and his name is used in those fines &c. as a judge of that court."

This address of the two houses of parliament which was in 1640, was made in consequence of a general jealousy conceived of the judges, and the general odium which had fallen upon them, for the opinion they gave in the case of ship money and other cases, and because there had been, not long before, changes and removals in the benches. To mention only one: "Sir Randolph Crew, not showing so much zeal for the advancement of the loan as the king was desirous he should, was removed from his place of lord chief justice, and Sir Nicholas Hyde succeeded in his room." And King Charles, in 1640, began to believe the discontents of his subjects to be a serious affair, and think it necessary to do something to appease them.*

But will it do to say that he had power to give away the prerogative of the crown, that had been established in his ancestors for eight hundred years, and no man can say how many centuries longer, without an act of parliament, against the express words of Lord Coke, which the General thanks me for quoting? "It is a rule in law that ancient offices must be granted in such

* See Rushworth, 420; 2 Rush. Append. 266.

forms and in such manner as they have used to be, unless the alteration was by authority of parliament."

As to King Charles II. his character is known to have been that of a man of pleasure and dissipation, who left most kinds of business to his ministers, and particularly in the beginning of his reign, to my Lord Clarendon, who had, perhaps, a large share in procuring that concession from Charles I., and therefore chose to continue it under the Second.

But notwithstanding all this, Charles II. soon discovered that by law his father's concession and his own had not divested him of the power of re-moving judges, even those to whom he had given patents *quamdiu se bene gesserint,* and he actually reassumed his prerogative, displaced Judge Archer and many others in the latter end of his reign, and so did his successor.* These examples show that those kings did not consider these concessions as legally binding on them; they also show that the judges in Westminster Hall were of the same mind, otherwise they would not have admitted the new judges in the room of those displaced; and it seems that even the judges themselves who were then displaced, Judge Archer himself, did not venture to demand his place, which he might have done if he had an estate for life in his office. Nay, it may be affirmed that the house of commons themselves were of the same mind; for in the year 1680, in the reign of Charles II. after the removal of Archer and many other judges, the commons brought in a bill to make the office of judge during good behavior.† Now I think they would not have taken this course if they had thought Archer had an estate for life in his office, but would have voted his removal illegal, and would have impeached the other judges for admitting another in his room.

Archer "continuing judge," and "receiving fees for fines," and "his name being used in the fines," I conjecture are to be accounted for in this manner. He refused to surrender his patent without a *scire facias.* The king would not have a *scire facias* brought, because that would occasion a solemn hearing, and much speculation, clamor, and heat, which he chose to avoid; and as his patent remained unsurrendered and uncancelled, and as by law there might be more judges of the common pleas than four, and therefore the appoint-ment of another judge might not be a *supersedeas* to Archer, they might think it safest to join his name in the fines, and give him a share in the fees. And no doubt this might be done in some instances to keep up the appearance of a claim to the place, and with a design to provoke the king's servants and

* See Skinner's Reports, and Raymond, 251.
† See 8 Hume, 143.

friends to bring a *scire facias,* and so occasion an odium on the administration, and hasten a revolution.

I have hazarded these conjectures unnecessarily, for it is incumbent upon General Brattle to show from good authorities, for the affirmative side of the issue is with him, that by common law the judges had estates for life in their offices. In order to do this, he ought to show that the king at common law, that is, from time immemorial, granted patents to these judges during good behavior, or that he, the king, had his election to grant them either *durante beneplacito,* or *quamdiu se bene gesserint,* as he pleased. Nay, it is incumbent on him to show that a patent without either of these clauses conveys an estate for life. None of these things has he done, or can he do.

It was never denied nor doubted by me, that a grant made in pursuance of immemorial custom, or of an act of parliament, to a man to hold, so long as he should behave himself well, would give him an estate for life. The unanimous judgment of the court in that case of Harcourt against Fox proves this. But then, in that case, an express act of parliament empowered the *custos rotulorum* to constitute a clerk of the peace for so long time as he should behave himself well. Nor have I any doubt that the patents to the barons of the exchequer, which are by immemorial usage, *quamdiu se bene gesserint,* convey to them an estate for life; but my difficulty lies here; no custom, no immemorial usage, no act of parliament, enabled the king to grant patents to the judges of king's bench, and common pleas, expressly *quamdiu se bene gesserint;* and therefore, if Lord Coke's rule is right, "that ancient offices must be granted in such forms and in such manner as they have used to be, unless the alteration be by authority of parliament," the king's grant at common law, to a judge of king's bench or common pleas, of his office, for life in terms, or during good behavior, which is tantamount, would have been void—void, I mean *quoad* an estate for life or good behavior, but good, as an estate at will; and I conceive, when we read that the king cannot make a lord chancellor for life, but that such a grant would be void, the meaning is, that the *habendum* for life or good behavior shall be void; but that this shall not vitiate the other parts of the patents, but that they shall convey such estate, and such estate only, as the king had power by custom or by statute to grant. I do not suppose that the writ to Lord Holt, or the patents to his brothers in the reign of King William were void, but I fear that, had the king seen fit to have removed them by writ, it would have been legally in his power, notwithstanding that clause in their commissions.

JOHN ADAMS

8 February, 1773

To the printers

TWO OR THREE ANECDOTES were omitted in my last for want of room, which may be here inserted, in order to show that General Brattle's "rule of the common law of England" originated in the reign of King Charles I. I say originated, because the example of Hubert de Burgh is so ancient and so uncertain that it is even doubted by Baron Gilbert whether he was ever chief justiciary or not.

In 1641, King Charles I. finding his affairs in a desperate condition, was obliged to consent to an act of the Scottish parliament, that no member of the privy council, no officer of state, none of the judges, should be appointed but by advice and approbation of parliament; and all the officers of state were to hold their places *quamdiu se bene gesserint.* Four of the present judges, who had been active on the side of prerogative, were displaced.

In 1642, the parliament of England transmitted to the king, at York, nineteen propositions, in order for an accommodation of the differences then subsisting, the twelfth of which was, that the judges should hold their places *quamdiu se bene gesserint.**

This was but about two years after the king had given orders, at the instance of parliament, and his royal promise in his public speech, that the judges' commissions should for the future be granted *quamdiu se bene gesserint.* And it proves incontestably one of these things, either that the parliament thought the king's promise was void, as being what he had not power by law to promise; or that the grants so made would be void, at least as to the *habendum* during good behavior; or, at least, that the crown had its election by law to make judges, at pleasure or at will, as it should see fit. Now, if either of these apprehensions was just, it could not be true that at common law the judges had their commissions *quamdiu se bene gesserint,* nor could it be true that by common law the judges had estates for life in their offices, whether *quamdiu se bene gesserint* was in their commissions or not.

I believe enough has been said concerning these dark sayings of Powis and Levinz. Let us now proceed to consider what was said by Lord Holt. And I must think, the General has discovered a degree of art in managing his lordship's words that is very remarkable; and I beg the reader's patience while I develop in some detail this complicated mystery. In order to this, I

* See Rapin and Mrs. Macaulay.

must state the case of Harcourt against Fox; for this will show that the decision of that case is no proof of any thing that I have ever denied, and that General Brattle has unaccountably misinterpreted Lord Holt's words.

The act of parliament made in the first year of William and Mary, says "the *custos rotulorum,* or other, having right to nominate a clerk of the peace, shall nominate and appoint a fit person for the same, for so long time only as such clerk of the peace shall demean himself well in his office."

The earl of Clare is made *custos* according to that statute. By his deed, he constituted the plaintiff, Harcourt, to be clerk of the peace, "to have and execute that office so long as he did well behave himself in it."

After this the earl of Clare was removed, and my lord of Bedford was made *custos;* and he, by his deed, appointed Fox, the defendant, to be clerk of the peace for so long time as he should continue *custos,* if the said Fox did behave himself well in the office. And the question, as stated by Lord Holt, was "whether or no by the motion of my lord of Clare from the office of *custos,* Harcourt ceased to be clerk of the peace; for then, the law was for the defendant; otherwise, it was for the plaintiff."

Lord Holt concurred with his brothers, that judgment should be for the plaintiff, and that he was still clerk of the peace; and, after explaining his reasons at great length, and with great learning and perspicuity, he hath these words,—

"All that the *custos* hath to do in reference to this office of clerk of the peace, is to point out the person that should have it; and as the other" (that is, the officer appointed by the chief justice) "is in by *custom,* so here *he is in by act of parliament;* the *custos,* when he hath named him, he hath executed his authority, and cannot qualify the interest which passeth by the act. I am the more inclined to be of this opinion, because I knew the *temper and inclination of the parliament* at the time when this act was made; *their design* was, that men should have places not to hold precariously or determinable upon will and pleasure, but have a certain, durable estate, that they might act in them without fear of losing them; *we all know it,* and our places as judges are so settled, only determinable upon misbehavior."

Now, I would ask any impartial person, to what those words, "we all know it," refer? We all know it; know what?—*that such was the temper and inclination of that parliament, and that such was* their design. Can it be said that these words refer to words that follow? We all know it; know what?— that our places as judges are so settled! Some new kind of grammar, logic, and common sense, must be invented, and applied to this paragraph, before this construction can be adopted.

I will now repeat the words of General Brattle:—"It is manifest to every one that doth not depend upon their memory, that Lord Chief Justice Holt, one of the sages of the law, apprehended that *for the judges' commissions being during good behavior, was upon the rule of the common law. He says,* after a cause had been argued upon a special verdict, after Sir T. Powis and Sergeant Levinz had most positively affirmed *that this was the rule of the common law,* not denied by the counsel for the other side, but rather conceded to, that, in giving his opinion upon the whole matter. '*We all know it,*' says that great lawyer, 'and our places as judges are so settled, only determinable by misbehavior.' "

Now, I will ask the same impartial person, to what those words, "we all know it," appear to refer, in the foregoing words of General Brattle. We all know it;—know what? *That this was the rule of the common law, as Powis and Levinz had most positively affirmed.*

In Lord Holt's own mouth, they referred to the temper, inclination, and design, of parliament; in General Brattle's writings, they are made to refer, seemingly, if not necessarily, to the sayings of Powis and Levinz, and to the rule of the common law. I hope this was the effect of haste, inadvertence, any thing rather than design in the General.

I must entreat every gentleman to look into that case of Harcourt and Fox, which is reported in Shower, at great length, and he must be convinced that, taken all together, it makes against General Brattle rather than for him. It was determined in that case, as it had been long before, that to hold an office during good behavior was to hold it for life, determinable upon misbehavior. This was never, and will never be, denied by me. But it was not determined that the judges' offices were held so, or that the king had power to grant them so. What was said by Lord Holt concerning the judges' offices had no direct relation to the point then in judgment before him, which concerned only the office of clerk of the peace. It was only said incidentally, and not explained. It might, and probably did, mean no more than it was so settled by King William in the patents he had given the judges, so far as it was in his power to settle it, and that it was the inclination and design of the parliament, and the then governing interest in the nation, that it should be so settled by act of parliament, as soon as it would bear. For it should be here observed, that although the friends of King William were most numerous and powerful, yet James had friends too, many and powerful friends, and the government was then weak; the revolution was so recent that they all had their fears. And the most sagacious of King William's friends might not choose to have this matter settled very suddenly; they might choose that the judges should remain subject to a revocation of their patents if they should fail in supporting King William; although they chose to have their patents granted *quamdiu bene se gesserint,* that they might have some hold of the royal word and honor, in order to obtain in due time a settlement of it by act of parliament.

Let me subjoin to this the authority of a very modern, though a very able and upright judge; I mean Sir Michael Foster: "The king, (Richard II.) and his ministers, soon after the dissolution of the parliament, entered into measures for defeating this commission. One expedient was to take the opinion of the judges upon the whole proceeding; a refuge constantly open to a corrupt administration, though—be it spoken to the honor of the profession—not always a sure one, *even while the judges' commissions were determinable at the pleasure of the crown.*" And in page 396, we find the eighth question propounded by the king to those judges was this:—"Since the king can, whenever he pleaseth, remove any of his judges and officers, and justify or punish them for their offences, whether the lords and commons can, without the will of the king, impeach in parliament any of the said judges or officers for any of their offences?" to which the judges answered unanimously, that "they cannot; and if any one should do so, he is to be punished as a traitor."*

It was said in a former paper, that the supreme jurisdiction in all causes, and the power of creating and annihilating magistrates, was an important branch of the *jura regalia principis* of the feudal law. These *regalia* were distributed into two principal divisions, the *regalia majora* and *minora.* The *majora* were those "quae personam et dignitatem principis et administrationem reipublicae concernunt, ut collatio dignitatum regalium, *et jurisdictio summa in causis ecclesiasticis et secularibus,* as well as the jus belli et pacis &c.; et haec alias jura majestatis dicuntur.†

Supreme, sovereign jurisdiction, therefore, in all causes temporal and spiritual, was one of the greater royalties, or sublimest prerogatives of the feudal princes, was inseparable from the feudal majesty, and could not be granted away by the prince to any subject, so as to be irrevocable. And the feudal law says expressly, if an infeudation of these *regalia majora* should be made, "majestas divisionem non recipiat, nec jura ab ea separari possint; distinguendum est inter ipsum jus, et exercitium hujus juris;—hoc alteri concedi potest, ut eodem utatur, *dependenter: illud, vero, penes principem remanet.*"‡

That this was one of the *regalia majora,* see the Consuetudines Feudo-

* See 1 State Trials,—the proceedings against Chief Justice Tresilian and others.

† Strykii, *Examen Juris Feudalis.*

‡ Stryk. 173.

rum, tit. 56: "Quae sint Regalia. Potestas constituendorum magistratuum ad justitiam expediendam."

It was this old feudal idea that such prerogatives were inseparable from majesty, and so incident and essential to the kingly office, that not even an act of parliament could divest it of them, which puzzled the heads of the two Jameses and the two Charleses, and cost them and the nations they governed very dear. It was this which was intended by Sir Edward Herbert and his brothers, who determined for Sir Edward Hales's case, mentioned in a former paper, and gave their opinions, and made it a general rule in law, that the dispensing power was an incident, inseparable prerogative of the kings of England, as of all other sovereign princes; and that this was not a trust invested in and granted to the king, but the *ancient remains* of the *sovereign power* of the kings of England, which was never yet taken from them, *nor can be.*

The way is now prepared for the most important question of all.

General Brattle declares his opinion in very strong terms, "that the governor and council cannot legally or constitutionally remove a justice of the superior court, as the commissions now are, unless there is a fair hearing and trial, and then a judgment that he hath behaved ill."

This I am content to make a question, after premising that we ought, in such inquiries, always to obtain precise ideas, and to give exact definitions of the terms we use, in order to arrive at truth. The question, then, appears to me to be different from what it would be, if we were to ask whether a justice of that court can be *constitutionally* removed, without a trial and judgment. Many people receive different ideas from the words *legally and constitutionally.* The law has certainly established in the crown many prerogatives, by the bare exertion of which, in their utmost extent, the nation might be undone. The prerogatives of war and peace, and of pardon, for examples, among many others. Yet it would be absurd to say that the crown can constitutionally ruin the nation, and overturn the constitution. The British constitution is a fine, a nice, a delicate machine; and the perfection of it depends upon such complicated movements, that it is as easily disordered as the human body; and in order to act constitutionally, every one must do his duty. If the king should suffer no parliament to sit for twelve years, by reason of continual prorogations, this would be an unconstitutional exercise of prerogative. If the commons should grant no supplies for twelve years, this would be an unconstitutional exertion of their privilege. Yet the king has power legally to do one, and the commons to do the other. I therefore shall not contend with General Brattle what the governor and council can constitutionally do, about removing justices, nor what they can do in honor, integrity, conscience, or Christianity: these things I shall leave to the internal sentiments of future governors and councils, and shall confine myself to the question, whether they can legally remove a judge.

And it is with great reluctance that I frankly say, I have not been able hitherto to find sufficient reason to convince me that the governor and council have not, as the law now stands, power to remove a judge, as the commissions now are, without a trial and judgment for ill behavior.

I believe it to be true that the judges in all King William's reign had their commissions *quamdiu se bene gesserint.* Our charter and our province law, erecting the superior court, were made in that reign. In the charter, the king grants power to the governor, with advice and consent of council, to nominate judges, &c., and to the general court to erect judicatories, &c.; "and that all and every of the subjects of us, our heirs and successors, which shall go to and inhabit within our said province and territory, and every of their children which shall happen to be born there, or on the seas in going thither or returning from thence, shall have and enjoy all liberties and immunities of free and natural subjects, within any of the dominions of us, our heirs and successors, to all intents, constructions, and purposes whatsoever, as if they and every of them were born within this our realm of England."

Now, admitting, for argument's sake, that the judges in England in that reign held their offices legally for life, determinable upon misbehavior, and that it was by law, in that reign, a liberty of free and natural subjects, born within the realms, that the judges should hold such an estate in their offices, what will be the consequence? Will it not be, that the governor and council have power, by charter and by law, to grant their commissions *quamdiu se bene gesserint?* and that, if the governor and council should grant their commissions in that manner, the judges would have estates for life in their offices? But will it follow that they have such estates, if the governor and council do not grant them in that manner? Here, then, if these principles are all just, let the just consequence be drawn. Let the governor and council—I speak with humble deference and submission—issue the commissions to the judges, *quamdiu se bene gesserint;* and if that is declined, let the province—I speak with all possible respect again—make their humble supplications to his majesty, that his governor may be permitted, or instructed, if you will, to grant them in that manner. I fear there is too much reason to think, as no judicature can be created but by the legislature, and the jurisdiction must appear in the erection, and as no judge at common law, or by the law of the province, can hold an office but by commission, that the duration of the judge's office or estate must appear in the commission itself.

However, all this reasoning in favor of an estate for life in our judges, is built upon the principle that Lord Holt, and the judges in England under King William, had estates for life, by law, in their offices. And this principle implies that the crown, at common law, had authority to make judges to hold for life or at will, at its pleasure; which is a problematical doctrine, at least. Some of the passages of law and history which I have quoted in former papers, seem to be evidence that, at some times, the houses of parliament and some of the ministers of the law had such an apprehension; but a multitude of others, produced in the same papers, betray an apprehension of the contrary; but I do not recollect a single circumstance, in law or history, that favors the opinion that a judge there had an estate for life, without the words *quamdiu se bene gesserit* in his commission.

General Brattle took the right way of establishing the independency of our judges, by affirming that they had estates for life by their nomination and appointment, and by common law, whether their commissions expressed *quamdiu se bene gesserint* or not, or whether they had any commissions at all or not; and if he could have proved these allegations, he would have got his cause. But he has been extremely unfortunate in having Bracton, Fortescue, Coke, Foster, Hume, Rapin, and Rushworth directly against him, and nothing in his favor but the say of a lawyer in arguing a cause for his client, and that say by no means so extensive as the General's assertions; for Powis himself does not say the judges at common law were in for their lives, without the clause *quamdiu se bene gesserint* in their commissions. The questions that have been considered are liberal, and of much importance. I have done little more than labor in the mines of ore and the quarries of stones. The materials are at the service of the public; and I leave them to the jeweller and lapidary, to refine, fabricate, and polish them.

JOHN ADAMS

15 February, 1773

TO THE PRINTERS

WE ARE NOW upon the commissions of our own judges; and we ought to examine well the tenure by which they are holden.

It may be depended on, that all the commissions of judges throughout America are without the words *quamdiu se bene gesserint* in them; and, consequently, that this horrid fragment of the feudal despotism hangs over the heads of the best of them to this hour. If this is the case, it is a common and a serious concern to the whole continent, and the several provinces will take such measures as they shall think fit to obtain a better security of their lives, liberties, and properties. One would think there never could happen a more favorable opportunity to procure a stable tenure of the judges' offices than the present reign, which was begun with his majesty's most gracious declaration from the throne, "that the independency and uprightness of the judges were essential to the impartial administration of justice." However, let us return and confine ourselves to this province. Our judges' commissions have neither the clause *quamdiu se bene gesserit,* nor the clause *durante beneplacito* in them. By what authority, and for what reasons, both these clauses were omitted, when the commission was first formed and digested, I know not; but the fact is certain, that they are not in it. But will it follow that, because both clauses are omitted, therefore the judges are in for life? Why should it not as well follow that they are in only at pleasure? Will it be said that the liberty of the subject and the independency of the judges are to be favored, and therefore, as there is no express clause to determine it otherwise, it must be presumed to be intended for life? If this is said, I answer that, by all rules, common law is to be favored; and, therefore, whatever was the rule at common law must be favored in this case; and if the judges at common law were in only at pleasure, it will follow that ours are so too, without express words; for there is no rule more established than this, that the prerogative is not to be taken away without express words, and that the king's grant is to be construed most favorably for the king, when it has not the clause *ex mero motu, speciali gratia, et certa scientia,* in it, as these commissions have not.

Why should the omission of both clauses make the commissions during good behavior, in the case of a superior judge, any more than in the case of a justice of the peace? The commission of a justice of the peace here is without both clauses, as much as the commission of a judge; yet it never was pretended here that a justice of peace might not be removed at pleasure by the governor and council, and without a hearing and judgment that he had misbehaved.

And I suppose it to be clearly settled so in England. By the form of the commission of the peace in England,* we find that both these clauses are omitted out of that commission, which was settled and reformed as it there stands by Sir Christopher Wray, Chief Justice of England, and all the other judges of England, in the 32 and 33 Elizabeth, upon perusal of the former commission of the peace, and upon conference within themselves.

Yet these commissions are determinable at pleasure.† "These commissioners of the peace, their authority doth determine by divers means, yet

---

* Which we have in Dalton, c. 5: and in 3 Burn, tit. Justices of the Peace; 1 Shaw's Inst. 13, 16, 17.

† See Dalton's Justice, c. 3.

more usually by three means: 1. By the death of the king, or by his resignation of his crown; for by the commission he maketh them *justiciarios nostros;* so that, he being once dead, or having given over his crown, they are no more his justices, and the justices of the next prince they cannot be, unless it shall please him afterwards so to make them. 2. At the king's pleasure, and that in two sorts. 1. Either by the king's pleasure, expressed, (as the king by express words may discharge them by his writ under the great seal,) or by *supersedeas;* but the *supersedeas* doth but suspend their authority, which may be revived by a *procedendo.* 2. Or by implication; as by making other commissioners of the same kind, and within the same limits, leaving out the ancient commissioners' names."

Thus, the argument arising from the omission of the clause in our judges' commissions, of *durante beneplacito,* seems to have no weight in it, because the same clause is omitted from the commission of the peace both at home and here, and yet the commission has been settled at home to be determinable at the pleasure of the king, and here, at the pleasure of the governor and council, particularly in a late instance, which General Brattle may possibly remember.

Let us now proceed to consider with more particular attention the principle upon which all colorable pretension of establishing the independency of our judges is founded. The principle is this, that Lord Holt and his brothers, under King William, had legal estates for life in their offices, determinable only on misbehavior and the demise of the crown; though, I apprehend, that even this principle will not serve the purpose. It is true that, if this principle is admitted, it will follow, that the governor and council here have power to issue the commissions *quamdiu se bene gesserint;* but it will not follow, that by law they are bound to do that, because King William was not bound by law to do it in England. If King William had his election to grant commissions *quamdiu se bene gesserint,* or *durante beneplacito,* then the natural subjects, born within the realm, had not a right to have the judges' patents granted *quamdiu se bene gesserint,* unless the king pleased. It is true, upon this supposition, that they had a right to have them granted so, if they were happy enough to persuade the crown to grant them so, not otherwise.

The same right and liberty will belong to the subject in this province. Not a right absolutely to have the judges' commissions granted *quamdiu se bene gesserint;* but to have them granted so, if the governor and council saw fit, and could be prevailed on to do it.

And, on the other hand, if King William had power to grant the commissions either way as he pleased, it will follow, that the governor and council have power to grant them either way. And if this is true, it is to be hoped

General Brattle will have influence enough to prevail that the commissions, for the future, may be granted expressly *quamdiu se bene gesserint;* but until that is done, even upon these principles, our judges hold their places only at will.

However, we must examine yet further, whether the crown, in King William's time, or any other, ever had its election to grant the patents either way.

Lord Coke's authority has been quoted before several times, and it seems to be very explicit, that a grant of a judicial office for life, which had usually been granted at will, is void. "Nay, it is said by some, that the king is so far restrained by the ancient forms, in all cases of this nature, that his grant of a judicial office for life, which has been accustomed to be granted only at will, is void." "And the law is so jealous of any kind of innovation, in a matter so highly concerning the safety of the subject, as not to endure any the least deviation from the old known stated forms, however immaterial it may seem, as will be more fully shown, c. 5, s. 1."*

I have not been able to find any direct adjudication of any of the courts of common law, or any absolute determination of all the judges in the exchequer chamber, that a grant to a judge of king's bench or common bench, *quamdiu se bene gesserit,* is void; but, besides what is before cited, from Coke and Hawkins, it is certain that, whenever such a grant has been made, the king who made it considered it as void. King Henry thought it was void, when he threw off his faithful Hubert de Burgh. Charles I. thought it void, and so did his parliament, in 1642, as appears by the twelfth article transmitted by them to the king at York; and Charles II. and James II. thought it void, as appears many ways,—by their displacing Judge Archer and others; and it appears also by King Charles's displacing the Earl of Clarendon; for there is no reason why a grant of the office of chancellor for life should be void, as Lord Coke says expressly that it is, and a grant of the office of chief justice, in the same manner, be good. "Note, that this vacation, Sir Edward Hyde, Earl of Clarendon and Lord Chancellor of England, was deposed by the king from being chancellor, although he had a patent for his life, because the taking away of the seal is a determination of the office, as 4 Inst."†

Here the grant for life is considered as void, and Lord Coke's authority is quoted for it, I suppose where he says, a grant of the office of chancellor for life is void, because it never was so granted, that is, as I understand it, never was customarily so granted; for it is not literally true that it never was

* 2 Hawkins's P. C. 2, § 5, 6.
† 1 Sid. 338, Mich. 19, Car. II. B. R.

so granted. It has been granted for life almost if not quite as often as the judges' offices ever were before the revolution. It may be proper to show this.

Thomas, Lord Ellesmere, in his Observations concerning the office of the lord chancellor, says: "The election or creation of chancellors and keepers, &c. was of more than one sort. Sometimes, and for the most part, the chancellor was elected by the king, *durante beneplacito,* and put in power of his office by the delivery of the seal; and sometimes the chancellor was made by patent *to hold that place or office during his life,* as Walter Grey, Bishop of Chester, in the time of King John, and others; some, and the most part, elected by the king only; some had patents of the king, and were confirmed chancellors by consent of the three estates, as were Ralph Nevil, Bishop of Chester, in the time of King Henry III., with whom the prince being offended, as reports Matthew Paris, and demanding the seal at his hands, he refused to yield the same unto him, affirming that, as he had received it by the common consent of the nobility, so he would not, without like warrant, resign the same; and in the days of the same king, it was told him by all the lords, spiritual and temporal, that of *ancient time* the election and disposition of the chief justice, chancellor, and treasurer belonged to the parliament; and, although the king in displeasure did take the seal from him, and deliver the same to the custody of others, yet did the aforesaid Nevil remain chancellor notwithstanding, and received the profits thereof, to whom the king would have restored the seal, but he refused to receive it."

Here, let me observe, that I have a long time expected from General Brattle some such authority as this; for I believe it was in the mind of Sir Thomas Powis, when he said, by the ancient constitution my lords the judges were in for their lives. But let it be considered, that there is no remaining record that the lords spiritual and temporal told the king so, nor any legal authority to prove it, nor any other authority for it but Matthew Paris, whose writings are not sufficient evidence of this; let it also be considered, that this King Henry would probably have been obliged to insert a clause in his *Magna Charta* to secure this privilege, if the claim of it had been then thought to be well founded; and, as this was not done, it is most likely (admitting Matthew Paris's fact to be true) that the lords spiritual and temporal meant no more than this, that some king of ancient time had, in some few instances, condescended to take the advice of his *wittenagemote,* or assembly of wise men, concerning the appointment and removal of such officers. But a few particular examples of royal condescension could form no established rule, and according to the notions of those feudal ages, could never alienate from the prince any of his *regalia majora.*

Lord Ellesmere goes on: "And let us note, by the way, three several patents were granted unto this Ralph Nevil, two whereby he is ordained to be chancellor, and the third for the custody of the seal, all remaining among the records of the tower *in haec verba:*

"Henricus Rex, &c. Archiepiscopis, &c. Sciatis, nos dedisse, concessisse, et hac charta nostra confirmasse, venerabili Randolpho cicestrensi episcopo cancellariam nostram habendam et tenendam *toto tempore vitae suae,* cum omnibus pertinentibus, &c."

His second patent was of this form:—"Henricus, &c. Archiepiscopis, &c. Sciatis nos concessisse, et hac charta nostra confirmasse, pro nobis et haeredibus nostris venerabili Randolpho cicestrensi episcopo, cancellario nostro, cancellariam Angliae, toto tempore vitae suae, cum omnibus pertinentibus, &c. Quare volumus et firmiter praecipimus pro nobis, et haeredibus nostris, quod praedictus episcopus habeat ipsam cancellariam, toto tempore vitae suae, &c."

This is the transcript of his third patent, the same day and year:— "Henricus, &c. Archiepiscopis, &c. Sciatis nos concessisse, et hac charta nostra confirmasse venerabili patri Randolpho cicestrensi episcopo cancellario nostro, custodiam sigilli nostri toto tempore vitae suae, cum omnibus, &c. ita quod sigillum portat et custodiat, in propria persona sua, quamdiu valuerit."

And in page 18, Lord Ellesmere says: "Sometimes the chancellors of England were elected by the nobility, as Nicolas of Eli was made chancellor by the barons, but this seemed a usurpation by them, for they were afterwards, the most of them, most sharply chastised, and the said Nicolas deprived by Henry III., disdaining to have officers of that estate appointed him by his subjects."

Thus we see that a few examples of appointments for life to the office of chancellor, have not been sufficient to establish the power of the crown to grant it in that manner, but it is often said in our books to be void, and in the case of Lord Clarendon was presumed to be so. Why, then, should a few examples of judges constituted *quamdiu se bene gesserint,* in the reigns of Charles I. and II., and King William, determine them to be good?

I think it has been determined by all the judges in England that time of memory should be limited to the reign of King Richard I.; and every rule of common law must be beyond the time of memory, that is, as ancient as the reign of that king, and continued down generally until it is altered by authority of parliament.

Sir James Dyer, at the end of his Reports, has given us the names of all the chief justices of the king's bench, from the twenty-second year of Edward III. to the sixteenth year of Queen Elizabeth, namely,—Thorpe, Shareshull,

Greene, Knyvett and Cavendish, under Edward III.; Tresilian and Clopton under Richard II.; Gascoigne under Henry IV.; Hankford under Henry V.; Cheyne, Ivyn, and Fortescue, under Henry VI.; Markham and Billing under Edward IV.; Hussey under Richard III.; Fineux under Henry VII.; Montague, Lyster, and Cholmley, under Henry VIII.; Bromley, Portmore, and Saunders under Queen Mary; Catlyne and Wray under Elizabeth.

And also the names of all the chief justices of the common pleas from the year 1399, namely,—the last year of the reign of Richard II. to the twenty-fourth of Queen Elizabeth, namely,—Thirninge under Henry IV.; Norton under Henry V.; Ivyn, Cottesmore, Newton, and Prisot, under Henry VI.; Danby and Brian, under Edward IV.; Woode, Frowicke and Rede, under Henry VII.; Erneley, Brudnell, Norwiche, Baldwin, Montague, under Henry VIII.; Morgan, Brooke and Browne, under Philip and Mary; Dyer and Anderson, under Elizabeth.

The writs or patents of all these chief justices remain enrolled in the courts of king's bench and common pleas, and also enrolled in chancery, and every one of them is *durante beneplacito,* as I conclude, because Dyer has given us the tenure of his own commission: "Ego, Jac. Dyer, constitutus fui unus justiciariorum ad placita coram rege et regina tenenda, per L. patentes gerentes datum apud Greenwich, 23 die Aprilis, durante beneplacito Regi, &c."; and because the foregoing lists, and the records from whence they were taken, were familiarly known to Sir Edward Coke; and he says, that form had been used and approved without any variation for many successions of ages, even from the time of Edward I. and long before. It may, therefore, be safely affirmed, that there is no record of any justiciary or chief justice of king's bench or common pleas whose writ or patent was not *durante bene-placito,* quite down to the year 1640, in the reign of Charles I. I say there is no record of any, because the story of Hubert de Burgh has no record extant to prove it, and rests upon no better evidence than Matthew Paris, which, in our present view of the matter, is no evidence at all, because he is no legal authority.

If there is no record, therefore, extant to warrant the crown in granting patents to the judges *quamdiu se bene gesserint,* anterior to 1640, it is in vain to look for any adjudged case, that a patent so granted is good anterior to that period, and I am equally confident to say there has been none since.

There is a case in the Year-Books, which was quoted by the attorney-general, in the argument of the case of Harcourt against Fox, to prove that a grant *quamdiu se bene gesserit* conveyed a frank tenement. But common sense, without a judicial decision, would be sufficient to determine that. It is but the necessary, natural import of the words. If a man has a lease of a house as long as he behaves well, if he behaves well as long as he lives, he must hold the house as long as he lives. That case is in 3 Ass. 4. pl. 9. That part of it which is to our present purpose is no more than this: "Note, that a grant of rent to be paid to another, as long as he wills or pleases, is a freehold clearly enough. Sicut dominus rex concessit alicui aliquam ballivam vel hujusmodi, donec bene et fideliter se gesserit in officio illo."

It is easy to see that this is no adjudication that the king's grant to a judge of king's bench or common pleas *quamdiu se bene gesserit* is good and valid, and I believe it may be depended on, that there never was such a judgment in Westminster Hall.

I have heretofore mentioned several instances of great, wise, and honest judges falling victims at the royal nod, and giving place to others, much their inferiors in all respects. To these let me add the case of the learned, firm, and upright Chief Justice Pemberton, who, in the thirty-fourth year of Charles II., was obliged to descend from the chief seat in the king's bench into the common pleas, to make way for the cunning chicanery of Saunders, who was elevated to his place in order to carry some court-points; and in the next year that great and honest man was deposed from his place in the common pleas, and after having been chief justice of both benches, was necessitated to take a place again at the bar, and to bear the sneers and railleries of young mooting barristers, who thought to recommend themselves at court by insulting him.

And here I cannot forbear introducing a curiosity. It is the speech of the Lord Chancellor to Sir Henry Montague, when he was sworn chief justice of the king's bench in the room of a man much greater and better; I mean Lord Coke. It is found at length in Sir Francis Moore's Reports, and I mention it because it is fraught with lessons of instruction. It shows the tendency of holding offices at pleasure. It shows what sordid, nauseous, and impious adulations to superiors, what malicious, envious, and cruel invectives against honest Coke, or any other brave and honest man whom the courtiers are determined to hunt down, are inspired by this dependent state of mind. It shows what a deep and lively sense they had upon their minds of their dependence, every moment of their existence, upon the royal will, and how carefully they cultivated in one another, as the highest virtue, this base servility of spirit.

"The king's majesty," (says the Chancellor to Sir Henry Montague,) "in the governing of his subjects, *representeth the divine majesty of Almighty God;* for it is truly said of God, that, infima per media ducit ad summa, &c." "You are called to a place vacant, not by *death* or *cession,* but by *amotion* and deposing of him that held the place before you, by the great King James, the great King of Great Britain; wherein you see the prophet David's words are true: '*He* putteth down one and setteth up another;' a lesson to be learned of all, and to be *remembered and feared of all that sit in judicial places, &c.* It is dangerous, in a monarchy, for a man holding a high and eminent place, to be ambitiously popular; take heed of it."

"Remember Sir Edward Montague, your worthy grandfather. You are called to succeed him in this high place, and called thereunto upon *amotion* and *deposing* of another by the great judgment and wisdom of the great King of Great Britain, whose royal virtues will be admired to all posterity." Then follows much abuse upon honest Coke.

"Your grandfather doubted not but if the king, by his writ under the great seal, commanded the judges that they should not proceed *rege inconsulto,* then they were dutifully to obey, and to consult with the king, not in this court but in another, that is, the court of chancery.

"Remember also the *removing* and putting down of your late predecessor, *and by whom,* which I often remember unto you,—that is, by the great King of Great Britain, whose great wisdom, royal virtues, and religious care for the weal of his subjects, and for the due administration of justice, can never be forgotten, but will remain admirable to all posterity." Who would think that this were a James? "Comfort yourself with this, that sithe the king's majesty hath enabled you, who shall or can disable you?"

Let us here subjoin a few clauses more from Hawkins: "All such justices must derive their authority from such instruments as are of a known, stated, and allowed form, warranted by ancient precedents," &c. "It seems clearly to be agreed, by all these books, that the best rule of judging of the validity of any such commissions, is their conformity to known and ancient precedents." "Such commissions may be determined expressly or impliedly; expressly by an absolute repeal or countermand from the king," &c.

JOHN ADAMS

22 February, 1773

TO THE PRINTERS

IN ALL GENERAL BRATTLE'S RESEARCHES HITHERTO, aided and assisted as he has been by mine, we have not been able to discover either that the judges at common law had their commissions *quamdiu se bene gesserint,* or for life, or that the crown had authority to grant them in that manner. Let us now examine, and see whether estates of life, determinable only on misbehavior or the demise of the crown, can be derived to the Massachusetts judges from any other source. If they can, they must be from the charter, from the nomination and appointment of the governor, with the advice and consent of council, from the judges' commissions, or from the law of the province; from one or more, or all these together, they must be derived, if from any thing. For, as the judges of the king's bench and common bench are in by the king's grant or by custom, or both; as justices of oyer and terminer, jail delivery, &c., are in by the king's grant; as the clerk of the peace is said by Lord Holt, in the case of Harcourt against Fox, to be in by the act of parliament, 1 William and Mary; and the officers, whose places are in the gift of the chief justice, are in by the custom; so the Massachusetts justices are in by one or more, or all of the four titles mentioned before.

And here the first inquiry is, what is meant by an officer's being in by custom or by statute, &c.? And I suppose the true answer to be this: he is invested with his powers, is obligated to his duties, and holds his estate by that custom or statute, &c. And the next inquiry is, by what are our judges in? that is, by what act or instrument are they clothed with their powers, bound to their duties, and entitled to their estates?

By the charter, there are no certain powers given them, no certain duties prescribed to them, nor any certain estate conferred upon them. The charter empowers the governor, with advice and consent of council, to nominate and appoint them, that is, to designate the persons; nothing more.

There are three sorts of officers in the charter. Those reserved to the nomination of the king, as the governor, lieutenant-governor, secretary, and judge of admiralty. And it is not limited how long they shall continue, excepting the first secretary, Addington, and he is constituted expressly during pleasure; and the duration of all these officers has been limited ever since expressly, by their commissions, to be during pleasure. The second sort of officers in the charter are those which the general court are to name and settle; and the charter expressly says they shall be named and settled annually, so that their duration is ascertained in the charter. The third sort are those which the governor, with advice and consent of council, is to nominate and appoint; and there are no duties imposed, no powers given, no estates limited to these, in the charter. But the power of erecting judicatories, stating the rights and duties, and limiting the estates, of all officers to the council and courts of justice belonging, is given to the general court; and the charter expressly requires that all these courts shall be held in the king's name, and that all officers shall take the oaths and subscribe the declarations appointed to be taken and subscribed, instead of the oaths of allegiance and supremacy. And it is in observance of this requisition in the charter,—namely, that all courts shall be held in the king's name,—that the judges' commissions are in the king's name. The governor and council designate a person, not to be the governor and council's justice, but the king's justice; not of the governor and council's court, but of the king's court. And the law of the province requires that the justices of the superior court should have a particular species of evidence of their nomination and appointment, namely, a commission; otherwise, as General Brattle says, a nomination and appointment recorded would be enough. And here I cannot refuse myself the pleasure of observing, that the opinion of Mr. Read concurred with, and, I humbly conceive, was founded on, these principles. Governor Belcher persuaded the council that, upon the appointment of a new governor, it was necessary to renew all civil commissions, and the same thing "was proposed in council by his successor; but Mr. Read, who was then a member of the council, brought such arguments against the practice, that the majority of the board refused to consent to it," and it never has been done since.* This was an important service rendered his country by that great lawyer and upright man, and it was grounded upon the principles I have mentioned. Civil officers are not nominated to be the governor's officers; they don't hold their courts nor commissions in his name, but in the king's; and therefore governors may come and go, as long as the same king reigns, and they continue the same officers. And, in conformity to the same principles, upon the demise of the crown, the commissions must be renewed, because the charter requires they should be in the king's name. The words are, "in the name of us, our heirs and successors;" and therefore, upon the accession of an heir apparent, that is, after six months from his accession, the commissions must be renewed, otherwise they cannot be held in his name, nor the requisition in the charter complied with. I said in six months, because the statute of 6 Anne, c. 7, s. 8, not the statute of the present king's reign, (as General Brattle supposes,) has provided, that "no office, place, or employment, civil or military, within the kingdoms of Great Britain or Ireland, dominion of Wales, town of Berwick-upon-Tweed, isles of Jersey, Guernsey, Alderney, or Sark, or any of her majesty's plantations, shall become void by reason of the demise or death of her majesty, her heirs or successors, kings or queens of this realm; but every person, &c., shall continue in their respective offices, places, and employments, for the space of six months next after such demise or death, unless sooner removed and discharged by the next in succession as aforesaid."

But, to return; our judges are not in merely by nomination and appointment of the governor and council, because they are not bound to their duties

* Hutchinson's *History of Massachusetts,* vol. 2, p. 375–6, note.

nor vested with their powers by the charter immediately, nor by that nomination and appointment. They are not in by the grant of the king merely, or by their commissions, because their court is not erected, their powers are not derived, their duties are not imposed, and no estate is limited by that grant. But their commission is nothing more than a particular kind of evidence, required by the province law, to show their conformity to the charter, in holding their court in the king's name, and to show their nomination and appointment, or the designation of their persons to those offices, by the governor and council.

It is the law of the province which gives them all the powers, and imposes upon them all the duties, of the courts of king's bench, common pleas, and exchequer; but it does not limit to them any estate in their offices. If it had said, as it ought to have said, that they shall be commissionated, *quamdiu se bene gesserint,* they would have been so commissionated, and would have held estates for life in their offices.

Whence, then, can General Brattle claim for them an estate for life in their offices? No such estate is given them by the charter, by their nomination and appointment, by their commissions, nor by the law of the province.

I cannot agree with General Brattle, that "supposing a corrupt governor and a corrupt council, whether the words in the commission are, so long as the governor and council please, or, during good behavior, will just come to the same thing." Because in the one case a judge may be removed suddenly and silently, in a council of seven only; in the other not without a hearing and trial, and an opportunity to defend himself before a fuller board, knowing his accuser and the accusation. And this would be a restraint even to corruption itself; for in the most abandoned state of it there is always some regard shown to appearances.

It is no part of my plan, in this rencounter with the General, to make my compliments to his excellency Governor Hutchinson, and the present council; but I may be permitted to say, that the governor differs in sentiment from his Major-General about the power of the governor and council. In a note in the second volume of the History of the Massachusetts Bay, we have these words:—"The freedom and independency of the judges of England is always enumerated among the excellencies of the constitution." The Massachusetts judges are far from independent. In Mr. Belcher's administration they were peculiarly dependent upon the governor. Before and since, they have been dependent upon the assembly for their salary granted annually, which sometimes has been delayed, sometimes diminished, and which rarely escapes being a subject of debate and altercation. The dependency in Mr.

Belcher's time is attributed to the pusillanimity of the council, as no appointment can be made without their advice.

And we are told, too, that the emoluments of a Massachusetts counsellor are very small, and can be but a poor temptation to sacrifice virtue. All this, however, has been found in many instances, by experience, to be but a poor consolation to the people. Four gentlemen, a majority of seven, have, since Mr. Belcher's day, been found under the influence of the same pusillanimity, and, for the sake of those emoluments, small as they are, or some other emoluments, have been seen to sacrifice virtue. And it is highly probable men will be composed of the same clay fifty years hence as they were forty years ago; and therefore they ought not to be left exposed to the same temptations.

The next thing observable in the General's last publication, is this. "The parliament grants," says he, "no salaries to the judges of England. The king settles the salaries, and pays his judges out of the civil list." How is it possible this gentleman should make such mistakes? What is the king's civil list? Whence do the moneys come to discharge it? Is it a mine of gold,—a quarry of precious stones? The king pays the judges! Whence does he get the money? The crown, without the gift of the people, is as poor as any of the subjects. But, to dwell no longer upon an error so palpable and gross, let us look into the book. The act of parliament of the 12 & 13 William III. expressly enacts, that the judges' salaries shall be ascertained and established, meaning, no doubt, at the sums which had then usually been allowed them. And another act of parliament was made in the thirty-second year of George II. c. 35, augmenting the salaries of the puisne judges five hundred pounds each, and granting and appropriating certain stamp duties to the payment of it. With what color of truth, then, can the General say, that parliament grants no salaries, but that the king settles the salaries?

Another thing that follows is more remarkable still. "The act of parliament," says the General, (meaning the late act empowering the crown to appropriate moneys for the administration of justice in such colonies where it shall be most needed,) "was made for no other reason than this, that the king might not pay them (that is, the judges) out of the civil list, but out of another fund, the revenue." The General seems to have in his mind a notion that the king's civil list is a magazine of gold and silver, and the crown a spot where diamonds grow. But I repeat it, the crown has no riches but from the gifts of the people. The civil list means an enumeration of the king's civil officers and servants, and the sums usually allowed them as salaries, &c. But the money to discharge these sums is, every farthing of it, granted by parliament. And without the aid of parliament the crown could not pay a porter.

Near the beginning of every reign, the civil list revenue is granted by parliament. But are the Massachusetts judges in the king's civil list? No more than the Massachusetts Major-General is. If a minister of state had taken money from the civil list revenue to pay our judges, would it not have been a misapplication of the public money? Would it not have been peculation? And in virtuous times, would not that minister have been compelled to refund it out of his own pocket? It is true, a minister who handles the public money may apply it to purposes for which it was never intended or appropriated. He may purchase votes and elections with it; and so he may rob the treasury-chests of their guineas; and he has as good a right to do one as the other, and to do either, as to apply moneys appropriated to the king's civil list to the payment of salaries to the Massachusetts judges.

Without the late act of parliament, therefore, as the king could not pay our judges out of the civil list, because the king can do no wrong, he could not pay them at all, unless he had given them presents out of his privy purse. The act must, therefore, have been made to enable the king to pay them, with what views of policy I leave to be conjectured by others.

I am very nearly of a mind with the General, that a lawyer who holds the judges' offices here to be during good behavior, must do it upon his principles; because I can see none much more solid to ground such an opinion upon. But I believe his principles appear by this time not to be infallible.

The General solemnly declares, that Mr. Read held this opinion and upon his principles. Mr. Read's opinion deserves great veneration, but not implicit faith; and, indeed, if it was certain that he held it, what resistance could it make against the whole united torrent of law, records, and history? However, we see, by the report the General was pleased to give the public of Lord Holt's words, that it is possible for him to mistake the words and opinion of a sage; and therefore it is possible he may have mistaken Mr. Read's words as well as his lordship's.

I believe the public is weary of my speculations, and the subject of them. I have bestowed more labor upon General Brattle's harangue in town meeting, and his writings in the newspaper, than was necessary to show their imperfection. I have now done with both,—and subscribe myself, Your, General Brattle's, and the Public's, well-wisher, and very humble servant,

JOHN ADAMS

Two Replies

of the

Massachusetts

House

of Representatives

to Governor

Hutchinson

GOVERNOR HUTCHINSON'S ANNOUNCEMENT that his salary and those of the judges would henceforth by paid out of crown revenue sent shock waves through Massachusetts. Fearing that Boston radicals were driving the colony to the brink of independence, Hutchinson called for two special joint sessions of the General Court in order to pacify the towns and to explain why Parliament must retain supreme authority over all British dominions. In theory and in practice, he argued, sovereignty cannot be divided and two independent legislative bodies could not exist in the same state.

Though not a member of the Massachusetts House at the time, Adams was asked by the committee charged with responding to the Governor's two speeches to assist them in drafting a response. Adams answered Hutchinson by arguing that the colonists were not and had never been under the sovereignty of Parliament. Their original charter was with the person of the king and their allegiance was to him and him only. Thus, if a workable line could not be drawn between Parliamentary sovereignty and the total independence of the colonies, the colonies would have no other choice but to choose independence.

This dramatic confrontation between Hutchinson and the Massachusetts House represents one of the most important debates of the Revolutionary period. The Massachusetts Assembly was the first colonial legislature to publicly reject the theory and practice of parliamentary sovereignty. It was not until after Parliament's passage of the Coercive Acts some eighteen months later that the other colonies followed the Massachusetts lead.

7

Two Replies of the Massachusetts House of Representatives to Governor Hutchinson

Answer to His Excellency's Speech at the Opening of the Session

May it please your Excellency,

Your Excellency's Speech to the General Assembly at the Opening of this Session, has been read with great Attention in this House.

We fully agree with your Excellency, that our own Happiness as well as his Majesty's Service, very much depends upon Peace and Order; and we shall at all Times take such Measures as are consistent with our Constitution and the Rights of the People to promote and maintain them. That the Government at present is in a very disturbed State is apparent! But we cannot ascribe it to the People's having adopted unconstitutional Principles, which seems to be the Cause assigned for it by your Excellency. It appears to us to have been occasioned rather, by the British House of Commons assuming and exercising a Power inconsistent with the Freedom of the Constitution to give and grant the Property of the Colonists, and appropriate the same without their Consent.

It is needless for us to enquire what were the Principles that induced the Councils of the Nation to so new and unprecedented a Measure. But when the Parliament by an Act of their own expressly declared, that the King, Lords and Commons of the Nation "have, had, and of Right ought to have full Power and Authority to make Laws and Statutes of sufficient Force and Validity to bind the Colonies and People of America, Subjects of the Crown of Great-Britain, in all Cases whatever," and in Consequence hereof another

Revenue Act was made, the Minds of the People were filled with Anxiety, and they were justly alarmed with Apprehensions of the total Extinction of their Liberties.

The Result of the free Enquiries of many Persons into the Right of the Parliament to exercise such a Power over the Colonies, seems in your Excellency's Opinion to be the Cause of what you are pleased to call the present "disturbed State of the Government;" upon which you "may not any longer consistent with your Duty to the King, and your Regard to the Interest of the Province, delay communicating your Sentiments." But that the Principles adopted in Consequence hereof, are unconstitutional, is a Subject of Enquiry. We know of no such Disorders arising therefrom as are mentioned by your Excellency. If Grand Jurors have not on their Oaths found such Offences, as your Excellency with the Advice of his Majesty's Council have *ordered* to be prosecuted, it is to be presumed they have followed the Dictates of good Conscience. They are the constitutional Judges of these Matters, and it is not to be supposed, that moved from corrupt Principles, they have suffered Offenders to escape a Prosecution, and thus supported and encouraged them to go on offending. If any Part of Authority, shall in an unconstitutional Manner, interpose in any Matter, it will be no wonder if it be brought into Contempt; to the lessening or confounding of that Subordination which is necessary to a well regulated State. Your Excellency's Representation that the Bands of Government are weakened, we humbly conceive to be without good Grounds; though we must own the heavy Burthens unconstitutionally brought upon the People have been and still are universally and very justly complained of as a Grievance.

You are pleased to say, that "when our Predecessors first took Possession of this Plantation or Colony, under a Grant and Charter from the Crown of England, it was their Sense and it was the Sense of the Kingdom, that they were to remain subject to the Supreme Authority of Parliament;" whereby we understand your Excellency to mean in the Sense of the Declaratory Act of Parliament aforementioned, in all Cases whatever. And indeed it is difficult, if possible, to draw a Line of Distinction between the universal Authority of Parliament over the Colonies and no Authority at all. It is therefore necessary for us to enquire how it appears, for your Excellency has not shown it to us, that when or at the Time that our Predecessors took Possession of this Plantation or Colony, under a Grant and Charter from the Crown of England, it was *their Sense,* and the Sense of *the Kingdom,* that they were to remain subject to the Supreme Authority of Parliament. In making this Enquiry, we shall, according to your Excellency's Recommendation, treat the Subject with Calmness and Candor, and also with a due Regard to Truth.

Previous to a direct Consideration of the Charter granted to this Province or Colony, and the better to elucidate the true Sense and Meaning of it, we would take a View of the State of the English North American Continent at the Time when and after Possession was first taken of any Part of it, by the Europeans. It was then possessed by Heathen and Barbarous People, who had nevertheless all that Right to the Soil and Sovereignty in and over the Lands they possessed, which God had originally given to Man. Whether their being Heathen, inferred any Right or Authority to Christian Princes, a Right which had long been assumed by the Pope, to dispose of their Lands to others, we will leave to your Excellency or any one of Understanding and impartial Judgment to consider. It is certain they had in no other Sense forfeited them to any Power in Europe. Should the Doctrine be admitted that the Discovery of Lands owned and possessed by Pagan People, gives to any Christian Prince a Right and Title to the Dominion and Property, still it is vested in the Crown alone. It was an Acquisition of Foreign Territory, not annexed to the Realm of England, and therefore at the absolute Disposal of the Crown. For we take it to be a settled Point, that the King has a constitutional Prerogative to dispose of and alienate any Part of his Territories not annexed to the Realm. In the Exercise of this Prerogative, Queen Elizabeth granted the first American Charter; and claiming a Right by Virtue of Discovery, then supposed to be valid, to the Lands which are now possessed by the Colony of Virginia, she conveyed to Sir Walter Rawleigh, the Property, Dominion and Sovereignty thereof, to be held of the Crown by Homage, and a certain Render, without any Reservation to herself of any Share in the Legislative and Executive Authority. After the Attainder of Sir Walter, King James the First created two Virginia Companies, to be governed each by Laws transmitted to them by his Majesty and not by the Parliament, with Power to establish and cause to be made a Coin to pass current among them; and vested with all Liberties, Franchises and Immunities within any of his other Dominions, to all Intents and Purposes, as if they had been abiding, and born *within the Realm*. A Declaration similar to this is contained in the first Charter of this Colony, and in those of other American Colonies, which shows that the Colonies were not intended or considered to be within the Realm of England, though within the Allegiance of the English Crown. After this, another Charter was granted by the same King James, to the Treasurer and Company of Virginia, vesting them with full Power and Authority, to make, ordain and establish all Manner of Orders, Laws, Directions, Instructions, Forms and Ceremonies of Government, and Magistracy, fit and necessary, and the same to abrogate, &c. without any Reservation for securing their Subjection to the Parliament and future Laws of England. A third

Charter was afterwards granted by the same King to the Treasurer and Company of Virginia, vesting them with Power and Authority to make Laws, with an Addition of this Clause, "so always that the same be not contrary to the Laws and Statutes of this our Realm of England." The same Clause was afterwards copied into the Charter of this and other Colonies, with certain Variations, such as that these Laws should be "consonant to Reason," "not repugnant to the Laws of England," "as nearly as conveniently may be to the Laws, Statutes and Rights of England," &c. These Modes of Expression convey the same Meaning, and serve to show an Intention that the Laws of the Colonies should be as much as possible, conformant in the Spirit of them to the Principles and fundamental Laws of the English Constitution, its Rights and Statutes then in Being, and by no Means to bind the Colonies to a Subjection to the Supreme Authority of the English Parliament. And that this is the true Intention, we think it further evident from this Consideration, that no Acts of any Colony Legislative, are ever brought into Parliament for Inspection there, though the Laws made in some of them, like the Acts of the British Parliament are laid before the King for his Assent or Disallowance.

We have brought the first American Charters into View, and the State of the Country when they were granted, to show that the Right of disposing of the Lands was in the Opinion of those Times vested solely in the Crown—that the several Charters conveyed to the Grantees, who should settle upon the Territories therein granted, all the Powers necessary to constitute them free and distinct States—and that the fundamental Laws of the English Constitution should be the certain and established Rule of Legislation, to which the Laws to be made in the several Colonies were to be as nearly as conveniently might be, conformable or similar, which was the true Intent and Import of the Words, "not repugnant to the Laws of England," "consonant to Reason," and other variant Expressions in the different Charters. And we would add, that the King in some of the Charters reserves the Right to judge of the Consonance and Similiarity of their Laws with the English Constitution to himself, and not to the Parliament; and in Consequence thereof to affirm, or within a limited Time, disallow them.

These Charters, as well as that afterwards granted to Lord Baltimore, and other Charters, are repugnant to the Idea of Parliamentary Authority. And to suppose a Parliamentary Authority over the Colonies under such Charters would necessarily induce that Solecism in Politics *Imperium in Imperio*. And the King's repeatedly exercising the Prerogative of disposing of the American Territory by such Charters, together with the Silence of the Nation, thereupon, is an Evidence that it was an acknowledged Prerogative.

But further to show the Sense of the English Crown and Nation that the American Colonists and our Predecessors in particular, when they first took Possession of this Country by a Grant and Charter, from the Crown did not remain subject to the Supreme Authority of Parliament, we beg Leave to observe; that when a Bill was offered by the two Houses of Parliament to King Charles the First, granting to the Subjects of England the free Liberty of Fishing on the Coast of America, he refused his Royal Assent, declaring as a Reason, that "the Colonies were *without the Realm and Jurisdiction of Parliament.*"

In like Manner, his Predecessor James the First, had before declared upon a similar Occasion, that "America *was not annexed to the Realm,* and it was not fitting that Parliament should make Laws for those Countries." This Reason was, not secretly, but openly declared in Parliament. If then the Colonies were not annexed to the Realm, at the Time when their Charters were granted, they never could be afterwards, without their own special Consent, which has never since been had, or even asked. If they are not now annexed to the Realm, they are not a Part of the Kingdom, and consequently not subject to the Legislative Authority of the Kingdom. For no Country, by the Common Law was subject to the Laws or to the Parliament, but the Realm of England.

We would, if your Excellency pleases, subjoin an Instance of Conduct in King Charles the Second, singular indeed, but important to our Purpose; who, in 1679, framed an Act for a permanent Revenue for the Support of Virginia, and sent it there by Lord Colpepper, the Governor of that Colony; which was afterwards passed into a Law, and "*Enacted by the King's most excellent Majesty, by and with the Consent of the General Assembly of Virginia.*" If the King had judged that Colony to be a Part of the Realm, he would not, nor could he consistently with Magna Charta, have placed himself at the Head of, and joined with any Legislative Body in making a Law to Tax the People there, other than the Lords and Commons of England.

Having taken a View of the several Charters of the first Colony in America, if we look into the old Charter of this Colony, we shall find it to be grounded on the same Principle: That the Right of disposing the Territory granted therein was vested in the Crown, as being that Christian Sovereign who first discovered it, when in the Possession of Heathen; and that it was considered as being not within the Realm, but only within the Fee and Seignory of the King. As therefore it was without the Realm of England, must not the King, if he had designed that the Parliament should have had any Authority over it, have made a special Reservation for that Purpose, which was not done.

Your Excellency says, it appears from the Charter itself, to have been the Sense of our Predecessors who first took Possession of this Plantation or Colony, that they were to remain subject to the Authority of Parliament. You have not been pleased to point out to us how this appears from the Charter, unless it be in the Observation you make on the above-mentioned Clause, viz. "That a favourable Construction has been put upon this Clause, when it has been allowed to intend such Laws of England only as are expresly made to respect us," which you say "is by Charter a Reserve of Power and Authority to Parliament to bind us by such Laws at least as are made expresly to refer to us, and consequently is a Limitation of the Power given to the General Court." But we would still recur to the Charter itself, and ask your Excellency, How this appears from thence to have been the Sense of our Predecessors? Is any Reservation of Power and Authority to Parliament thus to bind us, expressed or implied in the Charter? It is evident, that King Charles the first, the very Prince who granted it, as well as his Predecessor, had no such Idea of the supreme Authority of Parliament over the Colony, from their Declarations before recited. Your Excellency will then allow us further to ask, by what Authority in Reason or Equity the Parliament can enforce a Construction so *unfavourable* to us. *Quod ab initio injustum est, nullum potest habere juris effectum,* said *Grotius.* Which with Submission to your Excellency may be rendered thus, *Whatever is originally in its Nature wrong, can never be satisfied or made right by Reputation and Use.*

In solemn Agreements subsequent: Restrictions ought never to be allowed. The celebrated Author whom your Excellency has quoted, tells us that "neither the one or the other of the interested or contracting Powers hath a Right to interpret at Pleasure." This we mention to show, even upon a Supposition that the Parliament had been a Party to the Contract, the Invalidity of any of its subsequent Acts, to explain any Clause in the Charter; more especially to restrict or make void any Clause granted therein to the General Court. An Agreement ought to be interpreted "in such a Manner as that it may have *its Effect.*" But if your Excellency's Interpretation of this Clause is just, "that it is a Reserve of Power and Authority to Parliament to bind us by such Laws as are made expresly to refer to us," it is not only "a Limitation of the Power given to the General Court" to Legislate, but it may whenever the Parliament shall think fit, render it of *no Effect;* for it puts it in the Power of Parliament to bind us by as many Laws as they please, and even to restrain us from making any Laws at all. If your Excellency's Assertions in this and the next succeeding Part of your Speech were well grounded, the Conclusion would be undeniable, that the Charter even in this Clause, "does not confer or reserve any Liberties" worth enjoying "but what would have been enjoyed without it;" saving that within any of his Majesty's Dominions we are to be considered barely as *not Aliens*. You are pleased to say, it cannot "be contended that by the Liberties of free and natural Subjects" (which are expresly granted in the Charter to all Intents, Purposes and Constructions whatever) "is to be understood an Exemption from Acts of Parliament because not represented there; seeing it is provided by the same Charter that such Acts shall be in Force." If, says an eminent Lawyer, "the King grants to the Town of D. the same Liberties which London has, this shall be intended the like Liberties." A Grant of the Liberties of free and natural Subjects is equivalent to a Grant of the same Liberties. And the King in the first Charter to this Colony expressly grants that it "shall be construed, reputed and adjudged in all Cases most favourably on the Behalf and for the Benefit and Behoof of the said Governor and Company and their Successors—any Matter, Cause or Thing whatsoever to the contrary notwithstanding." It is one of the Liberties of free and natural Subjects, born and abiding within the Realm, to be governed as your Excellency observes, "by Laws made by Persons in whose Elections they from Time to Time have a Voice." This is an essential Right. For nothing is more evident, than that any People who are subject to the unlimited Power of another, must be in a State of abject Slavery. It was easily and plainly foreseen that the Right of Representation in the English Parliament could not be exercised by the People of this Colony. It would be impracticable, if consistent with the English Constitution. And for this Reason, that this Colony might have and enjoy all the Liberties and Immunities of free and natural Subjects within the Realm as stipulated in the Charter it was necessary, and a Legislative was accordingly constituted within the Colony; one Branch of which consists of Representatives chosen by the People, to make all Laws, Statutes, Ordinances, &c. for the well ordering & governing the same, not repugnant to the Laws of England, or, as nearly as conveniently might be, agreeable to the fundamental Laws of the English Constitution. We are therefore still at a Loss to conceive where your Excellency finds it "*provided* in the same Charter, that such Acts," viz. Acts of Parliament made expresly to refer to us "shall be in Force" in this Province. There is nothing to this Purpose expressed in the Charter, or in our Opinion even implied in it. And surely it would be very absurd, that a Charter, which is evidently formed upon a Supposition and Intention, that a Colony is and should be considered as not within the Realm; and declared by the very Prince who granted it, to be not within the Jurisdiction of Parliament, should yet *provide,* that the Laws which the same Parliament should make expressly to refer to that Colony, should be in Force therein. Your Excellency is pleased to ask, "Does it follow that the Government by their (our Ancestors) Removal from one Part of the Dominions to another, loses its Authority over that Part to which they remove; And that they are freed from the Subjection they were under before?" We answer, if that Part of the King's Dominions to which they removed was not then a Part of the Realm, and was never annexed to it, the Parliament lost no Authority over it, having never had such Authority; and the Emigrants were consequently freed from the Subjection they were under before their Removal: The Power and Authority of Parliament being constitutionally confined within the Limits of the Realm and the Nation collectively, of which alone it is the representing and legislative Assembly. Your Excellency further asks, "Will it not rather be said, that by this their voluntary Removal, they have relinquished for a Time at least, one of the Rights of an English Subject, which they might if they pleased have continued to enjoy, and may again enjoy, whenever they return to the Place where it can be exercised?" To which we answer; They never did relinquish the Right to be governed by Laws made by Persons in whose Election they had a Voice. The King stipulated with them that they should have and enjoy all the Liberties of free and natural Subjects born within the Realm, to all Intents, Purposes and Constructions whatsoever; that is, that they should be as free as those who were to abide within the Realm: Consequently he stipulated with them that they should enjoy and exercise this most essential Right, which discriminates Freemen from Vassals, uninterruptedly in its full Sense and Meaning; and they did and ought still to exercise it, without the Necessity of returning, for the Sake of exercising it, to the Nation or State of England.

We cannot help observing, that your Excellency's Manner of Reasoning on this Point, seems to us to render the most valuable Clauses in our Charter unintelligible: As if Persons going from the Realm of England to inhabit in America should hold and exercise there a certain Right of English Subjects; but in Order to exercise it in such Manner as to be of any Benefit to them, they must *not inhabit* there, but return to the Place where alone it can be exercised. By such Construction, the Words of the Charter can have no Sense or Meaning. We forbear remarking upon the Absurdity of a Grant to Persons born within the Realm, of the same Liberties which would have belonged to them if they had been born within the Realm.

Your Excellency is disposed to compare this Government to the Variety of Corporations, formed within the Kingdom, with Power to make and execute By-Laws, &c. And because they remain subject to the Supreme Authority of Parliament, to infer that this Colony is also subject to the same Authority: This Reasoning appears to us not just. The Members of those Corporations are Resident within the Kingdom; and Residence subjects them to the Authority of Parliament, in which they are also represented: Whereas the People of this Colony are not Resident within the Realm. The Charter was granted with the express Purpose to induce them to reside without the Realm; consequently they are not represented in Parliament there. But we would ask your Excellency; Are any of the Corporations formed within the Kingdom, vested with the Power of erecting other subordinate Corporations? Of enacting and determining what Crimes shall be Capital? And constituting Courts of Common Law with all their Officers, for the hearing, trying and punishing capital Offenders with Death? These and many other Powers vested in this Government, plainly show that it is to be considered as a Corporation in no other Light, than as every State is a Corporation. Besides, Appeals from the Courts of Law here, are not brought before the House of Lords; which shows that the Peers of the Realm are not the Peers of America: But all such Appeals are brought before the King in Council, which is a further Evidence that we are not within the Realm.

We conceive enough has been said to convince your Excellency, that "when our Predecessors first took Possession of this Plantation or Colony by a Grant and Charter from the Crown of England, it *was not* and never had been the Sense of the Kingdom, that they were to remain subject to the Supreme Authority of Parliament. We will now with your Excellency's Leave, enquire what *was* the Sense of our Ancestors of this very important Matter.

And as your Excellency has been pleased to tell us you have not discovered that the Supreme Authority of Parliament has been called in Question even by private and particular Persons, until within seven or eight Years past; except about the Time of the Anarchy and Confusion in England which preceeded the Restoration of King Charles the Second; we beg leave to remind your Excellency of some Parts of your own History of Massachusetts-Bay. Therein we are informed of the Sentiments of "Persons of Influence" after the Restoration, from which the Historian tells us, some Parts of their Conduct, that is of the General Assembly, "may be pretty well accounted for." By the History it appears to have been the Opinion of those Persons of Influence, "that the Subjects of any Prince or State had a natural Right to Remove to any other State or to another Quarter of the World unless the State was weakened or exposed by such Remove; and even in that Case, if they were deprived of the Right of all Mankind, Liberty of Conscience, it would justify a Separation, and *upon their Removal their Subjection determined and ceased*." That "the Country to which they had removed, was claimed and possessed by independent Princes, whose Right to the Lordship and Sovereignty thereof had been acknowledged by the Kings of England," an Instance of which is quoted in the Margin; "That they themselves had ac-

tually purchased for valuable Consideration, not only the Soil but the Dominion, the Lordship and Sovereignty of those Princes;" without which Purchase, "in the Sight of God and Men, they had no Right or Title to what
they possessed." That they had received a Charter of Incorporation from the
King, from whence arose a new Kind of Subjection, namely, "a voluntary,
civil Subjection;" and by this Compact "they were *to be governed by Laws
made by themselves.*" Thus it appears to have been the Sentiments of *private*
Persons, though Persons by whose Sentiments the public Conduct was influenced, that their Removal was a justifiable Separation from the Mother
State, upon which their Subjection to that State determined and ceased. The
Supreme Authority of Parliament, if it had then ever been asserted, must
surely have been called in Question, by Men who had advanced such Principles as these.

The first Act of Parliament made expressly to refer to the Colonies, was
after the Restoration. In the Reign of King Charles the Second, several such
Acts passed. And the same History informs us there was a Difficulty in
conforming to them; and the Reason of this Difficulty is explained in a Letter
of the General Assembly to their Agent, quoted in the following Words,
"They apprehended them to be an Invasion of the Rights, Liberties and
Properties of the Subjects of his Majesty in the Colony, *they not being represented in Parliament,* and according to the usual Sayings of the Learned in
the Law, the Laws of England were bounded within the four Seas, *and did
not reach America:* However as his Majesty had signified his Pleasure that
those Acts should be observed in the Massachusetts, they had made Provision
by a Law of the Colony that they should be strictly attended." Which Provision by a Law of their own would have been superfluous, if they had
admitted the supreme Authority of Parliament. In short, by the same History
it appears that those Acts of Parliament as such were disregarded; and the
following Reason is given for it; "It seems to have been a *general* Opinion
that Acts of Parliament had no other Force, than what they derived from
Acts made by the General Court to establish and confirm them."

But still further to show the Sense of our Ancestors respecting this Matter, we beg Leave to recite some Parts of a Narrative presented to the Lords
of Privy Council by Edward Randolph, in the Year 1676, which we find in
your Excellency's Collection of Papers lately published. Therein it is declared
to be the Sense of the Colony, "that no Law is in Force or Esteem there, but
such as are made by the General Court; and therefore it is accounted a Breach
of their Privileges, and a Betraying of the Liberties of their Commonwealth,
to urge the Observation of the Laws of England." And further, "That no
Oath shall be urged or required to be taken by any Person, but such Oath

as the General Court hath considered, allowed and required." And further, "there is no Notice taken of the Act of Navigation, Plantation or any other Laws made in England for the Regulation of Trade." "That the Government would make the World believe they are a free State and do act in all Matters accordingly." Again, "These Magistrates ever reserve to themselves a Power to alter, evade and disannul any Law or Command, not agreeing with their Humour or the absolute Authority of their Government, acknowledging no Superior." And further, "He (the Governor) freely declared to me, that the Laws made by your Majesty and your Parliament, obligeth them in nothing, but what consists with the Interests of that Colony, that the Legislative Power and Authority is and abides in them *solely.*" And in the same Mr. Randolph's Letter to the Bishop of London, July 14, 1682, he says, "This *Independency* in Government, claimed and daily practised." And your Excellency being *then* sensible that this was the Sense of our Ancestors, in a Marginal Note in the same Collection of Papers, observes, that "this," viz. the Provision made for observing the Acts of Trade, "is very extraordinary, for this Provision was an Act of the Colony declaring the Acts of Trade shall be in Force there." Although Mr. Randolph was very unfriendly to the Colony, yet as his Declarations are concurrent with those recited from your Excellency's History, we think they may be admitted for the Purpose for which they are now brought.

Thus we see, from your Excellency's History and Publications, the Sense our Ancestors had of the Jurisdiction of Parliament under the first Charter. Very different from that which your Excellency *in your Speech* apprehends it to have been.

It appears by Mr. Neal's History of New-England, that the Agents who had been employed by the Colony to transact its Affairs in England at the Time when the present Charter was granted, among other Reasons gave the following for their Acceptance of it, viz. "The General Court has with the King's Approbation as much Power in New-England, as the King and Parliament have in England; they have all English Privileges, and can be touched by *no Law,* and by no Tax but of their own making." This is the earliest Testimony that can be given of the Sense our Predecessors had of the Supreme Authority of Parliament under the present Charter. And it plainly shows, that they, who having been freely conversant with those who framed the Charter, must have well understood the Design and Meaning of it, supposed that the Terms in our Charter "full Power and Authority," intended and were considered as a *sole* and exclusive Power, and that there was no "Reserve in the Charter to the Authority of Parliament, to bind the Colony" by any Acts whatever.

Soon after the Arrival of the Charter, viz. in 1692, your Excellency's History informs us, "the first Act" of this Legislative was a Sort of Magna Charta, asserting and setting forth their general Privileges, and this Clause was among the rest, "No Aid, Tax, Tallage, Assessment, Custom, Loan, Benevolence, or Imposition whatever, shall be laid, assess'd, impos'd or levied on any of their Majesty's Subjects, or their Estates, on any Pretence whatever, but by the Act and Consent of the Governor, Council and Representatives of the People assembled in General Court." And though this Act was disallowed, it serves to show the Sense which the General Assembly contemporary with the granting the Charter had of their sole and exclusive Right to Legislate for the Colony. The History says, "the other Parts of the Act were copied from Magna Charta;" by which we may conclude that the Assembly then construed the Words "not repugnant to the Laws;" to mean, conformable to the fundamental Principles of the English Constitution. And it is observable that the Lords of Privy Council, so lately as in the Reign of Queen Anne, when several Laws enacted by the General Assembly, were laid before her Majesty for her Allowance, interpreted the Words in this Charter, "not repugnant to the Laws of England," by the Words "as nearly as conveniently may be agreeable to the Laws and Statutes of England." And her Majesty was pleased to disallow those Acts, not because they were repugnant to any Law or Statute of England, made expressly to refer to the Colony; but because divers Persons, by Virtue thereof, were punished without being tried by their Peers in the ordinary "Courts of Law," and "by the ordinary Rules and known Methods of Justice;" contrary to the express Terms of Magna Charta, which was a Statute in Force at the Time of granting the Charter, and declaratory of the Rights and Liberties of the Subjects within the Realm.

You are pleased to say, that "our Provincial or Local Laws have in numerous Instances had Relation to Acts of Parliament made to respect the Plantations and this Colony in particular." The Authority of the Legislature, says the same Author who is quoted by your Excellency, "does not extend so far as the Fundamentals of the Constitution." "They ought to consider the Fundamental Laws as sacred, if the Nation has not in very express Terms, given them the Power to change them. For the Constitution of the State ought to be fixed: And since that was first established by the Nation, which afterwards trusted certain Persons with the Legislative Power, the fundamental Laws are excepted from their Commission." Now the Fundamentals of the Constitution of this Province are stipulated in the Charter; the Reasoning therefore in this Case holds equally good. Much less then ought any Acts or Doings of the General Assembly, however numerous, to neither of which your Excellency has pointed us, which barely relate to Acts of Parliament made to respect the Plantations in general, or this Colony in particular, to be taken as an Acknowledgment of this People, or even of the Assembly, which inadvertently passed those Acts, that we are subject to the Supreme Authority of Parliament. And with still less Reason are the Decisions in the Executive Courts to determine this Point. If they have adopted that "as Part of the Rule of Law," which in Fact is not, it must be imputed to Inattention or Error in Judgment, and cannot justly be urged as an Alteration or Restriction of the Legislative Authority of the Province.

Before we leave this Part of your Excellency's Speech, we would observe, that the great Design of our Ancestors, in leaving the Kingdom of England, was to be freed from a Subjection to its spiritual Laws and Courts, and to worship God according to the Dictates of their Consciences. Your Excellency in your History observes, that their Design was "to obtain for themselves and their Posterity the Liberty of worshipping God in such Manner as appeared to them most agreeable to the sacred Scriptures." And the General Court themselves declared in 1651, that "seeing just Cause to fear the Persecution of the then Bishop, and High Commission for not conforming to the Ceremonies of those under their Power, they thought it their safest Course, to get to this Outside of the World, out of their View and *beyond their Reach.*" But if it had been their Sense, that they were still to be subject to the supreme Authority of Parliament, they must have known that their Design might and probably would be frustrated; that the Parliament, especially considering the Temper of those Times, might make what ecclesiastical Laws they pleased, expressly to refer to them, and place them in the same Circumstances with Respect to religious Matters, to be relieved from which was the Design of their Removal. And we would add, that if your Excellency's Construction of the Clause in our present Charter is just, another Clause therein, which provides for Liberty of Conscience for all Christians except Papists, may be rendered void by an Act of Parliament made to refer to us, requiring a Conformity to the Rites and Mode of Worship in the Church of England or any other.

Thus we have endeavoured to shew the Sense of the People of this Colony under both Charters; and if there have been in any late Instances a Submission to Acts of Parliament, it has been in our Opinion, rather from Inconsideration or a Reluctance at the Idea of contending with the Parent State, than from a Conviction or Acknowledgement of the Supreme Legislative Authority of Parliament.

Your Excellency tells us, "you know of no Line that can be drawn between the Supreme Authority of Parliament and the total Independence of the Colonies." If there be no such line, the Consequence is, either that the

Colonies are the Vassals of the Parliament, or, that they are totally independent. As it cannot be supposed to have been the Intention of the Parties in the Compact, that we should be reduced to a State of Vassallage, the Conclusion is, that it was their Sense, that we were thus Independent. "It is impossible, your Excellency says, that there should be two independent Legislatures in one and the same State." May we not then further conclude, that it was their Sense that the Colonies were by their Charters made distinct States from the Mother Country? Your Excellency adds, "For although there may be but one Head, the King, yet the two Legislative Bodies will make two Governments as distinct as the Kingdoms of England and Scotland before the Union." Very true, may it please your Excellency; and if they interfere not with each other, what hinders but that being united in one Head and common Sovereign, they may live happily in that Connection and mutally support and protect each other? Notwithstanding all the Terrors which your Excellency has pictured to us as the Affects of a total Independence, there is more Reason to dread the Consequences, of absolute uncontrouled Supreme Power, whether of a Nation or a Monarch, than those of a total Independence. It would be a Misfortune "to know by Experience, the Difference between the Liberties of an English Colonist and those of the Spanish, French and Dutch: And since the British Parliament has passed an Act which is executed even with Rigour, though not voluntarily submitted to, for raising a Revenue and appropriating the same without the Consent of the People who pay it, and have claimed a Power of making such Laws as they please to order and govern us, your Excellency will excuse us in asking, whether you do not think we already experience too much of such a Difference, and have not Reason to fear we shall soon be reduced to a worse Situation than that of the Colonies of France, Spain or Holland.

If your Excellency expects to have the Line of Distinction between the Supreme Authority of Parliament, and the total Independence of the Colonies drawn by us, we would say it would be an arduous Undertaking; and of very great Importance to all the other Colonies: And therefore, could we conceive of such a Line, we should be unwilling to propose it, without their Consent in Congress.

To conclude, These are great and profound Questions. It is the Grief of this House, that by the ill Policy of a late injudicious Administration, America has been driven into the Contemplation of them. And we cannot but express our Concern, that your Excellency by your Speech has reduced us to the unhappy Alternative, either of appearing by our Silence to acquiesce in your Excellency's Sentiments, or of thus freely discussing this Point.

After all that we have said, we would be far from being understood to have in the least abated that just Sense of Allegiance which we owe to the King of Great-Britain, our rightful Sovereign: And should the People of this Province be left to the free and full Exercise of all the Liberties and Immunities granted to them by Charter, there would be no Danger of an Independance on the Crown. Our Charters reserve great Power to the Crown in its Representative, fully sufficient to balance, analagous to the English Constitution, all the Liberties and Privileges granted to the People. All this your Excellency knows full well—And whoever considers the Power and Influence, in all their Branches, reserved by our Charter to the Crown, will be far from thinking that the Commons of this Province are too Independent.

Answer to His Excellency's Speech

May it please your Excellency,

In your Speech at the Opening of the present Session, your Excellency express'd your Displeasure at some late Proceedings of the Town of *Boston,* and other principal Towns in the Province. And in another Speech to both Houses we have your repeated Exceptions at the same Proceedings as being "unwarrantable," and of a dangerous Nature and Tendency; "against which you thought yourself bound to call upon us to join with you in bearing a proper Testimony." This House have not discovered any Principles advanced by the Town of *Boston,* that are unwarrantable by the Constitution; nor does it appear to us that they have "invited every other Town and District in the Province to adopt their Principles." We are fully convinced that it is our Duty to bear our Testimony against "Innovations of a dangerous Nature and Tendency:" but it is clearly our Opinion, that it is the indisputable Right of all or any of his Majesty's Subjects in this Province, regularly and orderly to meet together to state the Grievances they labor under; and to propose and unite in such constitutional Measures as they shall judge necessary or proper to obtain Redress. This Right has been frequently exercised by his Majesty's Subjects within the Realm; and we do not recollect an Instance, since the happy Revolution, when the two Houses of Parliament have been called upon to discountenance or bear their Testimony against it, in a Speech from the Throne.

Your Excellency is pleased to take Notice of some Things which we "alledge" in our Answer to your first Speech: And the Observation you make, we must confess, is as natural and as undeniably true, as any one that could have been made; that "if our Foundation shall fail us *in every Part of it,* the Fabrick we have rais'd upon it, must certainly fall." You think, this Foundation will fail us; but we with your Excellency had condescended to a Consideration of what we have "adduced in Support of our Principles." We might then perhaps have had some Things offered for our Conviction, more than bare Affirmations; which, we must beg to be excused if we say, are far from being sufficient, though they came with your Excellency's Authority, for which however we have a due Regard.

Your Excellency says that "as English Subjects and agreeable to the Doctrine of the Feudal Tenure all our Lands are held mediately or immediately of the Crown." We trust your Excellency does not mean to introduce the Feudal System in it's Perfection; which to use the Words of one of our greatest Historians, was "a State of perpetual War, Anarchy and Confusion; calculated solely for Defence against the Assaults of any foreign Power, but in it's Provision for the interior Order and Tranquility of Society extremely defective." "A Constitution so contradictory to all the Principles that govern Mankind, could never be brought about but by foreign Conquest or native Usurpation:" And a very celebrated Writer calls it "that most iniquitous and absurd Form of Government by which human Nature was so shamefully degraded." This System of Iniquity by a strange Kind of Fatility, "though originally form'd for an Encampment and for Military Purposes only, spread over a great Part of Europe:" and to serve the Purposes of Oppression and Tyranny "was adopted by Princes and wrought into their Civil Constitutions;" and aided by the Canon Law, calculated by the Roman Pontiff, to exalt himself above all that is called God, it prevailed to the almost utter Extinction of Knowledge, Virtue, Religion and Liberty from that Part of the Earth. But from the Time of the Reformation, in Proportion as Knowledge, which then darted its Rays upon the benighted World, increas'd and spread among the People, they grew impatient under this heavy Yoke: And the most virtuous and sensible among them, to whose Stedfastness we in this distant Age and Climate are greatly indebted, were determined to get rid of it: And tho' they have in a great Measure subdued it's Power and Influence in England, they have never yet totally eradicated its Principles.

Upon these Principles the King claimed an absolute Right to and a perfect Estate in all the Lands within his Dominions; but how he came by this absolute Right and perfect Estate is a Mystery which we have never seen unravelled, nor is it our Business or Design at present to enquire. He granted Parts or Parcels of it to his Friends the great Men, and they granted lesser Parcels to their Tenants: All therefore derived their Right and held their Lands, upon these Principles mediately or immediately of the King; which

Mr. *Blackstone* however calls "in Reality a meer Fiction of our English Tenures."

By what Right in Nature and Reason the Christian Princes in Europe claimed the Lands of Heathen People, upon a Discovery made by any of their Subjects, is equally mysterious: Such however was the Doctrine universally prevailing when the Lands in *America* were discovered; but as the People of England upon those Principles held all the Lands they possessed by Grants from the King, and the King had never granted the Lands in America *to them,* it is certain they could have no Sort of Claim to them: Upon the Principles advanced, the Lordship and Dominion like that of the Lands in England, was in the King solely: and a Right from thence accrued to him of disposing such Territories under such Tenure and for such Services to be performed, as the King or Lord thought proper. But how the Grantees *became* Subjects of England, that is the Supreme Authority of the Parliament, your Excellency has not explained to us. We conceive that upon the Feudal Principles all Power is in the King; they afford us no Idea *of Parliament.* "The Lord was in early Times the Legislator and Judge over all his Feudatories," says Judge Blackstone. By the Struggles for Liberty in England from the Days of King John to the last happy Revolution, the Constitution has been gradually changing for the better; and upon the more rational Principles that all Men by Nature are in a State of Equality in Respect of Jurisdiction and Dominion, Power in England has been more equally divided. And thus also in America, though we hold our Lands agreeably to the Feudal Principles of the King; yet our Predecessors wisely took Care to enter into Compact with the King that Power here should also be equally divided agreeable to the original fundamental Principles of the English Constitution, declared in Magna Charta, and other Laws and Statutes of England, made to confirm them.

Your Excellency says, "you can by no Means concede to us that it is now or was when the Plantations were first granted the Prerogative of the Kings of England to constitute a Number of new Governments altogether independent of the Sovereign Authority of the English Empire." By the Feudal Principles upon which you say "all the Grants which have been made of America are founded" "the Constitutions of the Emperor have the Force of Law." If our Government be considered as merely Feudatory, we are subject to the King's absolute Will, and there is no Room for the Authority of Parliament, as the Sovereign Authority of the British Empire. Upon these Principles, what could hinder the King's constituting a Number of Independent Governments in America? That King Charles the First did actually set up a Government in this Colony, conceding to it Powers of making and executing Laws, without any Reservation to the English Parliament, of Authority to make future Laws binding therein, is a Fact which your Excellency has not disproved if you have denied it. Nor have you shewn that the Parliament or Nation objected to it, from whence we have inferred that it was an acknowledged Right. And we cannot conceive, why the King has not the same Right to alienate and dispose of Countries acquired by the Discovery of his Subjects, as he has to "restore upon a Treaty of Peace Countries which have been acquired in War," carried on at the Charge of the Nation; or to "sell and deliver up any Part of his Dominions to a foreign Prince or State, against the General Sense of the Nation" which is "an Act of Power" or Prerogative which your Excellency allows. You tell us that "when any new Countries are discovered by English Subjects, according to the general Law and Usage of Nations, *they become Part of the State.*" The Law of Nations is or ought to be founded on the Law of Reason. It was the saying of Sir Edwin Sandis, in the the great Case of the Union of the Realm of Scotland with England, which is applicable to our present Purpose, that "there being no Precedent for this Case in the Law, the Law is deficient; and the Law being deficient, Recourse is to be had to Custom; and Custom being insufficient, we must recur to natural Reason," the greatest of all Authorities, which he adds "is the Law of Nations." The Opinions therefore, and Determinations of the greatest Sages and Judges of the Law in the Exchequer Chamber ought not to be considered as decisive or binding in our present Controversy with your Excellency, any further than they are consonant to *natural Reason.* If however we were to recur to such Opinions and Determinations we should find very great Authorities in our Favour, to show that the Statutes of England are not binding on those who are not represented in Parliament there. The Opinion of Lord Coke that Ireland was bound by Statutes of England wherein they *were named,* if compared with his other Writings, appears manifestly to be grounded upon a Supposition, that Ireland had by an Act of their own, in the Reign of King John, consented to be thus bound, and upon any other Supposition, this Opinion would be against *Reason;* for *Consent only* gives human Laws their Force. We beg Leave, upon what your Excellency has observed, of the Colony becoming Part of the State, to subjoin the Opinions of several learned Civilians, as quoted by a very able Lawyer in this Country; "Colonies, says Puffendorf, are settled in different Methods. For either the Colony *continues a Part* of the Common Wealth it was sent out from; or else is obliged to pay a dutiful Regard to the Mother Common Wealth, and to be in Readiness to defend and vindicate its Honor, and so is united by a Sort of unequal Confederacy; or lastly, is *erected into a separate Common Wealth* and *assumes the same Rights,* with the State it descended from." And King Tullius, as quoted by the same learned Author from Grotius, says "We look upon it to be neither Truth nor Justice that Mother Cities ought of Necessity and *by the Law of Nature* to *rule over the Colonies.*"

Your Excellency has misinterpreted what we have said, "that no Country by the Common Law, was subject to the Laws or the Parliament but the Realm of England," and are pleased to tell us that we have expressed ourselves "*Incautiously.*" We beg Leave to recite the Words of the Judges of England in the beforementioned Case to our Purpose. "If a King go out of England with a Company of his Servants, Allegiance remaineth among his Subjects and Servants, altho' he be out of his Realm *whereto his Laws are confined.*" We did not mean to say, as your Excellency would suppose, that "the Common Law prescribes Limits to the Extent of the Legislative Power," though we shall always affirm it to be true of the Law of Reason and natural Equity. Your Excellency thinks you have made it appear, that "the Colony of Massachusetts-Bay is holden as feudatory of the Imperial Crown of England;" and therefore you say, "to use the Words of a very great Authority in a Case in *some Respects* analogous to it," being feudatory it necessary follows, that "it is under the Government of the King's Laws." Your Excellency has not named this Authority; but we conceive his Meaning must be, that being Feudatory, it is under the Government of the King's Laws *absolutely;* for as we have before said the Feudal System admits of no Idea of the Authority of Parliament, and this would have been the Case of the Colony but for the Compact with the King in the Charter.

Your Excellency says, that "Persons thus holding *under the Crown* of England remain or *become* Subjects of England;" by which we suppose your Excellency to mean, subject to the Supreme Authority of Parliament "to all Intents and Purposes as fully as if any of the Royal Manors, &c. within the Realm had been granted to them upon the like Tenure." We apprehend with Submission, your Excellency is Mistaken in supposing that our Allegiance is due to the Crown of England. Every Man swears Allegiance for himself to his own King in his Natural Person. "Every Subject is presumed by Law to be Sworn to the King, which is to his Natural Person," says Lord Coke. *Rep. on Calvins Case.* "The Allegiance is due to his Natural Body." And he says "in the Reign of Edward II. the Spencers, the Father and the Son, to cover the Treason hatched in their Hearts, invented this damnable and damned Opinion, that *Homage* and Oath of Allegiance was more by Reason of the King's Crown, that is of his politick Capacity, than by Reason of the Person of the King; upon which Opinion they infer'd execrable and detestable Consequents." The Judges of England, all but one, in the Case of the Union between Scotland and England, declared that "Allegiance followeth the natural Person not the politick;" and "to prove the Allegiance to be tied to the Body natural of the King, and not to the Body politick, the Lord Coke cited the Phrases of diverse Statutes, mentioning our *natural* liege Sovereign."— If then the Homage and Allegiance is not to the Body politick of the King, then it is not to him as the Head or any Part of that Legislative Authority, which your Excellency says "is equally extensive with the Authority of the Crown throughout every Part of the Dominion;" and your Excellency's Observations thereupon must fail. The same Judges mention the Allegiance of a Subject to the Kings of England who is out of the Reach and Extent of the Laws of England; which is perfectly reconcileable with the Principles of our Ancestors quoted before from your Excellency's History, but upon your Excellency's Principles appears to us to be an Absurdity. The Judges, speaking of a Subject, say, "although his Birth was out of the Bounds of the Kingdom of England, and *out of the Reach and Extent of the Laws of England,* yet if it were *within the Allegiance of the King of England, &c.* Normandy, Acquitain, Gascoign, and other Places within the Limits of France, and consequently out of the Realm or Bounds of the Kingdom of England, were in Subjection to the Kings of England. And the Judges say, "*Rex et Regnum* be not so Relatives, as a King can be King but of one Kingdom, which clearly holdeth not but that his Kingly Power extending to divers Nations and Kingdoms, all owe him equal Subjection and are equally born to the Benefit of his Protection, and altho' he is to govern them *by their distinct Laws,* yet any one of the People coming into the other is to have the Benefit of the Laws wheresoever he cometh." So they are not to be deemed Aliens, as your Excellency in your Speech supposes in any of the Dominions; all which accords with the Principles our Ancestors held. "And he is to bear the Burden of Taxes of the *Place where he cometh,* but living in one or for his Livelihood in one, *he is not to be taxed in the other,* because Laws ordain Taxes, Impositions and Charges as a Discipline of Subjection particularized to every particular Nation:" Nothing we think, can be more clear to our Purpose than this Decision, of Judges, perhaps as learned as ever adorned the English Nation; or in Favor of America in her present Controversy with the Mother State.

Your Excellency says, that by our not distinguishing between the Crown of England and the Kings and Queens of England in their personal or natural Capacities, we have been led into a fundamental Error." Upon this very Distinction we have availed ourselves. We have said that our Ancestors considered the Land which they took Possession of in America as out of the Bounds of the Kingdom of England, and out of the Reach and Extent of the Laws of England; and that the King also even in the Act of granting the Charter, considered the Territory as *not within* the Realm; that the King had an absolute Right in himself to dispose of the Lands, and that this was not disputed by the Nation; nor could the Lands on any solid Grounds be claimed by the Nation, and therefore our Ancestors received the Lands by Grant from the King, and at the same Time compacted with him and promised him Homage and Allegiance, not in his publick or politick but natural Capacity only.—If it be difficult for us to show how the King acquired a Title to this Country in his natural Capacity, or separate from his Relation to his Subjects, which we confess, yet we conceive it will be equally difficult for your Excellency to show how the Body Politick and Nation of England acquired it. Our Ancestors supposed it was acquired by neither; and therefore they declared, as we have before quoted from your History, that saving their actual Purchase from the Natives, of the Soil, the Dominion, the Lordship, and Sovereignty, they had in the Sight of God and Man, no Right and Title to what they possessed. How much clearer then in natural Reason and Equity must our Title be, who hold Estates dearly purchased at the Expence of our own as well as our Ancestors Labour, and defended by them with Treasure and Blood.

Your Excellency has been pleased to confirm, rather than deny or confute a Piece of History which you say we took from an anonimous Pamphlet, and by which you "fear we have been too easily misled." It may be gathered from your own Declaration and other Authorities besides the anonimous Pamphlet, that the House of Commons took Exception, not at the King's having made an absolute Grant of the Territory, but at the Claim of an exclusive Right to the Fishery on the Banks and Sea-Coast, by Virtue of the Patent. At this you say "the House of Commons was alarmed, and a Bill was brought in for allowing a Fishery." And upon this Occasion your Excellency allows, that "one of the Secretaries of State declared that the Plantations were not annexed to the Crown, and so were not within the Jurisdiction of Parliament." If we should concede to what your Excellency supposes might possibly or "perhaps" be the Case, that the Secretary made this Declaration "as his own Opinion," the Event showed that it was the Opinion of the King too; for it is not to be accounted for upon any other Principle, that he would have denied his Royal Assent to a Bill formed for no other Purpose, but to grant his Subjects in England the Privileges of Fishing on the Sea Coasts in America. The Account published by Sir Ferdinando Gorges himself, of the Proceedings of Parliament *on this Occasion,* your Excellency thinks will remove all Doubt of the Sense of the Nation and of the Patentees of this Patent or Charter in 1620. "This Narrative, you say, has all the Appearance of Truth and Sincerity," which we do not deny: and to us it carries this Conviction with it, that "what was objected" in Parliament was, the exclusive Claim of

Fishing only. His imagining that he had satisfied the House after divers Attendances, that the Planting a Colony was of much more Consequence than a *simple disorderly Course of Fishing,* is sufficient for our Conviction. We know that the Nation was at that Time alarmed with Apprehensions of Monopolies; and if the Patent of New-England was presented by the two Houses as a Grievance, it did not show, as your Excellency supposes, "the Sense they then had of their Authority over this new-acquired Territory," but only their Sense of the Grievance of a Monopoly of the Sea.

We are happy to hear your Excellency say, that "our Remarks upon and Construction of the Words *not repugnant to the Laws of England,* are much the same with those of the Council." It serves to confirm us in our Opinion, in what we take to be the most important Matter of Difference between your Excellency and the two Houses. After saying, that the Statute of 7th and 8th of William and Mary favors the Construction of the Words as intending such Laws of England as are made more immediately to respect us, you tell us, that "the Province Agent Mr. Dummer in his much applauded Defence, says that *then* a Law of the Plantations may be said to be repugnant to a Law made in Great-Britain, when it flatly contradicts it so far as the Law made there mentions and relates to the Plantations." This is plain and obvious to common Sense, and therefore cannot be denied. But if your Excellency will read a Page or two further in that excellent Defence, you will see that he mentions this as the Sense of the Phrase, as taken from an Act of Parliament, rather than as the Sense he would chuse himself to put upon it; and he expresly designs to shew, in Vindication of the Charter, that in that Sense of the Words, there never was a Law made in the Plantations repugnant to the Laws of Great-Britain. He gives another Construction much more likely to be the true Intent of the Words; namely, "that the Patentees shall not presume under Colour of their particular Charters to make any Laws *inconsistent with the Great Charter and other Laws of England, by which the Lives, Liberties, and Properties of Englishmen are secured.*" This is the Sense in which our Ancestors understood the Words; and therefore they were unwilling to conform to the Acts of Trade, and disregarded them all till they made Provision to give them Force in the Colony by a Law of their own; saying, that "the Laws of England did not reach America: And those Acts were an Invasion of their Rights, Liberties and Properties," because they were not "represented in Parliament." The Right of being governed only by Laws which were made by Persons in whose Election they had a Voice, they looked upon as the Foundation of English Liberties. By the Compact with the King in the Charter, they were to be as free in America, as they would have been if they had remained within the Realm; and therefore they freely asserted that they "were to be governed by Laws made by themselves and by Officers chosen by themselves." Mr. Dummer says, "It seems reasonable enough to think that the Crown," and he might have added our Ancestors, "intended by this Injunction to provide for all its Subjects, that they might not be oppressed by arbitrary Power— but—being still Subjects, they should be protected by the same mild Laws, and enjoy the same happy Government as if they continued within the Realm." And considering the Words of the Charter in this Light, he looks upon them as designed to be a Fence against Oppression and despotic Power. But the Construction which your Excellency puts upon the Words, reduce us to a State of Vassallage, and exposes us to Oppression and despotic Power, whenever a Parliament shall see fit to make Laws for that Purpose and put them in Execution.

We flatter ourselves that from the large Extracts we have made from your Excellency's History of the Colony, it appears evidently, that under both Charters it hath been the Sense of the People and of the Government that they were not under the Jurisdiction of Parliament. We pray you again to recur to those Quotations and our Observations upon them: And we wish to have your Excellency's judicious Remarks. When we adduced that History to prove that the Sentiments of *private* Persons of Influence, four or five Years after the Restoration, were very different from what your Excellency apprehended them to be when you delivered your Speech, you seem to concede to it by telling us "it was, as you take it, from the *Principles imbibed* in those Times of Anarchy (preceeding the Restoration) that they disputed the Authority of Parliament;" but you add, "the Government would not venture to dispute it." We find in the same History a Quotation from a Letter of Mr. *Stoughton,* dated 17 Years after the Restoration, mentioning "the Country's not taking Notice of the Acts of Navigation *to observe them.*" And it was, as we take it, after that Time, that the Government declared in a Letter to their Agents, that they had not submitted to them; and they ventured to "dispute" the Jurisdiction, asserting that they apprehended the Acts to be an Invasion of the Rights, Liberties, and Properties of the Subjects of his Majesty in the Colony, *they not being represented in Parliament;* and that "the Laws of England *did not reach America.*" It very little avails in Proof that they conceded to the Supreme Authority of Parliament, their telling the Commissioners "that the Act of Navigation had for some Years before been observed here, that they knew not of its being greatly violated, and that such Laws as appeared to be against it were repealed." It may as truly be said now, that the Revenue Acts are observed by some of the People of this Province; but it cannot be said that the Government and People of this Province have conceded that the Parliament had Authority to make such Acts to be observed here. Neither does their Declarations to the Commissioners that such Laws as appeared to be against the Act of Navigation were repealed, prove their Concession of the Authority of Parliament, by any Means so much as their making Provision for giving Force to an Act of Parliament within this Province, by a deliberate and solemn Act or Law of their own, proves the contrary.

You tell us, that "the Government four or five Years before the Charter was vacated more explicitly," that is than by a Conversation with the Commissioners, "acknowledge the Authority of Parliament, and voted that their Governor should take the Oath required of him faithfully to do and perform all Matters and Things enjoined him by the Acts of Trade." But does this, may it please your Excellency, show their explicit Acknowledgment of the Authority of Parliament? Does it not rather show directly the contrary? For, what need could there be for their Vote or Authority to require him to take the Oath already required of him by the Act of Parliament, unless both he and they judged that an Act of Parliament was not of Force sufficient to bind him to take such Oath? We do not deny, but on the contrary are fully persuaded that your Excellency's Principles in Government are still the same with what they appear to be in the History; for you there say, that "the passing the Law plainly shows the wrong Sense they had of the Relation they stood in to England." But we are from hence convinced that your Excellency when you wrote the History was of our Mind in this Respect, that our Ancestors in passing the Law discovered their Opinion that they were without the Jurisdiction of Parliament: For it was upon this Principle alone that they shewed the wrong Sense they had in your Excellency's Opinion, of the Relation they stood in to England.

Your Excellency in your second Speech condescends to point out to us the Acts and Doings of the General Assembly which relates to Acts of Parliament, which you think "demonstrates that they have been acknowledged by the Assembly or submitted to by the People:" Neither of which in our Opinion shows that it was the Sense of the Nation, and our Predecessors when they first took Possession of this Plantation or Colony by a Grant and Charter from the Crown, that they were to remain subject to the Supreme Authority of the English Parliament.

Your Excellency seems chiefly to rely upon our Ancestors, after the Revolution "proclaiming King William and Queen Mary in the Room of King James," and taking the Oaths to them, "the Alteration of the Form of Oaths from Time to Time," and finally "the Establishment of the Form which every one of us has complied with, as the Charter in express Terms requires and makes our Duty." We do not know that it has ever been a Point in Dispute whether the Kings of England were ipso facto Kings in and over this Colony or Province, the Compact was made between King Charles the First, his Heirs and Successors, and the Governor and Company, their Heirs and Successors. It is easy upon this Principle to account for the Acknowledgment and Submission of King William and Queen Mary as Successors of Charles the First, in the Room of King James: Besides it is to be considered, that the People in the Colony as well as in England had suffered under the TYRANT James, by which he had alike forfeited his Right to reign over both. There had been a Revolution here as well as in England. The Eyes of the People here were upon William and Mary, and the News of their being proclaimed in England was as your Excellency's History tells us, "the most joyful News ever received in New-England." And if they were not proclaimed here "by Virtue of an Act of the Colony," it was, as we think may be concluded from the Tenor of your History, with the general or universal Consent of the People as apparently as if "such Act had passed." It is *Consent alone,* that makes any human Laws binding; and as a learned Author observes, a purely *voluntary* Submission to an Act, because it is highly in our Favor and for our Benefit, is in all Equity and Justice to be deemed as not at all proceeding from the *Right* we include in the Legislators, that they thereby obtain an *Authority* over us, and that ever hereafter we must obey them of *Duty*. We would observe that one of the first Acts of the General Assembly of this Province since the present Charter, was an Act requiring the taking the Oaths mentioned in an Act of Parliament, to which you refer us: For what Purpose was this Act of the Assembly passed, if it was the Sense of the Legislators that the Act of Parliament was in Force in the Province. And at the same Time another Act was made for the Establishment of other Oaths necessary to be taken; both which Acts have the Royal Sanction, and are now in Force. Your Excellency says, that when the Colony applied to King William for a second Charter, they knew the Oath the King had taken, which was to govern them according to the Statutes in Parliament, and (which your Excellency here omits) *the Laws and Customs of the same.* By the Laws and Customs of Parliament, the People of England freely debate and consent to such Statutes as are made by themselves or their chosen Representatives. This is a Law or Custom which all Mankind may justly challenge as their *inherent* Right. According to this Law the King has an undoubted Right to govern us. Your Excellency upon Recollection surely will not infer from hence, that it was the Sense of our Predecessors that there was to remain a Supremacy in the English Parliament, or a full Power and Authority to make Laws binding upon us in all Cases whatever, in that Parliament where we cannot *debate* and *deliberate* upon the Necessity or Expediency of any Law, and consequently without our Consent, and as it may probably happen destructive of the first Law of Society, the Good of the Whole. You tell us that "after the Assumption of all the Powers of Government, by Virtue of the new Charter, an Act passed for the reviving for a limited Time all the local Laws of the Massachusetts-Bay and New-Plymouth respectively, not repugnant to the Laws of England. And at the same Session an Act passed establishing Naval Officers, that all undue Trading contrary to an Act of Parliament—may be prevented." Among the Acts that were then revived we may reasonably suppose was that whereby Provision was made to give Force to this Act of Parliament in the Province. The Establishment therefore of the Naval Officers was to aid the Execution of an Act of Parliament; for the Observance of which within the Colony, the Assembly had before made Provision, after free Debates, with their own Consent and by their own Act.

The Act of Parliament passed in 1741, for putting an End to several unwarrantable Schemes, mentioned by your Excellency, was designed for the general Good, and if the Validity of it was not disputed, it cannot be urged as a Concession of the Supreme Authority, to make Laws binding on us *in all Cases whatever.* But if the Design of it was for the general Benefit of the Province, it was in one Respect at least greatly complained of by the Persons more immediately affected by it; and to remedy the Inconvenience, the Legislative of this Province pass'd an Act, directly militating with it; which is the strongest Evidence, that altho' they may have submitted *sub silentio* to some Acts of Parliament that they conceived might operate for their Benefit, they did not conceive themselves bound by any of its Acts which they judged would operate to the Injury even of Individuals.

Your Excellency has not thought proper to attempt to confute the Reasoning of a learned Writer on the Laws of Nature and Nations, quoted by us on this Occasion, to shew that the Authority of the Legislature does not extend so far as the Fundamentals of the Constitution. We are unhappy in not having your Remarks upon the Reasoning of that great Man; and until it is confuted, we shall remain of the Opinion, that the Fundamentals of the Constitution being excepted from the Commission of the Legislators, none of the Acts or Doings of the General Assembly, however deliberate and solemn, could avail to change them, if the People have not in very express Terms given them the Power to do it; and that much less ought their Acts and Doings however numerous, which barely refer to Acts of Parliament made expresly to relate us, to be taken as an Acknowledgment that we are subject to the Supreme Authority of Parliament.

We shall sum up our own Sentiments in the Words of that learned Writer Mr. Hooker, in his Ecclesiastical Policy, as quoted by Mr. Locke, "The lawful Power of making Laws to command whole political Societies of Men, belonging so properly to the same intire Societies, that for any Prince or Potentate of what kind soever, to exercise the same of himself, and not from express Commission immediately and personally received from God, is no better *than mere Tyranny.* Laws therefore they are not which *publick Approbation* hath not made so, for Laws human of what kind soever are available by Consent." "Since Men naturally have no full and perfect Power to command whole politick Multitudes of Men, therefore, utterly without our Consent we could in such Sort be at no Man's Commandment living. And to be commanded we do not consent when that Society whereof we be a Part, hath at any Time before consented." We think your Excellency has not proved, either that the Colony is a Part of the politick Society of England, or that it has ever consented that the Parliament of England or Great-Britain should make Laws binding upon us in all Cases whatever, whether made expresly to refer to us or not.

We cannot help before we conclude, expressing our great Concern, that your Excellency has thus repeatedly, in a Manner insisted upon our free Sentiments on Matters of so delicate a Nature, and weighty Importance. The Question appears to us to be no other, than Whether we are the Subjects of absolute unlimitted Power, or of a free Government formed on the Principles of the English Constitution. If your Excellency's Doctrine be true, the People of this Province hold their Lands of the Crown and People of England, and their Lives, Liberties and Properties are at their Disposal; and that even by Compact and their own Consent. They are subject to the King as the Head *alterius Populi* of another People, in whose Legislative they have no Voice or Interest. They are indeed said to have a Constitution and a Legislative of their own, but your Excellency has explained it into a mere Phantom; limitted, controuled, superceded and nullified at the Will of another. Is this the Constitution which so charmed our Ancestors, that as your Excellency has informed us, they kept a Day of solemn Thanksgiving to Almighty God when they received it? and were they Men of so little Discernment, such Children in Understanding, as to please themselves with the Imagination that they were blessed with the same Rights and Liberties which natural-born Subjects in England enjoyed? when at the same Time they had fully consented to be ruled and ordered by a Legislative a Thousand Leagues distant from them, which cannot be supposed to be sufficiently acquainted with their Circumstances, if concerned for their Interest, and in which they cannot be in any Sense represented.

Novanglus;

or, A History

of the Dispute

with America

UPON HIS RETURN FROM THE CONTINENTAL CONGRESS in the fall of 1774, Adams was met with a series of powerful and lucid essays in the *Massachusetts Gazette* defending the principles and policies of British officialdom and challenging the claims of the American Whigs. Writing over the pseudonym Massachusettensis, Daniel Leonard argued that the constitutional authority of Parliament did and must extend to the colonies. Theoretically, the colonies must be under the sovereignty of Parliament, Leonard insisted, because "two supreme or independent authorities cannot exist in the same state." Such an *imperium in imperio* was absurd and a contradiction in terms. According to Leonard, there could be "no possible medium between absolute independence" on the one hand, and "subjection to the authority of Parliament" on the other.

Historians have long recognized the importance of Adams's Novanglus letters to the Revolutionary cause. They were not only a close, point-by-point refutation of Leonard's argument, but they represent the most advanced Patriot argument against British imperial policy. The "Novanglus" letters were a systematic attempt by Adams to describe the origins, nature, and jurisdictional boundaries of the imperial British constitution. The central question that sparked Adams to write was clear and simple: Does the authority of Parliament extend to the colonies? In exhaustive and sometimes painstaking detail, Adams plumbs the depths of English and colonial legal history to demonstrate that the provincial legislatures are fully sovereign over their own internal affairs, and that the colonies are connected to Great Britain only through a modified feudal allegiance with the person of the King.

8

NOVANGLUS;

OR, A HISTORY OF

THE DISPUTE WITH AMERICA,

FROM ITS ORIGIN, IN 1754,

TO THE PRESENT TIME

ADDRESSED TO THE INHABITANTS OF
THE COLONY OF MASSACHUSETTS BAY

No. 1

MY FRIENDS,—A writer, under the signature of *Massachusettensis,* has addressed you, in a series of papers, on the great national subject of the present quarrel between the British administration and the Colonies. As I have not in my possession more than one of his essays, and that is in the Gazette of December 26, I will take the liberty, in the spirit of candor and decency, to bespeak your attention upon the same subject.

There may be occasion to say very severe things, before I shall have finished what I propose, in opposition to this writer, but there ought to be no reviling. *Rem ipsam dic, mitte male loqui,* which may be justly translated, speak out the whole truth boldly, but use no bad language.

It is not very material to inquire, as others have done, who is the author of the speculations in question. If he is a disinterested writer, and has nothing to gain or to lose, to hope or to fear, for himself more than other individuals of your community; but engages in this controversy from the purest principles, the noblest motives of benevolence to men, and of love to his country, he ought to have no influence with you, further than truth and justice will support his argument. On the other hand, if he hopes to acquire or preserve a lucrative employment, to screen himself from the just detestation of his countrymen, or whatever other sinister inducement he may have, so far as the truth of facts and the weight of argument are in his favor, he ought to be duly regarded.

He tells you, "that the temporal salvation of this province depends upon an entire and speedy change of measures, which must depend upon a change of sentiment respecting our own conduct and the justice of the British nation."

The task of effecting these great changes, this courageous writer has undertaken in a course of publications in a newspaper. *Nil desperandum* is a good motto, and *nil admirari* is another. He is welcome to the first, and I hope will be willing that I should assume the last. The public, if they are not mistaken in their conjecture, have been so long acquainted with this gentleman, and have seen him so often disappointed, that if they were not habituated to strange things, they would wonder at his hopes, at this time, to accomplish the most unpromising project of his whole life. In the character of *Philanthrop,* he attempted to reconcile you to Mr. Bernard. But the only fruit of his labor was, to expose his client to more general examination, and consequently to more general resentment and aversion. In the character of *Philalethes,* he essayed to prove Mr. Hutchinson a patriot, and his letters not only innocent but meritorious. But the more you read and considered, the more you were convinced of the ambition and avarice, the simulation and dissimulation, the hypocrisy and perfidy of that destroying angel.

This ill-fated and unsuccessful, though persevering writer, still hopes to change your sentiments and conduct, by which it is supposed that he means to convince you, that the system of colony administration which has been pursued for these ten or twelve years past is a wise, righteous, and humane plan; that Sir Francis Bernard and Mr. Hutchinson, with their connections, who have been the principal instruments of it, are your best friends; and that those gentlemen, in this province, and in all the other colonies, who have been in opposition to it, are, from ignorance, error, or from worse and baser causes, your worst enemies.

This is certainly an inquiry that is worthy of you; and I promise to accompany this writer in his ingenious labors to assist you in it. And I earnestly entreat you, as the result of all shall be, to change your sentiments or persevere in them, as the evidence shall appear to you, upon the most dispassionate and impartial consideration, without regard to his opinion or mine.

He promises to avoid personal reflections, but to "penetrate the arcana" and "expose the wretched policy of the whigs." The cause of the whigs is not conducted by intrigues at a distant court, but by constant appeals to a sensible and virtuous people; it depends entirely on their good-will, and cannot be pursued a single step without their concurrence, to obtain which, all their designs, measures, and means, are constantly published to the collective body. The whigs, therefore, can have no arcana; but if they had, I dare say they were never so left, as to communicate them to this writer; you will therefore be disappointed, if you expect from him any thing which is true, but what has been as public as records and newspapers could make it.

I, on my part, may, perhaps, in a course of papers, penetrate arcana too; show the wicked policy of the tories; trace their plan from its first rude sketches to its present complete draught; show that it has been much longer in contemplation than is generally known,—who were the first in it—their views, motives, and secret springs of action, and the means they have employed. This will necessarily bring before your eyes many characters, living and dead. From such a research and detail of facts, it will clearly appear, who were the aggressors, and who have acted on the defensive from first to last; who are still struggling, at the expense of their ease, health, peace, wealth, and preferment, against the encroachments of the tories on their country, and who are determined to continue struggling, at much greater hazards still, and, like the Prince of Orange, are resolved never to see its entire subjection to arbitrary power, but rather to die fighting against it in the last ditch.

It is true, as this writer observes, "that the bulk of the people are generally but little versed in the affairs of state;" that they "rest the affairs of government in the hands where accident has placed them." If this had not been true, the designs of the tories had been many years ago entirely defeated. It was clearly seen by a few, more than ten years since, that they were planning and pursuing the very measures we now see executing. The people were informed of it, and warned of their danger; but they had been accustomed to confide in certain persons, and could never be persuaded to believe, until prophecy became history. Now, they see and feel that the horrible calamities are come upon them, which were foretold so many years ago, and they now sufficiently execrate the men who have brought these things upon them. Now, alas! when perhaps it is too late. If they had withdrawn their confidence from them in season, they would have wholly disarmed them.

"The same game, with the same success, has been played in all ages and countries," as Massachusettensis observes. When a favorable conjuncture has presented, some of the most intriguing and powerful citizens have conceived the design of enslaving their country, and building their own greatness on its ruins. Philip and Alexander are examples of this in Greece; Caesar in Rome; Charles V. in Spain; Louis XII. in France; and ten thousand others.

"There is a latent spark in the breasts of the people, capable of being kindled into a flame, and to do this has always been the employment of the disaffected." What is this latent spark? The love of liberty. *A Deo hominis est indita naturae.* Human nature itself is evermore an advocate for liberty. There is also in human nature a resentment of injury and indignation against wrong; a love of truth, and a veneration for virtue. These amiable passions are the "latent spark" to which those whom this writer calls the "disaffected" apply. If the people are capable of understanding, seeing, and feeling the difference between true and false, right and wrong, virtue and vice, to what better principle can the friends of mankind apply, than to the sense of this difference? Is it better to apply, as this writer and his friends do, to the basest passions in the human breast—to their fear, their vanity, their avarice, ambition, and every kind of corruption? I appeal to all experience, and to universal history, if it has ever been in the power of popular leaders, uninvested with other authority than what is conferred by the popular suffrage, to persuade a large people, for any length of time together, to think themselves wronged, injured, and oppressed, unless they really were, and saw and felt it to be so.

"They," the popular leaders, "begin by reminding the people of the elevated rank they hold in the universe, as men; that all men by nature are equal; that kings are but the ministers of the people; that their authority is delegated to them by the people, for their good, and they have a right to resume it, and place it in other hands, or keep it themselves, whenever it is made use of to oppress them. Doubtless, there have been instances when these principles have been inculcated to obtain a redress of real grievances; but they have been much oftener perverted to the worst of purposes."

These are what are called revolution principles. They are the principles of Aristotle and Plato, of Livy and Cicero, and Sidney, Harrington, and Locke; the principles of nature and eternal reason; the principles on which the whole government over us now stands. It is therefore astonishing, if any thing can be so, that writers, who call themselves friends of government, should in this age and country be so inconsistent with themselves, so indiscreet, so immodest, as to insinuate a doubt concerning them.

Yet we find that these principles stand in the way of Massachusettensis and all the writers of his class. The Veteran, in his letter to the officers of the army, allows them to be noble and true; but says the application of them to particular cases is wild and utopian. How they can be in general true, and not applicable to particular cases, I cannot comprehend. I thought their being true in general, was because they were applicable in most particular cases.

Gravity is a principle in nature. Why? Because all particular bodies are found to gravitate. How would it sound to say, that bodies in general are heavy; yet to apply this to particular bodies, and say, that a guinea or a ball is heavy, is wild? "Adopted in private life," says the honest amiable veteran, "they would introduce perpetual discord." This I deny; and I think it plain, that there never was a happy private family where they were not adopted. "In the state, perpetual discord." This I deny; and affirm, that order, concord, and stability in this state, never was nor can be preserved without them. "The least failure in the reciprocal duties of worship and obedience in the matrimonial contract would justify a divorce." This is no consequence from these principles. A total departure from the ends and designs of the contract, it is true, as elopement and adultery, would by these principles justify a divorce; but not the least failure, or many smaller failures in the reciprocal duties, &c. "In the political compact, the smallest defect in the prince, a revolution." By no means; but a manifest design in the prince, to annul the contract on his part, will annul it on the part of the people. A settled plan to deprive the people of all the benefits, blessings, and ends of the contract, to subvert the fundamentals of the constitution, to deprive them of all share in making and executing laws, will justify a revolution.

The author of a "Friendly Address to all reasonable Americans" discovers his rancor against these principles in a more explicit manner; and makes no scruples to advance the principles of Hobbes and Filmer boldly, and to pronounce damnation, *ore rotundo,* on all who do not practise implicit, passive obedience to an established government, of whatever character it may be. It is not reviling, it is not bad language, it is strictly decent to say, that this angry bigot, this ignorant dogmatist, this foul-mouthed scold, deserves no other answer than silent contempt. Massachusettensis and the Veteran—I admire the first for his art, the last for his honesty.

Massachusettensis is more discreet than any of the others; sensible that these principles would be very troublesome to him, yet conscious of their truth, he has neither admitted nor denied them. But we have a right to his opinion of them, before we dispute with him. He finds fault with the application of them. They have been invariably applied, in support of the revolution and the present establishment, against the Stuarts, the Charleses, and the Jameses, in support of the Reformation and the Protestant religion; and against the worst tyranny that the genius of toryism has ever yet invented; I mean the Roman superstition. Does this writer rank the revolution and present establishment, the Reformation and Protestant religion, among his worst of purposes? What "worse purpose" is there than established tyranny? Were these principles ever inculcated in favor of such tyranny? Have they not always been used against such tyrannies, when the people have had knowledge enough to be apprized of them, and courage to assert them? Do not those who aim at depriving the people of their liberties, always inculcate opposite principles, or discredit these?

"A small mistake in point of policy," says he, "often furnishes a pretence to libel government, and persuade the people that their rulers are tyrants, and the whole government a system of oppression." This is not only untrue, but inconsistent with what he said before. The people are in their nature so gentle, that there never was a government yet in which thousands of mistakes were not overlooked. The most sensible and jealous people are so little attentive to government, that there are no instances of resistance, until repeated, multiplied oppressions have placed it beyond a doubt, that their rulers had formed settled plans to deprive them of their liberties; not to oppress an individual or a few, but to break down the fences of a free constitution, and deprive the people at large of all share in the government, and all the checks by which it is limited. Even Machiavel himself allows, that, not ingratitude to their rulers, but much love, is the constant fault of the people.

This writer is equally mistaken, when he says, the people are sure to be losers in the end. They can hardly be losers if unsuccessful; because, if they live, they can but be slaves, after an unfortunate effort, and slaves they would have been, if they had not resisted. So that nothing is lost. If they die, they cannot be said to lose, for death is better than slavery. If they succeed, their gains are immense. They preserve their liberties. The instances in antiquity which this writer alludes to are not mentioned, and therefore cannot be answered; but that in the country from whence we are derived, is the most unfortunate for his purpose that could have been chosen. No doubt he means, the resistance to Charles I. and the case of Cromwell. But the people of England, and the cause of liberty, truth, virtue, and humanity, gained infinite advantages by that resistance. In all human probability, liberty, civil and religious, not only in England, but in all Europe, would have been lost. Charles would undoubtedly have established the Romish religion, and a despotism as wild as any in the world. And as England has been a principal bulwark, from that period to this, of civil liberty and the Protestant religion in all Europe, if Charles's schemes had succeeded, there is great reason to apprehend that the light of science would have been extinguished, and mankind drawn back to a state of darkness and misery like that which prevailed from the fourth to the fourteenth century. It is true, and to be lamented, that Cromwell did not establish a government as free as he might and ought; but his government was infinitely more glorious and happy to the people than Charles's. Did not the people gain by the resistance to James II.? Did not the Romans gain by the resistance to Tarquin? Without that resistance, and the liberty that was restored by it, would the great Roman orators, poets, and historians, the great teachers of humanity and politeness, the pride of human nature, and the delight and glory of mankind for seventeen hundred years, ever have existed? Did not the Romans gain by resistance to the Decemvirs? Did not the English gain by resistance to John, when *Magna Charta* was obtained? Did not the Seven United Provinces gain by resistance to Philip, Alva, and Granvelle? Did not the Swiss Cantons, the Genevans, and Grisons gain by resistance to Albert and Gessler?

No. 11

I HAVE HERETOFORE INTIMATED my intention of pursuing the tories through all their dark intrigues and wicked machinations, and to show the rise and progress of their schemes for enslaving this country. The honor of inventing and contriving these measures is not their due. They have been but servile copiers of the designs of Andros, Randolph, Dudley, and other champions of their cause towards the close of the last century. These latter worthies accomplished but little; and their plans had been buried with them for a long course of years, until, in the administration of the late Governor Shirley, they were revived by the persons who are now principally concerned in carrying them into execution. Shirley was a crafty, busy, ambitious, intriguing, enterprising man; and, having mounted, no matter by what means, to the chair of this province, he saw, in a young, growing country, vast prospects of ambition opening before his eyes, and conceived great designs of aggrandizing himself, his family, and his friends. Mr. Hutchinson and Mr. Oliver, the two famous letter-writers, were his principal ministers of state; Russell, Paxton, Ruggles, and a few others, were *subordinate* instruments. Among other schemes of this junto, one was to have a revenue in America, by authority of parliament.

In order to effect their purpose, it was necessary to concert measures with the other colonies. Dr. Franklin, who was known to be an active and very able man, and to have great influence in the province of Pennsylvania, was in Boston in the year 1754, and Mr. Shirley communicated to him the profound secret,—the great design of taxing the colonies by act of parliament. This sagacious gentleman, this eminent philosopher and distinguished patriot, to his lasting honor, sent the Governor an answer in writing, with the following remarks upon his scheme, remarks which would have discouraged any honest man from the pursuit. The remarks are these:—

"That the people always bear the burden best, when they have, or think they have, some *share* in the direction.

"That when public measures are generally distasteful to the people, the wheels of government must move more heavily.

"That excluding the people of America from all share in the choice of a grand council for their own defence, and taxing them in parliament, where they have no representative, would probably give extreme dissatisfaction.

"That there was no reason to doubt the willingness of the colonists to contribute for their own defence. That the people themselves, whose all was at stake, could better judge of the force necessary for their defence, and of the means for raising money for the purpose, than a British parliament at so great distance.

"That natives of America would be as likely to consult wisely and faithfully for the safety of their native country, as the governors sent from Britain, whose object is generally to make fortunes, and then return home, and who might therefore be expected to carry on the war against France, rather in a way by which themselves were likely to be gainers, than for the greatest advantage of the cause.

"That compelling the colonies to pay money for their own defence, without their consent, would show a suspicion of their loyalty, or of their regard for their country, or of their common sense, and would be treating them as conquered enemies, and not as free Britons, who hold it for their undoubted right, not to be taxed but by their own consent, given through their representatives.

"That parliamentary taxes, once laid on, are often continued, after the necessity for laying them on ceases; but that if the colonists were trusted to tax themselves, they would remove the burden from the people as soon as it should become unnecessary for them to bear it any longer.

"That if parliament is to tax the colonies, their assemblies of representatives may be dismissed as useless.

"That taxing the colonies in parliament for their own defence against the French, is not more just, than it would be to oblige the cinque-ports, and other parts of Britain, to maintain a force against France, and tax them for this purpose, without allowing them representatives in parliament.

"That the colonists have always been indirectly taxed by the mother country, (besides paying the taxes necessarily laid on by their own assemblies); inasmuch as they are obliged to purchase the manufactures of Britain, charged with innumerable heavy taxes, some of which manufactures they could make, and others could purchase cheaper at markets.

"That the colonists are besides taxed by the mother country, by being obliged to carry great part of their produce to Britain, and accept a lower price than they might have at other markets. The difference is a tax paid to Britain.

"That the whole wealth of the colonists centres at last in the mother country, which enables her to pay her taxes.

"That the colonies have, at the hazard of their lives and fortunes, extended the dominions and increased the commerce and riches of the mother country; that therefore the colonists do not deserve to be deprived of the native right of Britons, the right of being taxed only by representatives chosen by themselves.

"That an adequate representation in parliament would probably be acceptable to the colonists, and would best raise the views and interests of the whole empire."

The last of these propositions seems not to have been well considered; because an adequate representation in parliament is totally impracticable; but the others have exhausted the subject.*

Whether the ministry at home, or the junto here, were discouraged by these masterly remarks, or by any other cause, the project of taxing the colonies was laid aside; Mr. Shirley was removed from this government, and Mr. Pownall was placed in his stead.

Mr. Pownall seems to have been a friend to liberty and to our constitution, and to have had an aversion to all plots against either; and, consequently, to have given his confidence to other persons than Hutchinson and Oliver, who, stung with envy against Mr. Pratt and others, who had the lead in affairs, set themselves, by propagating slanders against the Governor among the people, and especially among the clergy, to raise discontents, and make him uneasy in his seat. Pownall, averse to wrangling, and fond of the delights of England, solicited to be recalled, and after some time Mr. Bernard was removed from New Jersey to the chair of this province.

Bernard was the man for the purpose of the junto. Educated in the highest principles of monarchy; naturally daring and courageous; skilled enough in law and policy to do mischief, and avaricious to a most infamous degree; needy, at the same time, and having a numerous family to provide for, he was an instrument suitable in every respect, excepting one, for this junto to employ. The exception I mean was blunt frankness, very opposite to that cautious cunning, that deep dissimulation, to which they had, by long practice, disciplined themselves. However, they did not despair of teaching

---

* If any one should ask what authority or evidence I have of this anecdote, I refer to the second volume of the Political Disquisitions, pp. 276–9. A book which ought to be in the hands of every American who has learned to read.

him this necessary artful quality by degrees, and the event showed that they were not wholly unsuccessful in their endeavors to do it.

While the war lasted, these simple provinces were of too much importance in the conduct of it, to be disgusted by any open attempt against their liberties. The junto, therefore, contented themselves with preparing their ground, by extending their connection and correspondencies in England, and by conciliating the friendship of the crown-officers occasionally here, and insinuating their designs as necessary to be undertaken in some future favorable opportunity, for the good of the empire, as well as of the colonies.

The designs of Providence are inscrutable. It affords conjunctures, favorable for their designs, to bad men, as well as to good. The conclusion of the peace was the most critical opportunity for our junto that could have presented. A peace, founded on the destruction of that system of policy, the most glorious for the nation that ever was formed, and which was never equalled in the conduct of the English government, except in the interregnum, and perhaps in the reign of Elizabeth; which system, however, by its being abruptly broken off, and its chief conductor discarded before it was completed, proved unfortunate to the nation, by leaving it sinking in a bottomless gulf of debt, oppressed and borne down with taxes.

At this lucky time, when the British financier was driven out of his wits, for ways and means to supply the demands upon him, Bernard is employed by the junto, to suggest to him the project of taxing the colonies by act of parliament.

I do not advance this without evidence. I appeal to a publication made by Sir Francis Bernard himself, the last year, of his own Select Letters on the Trade and Government of America; and the Principles of Law and Polity applied to the American Colonies. I shall make use of this pamphlet before I have done.

In the year 1764, Mr. Bernard transmitted home to different noblemen and gentlemen, four copies of his Principles of Law and Polity, with a preface, which proves incontestably, that the project of new-regulating the American Colonies was not first suggested to him by the ministry, but by him to them. The words of this preface are these: "The present expectation, that a new regulation of the American governments will soon take place, probably arises more from the opinion the public has of the abilities of the present ministry, than from any thing that has transpired from the cabinet. It cannot be supposed that their penetration can overlook the necessity of such a regulation, nor their public spirit fail to carry it into execution. But it may be a question, whether the present is a proper time for this work; more urgent business may stand before it; some preparatory steps may be required to precede it; but these will only serve to postpone. As we may expect that this reformation, like all others, will be opposed by powerful prejudices, it may not be amiss to reason with them at leisure, and endeavor to take off their force before they become opposed to government."

These are the words of that arch-enemy of North America, written in 1764, and then transmitted to four persons, with a desire that they might be communicated to others.

Upon these words, it is impossible not to observe: First, that the ministry had never signified to him any intention of new-regulating the colonies, and therefore, that it was he who most officiously and impertinently put them upon the pursuit of this *will-with-a-wisp,* which has led him and them into so much mire; secondly, the artful flattery with which he insinuates these projects into the minds of the ministry, as matters of absolute necessity, which their great penetration could not fail to discover, nor their great regard to the public omit; thirdly, the importunity with which he urges a speedy accomplishment of his pretended reformation of the governments; and, fourthly, his consciousness that these schemes would be opposed, although he affects to expect from powerful prejudices only, that opposition, which all Americans say, has been dictated by sound reason, true policy, and eternal justice. The last thing I shall take notice of is, the artful, yet most false and wicked insinuation, that such new regulations were then generally expected. This is so absolutely false, that, excepting Bernard himself, and his junto, scarcely anybody on this side the water had any suspicion of it,—insomuch that, if Bernard had made public, at that time, his preface and principles, as he sent them to the ministry, it is much to be doubted whether he could have lived in this country; certain it is, he would have had no friends in this province out of the junto.

The intention of the junto was, to procure a revenue to be raised in America by act of parliament. Nothing was further from their designs and wishes, than the drawing or sending this revenue into the exchequer in England, to be spent there in discharging the national debt, and lessening the burdens of the poor people there. They were more selfish. They chose to have the fingering of the money themselves. Their design was, that the money should be applied, first, in a large salary to the governor. This would gratify Bernard's avarice; and then, it would render him and all other governors, not only independent of the people, but still more absolutely a slave to the will of the minister. They intended likewise a salary for the lieutenant-governor. This would appease in some degree the gnawings of Hutchinson's avidity, in which he was not a whit behind Bernard himself. In the next place, they intended a salary to the judges of the common law, as well as admiralty. And thus, the whole government, executive and judicial, was to be rendered wholly independent of the people, (and their representatives rendered useless, insignificant, and even burthensome,) and absolutely dependent upon, and under the direction of the will of the minister of state. They intended, further, to new-model the whole continent of North America; make an entire new division of it into distinct, though more extensive and less numerous colonies; to sweep away all the charters upon the continent with the destroying besom of an act of parliament; and reduce all the governments to the plan of the royal governments, with a nobility in each colony, not hereditary indeed at first, but for life. They did indeed flatter the ministry and people in England with distant hopes of a revenue from America, at some future period, to be appropriated to national uses there. But this was not to happen, in their minds, for some time. The governments must be new-modelled, new-regulated, reformed, first, and then the governments here would be able and willing to carry into execution any acts of parliament, or measures of the ministry, for fleecing the people here, to pay debts, or support pensioners on the American establishment, or bribe electors or members of parliament, or any other purpose that a virtuous ministry could desire.

But, as ill luck would have it, the British financier was as selfish as themselves, and, instead of raising money for them, chose to raise it for himself. He put the cart before the horse. He chose to get the revenue into the exchequer, because he had hungry cormorants enough about him in England, whose cawings were more troublesome to his ears than the croaking of the ravens in America. And he thought, if America could afford any revenue at all, and he could get it by authority of parliament, he might have it himself, to give to his friends, as well as raise it for the junto here, to spend themselves, or give to theirs. This unfortunate, preposterous improvement, of Mr. Grenville, upon the plan of the junto, had wellnigh ruined the whole.

I will proceed no further without producing my evidence. Indeed, to a man who was acquainted with this junto, and had any opportunity to watch their motions, observe their language, and remark their countenances, for these last twelve years, no other evidence is necessary; it was plain to such persons what this junto were about. But we have evidence enough now, under their own hands, of the whole of what was said of them by their opposers through the whole period.

Governor Bernard, in his letter of July 11, 1764, says, "that a general reformation of the American governments would become not only a desirable but a necessary measure." What his idea was, of a general reformation of the American governments, is to be learned from his Principles of Law and Polity, which he sent to the ministry in 1764. I shall select a few of them in his own words; but I wish the whole of them could be printed in the newspapers, that America might know more generally the principles, and designs, and exertions of our junto.

His 29th proposition is: "The rule that a British subject shall not be bound by laws, or liable to taxes, but what he has consented to by his representatives, must be confined to the inhabitants of Great Britain only; and is not strictly true even there.

"30. The Parliament of Great Britain, as well from its rights of sovereignty, as from occasional exigencies, has a right to make laws for, and impose taxes upon, its subjects in its external dominions, although they are not represented in such Parliament. But,

"31. Taxes imposed upon the external dominions ought to be applied to the use of the people from whom they are raised.

"32. The Parliament of Great Britain has a right and a duty to take care to provide for the defence of the American colonies; especially as such colonies are unable to defend themselves.

"33. The Parliament of Great Britain has a right and a duty to take care that provision be made for a sufficient support of the American governments." Because,

"34. The support of the government is one of the principal conditions upon which a colony is allowed the power of legislation." Also, because,

"35. Some of the American colonies have shown themselves deficient in the support of their several governments, both as to sufficiency and independency."

His 75th proposition is: "Every American government is capable of having its constitution altered for the better.

"76. The grants of the powers of government to the American colonies, by charters, cannot be understood to be intended for other than their infant or growing states.

"77. They cannot be intended for their mature state, that is, for perpetuity; because they are in many things unconstitutional, and contrary to the very nature of a British government. Therefore,

"78. They must be considered as designed only as temporary means, for settling and bringing forward the peopling the colonies; which being effected, the cause of the peculiarity of their constitution ceases.

"79. If the charters can be pleaded against the authority of parliament, they amount to an alienation of the dominions of Great Britain, and are, in effect, acts of dismembering the British empire, and will operate as such, if care is not taken to prevent it.

"83. The notion which has heretofore prevailed, that the dividing America into many governments, and different modes of government, will be the means to prevent their uniting to revolt, is ill-founded; since, if the governments were ever so much consolidated, it will be necessary to have so many distinct states, as to make a union to revolt impracticable." Whereas,

"84. The splitting America into many small governments, weakens the governing power and strengthens that of the people; and thereby makes revolting more probable and more practicable.

"85. To prevent revolts in future times, (for there is no room to fear them in the present,) the most effectual means would be, to make the governments large and respectable, and balance the powers of them.

"86. There is no government in America at present, whose powers are properly balanced; there not being in any of them a real and distinct third legislative power mediating between the king and the people, which is the peculiar excellence of the British constitution.

"87. The want of such a third legislative power adds weight to the popular, and lightens the royal scale, so as to destroy the balance between the royal and popular powers.

"88. Although America is not now, (and probably will not be for many years to come) ripe enough for a hereditary nobility, yet it is now capable of a nobility for life.

"89. A nobility appointed by the king for life, and made independent, would probably give strength and stability to the American governments as effectually as a hereditary nobility does to that of Great Britain.

"90. The reformation of the American governments should not be controlled by the present boundaries of the colonies, as they were mostly settled upon partial, occasional, and accidental considerations, without any regard to the whole.

"91. To settle the American governments to the greatest possible advantage, it will be necessary to reduce the number of them; in some places to unite and consolidate; in others to separate and transfer; and in general to divide by natural boundaries instead of imaginary lines.

"92. If there should be but one form of government established for all the North American provinces, it would greatly facilitate the reformation of them; since, if the mode of government was everywhere the same, people would be more indifferent under what division they were ranged.

"93. No objections ought to arise to the alteration of the boundaries of provinces from proprietors, on account of their property only; since there is no occasion that it should in the least affect the boundaries of properties.

"94. The present distinctions of one government being more free or more popular than another, tends to embarrass and to weaken the whole, and should not be allowed to subsist among people subject to one king and one law, and all equally fit for one form of government.

"95. The American colonies, in general, are at this time arrived at that state, which qualifies them to receive the most perfect form of government which their situation and relation to Great Britain make them capable of.

"96. The people of North America, at this time, expect a revisal and reformation of the American governments, and are better disposed to submit to it than ever they were, or perhaps ever will be again.

"97. This is, therefore, the proper and critical time to reform the American governments, upon a general, constitutional, firm, and durable plan; and if it is not done now, it will probably every day grow more difficult, till at last it becomes impracticable."

My friends, these are the words, the plans, principles, and endeavors of Governor Bernard, in the year 1764. That Hutchinson and Oliver, notwithstanding all their disguises, which you well remember, were in unison with him in the whole of his measures, can be doubted by no man. It appeared sufficiently in the part they all along acted, notwithstanding their professions. And it appears incontestably from their detected letters; of which more hereafter.

Now, let me ask you, if the Parliament of Great Britain had all the natural foundations of authority, wisdom, goodness, justice, power, in as great perfection as they ever existed in any body of men since Adam's fall; and if the English nation was the most virtuous, pure, and free that ever was; would not such an unlimited subjection of three millions of people to that parliament, at three thousand miles distance, be real slavery? There are but two sorts of men in the world, freemen and slaves. The very definition of a freeman is one who is bound by no law to which he has not consented. Americans would have no way of giving or withholding their consent to the acts of this parliament, therefore they would not be freemen. But when luxury, effeminacy, and venality are arrived at such a shocking pitch in England; when both electors and elected are become one mass of corruption; when the nation is oppressed to death with debts and taxes, owing to their own extravagance and want of wisdom, what would be your condition under such an absolute subjection to parliament? You would not only be slaves, but the most abject sort of slaves, to the worst sort of masters! at least this is my opinion.

Judge you for yourselves between Massachusettensis and Novanglus.

No. III

THE HISTORY OF THE TORIES, begun in my last, will be interrupted for some time; but it shall be resumed, and minutely related in some future papers. Massachusettensis, who shall now be pursued in his own serpentine path, in his first paper complains that the press is not free; that a party, by playing off the resentment of the populace against printers and authors, has gained the ascendency so far as to become the licenser of it; that the press is become an engine of oppression and licentiousness, much devoted to the partisans of liberty, who have been indulged in publishing what they pleased, *fas vel nefas,* while little has been published on the part of government.

The art of this writer, which appears in all his productions, is very conspicuous in this. It is intended to excite a resentment against the friends of liberty, for tyrannically depriving their antagonists of so important a branch of freedom; and a compassion towards the tories, in the breasts of the people, in the other colonies and in Great Britain, by insinuating that they have not had equal terms. But nothing can be more injurious, nothing farther from the truth. Let us take a retrospective view of the period since the last peace, and see whether they have not uniformly had the press at their service, without the least molestation to authors or printers. Indeed, I believe, that the Massachusetts Spy, if not the Boston Gazette, has been open to them as well as to others. The Evening Post, Massachusetts Gazette, and Boston Chronicle have certainly been always as free for their use as the air. Let us dismiss prejudice and passion, and examine impartially whether the tories have not been chargeable with at least as many libels, as much licentiousness of the press, as the whigs? Dr. Mayhew was a whig of the first magnitude,—a clergyman equalled by very few of any denomination in piety, virtue, genius, or learning, whose works will maintain his character as long as New England shall be free, integrity esteemed, or wit, spirit, humor, reason, and knowledge admired. How was he treated from the press? Did not the reverend tories, who were pleased to write against him, the missionaries of defamation, as well as bigotry and passive obedience, in their pamphlets and newspapers, bespatter him all over with their filth? Did they not, with equal falsehood and malice, charge him with every thing evil? Mr. Otis was in civil life, and a senator, whose parts, literature, eloquence, and integrity proved him a character in the world equal to any of the time in which he flourished of any party in the province. Now, be pleased to recollect the Evening Post. For a long course of years, that gentleman, his friends and connections, of whom the world has, and grateful posterity will have, a better opinion than Massachusettensis will acknowledge, were pelted with the most infernally malicious, false, and atrocious libels that ever issued from any press in Boston. I will mention no other names, lest I give too much offence to the modesty of some, and the envy and rancor of others.

There never was before, in any part of the world, a whole town insulted to their faces, as Boston was by the Boston Chronicle. Yet the printer was not molested for printing. It was his mad attack upon other printers with his clubs, and upon other gentlemen with his pistols, that was the cause, or rather the pretence, of his flight. The truth was, he became too polite to attend to his business; his shop was neglected; procurations were coming for more than two thousand pounds sterling, which he had no inclination to pay.

Printers may have been less eager after the productions of the tories than of the whigs, and the reason has been, because the latter have been more consonant to the general taste and sense, and consequently more in demand. Notwithstanding this, the former have ever found one press, at least, devoted to their service, and have used it as licentiously as they could wish. Whether the revenue-chest has kept it alive, and made it profitable against the general sense, or not, I wot not. Thus much is certain, that two, three, four, five, six, eight, fifteen hundred pounds sterling a-year, have been the constant reward of every scribbler who has taken up the pen on the side of the ministry with any reputation, and commissions have been given here for the most wretched productions of dulness itself; whereas, the writers on the side of liberty have been rewarded only with the consciousness of endeavoring to do good, with the approbation of the virtuous, and the malice of men in power.

But this is not the first time that writers have taken advantage of the times. Massachusettensis knows the critical situation of this province; the danger it is in, without government or law; the army in Boston; the people irritated and exasperated in such a manner as was never before borne by any people under heaven. Much depends upon their patience at this critical time; and such an example of patience and order this people have exhibited, in a state of nature, under such cruel insults, distresses, and provocations, as the history of mankind cannot parallel. In this state of things, protected by an army, the whole junto are now pouring forth the torrents of their billingsgate; propagating thousands of the most palpable falsehoods, when they know that the writers on the other side have been restrained by their prudence and caution from engaging in a controversy that must excite heats, lest it should have unhappy and tragical consequences.

There is nothing in this world so excellent that it may not be abused. The abuses of the press are notorious. It is much to be desired, that writers on all sides would be more careful of truth and decency; but, upon the most impartial estimate, the tories will be found to have been the least so of any party among us.

The honest Veteran, who ought not to be forgotten in this place, says: "If an inhabitant of Bern or Amsterdam could read the newspapers, &c., he would be at a loss how to reconcile oppression with such unbounded license of the press, and would laugh at the charge, as something much more than a paradox,—as a palpable contradiction." But, with all his taste and manly spirit, the Veteran is little of a statesman. His ideas of liberty are quite inadequate; his notions of government very superficial. License of the press is no proof of liberty. When a people are corrupted, the press may be made an engine to complete their ruin; and it is now notorious, that the ministry are daily employing it, to increase and establish corruption, and to pluck up virtue by the roots. Liberty can no more exist without virtue and independence, than the body can live and move without a soul. When these are gone, and the popular branch of the constitution is become dependent on the minister, as it is in England, or cut off, as it is in America, all other forms of the constitution may remain; but if you look for liberty, you will grope in vain; and the freedom of the press, instead of promoting the cause of liberty, will but hasten its destruction, as the best cordials taken by patients in some distempers become the most rancid and corrosive poisons.

The language of the Veteran, however, is like the style of the minister and his scribblers in England,—boasting of the unbounded freedom of the press, and assuring the people that all is safe while that continues; and thus the people are to be cheated with libels, in exchange for their liberties.

A stronger proof cannot be wished, of the scandalous license of the tory presses, than the swarms of pamphlets and speculations, in New York and Boston, since last October. "Madness, folly, delusion, delirium, infatuation, frenzy, high treason, and rebellion," are charged in every page, upon three millions of as good and loyal, as sensible and virtuous people as any in the empire; nay, upon that congress, which was as full and free a representative as ever was constituted by any people; chosen universally, without solicitation, or the least tincture of corruption; that congress which consisted of governors, counsellors, some of them by mandamus too, judges of supreme courts, speakers of assemblies, planters and merchants of the first fortune and character, and lawyers of the highest class, many of them educated at the temple, called to the bar in England, and of abilities and integrity equal to any there.

Massachusettensis, conscious that the people of this continent have the utmost abhorrence of treason and rebellion, labors to avail himself of the magic in these words. But his artifice is vain. The people are not to be intimidated by hard words from a necessary defence of their liberties. Their attachment to their constitution, so dearly purchased by their own and their ancestors' blood and treasure; their aversion to the late innovations; their horror of arbitrary power and the Romish religion, are much deeper rooted than their dread of rude sounds and unmannerly language. They do not want "the advice of an honest lawyer, if such an one could be found," nor will they be deceived by a dishonest one. They know what offence it is to assemble armed, and forcibly obstruct the course of justice. They have been many years considering and inquiring; they have been instructed by Massachusettensis and his friends, in the nature of treason, and the consequences of their own principles and actions. They know upon what hinge the whole dispute turns; that the *fundamentals* of the government over them are disputed; that the minister pretends, and had the influence to obtain the voice of the last parliament in his favor, that parliament is the only supreme, sovereign, absolute, and uncontrollable legislative over all the colonies; that, therefore, the minister and all his advocates will call resistance to acts of parliament by the names of treason and rebellion. But, at the same time, they know that, in their own opinions, and in the opinions of all the colonies, parliament has no authority over them, excepting to regulate their trade, and this not by any principle of common law, but merely by the consent of the colonies, founded on the obvious necessity of a case which was never in contemplation of that law, nor provided for by it; that, therefore, they have as good a right to charge that minister, Massachusettensis, and the whole army to which he has fled for protection, with treason and rebellion. For, if the parliament has not a legal authority to overturn their constitution, and subject them to such acts as are lately passed, every man who accepts of any commission, and takes any steps to carry those acts into execution, is guilty of overt acts of treason and rebellion against his majesty, his royal crown and dignity, as much as if he should take arms against his troops, or attempt his sacred life. They know that the resistance against the Stamp Act, which was made through all America, was, in the opinion of Massachusettensis and George Grenville, high treason; and that Brigadier Ruggles and good Mr. Ogden pretended at the congress of New York to be of the same mind, and have been held in utter contempt and derision by the whole continent for the same reason ever since; because, in their own opinion, that resistance was a noble stand against tyranny, and the only opposition to it which could have been effectual; that if the American resistance to the act for destroying your charter, and to the resolves for arresting persons here and sending them to England for trial, is treason, the lords and commons, and the whole nation, were traitors at the revolution. They know that all America is united in sentiment, and in the plan of opposition to the claims of administration and parliament. The junto, in Boston, with their little flocks of adherents in the country, are not worth taking into the account; and the army and navy, though these are divided among themselves, are no part of America.

In order to judge of this union, they begin at the commencement of the dispute, and run through the whole course of it. At the time of the Stamp Act, every colony expressed its sentiments by resolves of their assemblies, and every one agreed that parliament had no right to tax the colonies. The house of representatives of the Massachusetts Bay then consisted of many persons who have since figured as friends to government; yet every member of that house concurred most cheerfully in the resolves then passed. The congress which met that year at New York expressed the same opinion in their resolves, after the paint, paper, and tea act was passed. The several assemblies expressed the same sentiments; and when your colony wrote the famous circular letter, notwithstanding all the mandates and threats and cajoling of the minister and the several governors, and all the crown-officers through the continent, the assemblies, with one voice, echoed their entire approbation of that letter, and their applause to your colony for sending it. In the year 1768, when a non-importation was suggested and planned by a few gentlemen at a private club in one of our large towns, as soon as it was proposed to the public, did it not spread through the whole continent? Was it not regarded like the laws of the Medes and Persians in almost all the colonies? When the paint and paper act was repealed, the southern colonies agreed to depart from the association in all things but the dutied articles; but they have kept strictly to their agreement against importing them, so that no tea worth the mentioning has been imported into any of them from Great Britain to this day. In the year 1770, when a number of persons were slaughtered in King Street, such was the brotherly sympathy of all the colonies, such their resentment against a hostile administration, that the innocent blood then spilt has never been forgotten, nor the murderous minister and governors, who brought the troops here, forgiven by any part of the continent, and never will be. When a certain masterly statesman invented a committee of correspondence in Boston, which has provoked so much of the spleen of Massachusettensis, (of which much more hereafter) did not every colony, nay, every county, city, hundred, and town, upon the whole continent, adopt the measure, I had almost said, as if it had been a revelation from above, as the happiest means of cementing the union and acting in concert?

What proofs of union have been given since the last March? Look over the resolves of the several colonies, and you will see that one understanding governs, one heart animates the whole body. Assemblies, conventions, congresses, towns, cities, and private clubs and circles, have been actuated by one great, wise, active, and noble spirit, one masterly soul animating one vigorous body. The congress at Philadelphia have expressed the same sentiments with the people of New England; approved of the opposition to the late innovations; unanimously advised us to persevere in it; and assured us, that if force is attempted to carry these measures against us, all America ought to support us. Maryland and the lower counties on Delaware have already, to show to all the world their approbation of the measures of New England and their determination to join in them, with a generosity, a wisdom, and magnanimity which ought to make the tories consider, taken the power of the militia into the hands of the people, without the governor or minister, and established it by their own authority, for the defence of Massachusetts, as well as of themselves. Other colonies are only waiting to see if the necessity of it will become more obvious. Virginia and the Carolinas are preparing for military defence, and have been for some time. When we consider the variety of climate, soil, religion, civil government, commercial interests, &c. which were represented at the congress, and the various occupations, education, and characters of the gentlemen who composed it, the harmony and unanimity which prevailed in it can scarcely be paralleled in any assembly that ever met. When we consider that, at the revolution, such mighty questions, as whether the throne was vacant or not, and whether the Prince of Orange should be king or not, were determined in the convention of parliament by small majorities of two or three, and four or five only, the great majorities, the almost unanimity with which all great questions have been decided in your house of representatives and other assemblies, and especially in the continental congress, cannot be considered in any other light than as the happiest omens, indeed as providential dispensations, in our favor, as well as the clearest demonstrations of the cordial, firm, radical, and indissoluble union of the colonies.

The grand aphorism of the policy of the whigs has been to unite the people of America, and divide those of Great Britain. The reverse of this has been the maxim of the tories, namely,—to unite the people of Great Britain, and divide those of America. All the movements, marches, and countermarches of both parties, on both sides of the Atlantic, may be reduced to one or the other of these rules. I have shown, in opposition to Massachusettensis, that the people of America are united more perfectly than the most sanguine whig could ever have hoped, or than the most timid tory could have feared. Let us now examine whether the people of Great Britain are equally united against us. For, if the contending countries were equally united, the prospect of success in the quarrel would depend upon the comparative wisdom, firmness, strength, and other advantages of each. And if such a comparison was made, it would not appear to a demonstration that

Great Britain could so easily subdue and conquer. It is not so easy a thing for the most powerful state to conquer a country a thousand leagues off. How many years time, how many millions of money, did it take, with five-and-thirty thousand men, to conquer the poor province of Canada? And, after all the battles and victories, it never would have submitted, without a capitulation which secured to them their religion and properties.

But we know that the people of Great Britain are not united against us. We distinguish between the ministry, the house of commons, the officers of the army, navy, excise, customs, &c., who are dependent on the ministry, and tempted, if not obliged, to echo their voices, and the body of the people. We are assured, by thousands of letters from persons of good intelligence, by the general strain of publications in public papers, pamphlets, and magazines, and by some larger works written for posterity, that the body of the people are friends to America, and wish us success in our struggles against the claims of parliament and administration. We know, that millions in England and Scotland will think it unrighteous, impolitic, and ruinous to make war upon us; and a minister, though he may have a marble heart, will proceed with a diffident, desponding spirit. We know that London and Bristol, the two greatest commercial cities in the empire, have declared themselves, in the most decisive manner, in favor of our cause,—so explicitly, that the former has bound her members under their hands to assist us; and the latter has chosen two known friends of America, one attached to us by principle, birth, and the most ardent affection, the other an able advocate for us on several great occasions. We know that many of the most virtuous and independent of the nobility and gentry are for us, and among them, the best bishop that adorns the bench, as great a judge as the nation can boast, and the greatest statesman it ever saw. We know that the nation is loaded with debts and taxes, by the folly and iniquity of its ministers, and that, without the trade of America, it can neither long support its fleet and army, nor pay the interest of its debt.

But we are told that the nation is now united against us; that they hold they have a right to tax us and legislate for us, as firmly as we deny it; that we are a part of the British empire; that every state must have an uncon-trollable power coextensive with the empire; that there is little probability of serving ourselves by ingenious distinctions between external and internal taxes; that if we are not a part of the state, and subject to the supreme authority of parliament, Great Britain will make us so; that if this opportunity of reclaiming the colonies is lost, they will be dismembered from the empire; and, although they may continue their allegiance to the king, they will own none to the imperial crown.

To all this I answer, that the nation is not so united; that they do not so universally hold they have such a right. And my reasons I have given before; that the terms "British Empire" are not the language of the common law, but the language of newspapers and political pamphlets; that the dominions of the king of Great Britain have no power coextensive with them. I would ask, by what law the parliament has authority over America? By the law of God, in the Old and New Testament, it has none; by the law of nature and nations, it has none; by the common law of England, it has none, for the common law, and the authority of parliament founded on it, never extended beyond the four seas; by statute law it has none, for no statute was made before the settlement of the colonies for this purpose; and the declaratory act, made in 1766, was made without our consent, by a parliament which had no authority beyond the four seas. What religious, moral, or political obligations then are we under to submit to parliament as a supreme legislative? None at all. When it is said, that if we are not subject to the supreme authority of parliament, Great Britain will make us so, all other laws and obligations are given up, and recourse is had to the *ratio ultima* of Louis XIV. and the *suprema lex* of the king of Sardinia,—to the law of brickbats and cannon balls, which can be answered only by brickbats and balls.

This language, "the imperial crown of Great Britain," is not the style of the common law, but of court sycophants. It was introduced in allusion to the Roman empire, and intended to insinuate that the prerogative of the imperial crown of England was like that of the Roman emperor, after the maxim was established, *quod principi placuit legis habet vigorem;* and, so far from including the two houses of parliament in the idea of this imperial crown, it was intended to insinuate that the crown was absolute, and had no need of lords or commons to make or dispense with laws. Yet even these court sycophants, when driven to an explanation, never dared to put any other sense upon the words *imperial crown* than this, that the crown of England was independent of France, Spain, and all other kings and states in the world.

When he says, that the king's dominions must have an uncontrollable power coextensive with them, I ask whether they have such a power or not? and utterly deny that they have, by any law but that of Louis XIV. and the king of Sardinia. If they have not, and it is necessary that they should have, it then follows that there is a defect in what he calls the British empire; and how shall this defect be supplied? It cannot be supplied consistently with reason, justice, policy, morality, or humanity, without the consent of the colonies and some new plan of connection. But if Great Britain will set all these at defiance, and resort to the *ratio ultima,* all Europe will pronounce her a tyrant, and America never will submit to her, be the danger of disobedience as great as it will.

But there is no need of any other power than that of regulating trade, and this the colonies ever have been, and will be, ready and willing to concede to her. But she will never obtain from America any further concession while she exists. We are then asked, "for what she protected and defended the colonies against the maritime powers of Europe, from their first settlement to this day?" I answer, for her own interest; because all the profits of our trade centred in her lap. But it ought to be remembered, that her name, not her purse, nor her fleets and armies ever protected us, until the last war, and then the minister who conducted that war informed us that the annual millions from America enabled her to do it.

We are then asked, for what she purchased New York of the Dutch? I answer, she never did. The Dutch never owned it, were never more than trespassers and intruders there, and were finally expelled by conquest. It was ceded, it is true, by the treaty of Breda, and it is said in some authors, that some other territory in India was ceded to the Dutch in lieu of it. But this was the transaction of the king, not of parliament, and therefore makes nothing to the argument.

But admitting, for argument sake, (since the cautious Massachusettensis will urge us into the discussion of such questions,) what is not a supposable case, that the nation should be so sunk in sloth, luxury, and corruption, as to suffer their minister to persevere in his mad blunders, and send fire and sword against us, how shall we defend ourselves? The colonies south of Pennsylvania have no men to spare, we are told. But we know better; we know that all those colonies have a back country, which is inhabited by a hardy, robust people, many of whom are emigrants from New England, and habituated, like multitudes of New England men, to carry their fuzees or rifles upon one shoulder, to defend themselves against the Indians, while they carry their axes, scythes, and hoes upon the other, to till the ground. Did not those colonies furnish men the last war, excepting Maryland? Did not Virginia furnish men, one regiment particularly, equal to any regular regiment in the service? Does the soft Massachusettensis imagine, that in the unnatural, horrid war he is now supposing, their exertions would be less? If he does, he is very ill informed of their principles, their present sentiments and temper.

But, "have you arms and ammunition?" I answer, we have; but if we had not, we could make a sufficient quantity of both. What should hinder? We have many manufacturers of fire-arms now, whose arms are as good as any in the world. Powder has been made here, and may be again, and so may saltpetre. What should hinder? We have all the materials in great abundance, and the process is very simple. But if we neither had them nor could make them, we could import them.

But "the British navy!" ay, there's the rub. Let us consider, since the prudent Massachusettensis will have these questions debated, how many ships are taken to blockade Boston harbor! How many ships can Britain spare to carry on this humane and political war, the object of which is a pepper-corn! Let her send all the ships she has round her island; what if her ill-natured neighbors, France and Spain, should strike a blow in their absence? In order to judge what they could all do when they arrived here, we should consider what they are all able to do round the island of Great Britain. We know that the utmost vigilance and exertions of them, added to all the terrors of sanguinary laws, are not sufficient to prevent continual smuggling into their own island. Are there not fifty bays, harbors, creeks, and inlets upon the whole coast of North America, where there is one round the island of Great Britain? Is it to be supposed, then, that the whole British navy could prevent the importation of arms and ammunition into America, if she should have occasion for them to defend herself against the hellish warfare that is here supposed?

But what will you do for discipline and subordination? I answer, We will have them in as great perfection as the regular troops. If the provincials were not brought, in the last war, to a proper discipline, what was the reason? Because regular generals would not let them fight, which they ardently wished, but employed them in cutting roads. If they had been allowed to fight, they would have brought the war to a conclusion too soon. The provincials did submit to martial law, and to the mutiny and desertion act the last war, and such an act may be made here by a legislature which they will obey with much more alacrity than an act of parliament.

"The new-fangled militia," as the specious Massachusettensis calls it, is such a militia as he never saw. They are commanded through the province, not by men who procured their commissions from a governor as a reward for making themselves pimps to his tools, and by discovering a hatred of the people, but by gentlemen, whose estates, abilities, and benevolence have rendered them the delight of the soldiers; and there is an esteem and respect for them visible through the province, which has not been used in the militia. Nor is there that unsteadiness that is charged upon them. In some places, where companies have been split into two or three, it has only served, by exciting an emulation between the companies, to increase the martial spirit and skill. The plausible Massachusettensis may write as he will, but in a land war, this continent might defend itself against all the world. We have men enough, and those men have as good natural understandings, and as much natural courage as any other men. If they were wholly ignorant now, they might learn the art of war.

But at sea we are defenceless. A navy might burn our seaport towns. What then? If the insinuating Massachusettensis has ever read any speculations concerning an agrarian law, and I know he has, he will be satisfied that three hundred and fifty thousand landholders will not give up their rights, and the constitution by which they hold them, to save fifty thousand inhabitants of maritime towns. Will the minister be nearer his mark, after he has burned a beautiful town and murdered thirty thousand innocent people? So far from it, that one such event would occasion the loss of all the colonies to Great Britain forever. It is not so clear that our trade, fishery, and navigation could be taken from us. Some persons, who understand this subject better than Massachusettensis, with all his sprightly imaginations, are of a different opinion. They think that our trade would be increased. But I will not enlarge upon this subject, because I wish the trade of this continent may be confined to Great Britain, at least as much of it as it can do her any good to restrain.

The Canadians and savages are brought in to thicken the horrors of a picture with which the lively fancy of this writer has terrified him. But, although we are sensible that the Quebec act has laid a foundation for a fabric, which, if not seasonably demolished, may be formidable, if not ruinous, to the colonies, in future times, yet we know that these times are yet at a distance; at present we hold the power of the Canadians as nothing. But we know their dispositions are not unfriendly to us.

The savages will be more likely to be our friends than enemies; but if they should not, we know well enough how to defend ourselves against them.

I ought to apologize for the immoderate length of this paper; but general assertions are only to be confuted by an examination of particulars, which necessarily fills up much space. I will trespass on the reader's patience only while I make one observation more upon the art, I had almost said chicanery, of this writer.

He affirms that we are not united in this province, and that associations are forming in several parts of the province. The association he means has been laid before the public, and a very curious piece of legerdemain it is. Is there any article acknowledging the authority of parliament, the unlimited authority of parliament? Brigadier Ruggles himself, Massachusettensis himself, could not have signed it if there had been, consistent with their known declared opinions. They associate to stand by the king's laws, and this every whig will subscribe. But, after all, what a wretched fortune has this association made in the world! The numbers who have signed it would appear so inconsiderable, that I dare say the Brigadier will never publish to the world their numbers or names. But, "has not Great Britain been a nursing-mother to us?" Yes, and we have behaved as nurse-children commonly do,—been very fond of her, and rewarded her all along tenfold for all her care and expense in our nurture.

But "is not our distraction owing to parliament's taking off a shilling-duty on tea and imposing threepence, and is not this a more unaccountable frenzy, more disgraceful to the annals of America, than the witchcraft?"

Is the threepence upon tea our only grievance? Are we not in this province deprived of the privilege of paying our governors, judges, &c.? Are not trials by jury taken from us? Are we not sent to England for trial? Is not a military government put over us? Is not our constitution demolished to the foundation? Have not the ministry shown, by the Quebec bill, that we have no security against them for our religion, any more than our property, if we once submit to the unlimited claims of parliament? This is so gross an attempt to impose on the most ignorant of the people, that it is a shame to answer it.

Obsta principiis, nip the shoots of arbitrary power in the bud, is the only maxim which can ever preserve the liberties of any people. When the people give way, their deceivers, betrayers, and destroyers press upon them so fast, that there is no resisting afterwards. The nature of the encroachment upon the American constitution is such, as to grow every day more and more encroaching. Like a cancer, it eats faster and faster every hour. The revenue creates pensioners, and the pensioners urge for more revenue. The people grow less steady, spirited, and virtuous, the seekers more numerous and more corrupt, and every day increases the circles of their dependents and expectants, until virtue, integrity, public spirit, simplicity, and frugality, become the objects of ridicule and scorn, and vanity, luxury, foppery, selfishness, meanness, and downright venality swallow up the whole society.

No. iv

Massachusettensis, whose pen can wheedle with the tongue of King Richard III., in his first paper, threatens you with the vengence of Great Britain; and assures you, that if she had no authority over you, yet she would support her claims by her fleets and armies, Canadians and Indians. In his next, he alters his tone, and soothes you with the generosity, justice, and humanity of the nation.

I shall leave him to show how a nation can claim an authority which they have not by right, and support it by fire and sword, and yet be generous and just. The nation, I believe, is not vindictive, but the minister has discovered himself to be so in a degree that would disgrace a warrior of a savage tribe.

The wily Massachusettensis thinks our present calamity is to be attributed to the bad policy of a popular party, whose measures, whatever their intentions were, have been opposite to their profession, the public good. The present calamity seems to be nothing more nor less than reviving the plans of Mr. Bernard and the junto, and Mr. Grenville and his friends, in 1764. Surely this party are, and have been, rather unpopular. The popular party did not write Bernard's letters, who so long ago pressed for the demolition of all the charters upon the continent, and a parliamentary taxation to support government and the administration of justice in America. The popular party did not write Oliver's letters, who enforces Bernard's plans; nor Hutchinson's, who pleads with all his eloquence and pathos for parliamentary penalties, ministerial vengeance, and an abridgment of English liberties.

There is not in human nature a more wonderful phenomenon, nor in the whole theory of it a more intricate speculation, than the *shiftings, turnings, windings,* and *evasions* of a guilty conscience. Such is our unalterable moral constitution, that an internal inclination to do wrong is criminal; and a wicked thought stains the mind with guilt, and makes it tingle with pain. Hence it comes to pass, that the guilty mind can never bear to think that its guilt is known to God or man, no, nor to itself.

> "Cur tamen hos tu
> Evasisse putes, quos diri conscia facti
> Mens habet attonitos, et surdo verbere caedit
> Occultum quatiente animo tortore flagellum?
> Poena autem vehemeus ac multo saevior illis,
> Quas et Caeditius gravis invenit aut Rhadamanthus,
> Nocte dieque suum gestare in pectore testem."*

Massachusettensis and his friends the tories are startled at the calamities they have brought upon their country; and their conscious guilt, their smarting, wounded mind, will not suffer them to confess, even to themselves, what they have done. Their silly denials of their own share in it, before a people who, they know, have abundant evidence against them, never fail to remind me of an ancient *fugitive,* whose conscience could not bear the recollection of what he had done. "I know not; am I my brother's keeper?" he replies,

---

* Juv. Sat. xiii. 192.

with all the apparent simplicity of truth and innocence, to one from whom he was very sensible his guilt could not be hid. The still more absurd and ridiculous attempts of the tories, to throw off the blame of these calamities from themselves to the whigs, remind me of another story, which I have read in the Old Testament. When Joseph's brethren had sold him to the Ishmaelites for twenty pieces of silver, in order to conceal their own avarice, malice, and envy, they dip the coat of many colors in the blood of a kid, and say that an evil beast had rent him in pieces and devoured him. However, what the sons of Israel intended for ruin to Joseph, proved the salvation of the family; and I hope and believe that the whigs will have the magnanimity, like him, to suppress their resentment, and the felicity of saving their ungrateful brothers.

This writer has a faculty of insinuating errors into the mind almost imperceptibly, he dresses them so in the guise of truth. He says, that "the revenue to the crown from America amounted to but little more than the charges of collecting it," at the close of the last war. I believe it did not to so much. The truth is, there never was a pretence of raising a revenue in America before that time, and when the claim was first set up, it gave an alarm like a warlike expedition against us. True it is, that some duties had been laid before by parliament, under pretence of regulating our trade, and, by a collusion and combination between the West India planters and the North American governors, some years before, duties had been laid upon molasses &c. under the same pretence; but, in reality, merely to advance the value of the estates of the planters in the West India Islands, and to put some plunder, under the name of thirds of seizures, into the pockets of the governors. But these duties, though more had been collected in this province than in any other, in proportion, were never regularly collected in any of the colonies. So that the idea of an American revenue, for one purpose or another, had never, at this time, been formed in American minds.

Our writer goes on: "She (Great Britain) thought it as reasonable that the colonies should bear a part of the national burden, as that they should share in the national benefit."

Upon this subject Americans have a great deal to say. The national debt, before the last war, was near a hundred millions. Surely America had no share in running into that debt. What is the reason, then, that she should pay it? But a small part of the sixty millions spent in the last war was for her benefit. Did she not bear her full share of the burden of the last war in America? Did not the province pay twelve shillings in the pound in taxes for the support of it; and send a sixth or seventh part of her sons into actual service? And, at the conclusion of the war, was she not left half a million sterling in debt?

Did not all the rest of New England exert itself in proportion? What is the reason that the Massachusetts has paid its debt, and the British minister, in thirteen years of peace, has paid none of his? Much of it might have been paid in this time, had not such extravagance and speculation prevailed, as ought to be an eternal warning to America, never to trust such a minister with her money. What is the reason that the great and necessary virtues of simplicity, frugality, and economy cannot live in England, Scotland, and Ireland, as well as America?

We have much more to say still. Great Britain has confined all our trade to herself. We are willing she should, so far as it can be for the good of the empire. But we say, that we ought to be allowed as credit, in the account of public burdens and expenses, so much, paid in taxes, as we are obliged to sell our commodities to her cheaper than we could get for them at foreign markets. The difference is really a tax upon us for the good of the empire. We are obliged to take from Great Britain commodities that we could purchase cheaper elsewhere. This difference is a tax upon us for the good of the empire. We submit to this cheerfully; but insist that we ought to have credit for it in the account of the expenses of the empire, because it is really a tax upon us.

Another thing; I will venture a bold assertion,—let Massachusettensis or any other friend of the minister confute me,—the three million Americans, by the tax aforesaid, upon what they are obliged to export to Great Britain only, what they are obliged to import from Great Britain only, and the quantities of British manufactures which, in these climates, they are obliged to consume more than the like number of people in any part of the three kingdoms, ultimately pay more of the taxes and duties that are apparently paid in Great Britain, than any three million subjects in the three kingdoms. All this may be computed and reduced to stubborn figures by the minister, if he pleases. We cannot do it; we have not the accounts, records, &c. Now let this account be fairly stated, and I will engage for America, upon any penalty, that she will pay the overplus, if any, in her own constitutional way, provided it is to be applied for national purposes, as paying off the national debt, maintaining the fleet, &c., not to the support of a standing army in time of peace, placemen, pensioners, &c.

Besides, every farthing of expense which has been incurred, on pretence of protecting, defending, and securing America, since the last war, has been worse than thrown away; it has been applied to do mischief. Keeping an army in America has been nothing but a public nuisance.

Furthermore, we see that all the public money that is raised here, and have reason to believe all that will or can be raised, will be applied, not for public purposes, national or provincial, but merely to corrupt the sons of America, and create a faction to destroy its interest and happiness.

There are scarcely three sentences together, in all the voluminous productions of this plausible writer, which do not convey some error in fact or principle, tinged with a coloring to make it pass for truth. He says, "the idea that the stamps were a tax, not only exceeding our proportion, but beyond our utmost ability to pay, united the colonies generally in opposing it." That we thought it beyond our proportion and ability is true; but it was not this thought which united the colonies in opposing it. When he says that at first, we did not dream of denying the authority of parliament to tax us, much less to legislate for us, he discovers plainly either a total inattention to the sentiments of America, at that time, or a disregard of what he affirms.

The truth is, the authority of parliament was never generally acknowledged in America. More than a century since, Massachusetts and Virginia both protested against even the act of navigation, and refused obedience, for this very reason, because they were not represented in parliament and were therefore not bound; and afterwards confirmed it by their own provincial authority. And from that time to this, the general sense of the colonies has been, that the authority of parliament was confined to the regulation of trade, and did not extend to taxation or internal legislation.

In the year 1764, your house of representatives sent home a petition to the king against the plan of taxing them. Mr. Hutchinson, Oliver, and their relations and connections were then in the legislature, and had great influence there. It was by their influence that the two houses were induced to wave the word *rights* and an express denial of the right of parliament to tax us, to the great grief and distress of the friends of liberty in both houses. Mr. Otis and Mr. Thacher labored in the committee to obtain an express denial. Mr. Hutchinson expressly said, he agreed with them in opinion, that parliament had no right, but thought it ill policy to express this opinion in the petition. In truth, I will be bold to say, there was not any member of either house who thought that parliament had such a right at that time. The house of representatives, at that time, gave their approbation to Mr. Otis's Rights of the Colonies, in which it was shown to be inconsistent with the right of British subjects to be taxed but by their own representatives.

In 1765, our house expressly resolved against the right of parliament to tax us. The congress at New York resolved:

"3. That it is inseparably essential to the freedom of a people, and the undoubted right of Englishmen, that no tax be imposed on them, but with their own consent, given personally, or by their representatives.

"4. That the people of the colonies are not, and from their local circumstances cannot, be represented in the house of commons of Great Britain.

"5. That the only representatives of the people of the colonies are the persons chosen therein by themselves; and that no taxes ever have been, or can be constitutionally imposed on them, but by their respective legislatures."

Is it not a striking disregard to truth, in the artful Massachusettensis, to say, that, at first, we did not dream of denying the right of parliament to tax us? It was the principle that united the colonies to oppose it, not the *quantum* of the tax. Did not Dr. Franklin deny the right in 1754, in his remarks upon Governor Shirley's scheme, and suppose that all America would deny it? We had considered ourselves as connected with Great Britain, but we never thought parliament the supreme legislature over us. We never generally supposed it to have any authority over us, but from necessity, and that necessity we thought confined to the regulation of trade, and to such matters as concerned all the colonies together. We never allowed them any authority in our internal concerns.

This writer says, "acts of parliament for regulating our internal polity were familiar." This I deny. So far otherwise, that the Hatter's Act was never regarded; the act to destroy the Land Bank scheme raised a greater ferment in this province than the Stamp Act did, which was appeased only by passing province laws directly in opposition to it. The act against slitting-mills and tilt-hammers never was executed here. As to the postage, it was so useful a regulation, so few persons paid it, and they found such a benefit by it, that little opposition was made to it. Yet every man who thought about it, called it a usurpation. Duties for regulating trade we paid, because we thought it just and necessary that they should regulate the trade which their power protected. As for duties for a revenue, none were ever laid by parliament for that purpose, until 1764, when, and ever since, its authority to do it has been constantly denied. Nor is this complaisant writer near the truth when he says, "We knew that in all those acts of government, the good of the whole had been consulted." On the contrary, we know that the private interest of provincial governors and West India planters had been consulted in the duties on foreign molasses, &c., and the private interest of a few Portugal merchants, in obliging us to touch at Falmouth with fruit, &c., in opposition to the good of the whole, and in many other instances.

The resolves of the house of burgesses of Virginia upon the Stamp Act did great honor to that province, and to the eminent patriot, Patrick Henry, who composed them. But these resolves made no alteration in the opinion of the colonies, concerning the right of parliament to make that act. They expressed the universal opinion of the continent at that time; and the alacrity with which every other colony, and the congress at New York, adopted the same sentiment in similar resolves, proves the entire union of the colonies in it, and their universal determination to avow and support it. What follows here,—that it became so popular, that his life was in danger who suggested the contrary, and that the press was "open to one side only,"—are direct misrepresentations and wicked calumnies.

Then we are told by this sincere writer, that when we obtained a partial repeal of the statute imposing duties on glass, paper, and teas, "this was the lucky moment when to have closed the dispute." What? with a board of commissioners remaining, the sole end of whose creation was to form and conduct a revenue? With an act of parliament remaining, the professed design of which, expressed in the preamble, was to raise a revenue, and appropriate it to the payment of governors' and judges' salaries; the duty remaining, too, upon an article which must raise a large sum, the consumption of which would constantly increase? Was this a time to retreat? Let me ask this sincere writer a simple question,—does he seriously believe that the designs of imposing other taxes, and of new-modelling our governments, would have been laid aside by the ministry or by the servants of the crown here? Does he think that Mr. Bernard, Mr. Hutchinson, the commissioners, and others would have been content then to have desisted? If he really thinks so, he knows little of the human heart, and still less of those gentlemen's hearts. It was at this very time that the salary was given to the governor, and an order solicited for that to the judges.

Then we are entertained with a great deal of ingenious talk about whigs and tories, and at last are told, that some of the whigs owed all their importance to popularity. And what then? Did not as many of the tories owe their importance to popularity? And did not many more owe all their importance to unpopularity? If it had not been for their taking an active part on the side of the ministry, would not some of the most conspicuous and eminent of them have been unimportant enough? Indeed, through the two last administrations, to despise and hate the people, and to be despised and hated by them, were the principal recommendations to the favors of government, and all the qualification that was required.

"The tories," says he, "were for closing the controversy." That is, they were for contending no more; and it was equally true, that they never were for contending at all, but lying at mercy. It was the very end they had aimed at from the beginning. They had now got the governor's salary out of the revenue, a number of pensions and places; they knew they could at any time get the judges' salaries from the same fountain; and they wanted to get the people reconciled and familiarized to this, before they went upon any new projects.

"The whigs were averse to restoring government; they even refused to revive a temporary Riot Act which expired about this time." Government had as much vigor then as ever, excepting only in those cases which affected this dispute. The Riot Act expired in 1770, immediately after the massacre in King Street. It was not revived, and never will be in this colony; nor will any one ever be made in any other, while a standing army is illegally posted here to butcher the people, whenever a governor or a magistrate, who may be a tool, shall order it. "Perhaps the whigs thought that mobs were a necessary ingredient in their system of opposition." Whether they did or not, it is certain that mobs have been thought a necessary ingredient by the tories in their system of administration, mobs of the worst sort, with red coats, fuzees, and bayonets; and the lives and limbs of the whigs have been in greater danger from these, than ever the tories were from others.

"The scheme of the whigs flattered the people with the idea of independence; the tories' plan supposed a degree of subordination." This is artful enough, as usual, not to say jesuitical. The word independence is one of those which this writer uses, as he does treason and rebellion, to impose upon the undistinguishing on both sides of the Atlantic. But let us take him to pieces. What does he mean by independence? Does he mean independent of the crown of Great Britain, and an independent republic in America, or a confederation of independent republics? No doubt he intended the undistinguishing should understand him so. If he did, nothing can be more wicked, or a greater slander on the whigs; because he knows there is not a man in the province among the whigs, nor ever was, who harbors a wish of that sort. Does he mean that the people were flattered with the idea of total independence on parliament? If he does, this is equally malicious and injurious; because he knows that the equity and necessity of parliament's regulating trade has always been acknowledged; our determination to consent and submit to such regulations constantly expressed; and all the acts of trade, in fact, to this very day, much more submitted to and strictly executed in this province than any other in America.

There is equal ambiguity in the words "degree of subordination." The whigs acknowledge a subordination to the king, in as strict and strong a sense as the tories. The whigs acknowledge a voluntary subordination to parliament, as far as the regulation of trade. What degree of subordination, then, do the tories acknowledge? An absolute dependence upon parliament as their supreme legislative, in all cases whatever, in their internal polity, as well as taxation? This would be too gross, and would lose Massachusettensis all his readers; for there is nobody here who will expose his understanding so much, as explicitly to adopt such a sentiment. Yet it is such an absolute dependence and submission that these writers would persuade us to, or else there is no need of changing our sentiments and conduct. Why will not these gentlemen speak out, show us plainly their opinion, that the new government they have fabricated for this province is better than the old, and that all the other measures we complain of are for our and the public good, and exhort us directly to submit to them? The reason is, because they know they should lose their readers.

"The whigs were sensible that there was no oppression that could be seen or felt." The tories have so often said and wrote this to one another, that I sometimes suspect they believe it to be true. But it is quite otherwise. The castle of the province was taken out of their hands and garrisoned by regular soldiers. This they could see, and they thought it indicated a hostile intention and disposition towards them. They continually paid their money to collectors of duties; this they could both see and feel. A host of placemen, whose whole business it was to collect a revenue, were continually rolling before them in their chariots. These they saw. Their governor was no longer paid by themselves, according to their charter, but out of the new revenue, in order to render their assemblies useless, and indeed contemptible. The judges' salaries were threatened every day to be paid in the same unconstitutional manner. The dullest eyesight could not but see to what all this tended, namely,—to prepare the way for greater innovations and oppressions. They knew a minister would never spend his money in this way, if he had not some end to answer by it. Another thing they both saw and felt. Every man, of every character, who, by voting, writing, speaking, or otherwise, had favored the Stamp Act, the Tea Act, and every other measure of a minister or governor, who they knew was aiming at the destruction of their form of government, and introducing parliamentary taxation, was uniformly, in some department or other, promoted to some place of honor or profit for ten years together; and, on the other hand, every man who favored the people in their opposition to those innovations, was depressed, degraded, and persecuted, so far as it was in the power of the government to do it.

This they considered as a systematical means of encouraging every man of abilities to espouse the cause of parliamentary taxation and the plan of destroying their charter privilege, and to discourage all from exerting themselves in opposition to them. This they thought a plan to enslave them; for they uniformly think that the destruction of their charter, making the council and judges wholly dependent on the crown, and the people subject to the unlimited power of parliament as their supreme legislative, is slavery. They

were certainly rightly told, then, that the ministry and their governors together had formed a design to enslave them, and that when once this was
done, they had the highest reason to expect window-taxes, hearth-taxes, land-
taxes, and all others; and that these were only paving the way for reducing
the country to lordships. Were the people mistaken in these suspicions? Is it
not now certain, that Governor Bernard, in 1764, had formed a design of
this sort? Read his Principles of Polity. And that Lieutenant-Governor Oliver,
as late as 1768, or 9, enforced the same plan? Read his letters. Now, if Massachusettensis will be ingenuous, avow this design, show the people its utility,
and that it ought to be done by parliament, he will act the part of an honest
man. But to insinuate that there was no such plan, when he knows there
was, is acting the part of one of the junto.

It is true, that the people of this country in general, and of this province
in special, have a hereditary apprehension of and aversion to lordships, temporal and spiritual. Their ancestors fled to this wilderness to avoid them;
they suffered sufficiently under them in England. And there are few of the
present generation who have not been warned of the danger of them by their
fathers or grandfathers, and enjoined to oppose them. And neither Bernard
nor Oliver ever dared to avow before them, the designs which they had
certainly formed to introduce them. Nor does Massachusettensis dare to avow
his opinion in their favor. I do not mean that such avowal would expose their
persons to danger, but it would their character and writings to universal
contempt.

When you were told that the people of England were depraved, the
parliament venal, and the ministry corrupt, were you not told most melancholy truths? Will Massachusettensis deny any of them? Does not every man
who comes from England, whig or tory, tell you the same thing? Do they
make any secret of it, or use any delicacy about it? Do they not most of them
avow that corruption is so established there as to be incurable, and a necessary
instrument of government? Is not the British constitution arrived nearly to
that point where the Roman republic was when Jugurtha left it, and pronounced it, "a venal city, ripe for destruction, if it can only find a purchaser?"
If Massachusettensis can prove that it is not, he will remove from my mind
one of the heaviest loads which lie upon it.

Who has censured the tories for remissness, I know not. Whoever it was,
he did them great injustice. Every one that I know of that character has been,
through the whole tempestuous period, as indefatigable as human nature will
admit, going about seeking whom he might devour, making use of art, flattery, terror, temptation, and allurements, in every shape in which human wit
could dress it up, in public and private; but all to no purpose. The people

have grown more and more weary of them every day, until now the land mourns under them.

Massachusettensis is then seized with a violent fit of anger at the clergy. It is curious to observe the conduct of the tories towards this sacred body. If a clergyman, of whatever character, preaches against the principles of the revolution, and tells the people that, upon pain of damnation, they must submit to an established government, the tories cry him up as an excellent man and a wonderful preacher, invite him to their tables, procure him missions from the society and chaplainships to the navy, and flatter him with the hopes of lawn sleeves. But if a clergyman preaches Christianity, and tells the magistrates that they were not distinguished from their brethren for their private emolument, but for the good of the people; that the people are bound in conscience to obey a good government, but are not bound to submit to one that aims at destroying all the ends of government,—oh sedition! treason!

The clergy in all ages and countries, and in this in particular, are disposed enough to be on the side of government as long as it is tolerable. If they have not been generally in the late administration on that side, it is a demonstration that the late administration has been universally odious. The clergy of this province are a virtuous, sensible, and learned set of men, and they do not take their sermons from newspapers, but the Bible; unless it be a few, who preach passive obedience. These are not generally curious enough to read Hobbes. It is the duty of the clergy to accommodate their discourses to the times, to preach against such sins as are most prevalent, and recommend such virtues as are most wanted. For example,—if exorbitant ambition and venality are predominant, ought they not to warn their hearers against those vices? If public spirit is much wanted, should they not inculcate this great virtue? If the rights and duties of Christian magistrates and subjects are disputed, should they not explain them, show their nature, ends, limitations, and restrictions, how much soever it may move the gall of Massachusettensis?

Let me put a supposition. Justice is a great Christian, as well as moral, duty and virtue, which the clergy ought to inculcate and explain. Suppose a great man of a parish should, for seven years together, receive six hundred pounds sterling a year, for discharging the duties of an important office, but, during the whole time, should never do one act or take one step about it. Would not this be great injustice to the public? And ought not the parson of that parish to cry aloud and spare not, and show such a bold transgressor his sin; show that justice was due to the public as well as to an individual; and that cheating the public of four thousand two hundred pounds sterling is at least as great a sin as taking a chicken from a private hen-roost, or perhaps a watch from a fob?

Then we are told that newspapers and preachers have excited "outrages disgraceful to humanity." Upon this subject, I will venture to say, that there have been outrages in this province which I neither justify, excuse, nor extenuate; but these were not excited, that I know of, by newspapers or sermons; that, however, if we run through the last ten years, and consider all the tumults and outrages that have happened, and at the same time recollect the insults, provocations, and oppressions which this people have endured, we shall find the two characteristics of this people, religion and humanity, strongly marked on all their proceedings. Not a life, nor, that I have ever heard, a single limb, has been lost through the whole. I will take upon me to say, there is not another province on this continent, nor in his majesty's dominions, where the people, under the same indignities, would not have gone greater lengths. Consider the tumults in the three kingdoms; consider the tumults in ancient Rome, in the most virtuous of her periods; and compare them with ours. It is a saying of Machiavel no wise man ever contradicted, which has been literally verified in this province, that "while the mass of the people is not corrupted, tumults do no hurt." By which he means, that they leave no lasting ill effects behind.

But let us consider the outrages committed by the tories; half a dozen men shot dead in an instant in King Street; frequent resistance and affronts to civil officers and magistrates; officers, watchmen, citizens, cut and mangled in a most inhuman manner; not to mention the shootings for desertion, and the frequent cruel whippings for other faults, cutting and mangling men's bodies before the eyes of citizens, spectacles which ought never to be introduced into populous places. The worst sort of tumults and outrages ever committed in this province were excited by the tories. But more of this hereafter.

We are then told, that the whigs erected a provincial democracy, or republic, in the province. I wish Massachusettensis knew what a democracy or a republic is. But this subject must be considered another time.

No. v

WE ARE AT LENGTH ARRIVED at the paper on which I made a few strictures some weeks ago; these I shall not repeat, but proceed to consider the other part of it.

We are told: "It is a universal truth, that he that would excite a rebellion, is at heart as great a tyrant as ever wielded the iron rod of oppression." Be it so. We are not exciting a rebellion. Opposition, nay, open, avowed resistance by arms, against usurpation and lawless violence, is not rebellion by the law of God or the land. Resistance to lawful authority makes rebellion. Hampden, Russell, Sidney, Somers, Holt, Tillotson, Burnet, Hoadly, &c. were no tyrants nor rebels, although some of them were in arms, and the others undoubtedly excited resistance against the tories. Do not beg the question, Mr. Massachusettensis, and then give yourself airs of triumph. Remember the frank Veteran acknowledges, that "the word rebel is a convertible term."

This writer next attempts to trace the spirit of opposition through the general court and the courts of common law. "It was the policy of the whigs, to have their questions upon high matters determined by yea and nay votes, which were published in the gazettes." And ought not great questions to be so determined? In many other assemblies, New York particularly, they always are. What better can be devised to discover the true sense of the people? It is extremely provoking to courtiers, that they cannot vote as the cabinet direct them, against their consciences, the known sense of their constituents, and the obvious good of the community, without being detected. Generally, perhaps universally, no unpopular measure in a free government, particularly the English, ought ever to pass. Why have the people a share in the legislature, but to prevent such measures from passing, I mean such as are disapproved by the people at large? But did not these yea and nay votes expose the whigs, as well as tories, to the impartial judgment of the public? If the votes of the former were given for measures injurious to the community, had not the latter an equal opportunity of improving them to the disadvantage of their adversaries in the next election? Besides, were not those few persons in the house, who generally voted for unpopular measures, near the governor, in possession of his confidence? Had they not the absolute disposal in their towns and counties of the favor of government? Were not all the judges, justices, sheriffs, coroners, and military officers in their towns made upon their recommendation? Did not this give them a prodigious weight and influence? Had the whigs any such advantage? And does not the influence of these yea and nay votes, consequently, prove to a demonstration the unanimity of the people against the measures of the court?

As to what is said of "severe strictures, illiberal invectives, abuse, and scurrility, upon the dissentients," there was quite as much of all these published against the leading whigs. In truth, the strictures, &c. against the tories were generally nothing more than hints at the particular place or office, which was known to be the temptation to vote against the country. That "the dissentient was in danger of losing his bread and involving his family in ruin," is equally injurious. Not an instance can be produced of a member losing his bread or injuring his business by voting for unpopular measures. On the contrary, such voters never failed to obtain some lucrative employment, title, or honorary office, as a reward from the court.

If "one set of members in committee had always prepared the resolves," &c., which they did not, what would this prove, but that this set was thought by the house the fittest for the purpose? Can it ever be otherwise? Will any popular assembly choose its worst members for the best services? Will an assembly of patriots choose courtiers to prepare votes against the court? No resolves against the claims of parliament or administration, or the measures of the governor, (excepting those against the Stamp Act, and perhaps the answers to Governor Hutchinson's speeches upon the supremacy of parliament,) ever passed through the house without meeting an obstacle. The governor had, to the last hour of the house's existence, always some seekers and expectants in the house, who never failed to oppose, and offer the best arguments they could, and were always patiently heard. That "the lips of the dissentients were sealed up;" that "they sat in silence, and beheld with regret measures they dared not oppose," are groundless suggestions, and gross reflections upon the honor and courage of those members. The debates of this house were public, and every man who has attended the gallery, knows there never was more freedom of debate in any assembly.

Massachusettensis, in the next place, conducts us to the agent, and tells us "there cannot be a provincial agent without an appointment by the three branches of the assembly. The whigs soon found that they could not have such services rendered them from a provincial agent as would answer their purposes."

The treatment this province has received respecting the agency, since Mr. Hutchinson's administration commenced, is a flagrant example of injustice. There is no law which requires the province to maintain any agent in England; much less is there any reason which necessarily requires that the three branches should join in the appointment. In ordinary times, indeed, when a harmony prevails among the branches, it is well enough to have an agent constituted by all. But in times when the foundations of the constitution are disputed, and certainly attacked by one branch or the other, to pretend that the house ought to join the governor in the choice, is a palpable absurdity. It is equivalent to saying, that the people shall have no agent at all; that all communication shall be cut off; and that there shall be no channel through which complaints and petitions may be conveyed to the royal ear. Because a governor will not concur in an agent whose sentiments are not like his; nor will an agent of the governor's appointment be likely to urge accusations against him with any diligence or zeal, if the people have occasion to complain against him.

Every private citizen, much more, every representative body, has an un-doubted right to petition the king, to convey such petition by an agent, and to pay him for his service. Mr. Bernard, to do him justice, had so much regard to these principles, as to consent to the payment of the people's agents while he staid; but Mr. Hutchinson was scarcely seated in the chair, as lieutenant-governor, before we had intelligence from England, that my Lord Hillsborough told Dr. Franklin, he had received a letter from Governor Hutchinson against consenting to the salary of the agent. Such an instruction was accordingly soon sent, and no agent for the board or house has received a farthing for services since that time, though Dr. Franklin and Mr. Bollan have taken much pains, and one of them expended considerable sums of money. There is a meanness in this play that would disgrace a gambler,—a manifest fear that the truth should be known to the sovereign or the people. Many persons have thought that the province ought to have dismissed all agents from that time, as useless and nugatory; this behavior amounting to a declaration, that we had no chance or hopes of justice from a minister.

But this province, at least as meritorious as any, has been long accus-tomed to indignities and injustice, and to bear both with unparalleled pa-tience. Others have pursued the same method before and since; but we have never heard that their agents are unpaid. They would scarcely have borne it with so much resignation.

It is great assurance to blame the house for this, which was both their right and duty; but it is a stain in the character of his patron which will not be soon worn out. Indeed this passage seems to have been brought in chiefly for the sake of a stroke or two, addressed to the lowest and meanest of the people; I mean the insinuation, that the two agents doubled the *expense,* which is as groundless as it is contracted; and that the ostensible agent for the province was only agent for a few individuals that had got the art of wielding the house; and that several hundred sterling a year, for attending levees and writing letters, were worth preserving. We, my friends, know that no members have the art of wielding us or our house, but by concurring in our principles, and assisting us in our designs. Numbers in both houses have turned about, and expected to wield us round with them, but they have been disappointed, and ever will be. Such apostates have never yet failed of our utter contempt, whatever titles, places, or pensions they might obtain.

The agent has never echoed back, or transmitted to America, any sen-timents which he did not give in substance to Governor Shirley, twenty years ago; and, therefore, this insinuation is but another slander. The remainder of what is said of the agency is levelled at Dr. Franklin, and is but a dull appendix to Wedderburn's ribaldry, having all his malice, without any of his wit or spirit. Nero murdered Seneca, that he might pull up virtue by the roots; and the same maxim governs the scribblers and speechifiers on the side of the minister. It is sufficient to discover that any man has abilities and integrity, a love of virtue and liberty, he must be run down at all events. Witness Pitt, Franklin, and too many others.

My design in pursuing this malicious slanderer, concealed as he is under so soft and oily an appearance, through all the doublings of his tedious course, is to vindicate this colony from his base aspersions; that strangers now among us, and the impartial public, may see the wicked arts, which are still employed against us. After the vilest abuse upon the agent of the province, and the house that appointed him, we are brought to his majesty's council, and are told that the "whigs reminded them of their mortality. If any one opposed the violent measures, he lost his election the next May. Half the whole number, mostly men of the first families, note, and abilities, attached to their native country, wealthy, and independent, were tumbled from their seats in disgrace. Thus the board lost its weight, and the political balance was destroyed."

It is impossible for any man acquainted with this subject to read this zealous rant without smiling, until he attends to the wickedness of it, which will provoke his utmost indignation. Let us, however, consider it soberly.

From the date of our charter to the time of the Stamp Act, and indeed since that time, (notwithstanding the misrepresentations of our charter constitution, as too popular and republican,) the council of this province have been generally on the side of the governor and the prerogative. For the truth of this, I appeal to our whole history and experience. The art and power of governors, and especially the negative, have been a stronger motive on the one hand, than the annual election of the two houses on the other. In disputes between the governor and the house, the council have generally adhered to the former, and in many cases have complied with his humor, when scarcely any council by mandamus, upon this continent, would have done it.

But in the time of the Stamp Act, it was found productive of many mischiefs and dangers, to have officers of the crown, who were dependent on the ministry, and judges of the superior court, whose offices were thought incompatible with a voice in the legislature, members of council.

In May, 1765, Lieutenant-Governor Hutchinson, Secretary Oliver, and Mr. Belcher, officers of the crown, the judges of the superior court, and some other gentlemen, who held commissions under the governor, were members of council. Mr. Hutchinson was chief justice, and a judge of probate for the first county, as well as lieutenant-governor, and a counsellor; too many offices for the greatest and best man in the world to hold, too much business for any man to do; besides, that these offices were frequently clashing and interfering with each other. Two other justices of the superior court were counsellors, and nearly and closely connected with him by family alliances. One other justice was judge of admiralty during pleasure. Such a jumble of offices never got together before in any English government. It was found, in short, that the famous triumvirate, Bernard, Hutchinson, and Oliver, the ever-memorable, secret, confidential letter-writers, whom I call the junto, had, by degrees, and before the people were aware of it, erected a tyranny in the province. Bernard had all the executive, and a negative on the legislative; Hutchinson and Oliver, by their popular arts and secret intrigues, had elevated to the board such a collection of crown-officers and their own relations, as to have too much influence there; and they had three of a family on the superior bench, which is the supreme tribunal in all causes, civil and criminal, vested with all the powers of the king's bench, common pleas, and exchequer, which gave them power over every act of this court. This junto, therefore, had the legislative and executive in their control, and more natural influence over the judicial than is ever to be trusted to any set of men in the world. The public, accordingly, found all these springs and wheels in the constitution set in motion to promote submission to the Stamp Act, and to discountenance resistance to it; and they thought they had a violent presumption, that they would forever be employed to encourage a compliance with all ministerial measures and parliamentary claims, of whatever character they might be.

The designs of the junto, however, were concealed as carefully as possible. Most persons were jealous; few were certain. When the assembly met, in May, 1766, after the Stamp Act was repealed, the whigs flattered themselves with hopes of peace and liberty for the future. Mr. Otis, whose abilities and integrity, whose great exertions, and most exemplary sacrifices of his private interest to the public service, had entitled him to all the promotion which the people could bestow, was chosen speaker of the house. Bernard negatived the choice. It can scarcely be conceived by a stranger what an alarm this manoeuvre gave to the public. It was thought equivalent to a declaration that, although the people had been so successful as to obtain a repeal of the Stamp Act, yet they must not hope to be quiet long; for parliament, by the Declaratory Act, had asserted its supreme authority, and new taxations and regulations should be made, if the junto could obtain them; and every man who should dare to oppose such projects, let his powers or virtues, his family or fortune, be what they would, should be surely cut off from all hopes of advancement. The electors thought it high time to be upon their guard. All the foregoing reasons and motives prevailed with the electors; and the crown officers and justices of the supreme court were left out of council in the new choice. Those who were elected in their places were all negatived by Bernard, which was considered as a fresh proof, that the junto still persevered in their designs of obtaining a revenue to divide among themselves.

The gentlemen elected anew were of equal fortune and integrity, at least, and not much inferior in abilities, to those left out; and indeed, in point of fortune, family, note, or abilities, the councils which have been chosen from that time to this, taken on an average, have been very little inferior, if any, to those chosen before. Let Massachusettensis descend, if he will, to every particular gentleman by name through the whole period, and I will make out my assertion.

Every impartial person will not only think these reasons a full vindication of the conduct of the two houses, but that it was their indispensable duty to their country, to act the part they did; and the course of time, which has developed the dark intrigues of the junto, before and since, has confirmed the rectitude and necessity of the measure. Had Bernard's Principles of Polity been published and known at that time, no member of the house, who should have voted for any of the persons then left out, if it was known to his constituents, would ever have obtained another election.

By the next step we rise to the chair. "With the board, the chair fell likewise," he says. But what a slander is this! Neither fell; both remained in as much vigor as ever. The junto, it is true, and some other gentlemen who were not in their secret, but however, had been misled to concur in their measures, were left out of council. But the board had as much authority as ever. The board of 1766 could not have influenced the people to acknowledge the supreme, uncontrollable authority of parliament, nor could that of 1765 have done it. So that, by the chair and the board's falling, he means no more, if his meaning has any truth in it, than that the junto fell; the designs of taxing the colonies fell, and the schemes for destroying all the charters on the continent, and for erecting lordships fell. These, it must be acknowledged, fell very low indeed in the esteem of the people, and the two houses.

"The governor," says our wily writer, "by the charter, could do little or nothing without the council. If he called upon a military officer to raise the militia, he was answered, they were there already," &c. The council, by the charter, had nothing to do with the militia; the governor alone had all authority over them. The council, therefore, are not to blame for their conduct. If the militia refused obedience to the captain-general, or his subordinate officer, when commanded to assist in carrying into execution the Stamp Act, or in dispersing those who were opposing it, does not this prove the universal sense and resolution of the people not to submit to it? Did not a regular army do more to James II.? If those, over whom the Governor had the most absolute authority and decisive influence, refused obedience, does not this show how deeply rooted in all men's minds was the abhorrence of that unconstitutional power which was usurping over them? "If he called upon the council for their assistance, they must first inquire into the cause." An unpardonable crime, no doubt! But is it the duty of a middle branch of legislature to do as the first shall command them implicitly, or to judge for themselves? Is it the duty of a privy council to understand the subject before they give advice, or only to lend their names to any edict, in order to make it less unpopular? It would be a shame to answer such observations as these, if it was not for their wickedness. Our council, all along however, did as much as any council could have done. Was the mandamus council at New York able to do more to influence the people to a submission to the Stamp Act? Was the chair, the board, the septennial house, with the assistance of General Gage and his troops, able to do more in that city, than our branches did in this province? Not one iota. Nor could Bernard, his council, and house, if they had been unanimous, have induced submission. The people would have spurned them all, for they are not to be wheedled out of their liberties by their own representatives, any more than by strangers. "If he wrote to government at home to strengthen his hands, some officious person procured and sent back his letters." At last, it seems to be acknowledged, that the governor did write for a military force to strengthen government. For what? To enable it to enforce stamp acts, tea acts, and other internal regulations, the authority of which the people were determined never to acknowledge.

But what a pity it was, that these worthy gentlemen could not be allowed, from the dearest affection to their native country, to which they had every possible attachment, to go on in profound confidential secrecy, procuring troops to cut our throats, acts of parliament to drain our purses, destroy our charters and assemblies, getting estates and dignities for themselves and their own families, and all the while most devoutly professing to be friends to our charter, enemies to parliamentary taxation, and to all pensions, without being detected! How happy if they could have annihilated all our charters, and yet have been beloved, nay, deified by the people, as friends and advocates of their charters! What masterly politicians, to have made themselves nobles for life, and yet have been thought very sorry, that the two houses were denied the privilege of choosing the council! How sagacious, to get large pensions for themselves, and yet be thought to mourn that pensions and venality were introduced into the country! How sweet and pleasant, to have been the most popular men in the community, for being staunch and zealous dissenters, true blue Calvinists, and able advocates for public virtue and popular government, after they had introduced an American episcopate, universal corruption among the leading men, and deprived the people of all share in their supreme legislative council! I mention an episcopate, for, although I do not know that Governors Hutchinson and Oliver ever directly solicited for bishops, yet they must have seen, that these would have been one effect, very soon, of establishing the unlimited authority of parliament!

I agree with this writer, that it was not the persons of Bernard, Hutchinson, or Oliver, that made them obnoxious; but their principles and practices. And I will agree that, if Chatham, Camden, and St. Asaph, (I beg pardon for introducing these reverend names into such company, and for making a supposition which is absurd,) had been here, and prosecuted such schemes, they would have met with contempt and execration from this people. But when he says, "that had the intimations in those letters been attended to, we had now been as happy a people as good government could make us," it is too gross to make us angry. We can do nothing but smile. Have not these intimations been attended to? Have not fleets and armies been sent here whenever they requested? Have not governor's, lieutenant-governor's, secretary's, judge's, attorney-general's, and solicitor-general's salaries been paid out of the revenue, as they solicited? Have not taxes been laid and continued? Have not English liberties been abridged, as Hutchinson desired? Have not "penalties of another kind" been inflicted, as he desired? Has not our charter been destroyed, and the council put into the king's hands, as Bernard requested? In short, almost all the wild mock pranks of this desperate triumvirate have been attended to and adopted, and we are now as miserable as tyranny can well make us. That Bernard came here with the affections of New Jersey, I never heard nor read but in this writer. His abilities were considerable, or he could not have done such extensive mischief. His true British honesty and punctuality will be acknowledged by none, but such as owe all their importance to flattering him.

That Hutchinson was amiable and exemplary in some respects, and very unamiable and unexemplary in others, is a certain truth; otherwise he never would have retained so much popularity on one hand, nor made so pernicious a use of it, on the other. His behavior, in several important departments, was with ability and integrity, in cases which did not affect his political system; but he bent all his offices to that. Had he continued steadfast to those principles in religion and government, which, in his former life, he professed, and which alone had procured him the confidence of the people and all his importance, he would have lived and died, respected and beloved, and have done honor to his native country. But, by renouncing these principles and that conduct, which had made him and all his ancestors respectable, his character is now considered by all America, and the best part of the three kingdoms, notwithstanding the countenance he receives from the ministry, as a reproach to the province that gave him birth; as that of a man who by all his actions aimed at making himself great at the expense of the liberties of his native country. This gentleman was open to flattery in so remarkable a degree, that any man who would flatter him was sure of his friendship, and every one who would not was sure of his enmity. He was credulous in a ridiculous degree, of every thing that favored his own plans, and equally incredulous of every thing which made against them. His natural abilities, which have been greatly exaggerated by persons whom he had advanced to power, were far from being of the first rate. His industry was prodigious. His knowledge lay chiefly in the laws and politics and history of this province, in which he had a long experience. Yet, with all his advantages, he never was master of the true character of his native country, not even of New England and the Massachusetts Bay. Through the whole troublesome period, since the last war, he manifestly mistook the temper, principles, and opinions of this people. He had resolved upon a system, and never could or would see the impracticability of it.

It is very true, that "all his abilities, virtues, interests, and connections were insufficient." But for what? To prevail on the people to acquiesce in the mighty claim of parliamentary authority. "The constitution was" *not* "gone." The suggestion that it was is a vile slander. It had as much vigor as ever, and even the governor had as much power as ever, excepting in cases which affected that claim. "The spirit," says this writer, "was truly republican." It was not so in any one case whatever, any further than the spirit of the British constitution is republican. Even in the grand fundamental dispute, the people arranged themselves under their house of representatives and council, with as much order as ever, and conducted their opposition as much by the constitution as ever. It is true, their constitution was employed against the measures of the junto, which created their enmity to it. However, I have not such a horror of republican spirit, which is a spirit of true virtue and honest independence; I do not mean on the king, but on men in power. This spirit is so far from being incompatible with the British constitution, that it is the greatest glory of it; and the nation has always been most prosperous, when it has most prevailed and been most encouraged by the crown. I wish it increased in every part of the world, especially in America; and I think the measures the tories are now pursuing will increase it to a degree that will insure us, in the end, redress of grievances, and a happy reconciliation with Great Britain.

"Governor Hutchinson strove to convince us, by the principles of government, our charters, and acknowledgments, that our claims were inconsistent with the subordination due to Great Britain," &c., says this writer.

Suffer me to introduce here a little history. In 1764, when the system of taxing and new-modelling the colonies was first apprehended, Lieutenant-Governor Hutchinson's friends struggled, in several successive sessions of the general court, to get him chosen agent for the province at the court of Great Britain. At this time, he declared freely, *that he was of the same sentiment with the people, that parliament had no right to tax them; but differed from the country party only in his opinion of the policy of denying that right in their petitions,* &c. I would not injure him; I was told this by three gentlemen, who were of the committee of both houses, to prepare that petition, that he made this declaration explicitly before that committee. I have been told by other gentlemen, that he made the same declaration to them. It is possible that he might make use of expressions studied for the purpose, which would not strictly bear this construction. But it is certain that they understood him so, and that this was the general opinion of his sentiments until he came to the chair.

The country party saw that this aspiring genius aimed at keeping fair with the ministry, by supporting their measures, and with the people, by pretending to be of our principles, and between both, to trim himself up to the chair. The only reason why he did not obtain an election at one time, and was excused from the service at another, after he had been chosen by a small majority, was because the members knew he would not openly deny the right, and assure his majesty, the parliament, and ministry, that the people never would submit to it. For the same reason he was left out of council. But he continued to cultivate his popularity, and to maintain a general opinion among the people that he denied the right in his private judgment, and this idea preserved most of those who continued their esteem for him.

But upon Bernard's removal, and his taking the chair as lieutenant-governor, he had no further expectations from the people, nor complaisance for their opinions. In one of his first speeches he took care to advance the supreme authority of parliament. This astonished many of his friends. They were heard to say, we have been deceived. We thought he had been abused, but we now find what has been said of him is true. He is determined to join in the designs against this country. After his promotion to the government, finding that the people had little confidence in him, and knowing that he had no interest at home to support him, but what he had acquired by joining with Bernard in kicking up a dust, he determined to strike a bold stroke, and, in a formal speech to both houses, became a champion for the unbounded authority of parliament over the colonies. This, he thought, would lay the ministry under obligation to support him in the government, or else to provide for him out of it, not considering that starting that question before that assembly, and calling upon them, as he did, to dispute with him upon it, was scattering firebrands, arrows, and death in sport. The arguments he then advanced were inconclusive indeed; but they shall be considered, when I come to the feeble attempt of Massachusettensis to give a color to the same position.

The house, thus called upon either to acknowledge the unlimited authority of parliament, or confute his arguments, were bound, by their duty to God, their country, and posterity, to give him a full and explicit answer. They proved incontestably that he was out in his facts, inconsistent with himself, and in every principle of his law he had committed a blunder. Thus the fowler was caught in his own snare; and although this country has suffered severe temporary calamities in consequence of this speech, yet I hope they will not be durable; but his ruin was certainly in part owing to it. Nothing ever opened the eyes of the people so much, as to his designs, excepting his letters. Thus it is the fate of Massachusettensis to praise this gentleman for those things which the wise part of mankind condemn in him, as the most insidious and mischievous of actions. If it was out of his power to do us any more injuries, I should wish to forget the past; but, as there is reason to fear he is still to continue his malevolent labors against this country, although he is out of our sight, he ought not to be out of our minds. This country has every thing to fear, in the present state of the British court, while the lords Bute, Mansfield, and North have the principal conduct of affairs, from the deep intrigues of that artful man.

To proceed to his successor, whom Massachusettensis has been pleased to compliment with the epithet of "amiable." I have no inclination to detract from this praise; but have no panegyrics or invectives for any man, much less for any governor, until satisfied of his character and designs. This gentleman's conduct, although he came here to support the systems of his two predecessors, and contracted to throw himself into the arms of their connections, when he has acted himself, and not been teased by others much less amiable and judicious than himself, into measures which his own inclination would have avoided, has been in general as unexceptionable as could be expected, in his very delicate, intricate, and difficult situation.

We are then told, "that disaffection to Great Britain was infused into the body of the people." The leading whigs have ever, systematically and upon principle, endeavored to preserve the people from all disaffection to the king, on the one hand, and the body of the people of England, on the other; but to lay the blame, where it is justly due, on the ministry and their instruments.

We are next conducted into the superior court, and informed "that the judges were dependent on the annual grants of the general court; that their salaries were small, in proportion to the salaries of other officers of less importance; that they often petitioned the assembly to enlarge them, without success, and were reminded of their dependence; that they remained unshaken amid the raging tempests, which is to be attributed rather to their firmness than situation."

That the salaries were small must be allowed; but not smaller in proportion than those of other officers. All salaries in this province have been and are small. It has been the policy of the country to keep them so; not so much from a spirit of parsimony, as an opinion, that the service of the public ought to be an honorary, rather than a lucrative employment; and that the great men ought to be obliged to set examples of simplicity and frugality before the people.

But, if we consider things maturely, and make allowance for all circumstances, I think the country may be vindicated. This province, during the last war, had such overbearing burdens upon it, that it was necessitated to use economy in every thing. At the peace she was half a million sterling in debt, nearly. She thought it the best policy to get out of debt before she raised the wages of her servants; and if Great Britain had thought as wisely, she would not now have had one hundred and forty millions to pay; and she would never have thought of taxing America. Low as the wages were, it was found that, whenever a vacancy happened, the place was solicited with much more anxiety and zeal than the kingdom of heaven.

Another cause which had its effect was this. The judges of that court had almost always enjoyed some other office. At the time of the Stamp Act the chief justice was lieutenant-governor, which yielded him a profit; and a judge of probate for the county of Suffolk, which yielded him another profit; and a counsellor, which, if it was not very profitable, gave him an opportunity of promoting his family and friends to other profitable offices, an opportunity which the country saw he most religiously improved. Another justice of this court was a judge of admiralty, and another was judge of probate for the county of Plymouth. The people thought, therefore, that as their time was not wholly taken up by their offices, as judges of the superior court, there was no reason why they should be paid as much as if it had been.

Another reason was this. Those justices had not been bred to the bar, but taken from merchandise, husbandry, and other occupations; had been at no great expense for education or libraries, and therefore, the people thought that equity did not demand large salaries.

It must be confessed that another motive had its weight. The people were growing jealous of the chief justice, and two other justices at least, and therefore thought it imprudent to enlarge their salaries, and, by that means, their influence.

Whether all these arguments were sufficient to vindicate the people for not enlarging their salaries, I shall leave to you, my friends, whose right it is to judge. But that the judges petitioned "often" to the assembly I do not remember. I knew it was suspected by many, and confidently affirmed by some, that Judge Russell carried home with him, in 1766, a petition to his majesty, subscribed by himself and Chief Justice Hutchinson at least, praying his majesty to take the payment of the judges into his own hands; and that this petition, together with the solicitations of Governor Bernard and others, had the success to procure the act of parliament, to enable his majesty to appropriate the revenue to the support of the administration of justice, &c., from whence a great part of the present calamities of America have flowed.

That the high whigs took *care* to get themselves chosen of the grand juries, I do not believe. Nine tenths of the people were high whigs; and therefore it was not easy to get a grand jury without nine whigs in ten, in it. And the matter would not be much mended by the new act of parliament. The sheriff must return the same set of jurors, court after court, or else his juries would be, nine tenths of them, high whigs still. Indeed the tories are so envenomed now with malice, envy, revenge and disappointed ambition, that they would be willing, for what I know, to be jurors for life, in order to give verdicts against the whigs. And many of them would readily do it, I doubt not, without any other law or evidence than what they found in their own breasts. The suggestion of legerdemain, in drawing the names of petit jurors out of the box, is scandalous. Human wisdom cannot devise a method of obtaining petit jurors more fairly, and better secured against a possibility of corruption of any kind, than that established by our provincial law. They were drawn by chance out of a box in open town meeting, to which the tories went, or might have gone, as well as the whigs, and have seen with their own eyes, that nothing unfair ever did or could take place. If the jurors consisted of whigs, it was because the freeholders were whigs, that is honest men. But now, it seems, if Massachusettensis can have his will, the sheriff, who will be a person properly qualified for the purpose, is to pick out a tory jury, if he can find one in ten, or one in twenty, of that character among the freeholders; and it is no doubt expected, that every newspaper that presumes to deny the right of parliament to tax us, or destroy our charter, will be presented as a libel, and every member of a committee of correspondence, or a congress, &c. &c. &c., is to be indicted for rebellion. These would be pleasant times to Massachusettensis and the junto, but they will never live to see them.

"The judges pointed out seditious libels on governors, magistrates, and the whole government to no effect." They did so; but the jurors thought some of these no libels, but solemn truths. At one time, I have heard that all the newspapers for several years, the Massachusetts Gazette, Evening Post, Boston Chronicle, Boston Gazette, and Massachusetts Spy, were laid before a grand jury at once. The jurors thought there were multitudes of libels written by the tories, and they did not know whom they should attack, if they presented them; perhaps Governor Bernard, Lieutenant-Governor Hutchinson, Secretary Oliver—possibly, the Attorney-General. They saw so many difficulties they knew not what to do.

As to the riots and insurrections, it is surprising that this writer should say,—"Scarce one offender was indicted, and I think not one convicted." Were not many indicted, convicted, and punished too, in the counties of Essex, and Middlesex, and indeed, in every other country? But, perhaps he will say, he means such as were connected with politics. Yet this is not true; for a large number in Essex were punished for abusing an informer, and others were indicted and convicted in Boston for a similar offense. None were indicted for pulling down the stamp office, because this was thought an honorable and glorious action, not a riot. And so it must be said of several other tumults. But was not this the case in royal as well as charter governments? Nor will this inconvenience be remedied by a sheriff's jury, if such a one should ever sit. For if such a jury should convict, the people will never bear the punishment. It is in vain to expect or hope to carry on government against the universal bent and genius of the people; we may whimper and whine as much as we will, but nature made it impossible when she made men.

If "causes of *meum* and *tuum* were not always exempt from party influence," the tories will get no credit by an examination into particular cases. Though I believe there was no great blame on either party in this respect, where the case was not connected with politics.

We are then told,—"The whigs once flattered themselves they should be able to divide the province between them." I suppose he means, that they should be able to get the honorable and lucrative offices of the province into their hands. If this was true, they would be chargeable with only designing what the tories have actually done; with this difference, that the whigs would have done it by saving the liberties and the constitution of the province, whereas the tories have done it by the destruction of both. That the whigs have ambition, a desire of profit, and other passions, like other men, it would be foolish to deny. But this writer cannot name a set of men, in the whole British empire, who have sacrificed their private interest to their nation's honor and the public good in so remarkable a manner, as the leading whigs have done in the two last administrations.

As to "cutting asunder the sinews of government, and breaking in pieces the ligament of social life," so far as this has been done, I have proved by incontestable evidence from Bernard's, Hutchinson's, and Oliver's letters, that the tories have done it, against all the endeavors of the whigs to prevent them from first to last.

The public is then amused with two instances of the weakness of our government, and these are, with equal artifice and injustice, insinuated to be chargeable upon the whigs. But the whigs are as innocent of these as the tories. Malcolm was injured as much against the inclinations and judgment of the whigs as the tories. But the real injury he received is exaggerated by this writer. The cruelty of his whipping and the danger of his life, are too highly colored.

Malcolm was such an oddity as naturally to excite the curiosity and ridicule of the lowest class of people wherever he went; had been active in battle against the regulators in North Carolina, who were thought in Boston to be an injured people. A few weeks before, he had made a seizure at Kennebec River, a hundred and fifty miles from Boston, and by some imprudence had excited the wrath of the people there in such a degree that they tarred and feathered him over his clothes. He comes to Boston to complain. The news of it was spread in town. It was a critical time, when the passions of the people were warm. Malcolm attacked a lad in the street, and cut his head with a cutlass, in return for some words from the boy, which I suppose were irritating. The boy ran bleeding through the street to his relations, of whom he had many. As he passed the street, the people inquired into the cause of his wounds; and a sudden heat arose against Malcolm, which neither whigs nor tories, though both endeavored it, could restrain, and produced the injuries of which he justly complained. But such a coincidence of circumstances might at any time, and in any place, have produced such an effect; and therefore it is no evidence of the weakness of government. Why he petitioned the general court, unless he was advised to it by the tories, to make a noise, I know not. That court had nothing to do with it. He might have brought his action against the trespassers, but never did. He chose to go to England, and get two hundred pounds a year, which would make his tarring the luckiest incident of his life.

The hospital at Marblehead is another instance, no more owing to the politics of the times than the burning of the temple at Ephesus. This hospital was newly erected, much against the will of the multitude. The patients were careless, some of them wantonly so; and others were suspected of designing to spread the smallpox in the town, which was full of people who had not passed through the distemper. It is needless to be particular; but the apprehension became general; the people arose and burnt the hospital. But the whigs are so little blamable for this, that two of the principal whigs in the province, gentlemen highly esteemed and beloved in the town, even by those who burnt the building, were owners of it. The principles and temper of the times had no share in this, any more than in cutting down the market in Boston, or in demolishing mills and dams in some parts of the country, in order to let the alewives pass up the streams, forty years ago. Such incidents happen in all governments at times; and it is a fresh proof of the weakness of this writer's cause, that he is driven to such wretched shifts to defend it.

Towards the close of this long speculation, Massachusettensis grows more and more splenetical, peevish, angry, and absurd.

He tells us, that in order to avoid the necessity of altering our provincial constitution, government at home made the judges independent of the grants of the general assembly. That is, in order to avoid the hazard of taking the fort by storm, they determined to take it by sap. In order to avoid altering our constitution, they changed it in the most essential manner; for, surely, by our charter, the province was to pay the judges as well as the governor. Taking away this privilege, and making them receive their pay from the crown, was destroying the charter so far forth, and making them dependent on the minister. As to their being dependent on the leading whigs, he means they were dependent on the province. And which is fairest to be dependent on, the province or the minister? In all this troublesome period, the leading whigs had never hesitated about granting their salaries, nor ever once moved to have them lessened; nor would the house have listened to them if they had. "This was done," he says, "to make them steady." We know that very well. Steady to what? Steady to the plans of Bernard, Hutchinson, Oliver, North, Mansfield, and Bute, which the people thought was steadiness to their ruin; and therefore it was found that a determined spirit of opposition to it arose in every part of the province, like that to the Stamp Act.

The chief justice, it is true, was accused by the house of representatives, of receiving a bribe,—a ministerial, not a royal bribe. For the king can do no wrong, although he may be deceived in his grant. The minister is accountable. The crime of receiving an illegal patent is not the less for purchasing it even of the king himself. Many impeachments have been for such offences.

He talks about "attempts to strengthen government and save our charter." With what modesty can he say this, when he knows that the overthrow of our charter was the very object which the junto had been invariably pursuing for a long course of years? Does he think his readers are to be deceived by such gross arts? But he says, "the whigs subverted the charter constitution, abridged the freedom of the house, annihilated the freedom of the board, and rendered the governor a doge of Venice." The freedom of the house was never abridged; the freedom of the board was never lessened. The governor had as much power as ever. The house and board, it is true, would do nothing in favor of parliamentary taxation. Their judgments and consciences were against it; and if they ever had done any thing in favor of it, it would have been through fear and not freedom. The governor found he could do nothing in favor of it, excepting to promote, in every department in the state, men who hated the people, and were hated by them. Enough of this he did in all conscience; and, after filling offices with men who were despised, he wondered that the officers were not revered. "They, the whigs, engrossed all the power of the province into their own hands." That is, the house and board were whigs; the grand juries and petit juries were whigs; towns were whigs; the clergy were whigs; the agents were whigs; and wherever you found people, you found all whigs; excepting those who had commissions from the crown or the governor. This is almost true; and it is to the eternal shame of the tories that they should pursue their *ignis fatuus* with such ungovernable fury as they have done, after such repeated and multiplied demonstrations, that the whole people were so universally bent against them. But nothing will satisfy them still but blood and carnage. The destruction of the whigs, charters, English liberties, and all, they must and will have, if it costs the blood of tens of thousands of innocent people. This is the benign temper of the tories.

This influence of the whigs he calls a democracy or republic, and then a despotism; two ideas incompatible with each other. A democratical despotism is a contradiction in terms.

He then says, that "the good policy of the act for regulating the government in this province will be the subject of some future paper." But that paper is still to come, and I suspect ever will be. I wish to hear him upon it, however.

With this, he and the junto ought to have begun. Bernard and the rest, in 1764, ought to have published their objections to this government, if they had been honest men, and produced their arguments in favor of the alteration, convinced the people of the necessity of it, and proposed some constitutional plan for effecting it. But the same motives which induced them to take another course, will prevail with Massachusettensis to wave the good policy of the act. He will be much more cunningly employed in laboring to terrify women and children with the horrors of a civil war, and the dread of a division among the people. There lies your forte, Massachusettensis; make the most of it.

No. VI

SUCH EVENTS as the resistance to the Stamp Act, and to the Tea Act, particularly the destruction of that which was sent by the ministry, in the name of the East India Company, have ever been cautiously spoken of by the whigs, because they knew the delicacy of the subject, and they lived in continual hopes of a speedy restoration of liberty and peace. But we are now thrown into a situation, which would render any further delicacy upon this point criminal.

Be it remembered, then, that there are tumults, seditions, popular commotions, insurrections, and civil wars, upon just occasions as well as unjust.

Grotius B. 1, c. 3, § 1, observes, "that some sort of private war may be lawfully waged. It is not repugnant to the law of nature, for any one to repel injuries by force."

§ 2. "The liberty allowed before is much restrained since the erecting of tribunals. Yet there are some cases wherein that right still subsists; that is, when the way to legal justice is not open; for the law which forbids a man to pursue his right any other way, ought to be understood with this equitable restriction, that one finds judges to whom he may apply," &c.

"*It is in vain to seek a government in all points free from a possibility of civil wars, tumults, and seditions; that is a blessing denied to this life, and reserved to complete the felicity of the next. Seditions, tumults, and wars do arise from mistake or from malice; from just occasions or unjust. . . . Seditions proceeding from malice are seldom or never seen in popular governments; for they are hurtful to the people, and none have ever willingly and knowingly hurt themselves. There may be, and often is, malice in those who excite them; but the people is ever deceived, and whatever is thereupon done, ought to be imputed to error, &c. But in absolute monarchies, almost all the troubles that arise proceed from malice; they cannot be reformed; the extinction of them is exceeding difficult, if they have continued long enough to corrupt the people; and those who appear against them seek only to set up themselves or their friends. The mischiefs designed are often dissembled or denied, till they are past all possibility of being cured by any other way

* Sidney's *Discourses upon Government*, c. 2, § 24.

than force; and such as are by necessity driven to use that remedy, know they must perfect their work or perish. He that draws his sword against the prince, say the French, ought to throw away the scabbard; for though the design be never so just, yet the authors are sure to be ruined if it miscarry. Peace is seldom made, and never kept, unless the subject retain such a power in his hands as may oblige the prince to stand to what is agreed; and, in time, some trick is found to deprive him of that benefit.

"It may seem strange to some that I mention seditions, tumults, and wars, upon just occasions; but I can find no reason to retract the terms. God, intending that men should live justly with one another, does certainly intend that he or they, who do no wrong, should suffer none; and the law that forbids injuries were of no use if no penalty might be inflicted on those that will not obey it. If injustice, therefore, be evil, and injuries be forbidden, they are also to be punished; and the law instituted for their prevention must necessarily intend the avenging of such as cannot be prevented. The work of the magistracy is to execute this law; the sword of justice is put into their hands to restrain the fury of those within the society who will not be a law to themselves; and the sword of war to protect the people against the violence of foreigners. This is without exception, and would be in vain if it were not. But the magistrate who is to protect the people from injury, may, and is often known not to have done it; he renders his office sometimes *useless by neglecting to do justice,* sometimes *mischievous by overthrowing it.* This strikes at the root of God's general ordinance, that there should be laws; and the particular ordinances of all societies, that appoint such as seem best to them. *The magistrate, therefore, is comprehended under both, and subject to both, as well as private men.*

"The ways of preventing or punishing injuries, are judicial or extrajudicial. Judicial proceedings are of force against those who submit, or may be brought to trial, but are of no effect against those who resist, and are of such power that they cannot be constrained. It were absurd to cite a man to appear before a tribunal, *who can awe the judges, or has armies to defend him;* and impious to think that he who has added treachery to his other crimes, and usurped a power above the law, should be protected by the enormity of his wickedness. Legal proceedings, therefore, are to be used when the delinquent submits to the law; *and all are just, when he will not be kept in order by the legal.*

"The word *sedition* is generally applied to all numerous assemblies without or against the authority of the magistrate, or of those who assume that power. Athaliah and Jezebel were more ready to cry out treason than David, &c. Tumult is from the disorderly manner of those assemblies, where things can seldom be done regularly; and war is that "*decertatio per vim,*" or trial by force, to which men come when other ways are ineffectual.

"If the laws of God and men are therefore of no effect when the magistracy is left at liberty to break them, and if the lusts of those who are too strong for the tribunals of justice, cannot be otherwise restrained than by sedition, tumults, and war; those seditions, tumults, and wars, are justified by the laws of God and man.

"I will not take upon me to enumerate all the cases in which this may be done; but content myself with three, which have most frequently given occasion for proceedings of this kind. The first is, when one or more men take upon them the power and name of a magistracy to which they are not justly called. The second, when one or more, being justly called, continue in their magistracy longer than the laws by which they are called do prescribe. And the third, when he, or they, who are rightly called, do assume a power, though within the time prescribed, that the law does not give, or turn that which the law does give, to an end different and contrary to that which is intended by it.

"The same course is justly used against a legal magistrate who takes upon him to exercise a power which the law does not give; for in that respect he is a private man,—"*Quia,*" as Grotius says, "*eatenus non habet imperium,*"—and may be restrained as well as any other; because he is not set up to do what he lists, but what the law appoints for the good of the people; and as he has no other power than what the law allows, so the same law limits and directs the exercise of that which he has."

"*When we speak of a tyrant that may lawfully be dethroned by the people, we do not mean by the word *people,* the vile populace or rabble of the country, nor the cabal of a small number of factious persons, but the greater and more judicious part of the subjects, of all ranks. Besides, the tyranny must be so notorious, and evidently clear, as to leave nobody any room to doubt of it, &c. Now, a prince may easily avoid making himself so universally suspected and odious to his subjects; for, as Mr. Locke says in his Treatise of Civil Government, c. 18, §209,—'It is as impossible for a governor, if he really means the good of the people, and the preservation of them and the laws together, not to make them see and feel it, as it is for the father of a family not to let his children see he loves and takes care of them.' And therefore the general insurrection of a whole nation does not deserve the name of a rebellion. We may see what Mr. Sidney says upon this subject in his Discourse concerning Government:—'Neither are subjects bound to stay

* Pufendorf's *Law of Nature and Nations,* 1. vii. c. viii. § 5, 6. Barbeyrac's note on section 6.

till the prince has entirely finished the chains which he is preparing for them, and put it out of their power to oppose. It is sufficient that all the advances which he makes are manifestly tending to their oppression, that he is march-ing boldly on to the ruin of the State.' In such a case, says Mr. Locke, admirably well,—'How can a man any more hinder himself from believing, in his own mind, which way things are going, or from casting about to save himself, than he could from believing the captain of the ship he was in was carrying him and the rest of his company to Algiers, when he found him always steering that course, though cross winds, leaks in his ship, and want of men and provisions, did often force him to turn his course another way for some time, which he steadily returned to again, as soon as the winds, weather, and other circumstances would let him?' This chiefly takes place with respect to kings, whose power is limited by fundamental laws.

"If it is objected that the people, being ignorant and always discontented, to lay the foundation of government in the unsteady opinion and the un-certain humor of the people, is to expose it to certain ruin; the same author will answer you, that 'on the contrary, people are not so easily got out of their old forms as some are apt to suggest. England, for instance, notwith-standing the many revolutions that have been seen in that kingdom, has always kept to its old legislative of king, lords, and commons; and whatever provocations have made the crown to be taken from some of their princes' heads, they never carried the people so far as to place it in another line.' But it will be said, this hypothesis lays a ferment for frequent rebellion. 'No more,' says Mr. Locke, 'than any other hypothesis. For when the people are made miserable, and find themselves exposed to the ill usage of arbitrary power, cry up their governors as you will for sons of Jupiter; let them be sacred and divine, descended or authorized from heaven; give them out for whom or what you please, the same will happen. The people generally ill treated, and contrary to right, will be ready upon any occasion to ease themselves of a burden that sits heavy upon them. 2. Such revolutions happen not upon every little mismanagement in public affairs. Great mistakes in the ruling part, many wrong and inconvenient laws, and all the slips of human frailty will be borne by the people without mutiny and murmur. 3. This power in the people of providing for their safety anew by a legislative, when their legislators have acted contrary to their trust by invading their property, is the best fence against rebellion, and the probablest means to hinder it; for re-bellion being an opposition, not to persons, but authority, which is founded only in the constitutions and laws of the government; those, whoever they be, *who by force break through, and by force justify the violation of them, are truly and properly rebels.* For when men, by entering into society and civil government, have excluded force, and introduced laws for the preservation of property, peace, and unity, among themselves; those who set up force again, in opposition to the laws, do *rebellare,* that is, do bring back again the state of war, and are properly, rebels,' as the author shows. In the last place, he demonstrates that there are also greater inconveniences in allowing all to those that govern, than in granting something to the people. But it will be said, that ill affected and factious men may spread among the people, and make them believe that the prince or legislative act contrary to their trust, when they only make use of their due prerogative. To this Mr. Locke answers, that the people, however, is to judge of all that; because nobody can better judge whether his trustee or deputy acts well, and according to the trust reposed in him, than he who deputed him. 'He might make the like query,' (says Mr. Le Clerc, from whom this extract is taken) 'and ask, whether the people being oppressed by an authority which they set up, but for their own good, it is just that those who are vested with this authority, and of which they are complaining, should themselves be judges of the complaints made against them. The greatest flatterers of kings dare not say, that the people are obliged to suffer absolutely all their humors, how irregular soever they be; and therefore must confess, that when no regard is had to their complaints, the very foundations of society are destroyed; the prince and people are in a state of war with each other, like two independent states, that are doing themselves justice, and acknowledge no person upon earth, who, in a sovereign manner, can determine the disputes between them," &c.

If there is any thing in these quotations, which is applicable to the destruction of the tea, or any other branch of our subject, it is not my fault; I did not make it. Surely Grotius, Pufendorf, Barbeyrac, Locke, Sidney, and Le Clerc, are writers of sufficient weight to put in the scale against the mercenary scribblers in New York and Boston, who have the unexampled impudence and folly, to call these, which are revolution principles, in question, and to ground their arguments upon passive obedience as a corner stone. What an opinion must these writers have of the principles of their patrons, the lords Bute, Mansfield, and North, when they hope to recommend themselves by reviving that stupid doctrine, which has been infamous so many years. Dr. Sacheverel himself tells us that his sermons were burnt by the hands of the common hangman, by the order of the king, lords, and commons, in order to fix an eternal and indelible brand of infamy on that doctrine.

In the Gazette of January the 2d, Massachusettensis entertains you with an account of his own important self. This is a subject which he has very much at heart, but it is of no consequence to you or me, and therefore little need be said of it. If he had such a stand in the community, that he could have seen all the political manoeuvres, it is plain he must have shut his eyes, or he never could have mistaken so grossly, causes for effects, and effects for causes.

He undertakes to point out the principles and motives upon which the Blockade Act was made, which were, according to him, the destruction of the East India Company's tea. He might have said more properly, the ministerial tea; for such it was, and the company are no losers; they have received from the public treasury compensation for it.

Then we are amused with a long discourse about the nature of the British government, commerce, agriculture, arts, manufactures, regulations of trade, custom-house officers, which, as it has no relation to the subject, I shall pass over.

The case is shortly this,—the East India Company, by their contract with government, in their charter and statute, are bound, in consideration of their important profitable privileges, to pay to the public treasury a revenue annually, of four hundred thousand pounds sterling, so long as they can hold up their dividends at twelve per cent., and no longer.

The mistaken policy of the ministry, in obstinately persisting in their claim of right to tax America, and refusing to repeal the duty on tea, with those on glass, paper, and paint, had induced all America, except a few merchants in Boston, most of whom were closely connected with the junto, to refuse to import tea from Great Britain; the consequence of which was a kind of stagnation in the affairs of the company, and an immense accumulation of tea in their stores, which they could not sell. This, among other causes, contributed to affect their credit, and their dividends were on the point of falling below twelve per cent., and consequently the government was upon the point of losing four hundred thousand pounds sterling a year of revenue. The company solicited the ministry to take off the duty in America; but they, adhering to their plan of taxing the colonies and establishing a precedent, framed an act to enable the company to send their tea directly to America. This was admired as a masterpiece of policy. It was thought they would accomplish four great purposes at once,—establish their precedent of taxing America; raise a large revenue there by the duties; save the credit of the company, and the four hundred thousand pounds to the government. The company, however, were so little pleased with this, that there were great debates among the directors, whether they should risk it, which were finally determined by a majority of one only; and that one, the chairman, being unwilling, as it is said, to interfere in the dispute between the minister and the colonies, and uncertain what the result would be; and this small majority was not obtained, as it is said, until a sufficient intimation was given, that the company should not be losers.

When these designs were made known, it appeared that American politicians were not to be deceived; that their sight was as quick and clear as the minister's; and that they were as steady to their purpose as he was to his. This was thought by all the colonies to be the precise point of time when it became absolutely necessary to make a stand. If the tea should be landed, it would be sold; if sold, the duties would amount to a large sum, which would be instantly applied to increase the friends and advocates for more duties, and to divide the people; and the company would get such a footing, that no opposition afterwards could ever be effectual. And as soon as the duties on tea should be established, they would be ranked among post-office fees and other precedents, and used as arguments both of the right and expediency of laying on others, perhaps on all the necessaries, as well as conveniences and luxuries of life. The whole continent was united in the sentiment, that all opposition to parliamentary taxation must be given up forever, if this critical moment was neglected. Accordingly, New York and Philadelphia determined that the ships should be sent back; and Charleston, that the tea should be stored and locked up. This was attended with no danger in that city, because they are fully united in sentiment and affection, and have no junto to perplex them. Boston was under greater difficulties. The consignees at New York and Philadelphia most readily resigned. The consignees at Boston, the children, cousins, and most intimate connections of Governor Hutchinson, refused. I am very sorry that I cannot stir a single step in developing the causes of my country's miseries without stumbling upon this gentleman. But so it is. From the near relation and most intimate connection of the consignees with him, there is great cause of jealousy, if not a violent presumption, that he was at the bottom of all this business; that he had planned it in his confidential letters with Bernard, and both of them joined in suggesting and recommending it to the ministry. Without this supposition, it is difficult to account for the obstinacy with which the consignees refused to resign, and the governor to let the vessel go. However this might be, Boston is the only place upon the continent, perhaps in the world, which ever breeds a species of misanthropes, who will persist in their schemes for their private interest with such obstinacy, in opposition to the public good; disoblige all their fellow-citizens for a little pelf, and make themselves odious and infamous, when they might be respected and esteemed. It must be said, however, in vindication of the town, that this breed is spawned chiefly by the junto. The consignees would not resign; the custom-house refused clearances; Governor Hutchinson refused passes by the castle. The question then was with many, whether the governor, officers, and consignees should be compelled to send the ships hence? An army and navy was at hand, and bloodshed was apprehended. At last, when the continent, as well as the town and province, were waiting the issue of this deliberation with the utmost anxiety, a number of persons, in the night, put them out of suspense, by an oblation to Neptune. I have heard some gentlemen say, "this was a very unjustifiable proceeding,"—"that if they had gone at noon-day, and in their ordinary habits, and drowned it in the face of the world, it would have been a meritorious, a most glorious action; but, to go in the night, and, much more, in disguise, they thought very inexcusable."

"The revenue was not the consideration before parliament," says Massachusettensis. Let who will believe him. But if it was not, the danger to America was the same. I take no notice of the idea of a monopoly. If it had been only a monopoly, (though in this light it would have been a very great grievance) it would not have excited, nor, in the opinion of any one, justified the step that was taken. It was an attack upon a fundamental principle of the constitution, and upon that supposition was resisted, after multitudes of petitions to no purpose, and because there was no tribunal in the constitution, from whence redress could have been obtained.

There is one passage so pretty, that I cannot refuse myself the pleasure of transcribing it. "A smuggler and a whig are cousin germans, the offspring of two sisters, avarice and ambition. They had been playing into each other's hands a long time. The smuggler received protection from the whig; and he in his turn received support from the smuggler. The illicit trader now demanded protection from his kinsman; and it would have been unnatural in him to have refused it; and, besides, an opportunity presented of strengthening his own interest."

The wit and beauty of the style in this place, seem to have quite enraptured the lively juvenile imagination of this writer.

The truth of the fact he never regards, any more than the justice of the sentiment. Some years ago, the smugglers might be pretty equally divided between the whigs and the tories. Since that time, they have almost all married into the tory families, for the sake of dispensations and indulgences. If I were to let myself into secret history, I could tell very diverting stories of smuggling tories in New York and Boston. Massachusettensis is quarrelling with some of his best friends. Let him learn more discretion.

We are then told that "the consignees offered to store the tea, under the care of the selectmen, or a committee of the town." This expedient might have answered, if none of the junto, nor any of their connections had been in Boston. But is it a wonder, that the selectmen declined accepting such a deposit? They supposed they should be answerable; and nobody doubted that tories might be found who would not scruple to set fire to the store, in order to make them liable. Besides, if the tea was landed, though only to be stored, the duty must be paid, which, it was thought, was giving up the point.

Another consideration, which had great weight, was, that the other colonies were grown jealous of Boston, and thought it already deficient in point of punctuality, against the duties articles; and if the tea was once stored, artifices might be used, if not violence, to disperse it abroad. But if through the continual vigilance and activity of the committee and the people, through a whole winter, this should be prevented, yet one thing was certain, that the tories would write to the other colonies, and to England, thousands of falsehoods concerning it, in order to induce the ministry to persevere, and to sow jealousies, and create divisions among the colonies.

Our acute logician then undertakes to prove the destruction of the tea unjustifiable, even upon the principle of the whigs, that the duty was unconstitutional. The only argument he uses is this,—that "unless we purchase the tea, we shall never pay the duty." This argument is so frivolous, and has been so often confuted and exposed, that if the party had any other, I think they would relinquish this. Where will it carry us? If a duty was laid upon our horses, we may walk; if upon our butcher's meat, we may live upon the produce of the dairy; and if that should be taxed, we may subsist as well as our fellow slaves in Ireland, upon Spanish potatoes and cold water. Were a thousand pounds laid upon the birth of every child, if children are not begotten none will be born; if upon every marriage, no duties will be paid if all the young gentlemen and ladies agree to live bachelors and maidens.

In order to form a rational judgment of the quality of this transaction, and determine whether it was good or evil, we must go to the bottom of this great controversy. If parliament has a right to tax us, and legislate for us in all cases, the destruction of the tea was unjustifiable; but if the people of America are right in their principle, that parliament has no such right, that the act of parliament is null and void, and it is lawful to oppose and resist it, the question then is, whether the destruction was necessary; for every principle of reason, justice, and prudence, in such cases, demands that the least mischief shall be done, the least evil, among a number, shall always be preferred.

All men are convinced that it was impracticable to return it, and rendered so by Mr. Hutchinson and the Boston consignees. Whether to have stored it would have answered the end, or been a less mischief than drowning it, I shall leave to the judgment of the public. The other colonies, it seems, have no scruples about it; for we find that whenever tea arrives in any of them, whether from the East India Company or any other quarter, it never fails to share the fate of that in Boston. All men will agree that such steps ought not to be taken but in cases of absolute necessity, and that such necessity must be very clear. But most people in America now think the destruction of the Boston tea was absolutely necessary, and therefore right and just. It is very true, they say, if the whole people had been united in sentiment, and equally stable in their resolution not to buy or drink it, there might have been a reason for preserving it; but the people here were not so virtuous or so happy. The British ministry had plundered the people by illegal taxes, and applied the money in salaries and pensions, by which devices they had insidiously attached to their party no inconsiderable number of persons, some of whom were of family, fortune, and influence, though many of them were of desperate fortunes, each of whom, however, had his circle of friends, connections, and dependants, who were determined to drink tea, both as evidence of their servility to administration, and their contempt and hatred of the people. These it was impossible to restrain without violence, perhaps bloodshed, certainly without hazarding more than the tea was worth. To this tribe of the *wicked*, they say must be added another, perhaps more numerous, of the *weak;* who never could be brought to think of the consequences of their actions, but would gratify their appetites if they could come at the means. What numbers are there in every community, who have no providence or prudence in their private affairs, but will go on indulging the present appetite, prejudice, or passion, to the ruin of their estates and families, as well as their own health and characters! How much larger is the number of those who have no foresight for the public, or consideration of the freedom of posterity! Such an abstinence from the tea as would have avoided the establishment of a precedent, dependent on the unanimity of the people, was a felicity that was unattainable. Must the wise, the virtuous and worthy part of the community, who constituted a very great majority, surrender their liberty, and involve their posterity in misery, in complaisance to a detestable, though small, party of knaves, and a despicable, though more numerous, company of fools?

If Boston could have been treated like other places, like New York and Philadelphia, the tea might have gone home from thence, as it did from those cities. That inveterate, desperate junto, to whom we owe all our calamities, were determined to hurt us in this, as in all other cases, as much as they could. It is to be hoped they will one day repent and be forgiven; but it is very hard to forgive without repentance. When the news of this event arrived in England, it excited such passions in the minister as nothing could restrain;

his resentment was enkindled into revenge, rage, and madness; his veracity was piqued, as his masterpiece of policy proved but a bubble. The bantling was the fruit of a favorite amour, and no wonder that his natural affection was touched, when he saw it despatched before his eyes. His grief and ingenuity, if he had any, were affected at the thought that he had misled the East India Company so much nearer to destruction, and that he had rendered the breach between the kingdom and the colonies almost irreconcilable. His shame was excited because opposition had gained a triumph over him, and the three kingdoms were laughing at him for his obstinacy and his blunders; instead of relieving the company, he had hastened its ruin; instead of establishing the absolute and unlimited sovereignty of parliament over the colonies, he had excited a more decisive denial of, and resistance to it. An election drew nigh, and he dreaded the resentment even of the corrupted electors.

In this state of mind, bordering on despair, he determines to strike a bold stroke. Bernard was near, and did not fail to embrace the opportunity to push the old systems of the junto. By attacking all the colonies together, by the Stamp Act, and the Paint and Glass Act, they had been defeated. The charter constitution of the Massachusetts Bay, had contributed greatly to both these defeats. Their representatives were too numerous, and too frequently elected, to be corrupted; their people had been used to consider public affairs in their town meetings; their counsellors were not absolutely at the nod of a minister or governor, but were once a year equally dependent on the governor and the two houses. Their grand jurors were elective by the people; their petit jurors were returned merely by lot. Bernard and the junto rightly judged, that by this constitution the people had a check on every branch of power, and, therefore, as long as it lasted, parliamentary taxations, &c. could never be enforced.

Bernard publishes his select letters, and his principles of polity; his son writes in defence of the Quebec bill; hireling garreteers are employed to scribble millions of lies against us, in pamphlets and newspapers; and setters employed in the coffee-houses, to challenge or knock down all the advocates for the poor Massachusetts. It was now determined, instead of attacking the colonies together, though they had been all equally opposed to the plans of the ministry and the claims of parliament, and therefore, upon ministerial principles, equally guilty, to handle them one by one, and to begin with Boston and the Massachusetts. The destruction of the tea was a fine event for scribblers and speechifiers to declaim upon; and there was a hereditary hatred of New England in the minds of many in England, on account of their non-conforming principles. It was likewise thought there was a similar jealousy and animosity in the other colonies against New England; that they would, therefore, certainly desert her; that she would be intimidated and submit; and then the minister, among his own friends, would acquire immortal honor, as the most able, skilful and undaunted statesman of the age.

The port bill, charter bill, murder bill, Quebec bill, making altogether such a frightful system, as would have terrified any people, who did not prefer liberty to life, were all concerted at once; but all this art and violence have not succeeded. This people, under great trials and dangers, have discovered great abilities and virtues, and that nothing is so terrible to them as the loss of their liberties. If these arts and violences are persisted in, and still greater, concerted and carried on against them, the world will see that their fortitude, patience, and magnanimity will rise in proportion.

"Had Cromwell," says our—what shall I call him? "had the guidance of the national ire, your proud capital had been levelled with the dust." Is it any breach of charity to suppose that such an event as this would have been a gratification to this writer? Can we otherwise account for his indulging himself in a thought so diabolical? Will he set up Cromwell as a model for his deified lords, Bute, Mansfield, and North? If he should, there is nothing in the whole history of him so cruel as this. All his conduct in Ireland, as exceptionable as any part of his whole life, affords nothing that can give the least probability to the idea of this writer. The rebellion in Ireland was most obstinate, and of many years duration; one hundred thousand Protestants had been murdered in a day, in cold blood, by papists, and therefore Cromwell might plead some excuse, that cruel severities were necessary in order to restore any peace to that kingdom. But all this will not justify him; for, as has been observed by a historian, upon his conduct in this instance, "men are not to divest themselves of humanity, and turn themselves into devils, because policy may suggest that they will succeed better as devils than as men!" But is there any parity or similitude between a rebellion of a dozen years standing, in which many battles had been fought, many thousands fallen in war, and one hundred thousand massacred in a day; and the drowning three cargoes of tea? To what strains of malevolence, to what flights of diabolical fury, is not tory rage capable of transporting men?

"The whigs saw their ruin connected with a compliance with the terms of opening the port." They saw the ruin of their country connected with such a compliance, and their own involved in it. But they might have easily voted a compliance, for they were undoubtedly a vast majority, and have enjoyed the esteem and affection of their fellow-slaves to their last hours. Several of them could have paid for the tea and never have felt the loss. They knew they must suffer vastly more than the tea was worth; but they thought they acted for America and posterity; and that they ought not to take such a step without the advice of the colonies. They have declared our cause their own; that they never will submit to a precedent in any part of the united colonies, by which parliament may take away wharves and other lawful estates, or demolish charters; for if they do, they have a moral certainty that, in the course of a few years, every right of Americans will be taken away, and governors and councils, holding at the will of the minister, will be the only legislatives in the colonies.

A pompous account of the addressers of Mr. Hutchinson then follows. They consisted of his relations, his fellow-laborers in the tory vineyard, and persons whom he had raised in the course of four administrations, Shirley's, Pownal's, Bernard's, and his own, to places in the province. Considering the industry that was used, and the vast number of persons in the province who had received commissions under government upon his recommendation, the small number of subscribers that was obtained, is among a thousand demonstrations of the unanimity of this people. If it had been thought worth while to have procured a remonstrance against him, fifty thousand subscribers might have been easily found. Several gentlemen of property were among these addressers, and some of fair character; but their acquaintance and friendships lay among the junto and their subalterns entirely. Besides, did these addressers approve the policy or justice of any one of the bills, which were passed the last session of the late parliament? Did they acknowledge the unlimited authority of parliament? The Middlesex magistrates remonstrated against taxation; but they were flattered with hopes, that Mr. Hutchinson would get the Port Bill, &c. repealed; that is, that he would have undone all, which every one but themselves knew he has been doing these fifteen years.

But these patriotic endeavors were defeated. By what? By "an invention of the fertile brain of one of our party agents, called a committee of correspondence. *This is the foulest, subtlest, and most venomous serpent that ever issued from the eggs of sedition.*"

I should rather call it the *ichneumon,* a very industrious, active, and useful animal, which was worshipped in Egypt as a divinity, because it defended the country from the ravages of the crocodiles. It was the whole occupation of this little creature to destroy those wily and ravenous monsters. It crushed their eggs, wherever they laid them, and, with a wonderful address and courage, would leap into their mouths, penetrate their entrails, and never leave until it destroyed them.

If the honor of this invention is due to the gentleman who is generally understood by the "party agent" of Massachusettensis, it belongs to one to whom America has erected a statue in her heart, for his integrity, fortitude, and perseverance in her cause. That the invention itself is very useful and important, is sufficiently clear, from the unlimited wrath of the tories against it, and from the gall which this writer discharges upon it. Almost all mankind have lost their liberties through ignorance, inattention, and disunion. These committees are admirably calculated to diffuse knowledge, to communicate intelligence, and promote unanimity. If the high whigs are generally of such committees, it is because the freeholders who choose them are such, and therefore prefer their peers. The tories, high or low, if they can make interest enough among the people, may get themselves chosen, and promote the great cause of parliamentary revenues, and the other sublime doctrines and mysteries of toryism. That these committees think themselves "amenable to none," is false; for there is not a man upon any one of them who does not acknowledge himself to hold his place at the pleasure of his constituents, and to be accountable to them, whenever they demand it. If the committee of the town of Boston was appointed for a special purpose, at first, their commission has been renewed from time to time; they have been frequently thanked by the town for their vigilance, activity, and disinterested labors in the public service. Their doings have been laid before the town, and approved of by it. The malice of the tories has several times swelled open their bosoms, and broken out into the most intemperate and illiberal invectives against it; but all in vain. It has only served to show the impotence of the tories, and increase the importance of the committee.

These committees cannot be too religiously careful of the exact truth of the intelligence they receive or convey; nor too anxious for the rectitude and purity of the measures they propose or adopt; they should be very sure that they do no injury to any man's person, property, or character; and they are generally persons of such worth, that I have no doubt of their attention to these rules; and therefore, that the reproaches of this writer are mere slanders.

If we recollect how many states have lost their liberties, merely from want of communication with each other, and union among themselves, we shall think that these committees may be intended by Providence to accomplish great events. What the eloquence and talents of negotiation of Demosthenes himself could not effect, among the states of Greece, might have been effected by so simple a device. Castile, Arragon, Valencia, Majorca, &c. all complained of oppression under Charles V., flew out into transports of rage, and took arms against him. But they never consulted or communicated with each other. They resisted separately, and were separately subdued. Had Don Juan Padilla, or his wife, been possessed of the genius to invent a committee of correspondence, perhaps the liberties of the Spanish nation might have remained to this hour, without any necessity to have had recourse to arms.

Hear the opinion of Dr. Robertson:—"While the spirit of disaffection was so general among the Spaniards, and so many causes concurred in precipitating them into such violent measures in order to obtain the redress of their grievances, it may appear strange that the malecontents in the different kingdoms should have carried on their operations without any mutual concert, or even any intercourse with each other. By uniting their councils and arms, they might have acted both with greater force and with more effect. The appearance of a national confederacy would have rendered it no less respectable among the people, than formidable to the crown; and the emperor, unable to resist such a combination, must have complied with any terms which the members of it should have thought fit to prescribe."

That it is owing to those committees that so many persons have been found to recant and resign, and so many others to fly to the army, is a mistake; for the same things would have taken place if such a committee had never been in being, and such persons would probably have met with much rougher usage. This writer asks,—"Have not these persons as good a right to think and act for themselves as the whigs?" I answer, yes. But if any man, whig or tory, shall take it into his head to think for himself, that he has a right to take my property without my consent, however tender I may be of the right of private judgment and the freedom of thought, this is a point in which I shall be very likely to differ from him, and to think for myself, that I have a right to resist him. If any man should think ever so conscientiously, that the Roman Catholic religion is better than the Protestant, or that the French government is preferable to the British constitution in its purity, Protestants and Britons will not be so tender of that man's conscience as to suffer him to introduce his favorite religion and government. So, the well-bred gentlemen, who are so polite as to think that the charter constitution of this province ought to be abolished, and another introduced, wholly at the will of a minister or the crown, or that our ecclesiastical constitution is bad, and high church ought to come in; few people will be so tender of these consciences, or complaisant to such polite taste, as to suffer the one or the other to be established. There are certain prejudices among the people so strong as to be irresistible. Reasoning is vain, and opposition idle. For example, there are certain popular maxims and precepts called the ten commandments. Suppose a number of fine gentlemen, superior to the prejudices of education, should discover that these were made for the common people, and are too illiberal for gentlemen of refined taste to observe, and accordingly, should engage in secret, confidential correspondences to procure an act of parliament to abolish the whole decalogue, or to exempt them from all obligation to observe it; if they should succeed, and their letters be detected, such is the force of prejudice and deep habits among the lower sort of people, that it is much to be questioned whether those refined geniuses would be allowed to enjoy themselves in the latitude of their sentiments. I once knew a man who had studied Jacob Behmen, and other mystics, until he conscientiously thought the millennium commenced, and all human authority at an end; that the saints only had a right to property, and to take from sinners any thing they wanted. In this persuasion, he very honestly stole a horse. Mankind pitied the poor man's infirmity, but thought it, however, their duty to confine him, that he might steal no more.

The freedom of thinking was never yet extended in any country so far as the utter subversion of all religion and morality, nor as the abolition of the laws and constitution of the country.

But "are not these persons as closely connected with the interest of their country as the whigs?" I answer, they are not; they have found an interest in opposition to that of their country, and are making themselves rich and their families illustrious by depressing and destroying their country. But "do not their former lives and conversations appear to have been regulated by principles, as much as those of the whigs?" A few of them, it must be acknowledged, until seduced by the bewitching charms of wealth and power, appeared to be men of principle. But taking the whigs and tories on an average, the balance of principle, as well as genius, learning, wit, and wealth, is infinitely in favor of the former. As to some of these fugitives, they are known to be men of no principles at all, in religion, morals, or government.

But the "policy" is questioned, and you are asked if you expect to make converts by it? As to the policy or impolicy of it, I have nothing to say; but we do not expect to make converts of most of those persons by any means whatever, as long as they have any hopes that the ministry will place and pension them. The instant these hopes are extinguished, we all know they will be converted of course. Converts from places and pensions are only to be made by places and pensions; all other reasoning is idle; these are the *penultima ratio* of the tories, as field-pieces are the *ultima*.

That we are "not unanimous" is certain. But there are nineteen on one side to one on the other, through the province; and ninety-nine out of a hundred of the remaining twentieth part, can be fairly shown to have some sinister private view, to induce them to profess his opinion.

Then we are threatened high, that "this is a changeable world, and time's rolling wheel may ere long bring them uppermost, and, in that case, we should not wish to have them fraught with resentment."

To all this we answer, without ceremony, that they always have been uppermost, in every respect, excepting only the esteem and affection of the people; that they always have been fraught with resentment, (even their cunning and policy have not restrained them,) and we know they always will be; that they have indulged their resentment and malice, in every instance in which they had power to do it; and we know that their revenge will never have other limits than their power.

Then this consistent writer begins to flatter the people; he "appeals to their good sense; he knows they have it;" the same people whom he has so many times represented as mad and foolish.

"I know you are loyal, and friends to good order." This is the same people that, in the whole course of his writings, he has represented as continuing for ten years together in a continual state of disorder, demolishing the chair, board, supreme court, and encouraging all sorts of riots, insurrections, treason, and rebellion. Such are the shifts to which a man is driven, when he aims at carrying a point, not at discovering truth!

The people are then told that "they have been insidiously taught to believe, that Great Britain is rapacious, cruel, and vindictive, and envies us the inheritance purchased by the sweat and blood of our ancestors." The people do not believe this; they will not believe it. On the contrary, they believe, if it was not for scandals constantly transmitted from this province by the tories, the nation would redress our grievances. Nay, as little as they reverence the ministry, they even believe that the lords North, Mansfield, and Bute, would relieve them, and would have done it long ago, if they had known the truth. The moment this is done, "long live our gracious king, and happiness to Britain," will resound from one end of the province to the other; but it requires very little foresight to determine, that no other plan of governing the province and the colonies will ever restore a harmony between two countries, but desisting from the plan of taxing them and interfering with their internal concerns, and returning to that system of colony administration, which nature dictated, and experience for one hundred and fifty years found useful.

No. VII

OUR RHETORICAL MAGICIAN, in his paper of January the 9th, continues to *wheedle:* You want nothing but "to know the true state of facts, to rectify whatever is amiss." He becomes an advocate for the poor of Boston! is for making great allowance for the whigs. "The whigs are too valuable a part of the community to lose. He would not draw down the vengeance of Great Britain. He shall become an advocate for the leading whigs," &c. It is in vain for us to inquire after the *sincerity* or *consistency* of all this. It is agreeable to the precept of Horace:

Irritat, mulcet, falvis terroribus implet,
Ut magus,

And that is all he desires.

After a long discourse, which has nothing in it but what has been answered already, he comes to a great subject indeed, the British constitution; and undertakes to prove, that "the authority of parliament extends to the colonies."

Why will not this writer state the question fairly? The whigs allow that, from the necessity of a case not provided for by common law, and to supply a defect in the British dominions, which there undoubtedly is, if they are to be governed only by that law, America has all along consented, still consents, and ever will consent, that parliament, being the most powerful legislature in the dominions, should regulate the trade of the dominions. This is founding the authority of parliament to regulate our trade, upon *compact* and *consent* of the colonies, not upon any principle of common or statute law; not upon any original principle of the English constitution; not upon the principle that parliament is the supreme and sovereign legislature over them in all cases whatsoever. The question is not, therefore, whether the authority of parliament extends to the colonies in any case, for it is admitted by the whigs, that it does in that of commerce; but whether it extends in all cases.

We are then detained with a long account of the three simple forms of government; and are told, that "the British constitution, consisting of king, lords, and commons, is formed upon the principles of monarchy, aristocracy, and democracy, in due proportion; that it includes the principal excellences, and excludes the principal defects of the other kinds of government,—the most perfect system that the wisdom of ages has produced, and Englishmen glory in being subject to, and protected by it."

Then we are told, "that the colonies are a part of the British empire." But what are we to understand by this? Some of the colonies, most of them, indeed, were settled before the kingdom of Great Britain was brought into existence. The union of England and Scotland was made and established by act of parliament in the reign of Queen Anne, and it was this union and statute which erected the kingdom of Great Britain. The colonies were settled long before, in the reigns of the Jameses and Charleses. What authority over them had Scotland? Scotland, England, and the colonies were all under one king before that; the two crowns of England and Scotland united on the head of James I., and continued united on that of Charles I., when our first charter was granted. Our charter, being granted by him, who was king of both nations, to our ancestors, most of whom were *post nati,* born after the union of the two crowns, and consequently, as was adjudged in Calvin's case, free, natural subjects of Scotland, as well as England,—had not the king as good a right to have governed the colonies by his Scottish, as by his English parliament, and to have granted our charters under the seal of Scotland, as well as that of England?

But to wave this. If the English parliament were to govern us, where did they get the right, without our consent, to take the Scottish parliament into a participation of the government over us? When this was done, was the American share of the democracy of the constitution consulted? If not, were not the Americans deprived of the benefit of the democratical part of the constitution? And is not the democracy as essential to the English constitution as the monarchy or aristocracy? Should we have been more effectually deprived of the benefit of the British or English constitution, if one or both houses of parliament, or if our house and council, had made this union with the two houses of parliament in Scotland, without the king?

If a new constitution was to be formed for the whole British dominions, and a supreme legislature coextensive with it, upon the general principles of the English constitution, an equal mixture of monarchy, aristocracy, and democracy, let us see what would be necessary. England has six millions of people, we will say; America had three. England has five hundred members in the house of commons, we will say; America must have two hundred and fifty. Is it possible she should maintain them there, or could they at such a distance know the state, the sense, or exigencies of their constituents? Ireland, too, must be incorporated, and send another hundred or two of members. The territory in the East Indies and West India Islands must send members. And after all this, every navigation act, every act of trade must be repealed. America, and the East and West Indies, and Africa too, must have equal liberty to trade with all the world, that the favored inhabitants of Great Britain have now. Will the ministry thank Massachusettensis for becoming an advocate for such a union, and incorporation of all the dominions of the King of Great Britain? Yet, without such a union, a legislature which shall be sovereign and supreme in all cases whatsoever, and coextensive with the empire, can never be established upon the general principles of the English constitution which Massachusettensis lays down, namely,—an equal mixture of monarchy, aristocracy, and democracy. Nay, further, in order to comply with this principle, this new government, this mighty colossus, which is to bestride the narrow world, must have a house of lords, consisting of Irish,

East and West Indian, African, American, as well as English and Scottish noblemen; for the nobility ought to be scattered about all the dominions, as well as the representatives of the commons. If in twenty years more America should have six millions of inhabitants, as there is a boundless territory to fill up, she must have five hundred representatives. Upon these principles, if in forty years she should have twelve millions, a thousand; and if the inhabitants of the three kingdoms remain as they are, being already full of inhabitants, what will become of your supreme legislative? It will be translated, crown and all, to America. This is a sublime system for America. It will flatter those ideas of independency which the tories impute to them, if they have any such, more than any other plan of independency that I have ever heard projected.

"The best writers upon the law of nations tell us, that when a nation takes possession of a distant country, and settles there, that country, though separated from the principal establishment, or mother country, naturally becomes a part of the state, equal with its ancient possessions." We are not told who these "best writers" are. I think we ought to be introduced to them. But their meaning may be no more, than that it is best they should be incorporated with the ancient establishment by contract, or by some new law and institution, by which the new country shall have equal right, powers, and privileges, as well as equal protection, and be under equal obligations of obedience, with the old. Has there been any such contract between Britain and the colonies? Is America incorporated into the realm? Is it a part of the realm? Is it a part of the kingdom? Has it any share in the legislative of the realm? The constitution requires that every foot of land should be represented in the third estate, the democratical branch of the constitution. How many millions of acres in America, how many thousands of wealthy landholders, have no representatives there?

But let these "best writers" say what they will, there is nothing in the law of nations, which is only the law of right reason applied to the conduct of nations, that requires that emigrants from a state should continue, or be made, a part of the state.

The practice of nations has been different. The Greeks planted colonies, and neither demanded nor pretended any authority over them; but they became distinct, independent commonwealths. The Romans continued their colonies under the jurisdiction of the mother commonwealth; but, nevertheless, they allowed them the privileges of cities. Indeed, that sagacious city seems to have been aware of difficulties similar to those under which Great Britain is now laboring. She seems to have been sensible of the impossibility of keeping colonies planted at great distances, under the absolute control of her *senatus-consulta*. Harrington tells us, that "the commonwealth of Rome, by planting colonies of its citizens within the bounds of Italy, took the best way of propagating itself and naturalizing the country; whereas, if it had planted such colonies without the bounds of Italy, it would have alienated the citizens, and given a root to liberty abroad, that might have sprung up foreign, or savage, and hostile to her; *wherefore it never made any such dispersion of itself and its strength* till it was under the yoke of the emperors, who, disburdening themselves of the people, as having less apprehension of what they could do abroad than at home, took a contrary course."* But these Italian cities, although established by decrees of the senate of Rome, to which the colonist was always party, either as a Roman citizen about to emigrate, or as a conquered enemy treating upon terms, were always allowed all the rights of Roman citizens, and were governed by senates of their own. It was the policy of Rome to conciliate her colonies by allowing them equal liberties with her citizens. Witness the example of the Privernates. This people had been conquered, and, complaining of oppressions, revolted. At last they sent ambassadors to Rome to treat of peace. The senate was divided in opinion. Some were for violent, others for lenient measures. In the course of the debate, a senator, whose opinion was for *bringing them to his feet*, proudly asked one of the ambassadors what punishment he thought his countrymen deserved. "*Eam, inquit, quam merentur, qui se libertate dignos censent.*" That punishment which those deserve who think themselves worthy of liberty. Another senator, seeing that the *ministerial members* were exasperated with the honest answer, in order to divert their anger, asks another question:— What if we remit all punishment? What kind of a peace may we hope for with you? "*Si bonam dederitis, inquit, et fidam et perpetuam; si malam, haud diuturnam.*" If you give us a just peace, it will be faithfully observed, and perpetually; but if a bad one, it will not last long. The *ministerial* senators all on fire at this answer, cried out sedition and rebellion; but the wiser majority decreed,—"*Viri et liberi, vocem auditam; an credi posse ullum populum, aut hominem denique, in ea conditione, cujus eum paeniteat, diutius quam necesse sit mansurum? Ibi pacem esse fidam, ubi voluntarii pacati sint; neque eo loco, ubi servitutem esse velint, fidem sperandam esse.*" That they had heard the voice of a man, and a son of liberty; that it was not natural or credible that any people, or any man, would continue longer than necessity should compel him in a condition that grieved and displeased him. A faithful peace was to be expected from men whose affections were conciliated; nor was any kind of fidelity to be expected from slaves. The consul exclaimed,—

* Oceana, p. 43.

"*Eos demum, qui nihil praeterquam de libertate cogitent, dignos esse qui Romani fiant.*" That they who regarded nothing so much as their liberty, deserved to be Romans. "*Itaque et in senatu causam obtinuere; et ex auctoritate patrum, latum ad populum est, ut Privernatibus civitas daretur.*" Therefore the Privernates obtained their cause in the senate; and it was, by the authority of those fathers, recommended to the people, that the privileges of a city should be granted them. The practice of free nations only can be adduced, as precedents of what the law of nature has been thought to dictate upon this subject of colonies. Their practice is different. The senate and people of Rome did not interfere commonly by making laws for their colonies, but left them to be ruled by governors and senates. Can Massachusettensis produce from the whole history of Rome, or from the Digest, one example of a *senatus-consultum,* or a *plebiscitum,* laying taxes on the colony?

Having mentioned the wisdom of the Romans, for not planting colonies out of Italy, and their reasons for it, I cannot help recollecting an observation of Harrington:—"For the colonies in the Indies," says he, "they are yet babes, that cannot live without sucking the breasts of their mother cities, but such as I mistake, if, when they come of age, they do not wean themselves, which causes me to wonder at princes that delight to be exhausted in that way." This was written one hundred and twenty years ago; the colonies are now nearer manhood than ever Harrington foresaw they would arrive in such a period of time. Is it not astonishing, then, that any British minister should ever have considered this subject so little as to believe it possible for him to new-model all our governments, to tax us by an authority that never taxed us before, and subdue us to an implicit obedience to a legislature that millions of us scarcely ever thought any thing about?

I have said, that the practice of free governments alone can be quoted with propriety to show the sense of nations. But the sense and practice of nations is not enough. Their practice must be reasonable, just, and right, or it will not govern Americans.

Absolute monarchies, whatever their practice may be, are nothing to us; for, as Harrington observes, "Absolute monarchy, as that of the Turks, neither plants its people at home nor abroad, otherwise than as tenants for life or at will; wherefore, its national and provincial government is all one."

I deny, therefore, that the practice of free nations, or the opinions of the best writers upon the law of nations, will warrant the position of Massachusettensis, that, "when a nation takes possession of a distant territory, that becomes a part of the state equally with its ancient possessions." The practice of free nations and the opinions of the best writers are in general on the contrary.

I agree, that "two supreme and independent authorities cannot exist in the same state," any more than two supreme beings in one universe; and, therefore, I contend, that our provincial legislatures are the only supreme authorities in our colonies. Parliament, notwithstanding this, may be allowed an authority supreme and sovereign over the ocean, which may be limited by the banks of the ocean, or the bounds of our charters; our charters give us no authority over the high seas. Parliament has our consent to assume a jurisdiction over them. And here is a line fairly drawn between the rights of Britain and the rights of the colonies, namely, the banks of the ocean, or low-water mark; the line of division between common law, and civil or maritime law. If this is not sufficient,—if parliament are at a loss for any principle of natural, civil, maritime, moral, or common law, on which to ground any authority over the high seas, the Atlantic especially, let the colonies be treated like reasonable creatures, and they will discover great ingenuity and modesty. The acts of trade and navigation might be confirmed by provincial laws, and carried into execution by our own courts and juries, and in this case, illicit trade would be cut up by the roots forever. I knew the smuggling tories in New York and Boston would cry out against this, because it would not only destroy their profitable game of smuggling, but their whole place and pension system. But the whigs, that is, a vast majority of the whole continent, would not regard the smuggling tories. In one word, if public principles, and motives, and arguments were alone to determine this dispute between the two countries, it might be settled forever in a few hours; but the everlasting clamors of prejudice, passion, and private interest drown every consideration of that sort, and are precipitating us into a civil war.

"If, then, we are a part of the British empire, we must be subject to the supreme power of the state, which is vested in the estates in parliament."

Here, again, we are to be conjured out of our senses by the magic in the words "British empire," and "supreme power of the state." But, however it may sound, I say we are not a part of the British empire; because the British government is not an empire. The governments of France, Spain, &c. are not empires, but monarchies, supposed to be governed by fixed fundamental laws, though not really. The British government is still less entitled to the style of *an empire*. It is a limited monarchy. If Aristotle, Livy, and Harrington knew what a republic was, the British constitution is much more like a republic than an empire. They define a republic to be a *government of laws, and not of men*. If this definition be just, the British constitution is nothing more nor less than a republic, in which the king is first magistrate. This office being hereditary, and being possessed of such ample and splendid prerogatives, is no objection to the government's being a republic, as long as it is bound by fixed laws, which the people have a voice in making, and a right to defend. An empire is a despotism, and an emperor a despot, bound by no law or limitation but his own will; it is a stretch of tyranny beyond absolute monarchy. For, although the will of an absolute monarch is law, yet his edicts must be registered by parliaments. Even this formality is not necessary in an empire. There the maxim is *quod principi placuit legis habet rigorem,* even without having that will and pleasure recorded. There are but three empires now in Europe, the German or Holy Roman, the Russian, and the Ottoman.

There is another sense, indeed, in which the word *empire* is used, in which it may be applied to the government of Geneva, or any other republic, as well as to monarchy or despotism. In this sense it is synonymous with *government, rule,* or *dominion.* In this sense we are within the dominion, rule, or government of the King of Great Britain.

The question should be, whether we are a part of the kingdom of Great Britain. This is the only language known in English laws. We are not then a part of the British kingdom, realm, or state; and therefore the supreme power of the kingdom, realm, or state is not, upon these principles, the supreme power of us. That "supreme power over America is vested in the estates in parliament," is an affront to us; for there is not an acre of American land represented there; there are no American estates in parliament.

To say, that we "must be" subject, seems to betray a consciousness that we are not by any law, or upon any principles but those of mere power; and an opinion that we ought to be, or that it is necessary that we should be. But if this should be admitted for argument's sake only, what is the consequence? The consequences that may fairly be drawn are these; that Britain has been imprudent enough to let colonies be planted, until they are become numerous and important, without ever having wisdom enough to concert a plan for their government, consistent with her own welfare; that now it is necessary to make them submit to the authority of parliament; and, because there is no principle of law, or justice, or reason, by which she can effect it, therefore she will resort to war and conquest—to the maxim, *delenda est Carthago.* These are the consequences, according to this writer's idea. We think the consequences are, that she has, after one hundred and fifty years, discovered a defect in her government, which ought to be supplied by some just and reasonable means, that is, by the consent of the colonies; for metaphysicians and politicians may dispute forever, but they will never find any other moral principle or foundation of rule or obedience, than the consent of governors and governed. She has found out that the great machine will not go any longer without a new wheel. She will make this herself. We think she is making it of such materials and workmanship as will tear the whole machine to pieces. We are willing, if she can convince us of the necessity of such a wheel, to assist with artists and materials in making it, so that it may answer the end. But she says, we shall have no share in it; and if we will not let her patch it up as she pleases, her Massachusettensis and other advocates tell us, she will tear it to pieces herself, by cutting our throats. To this kind of reasoning, we can only answer, that we will not stand still to be butchered. We will defend our lives as long as Providence shall enable us.

"It is beyond doubt, that it was the sense both of the *parent country* and *our ancestors,* that they were to remain subject to parliament."

This has been often asserted, and as often contradicted and fully confuted. The confutation may not, however, have come to every eye which has read this newspaper.

The public acts of kings and ministers of state, in that age when our ancestors emigrated, which were not complained of, remonstrated and protested against by the commons, are looked upon as sufficient proof of the "sense" of the parent country.

The charter to the treasurer and company of Virginia, 23 May, 1609, grants ample powers of government, legislative, executive, and judicial, and then contains an express covenant, "to and with the said treasurer and company, their successors, factors, and assigns, that they, and every of them, shall be free from all taxes and impositions forever, upon any goods or merchandises, at any time or times hereafter, either upon importation thither, or exportation from thence, into our realm of England, or into any other of our realms or dominions."

I agree with this writer, that the authority of a supreme legislature includes the right of taxation. Is not this quotation, then, an irresistible proof, that it was not "the sense of King James or his ministers, or of the ancestors of the Virginians, that they were to remain subject to parliament as a supreme legislature?"

After this, James issued a proclamation recalling the patent, but this was never regarded. Then Charles issued another proclamation, which produced a remonstrance from Virginia, which was answered by a letter from the lords of the privy council, 22 July, 1634, containing the royal assurance, that "all their estates, trade, freedom, and privileges should be enjoyed by them in as extensive a manner as they enjoyed them before those proclamations."

Here is another evidence of the sense of the king and his ministers.

Afterwards, parliament sent a squadron of ships to Virginia; the colony rose in open resistance, until the parliamentary commissioners granted them conditions, that they should enjoy the privileges of Englishmen; that their assembly should transact the affairs of the colonies; that they should have a free trade to all places and nations, as the people of England; and fourthly, that "Virginia shall be free from all *taxes,* customs, and impositions whatever, and none to be imposed on them without consent of the grand assembly; and so that neither forts nor castles be erected, or garrisons maintained, without their consent."

One would think this was evidence enough of the sense both of the parent country and our ancestors.

After the acts of navigation were passed, Virginia sent agents to England, and a remonstrance against those acts. Charles, in answer, sent a declaration under the privy seal, 19 April, 1676, affirming "that taxes ought not to be laid upon the inhabitants and proprietors of the colony, but by the common consent of the general assembly; except such impositions as the parliament should lay on the commodities imported into England from the colony." And he ordered a charter under the great seal, to secure this right to the Virginians.

What becomes of the "sense of the parent country and our ancestors"? for the ancestors of the Virginians are our ancestors, when we speak of ourselves as Americans.

From Virginia let us pass to Maryland. Charles I., in 1633, gave a charter to the Baron of Baltimore, containing ample powers of government, and this express covenant: "to and with the said Lord Baltimore, his heirs and assigns, that we, our heirs and successors, shall at no time hereafter, set or make, or cause to be set, any imposition, custom, or other taxation, rate, or contribution whatsoever, in and upon the dwellings and inhabitants of the aforesaid province, for their lands, tenements, goods, or chattels within the said province; or to be laden or unladen, within the ports or harbors of the said province."

What, then, was the "sense of the parent country and the ancestors" of Maryland? But if, by "our ancestors," he confines his idea to New England, or this province, let us consider. The first planters of Plymouth were "our ancestors" in the strictest sense. They had no charter or patent for the land they took possession of; and derived no authority from the English parliament or crown to set up their government. They purchased land of the Indians, and set up a government of their own, on the simple principle of nature; and afterwards purchased a patent for the land of the council at Plymouth; but never purchased any charter for government, of the crown or the king, and continued to exercise all the powers of government, legislative, executive, and judicial, upon the plain ground of an original contract among independent individuals for sixty-eight years, that is, until their incorporation with Massachusetts by our present charter. The same may be said of the colonies which emigrated to Say-Brook, New Haven, and other parts of Connecticut. They seem to have had no idea of dependence on parliament, any more than on the conclave. The Secretary of Connecticut has now in his possession an original letter from Charles II. to that colony, in which he considers them rather as friendly allies, than as subjects to his English parliament; and even requests them to pass a law in their assembly relative to piracy.

The sentiments of your ancestors in the Massachusetts, may be learned from almost every ancient paper and record. It would be endless to recite all the passages, in which it appears that they thought themselves exempt from the authority of parliament, not only in the point of taxation, but in all cases whatsoever. Let me mention one. Randolph, one of the predecessors of Massachusettensis, in a representation to Charles II., dated 20 September, 1676, says, "I went to visit the governor at his house, and, among other discourse, I told him, I took notice of several ships that were arrived at Boston, some since my being there, from Spain, France, Straits, Canaries, and other parts of Europe, contrary to your majesty's laws for encouraging navigation and regulating the trade of the plantations. He freely declared to me, that the law made by your majesty and your parliament, obligeth them in nothing but what consists with the interest of that colony; that the legislative power is and abides in them solely to act and make laws by virtue of a charter from your majesty's royal father." Here is a positive assertion of an exemption from the authority of parliament, even in the case of the regulation of trade.

Afterwards, in 1677, the general court passed a law which shows the sense of our ancestors in a very strong light. It is in these words:—

"This court being informed, by letters received this day from our messengers, of his majesty's expectation, that the acts of trade and navigation be exactly and punctually observed by this his majesty's colony, his pleasure therein not having before now been signified unto us, either by express from his majesty or any of his ministers of state:

"It is therefore hereby ordered, and by the authority of this court enacted, that henceforth, all masters of ships, ketches, or other vessels, of greater or lesser burthen, arriving in, or sailing from any of the ports in this jurisdiction, do, without coven or fraud, yield faithful and constant obedience unto, and observation of, all the said acts of navigation and trade, on penalty of suffering such forfeitures, loss, and damage, as in the said acts are particularly expressed. And the governor and council, and all officers commissionated and authorized by them, are hereby ordered and required to see to the strict observation of the said acts."

As soon as they had passed this law, they wrote a letter to their agent, in which they acknowledge they had not conformed to the acts of trade; and they say, they "apprehended them to be an invasion of the rights, liberties, and properties of the subjects of his majesty in the colony, they not being represented in parliament; and, according to the usual sayings of the learned in the law, *the laws of England were bounded within the four seas, and did not reach America.* However, as his majesty had signified his pleasure that these acts should be observed in the Massachusetts, they had made provision, by a law of the colony, that they should be strictly attended to from time to time, although it greatly discouraged trade, and was a great damage to his majesty's plantation."

Thus, it appears, that the ancient Massachusettensians and Virginians had precisely the same sense of the authority of parliament, namely,—that it had none at all; and the same sense of the necessity that, by the voluntary act of the colonies—their free, cheerful consent—it should be allowed the power of regulating trade; and this is precisely the idea of the late congress at Philadelphia, expressed in the fourth proposition in their Bill of Rights.

But this was the sense of the parent country, too, at that time; for King Charles II., in a letter to the Massachusetts, after this law had been laid before him, has these words: "We are informed that you have lately made *some good provision* for observing the acts of trade and navigation, which is well pleasing unto us." Had he or his ministers an idea that parliament was the sovereign legislative over the colony? If he had, would he not have censured this law, as an insult to that legislative?

I sincerely hope we shall see no more such round affirmations, that "it was the sense of the parent country and our ancestors, that they were to remain subject to parliament." So far from thinking themselves subject to parliament, it is clear that, during the interregnum, it was their desire and design to have been a free commonwealth, an independent republic; and after the restoration, it was with the utmost reluctance that, in the course of sixteen or seventeen years, they were brought to take the oaths of allegiance; and for some time after this, they insisted upon taking an oath of fidelity to the country, before that of allegiance to the king.

That "it is evident, from the charter itself, that they were to remain subject to parliament," is very unaccountable, when there is not one word in either charter concerning parliament.

That the authority of parliament "has been exercised almost ever since the first settlement of the country," is a mistake; for there is no instance, until the first Navigation Act, which was in 1660, more than forty years after the first settlement. This act was never executed nor regarded until seventeen years afterwards, and then it was not executed as an act of parliament, but as a law of the colony, to which the king agreed.

This "has been expressly acknowledged by our provincial legislatures." There is too much truth in this. It has been twice acknowledged by our house of representatives, that parliament was the supreme legislative; but this was directly repugnant to a multitude of other votes, by which it was denied. This was in conformity to the distinction between taxation and legislation, which has since been found to be a distinction without a difference.

When a great question is first started, there are very few, even of the greatest minds, which suddenly and intuitively comprehend it, in all its consequences.

It is both "our interest and our duty to continue subject to the authority of parliament," as far as the regulation of our trade, if it will be content with that, but no longer.

"If the colonies are not subject to the authority of parliament, Great Britain and the colonies must be distinct states, as completely so as England and Scotland were before the union, or as Great Britain and Hanover are now." There is no need of being startled at this consequence. It is very harmless. There is no absurdity at all in it. Distinct states may be united under one king. And those states may be further cemented and united together by a treaty of commerce. This is the case. We have, by our own express consent, contracted to observe the Navigation Act, and by our implied consent, by long usage and uninterrupted acquiescence, have submitted to the other acts of trade, however grievous some of them may be. This may be compared to a treaty of commerce, by which those distinct states are cemented together, in perpetual league and amity. And if any further ratifications of this pact or treaty are necessary, the colonies would readily enter into them, provided their other liberties were inviolate.

That "the colonies owe no allegiance to any imperial crown," provided such a crown involves in it a house of lords and a house of commons, is certain. Indeed, we owe no allegiance to any crown at all. We owe allegiance to the person of his majesty, King George III., whom God preserve. But allegiance is due universally, both from Britons and Americans to the person of the king, not to his crown; to his natural, not his politic capacity, as I will undertake to prove hereafter, from the highest authorities, and the most solemn adjudications, which were ever made within any part of the British dominions.

If his majesty's title to the crown is "derived from an act of parliament, made since the settlement of these colonies," it was not made since the date of our charter. Our charter was granted by King William and Queen Mary, three years after the revolution; and the oaths of allegiance are established by a law of the province. So that our allegiance to his majesty is not due by virtue of any act of a British parliament, but by our own charter and province laws. It ought to be remembered that there was a revolution here, as well as in England, and that we, as well as the people of England, made an original, express contract with King William.

If it follows from thence, that he appears "King of Massachusetts, King of Rhode Island, King of Connecticut, &c." this is no absurdity at all. He will appear in this light, and does appear so, whether parliament has authority over us or not. He is King of Ireland, I suppose, although parliament is allowed to have authority there. As to giving his majesty those titles, I have no objection at all; I wish he would be graciously pleased to assume them.

The only proposition in all this writer's long string of pretended absurdities, which he says follows from the position that we are distinct states, is this:—That "as the king must govern each state by its parliament, those several parliaments would pursue the particular interest of its own state; and however well disposed the king might be to pursue a line of interest that was common to all, the checks and control that he would meet with would render it impossible." Every argument ought to be allowed its full weight; and therefore candor obliges me to acknowledge, that here lies all the difficulty that there is in this whole controversy. There has been, from first to last, on both sides of the Atlantic, an idea, an apprehension, that it was necessary there should be some superintending power, to draw together all the wills, and unite all the strength of the subjects in all the dominions, in case of war, and in the case of trade. The necessity of this, in case of trade, has been so apparent, that, as has often been said, we have consented that parliament should exercise such a power. In case of war, it has by some been thought necessary. But in fact and experience, it has not been found so. What though the proprietary colonies, on account of disputes with the proprietors, did not come in so early to the assistance of the general cause in the last war as they ought, and perhaps one of them not at all? The inconveniences of this were small, in comparison of the absolute ruin to the liberties of all which must follow the submission to parliament, in all cases, which would be giving up all the popular limitations upon the government. These inconveniences fell chiefly upon New England. She was necessitated to greater exertions; but she had rather suffer these again and again than others infinitely greater. However, this subject has been so long in contemplation, that it is fully understood now in all the colonies; so that there is no danger, in case of another war, of any colony's failing of its duty.

But, admitting the proposition in its full force, that it is absolutely necessary there should be a supreme power, coextensive with all the dominions, will it follow that parliament, as now constituted, has a right to assume this supreme jurisdiction? By no means.

A union of the colonies might be projected, and an American legislature; for, if America has three millions of people, and the whole dominions, twelve millions, she ought to send a quarter part of all the members to the house of commons; and, instead of holding parliaments always at Westminster, the haughty members for Great Britain must humble themselves, one session in four, to cross the Atlantic, and hold the parliament in America.

There is no avoiding all inconveniences in human affairs. The greatest possible, or conceivable, would arise from ceding to parliament power over us without a representation in it. The next greatest would accrue from any plan that can be devised for a representation there. The least of all would arise from going on as we began, and fared well for one hundred and fifty years, by letting parliament regulate trade, and our own assemblies all other matters.

As to "the prerogatives not being defined, or limited," it is as much so in the colonies as in Great Britain, and as well understood, and as cheerfully submitted to in the former as the latter.

But "where is the British constitution, that we all agree we are entitled to?" I answer, if we enjoy, and are entitled to more liberty than the British constitution allows, where is the harm? Or if we enjoy the British constitution in greater purity and perfection than they do in England, as is really the case, whose fault is this? Not ours.

We may find all the blessings of this constitution "in our provincial assemblies." Our houses of representatives have, and ought to exercise every power of the house of commons. The first charter to this colony is nothing to the present argument; but it did grant a power of taxing the people, implicitly, though not in express terms. It granted all the rights and liberties of Englishmen, which include the power of taxing the people.

"Our council boards" in the royal governments, "are destitute of the noble independence and splendid appendages of peerage." Most certainly, they are the meanest creatures and tools in the political creation, dependent every moment for their existence on the tainted breath of a prime minister. But they have the authority of the house of lords, in our little models of the English constitution; and it is this which makes them so great a grievance. The crown has really two branches of our legislature in its power. Let an act of parliament pass at home, putting it in the power of the king to remove any peer from the house of lords at his pleasure, and what will become of the British constitution? It will be overturned from the foundation. Yet we are perpetually insulted by being told, that making our council by mandamus brings us nearer to the British constitution. In this province, by charter, the council certainly hold their seats for the year, after being chosen and approved, independent of both the other branches. For their creation, they are equally obliged to both the other branches; so that there is little or no bias in favor of either; if any, it is in favor of the prerogative. In short, it is not easy, without an hereditary nobility, to constitute a council more independent, more nearly resembling the house of lords, than the council of this province has ever been by charter.

But perhaps it will be said, that we are to enjoy the British constitution in our supreme legislature, the parliament, not in our provincial legislatures. To this I answer, if parliament is to be our supreme legislature, we shall be under a complete oligarchy or aristocracy, not the British constitution, which this writer himself defines a mixture of monarchy, aristocracy, and democracy. For king, lords, and commons, will constitute one great oligarchy, as they will stand related to America, as much as the decemvirs did in Rome; with this difference for the worse, that our rulers are to be three thousand miles off. The definition of an oligarchy is a government by a number of grandees, over whom the people have no control. The States of Holland were once chosen by the people frequently, then chosen for life; now they are not chosen by the people at all. When a member dies, his place is filled up, not by the people he is to represent, but by the States. Is not this depriving the Hollanders of a free constitution, and subjecting them to an aristocracy, or oligarchy? Will not the government of America be like it? Will not representatives be chosen for them by others, whom they never saw nor heard of? If our provincial constitutions are in any respect imperfect, and want alteration, they have capacity enough to discern it, and power enough to effect it, without the interposition of parliament. There never was an American constitution attempted by parliament before the Quebec bill, and Massachusetts bill. These are such *samples* of what they may, and probably will be, that few Americans are in love with them. However, America will never allow that parliament has any authority to alter their constitution at all. She is wholly penetrated with a sense of the necessity of resisting it at all hazards. And she would resist it, if the constitution of the Massachusetts had been altered as much for *the better* as it is for the worse. The question we insist on most is, not whether the alteration is for the better or not, but whether parliament has any right to make any alteration at all. And it is the universal sense of America, that it has none.

We are told, that "the provincial constitutions have no principle of stability within themselves." This is so great a mistake, that there is not more order or stability in any government upon the globe, than there ever has been in that of Connecticut. The same may be said of the Massachusetts and Pennsylvania; and, indeed, of the others very nearly. "That these constitutions, in turbulent times, would become wholly monarchical, or wholly republican," they must be such times as would have a similar effect upon the constitution at home. But in order to avoid the danger of this, what is to be done? Not give us an English constitution, it seems, but make sure of us at once, by giving us constitutions wholly monarchical, annihilating our houses of representatives first, by taking from them the support of government, &c., and then making the council and judges wholly dependent on the crown.

That a representation in parliament is impracticable, we all agree; but the consequence is, that we must have a representation in our supreme legislatures here. This was the consequence that was drawn by kings, ministers, our ancestors, and the whole nation, more than a century ago, when the colonies were first settled, and continued to be the general sense until the last peace; and it must be the general sense again soon, or Great Britain will lose her colonies.

"This is apparently the meaning of that celebrated passage in Governor Hutchinson's letter, that rung through the continent, namely, — 'There must be an abridgment of what is called English liberties.'" But all the art and subtlety of Massachusettensis will never vindicate or excuse that expression. According to this writer, it should have been, "there is an abridgment of English liberties, and it cannot be otherwise." But every candid reader must see that the letter-writer had more than that in his *view* and in his *wishes*. In the same letter, a little before, he says, "what marks of resentment the parliament will show, whether they will be upon the province in general, or particular persons, is extremely uncertain; but that they will be placed somewhere is most certain; and I add, *because I think it ought to be so.*" Is it possible to read this, without thinking of the Port Bill, the Charter Bill, and the resolves for sending persons to England, by the statute of Henry VIII., to be tried? But this is not all: "This is most certainly a crisis," says he, &c. "If no measure shall have been taken to secure this dependence, (that is, the dependence which a colony ought to have upon the parent state,) it is all over with us." "The friends of government will be utterly disheartened; and the friends of anarchy will be afraid of nothing, be it ever so extravagant." But this is not all: "I never think of the measures necessary for the peace and good order of the colonies without pain." "There must be an abridgment of what are called English liberties." What could he mean? Any thing less than depriving us of trial by jury? Perhaps he wanted an act of parliament to try persons here for treason, by a court of admiralty. Perhaps an act, that the province should be governed by a governor and a mandamus council, without a house of representatives. But to put it out of all doubt, that his meaning was much worse than Massachusettensis endeavors to make it, he explains himself in a subsequent part of the letter: "I wish," says he, "the good of the colony, *when I wish to see some further restraint of liberty.*" Here it is rendered certain, that he is pleading for a further restraint of liberty, not explaining the restraint he apprehended the constitution had already laid us under.

My indignation at this letter has sometimes been softened by compassion. It carries on the face of it evident marks of *madness*. It was written in such a transport of passions, *ambition* and *revenge* chiefly, that his reason was manifestly overpowered. The vessel was tost in such a hurricane, that she could not feel her helm. Indeed, he seems to have had a confused consciousness of this himself. "Pardon me this excursion," says he; "it really proceeds from the state of mind into which our perplexed affairs often throw me."

"It is our highest interest to continue a part of the British empire; and equally our duty to remain subject to the authority of parliament," says Massachusettensis.

We are a part of the British dominions, that is, of the King of Great Britain, and it is our interest and duty to continue so. It is equally our interest and duty to continue subject to the authority of parliament, in the regulation of our trade, as long as she shall leave us to govern our internal policy, and to give and grant our own money, and no longer.

This letter concludes with an agreeable flight of fancy. The time may not be so far off, however, as this writer imagines, when the colonies may have the balance of numbers and wealth in their favor. But when that shall happen, if we should attempt to rule her by an American parliament, without an adequate representation in it, she will infallibly resist us by her arms.

No. VIII

It has often been observed by me, and it cannot be too often repeated, that *colonization* is *casus omissus* at common law. There is no such title known in that law. By common law, I mean that system of customs written and unwritten, which was known and in force in England in the time of King Richard I. This continued to be the case down to the reign of Elizabeth and King James I. In all that time, the laws of England were confined to the realm, and within the four seas. There was no provision made in this law for governing colonies beyond the Atlantic, or beyond the four seas, by authority of parliament; no, nor for the king to grant charters to subjects to settle in foreign countries. It was the king's prerogative to prohibit the emigration of any of his subjects, by issuing his writ *ne exeat regno*. And, therefore, it was in the king's power to permit his subjects to leave the kingdom. "It is a high crime to disobey the king's lawful commands or prohibitions, as not returning from beyond sea upon the king's letters to that purpose; for which the offender's lands shall be seized until he return; and when he does return, he shall be fined, &c.; or going beyond sea against the king's will, expressly signified, either by the writ *ne exeat regno,* or under the great or privy seal, or signet, or by proclamation." When a subject left the kingdom by the king's permission, and if the nation did not remonstrate against it, by the nation's permission too, at least connivance, he carried with him, as a man, all the rights of nature. His allegiance bound him to the king, and entitled him to protection. But how? Not in France; the King of England was not bound to protect him in France. Nor in America. Nor in the dominions of Louis. Nor of Sassacus, or Massachusetts. He had a right to protection and the liberties of England, upon his return there, not otherwise. How, then, do we New Englandmen derive our laws? I say, not from parliament, not from common law, but from the law of nature, and the compact made with the king in our charters. Our ancestors were entitled to the common law of England when they emigrated, that is, to just so much of it as they pleased to adopt, and no more. They were not bound or obliged to submit to it, unless they chose it. By a positive principle of the common law they were bound, let them be in what part of the world they would, to do nothing against the allegiance of the king. But no kind of provision was ever made by common law for punishing or trying any man, even for treason committed out of the realm. He must be tried in some county of the realm by that law, the county where the overt act was done, or he could not be tried at all. Nor was any provision ever made, until the reign of Henry VIII., for trying treasons committed abroad, and the acts of that reign were made on purpose to catch Cardinal Pole.

So that our ancestors, when they emigrated, having obtained permission of the king to come here, and being never commanded to return into the realm, had a clear right to have erected in this wilderness a British constitution, or a perfect democracy, or any other form of government they saw fit. They, indeed, while they lived, could not have taken arms against the King of England, without violating their allegiance; but their children would not have been born within the king's allegiance, would not have been natural subjects, and consequently not entitled to protection, or bound to the king.

Massachusettensis seems possessed of these ideas, and attempts in the most awkward manner to get rid of them. He is conscious that America must be a part of the realm, before it can be bound by the authority of parliament; and, therefore, is obliged to suggest that we are annexed to the realm, and to endeavor to confuse himself and his readers, by confounding the realm with the empire and dominions.

But will any man soberly contend, that America was ever annexed to the realm? to what realm? When New England was settled, there was a realm of England, a realm of Scotland, and a realm of Ireland. To which of these three realms was New England annexed? To the realm of England, it will be said. But by what law? No territory could be annexed to the realm of England but by an act of parliament. Acts of parliament have been passed to annex Wales, &c. &c. to the realm; but none ever passed to annex America. But if New England was annexed to the realm of England, how came she annexed to the realm of, or kingdom of Great Britain? The two realms of England and Scotland were, by the act of union, incorporated into one kingdom, by the name of Great Britain; but there is not one word about America in that act.

Besides, if America was annexed to the realm, or a part of the kingdom, every act of parliament that is made would extend to it, named or not named. But everybody knows, that every act of parliament, and every other record, constantly distinguishes between this kingdom and his majesty's other dominions. Will it be said that Ireland is annexed to the realm, or a part of the kingdom of Great Britain? Ireland is a distinct kingdom, or realm, by itself, notwithstanding British parliament claims a right of binding it in all cases, and exercises it in some. And even so, the Massachusetts is a realm, New York is a realm, Pennsylvania another realm, to all intents and purposes, as much as Ireland is, or England or Scotland ever were. The King of Great Britain is the sovereign of all these realms.

This writer says, "that in denying that the colonies are annexed to the realm, and subject to the authority of parliament, individuals and bodies of men subvert the fundamentals of government, deprive us of British liberties, and build up absolute monarchy in the colonies."

This is the first time that I ever heard or read that the colonies are annexed to the realm. It is utterly denied that they are, and that it is possible they should be, without an act of parliament and acts of the colonies. Such an act of parliament cannot be produced, nor any such law of any one colony. Therefore, as this writer builds the whole authority of parliament upon this fact, namely,—that the colonies are annexed to the realm, and as it is certain they never were so annexed, the consequence is, that his whole superstructure falls.

When he says, that they subvert the fundamentals of government, he begs the question. We say, that the contrary doctrines subvert the fundamentals of government. When he says, that they deprive us of British liberties, he begs the question again. We say, that the contrary doctrine deprives us of English liberties; as to British liberties, we scarcely know what they are, as the liberties of England and Scotland are not precisely the same to this day. English liberties are but certain rights of nature, reserved to the citizen by the English constitution, which rights cleaved to our ancestors when they crossed the Atlantic, and would have inhered in them if, instead of coming to New England, they had gone to Otaheite or Patagonia, even although they had taken no patent or charter from the king at all. These rights did not adhere to them the less, for their purchasing patents and charters, in which the king expressly stipulates with them, that they and their posterity should forever enjoy all those rights and liberties.

The human mind is not naturally the clearest atmosphere; but the clouds and vapors which have been raised in it by the artifices of temporal and spiritual tyrants, have made it impossible to see objects in it distinctly. Scarcely any thing is involved in more systematical obscurity than the rights of our ancestors, when they arrived in America. How, in common sense, came the dominions of King Philip, King Massachusetts, and twenty other sovereigns, independent princes here, to be within the allegiance of the Kings of England, James and Charles? America was no more within the allegiance of those princes, by the common law of England, or by the law of nature, than France and Spain were. Discovery, if that was incontestable, could give no title to the English king, by common law, or by the law of nature, to the lands, tenements, and hereditaments of the native Indians here. Our ancestors were sensible of this, and, therefore, honestly purchased their lands of the natives. They might have bought them to hold allodially, if they would.

But there were two ideas, which confused them, and have continued to confuse their posterity; one derived from the feudal, the other from the canon law. By the former of these systems, the prince, the general, was supposed to be sovereign lord of all the lands conquered by the soldiers in his army; and upon this principle, the King of England was considered in law as sovereign lord of all the land within the realm. If he had sent an army here to conquer King Massachusetts, and it had succeeded, he would have been sovereign lord of the land here upon these principles; but there was no rule of the common law that made the discovery of the country by a subject a title to that country in the prince. But conquest would not have annexed the country to the realm, nor have given any authority to the parliament. But there was another mist cast before the eyes of the English nation from another source. The pope claimed a sovereign propriety in, as well as authority over, the whole earth. As head of the Christian church, and vicar of God, he claimed this authority over all Christendom; and, in the same character, he claimed a right to all the countries and possessions of heathens and infidels; a right divine to exterminate and destroy them at his discretion, in order to propagate the Catholic faith. When King Henry VIII. and his parliament threw off the authority of the pope, stripped his holiness of his supremacy, and invested it in himself by an act of parliament, he and his courtiers seemed to think that all the rights of the holy see were transferred to him; and it was a union of these two, (the most impertinent and fantastical ideas that ever got into a human pericranium, namely,—that, as feudal sovereign and supreme head of the church together, a king of England had a right to all the land his subjects could find, not possessed by any Christian state or prince, though possessed by heathen or infidel nations,) which seems to have deluded the nation about the time of the settlement of the colonies. But none of these ideas gave or inferred any right in parliament, over the new countries conquered or discovered; and, therefore, denying that the colonies are a part of the realm, and that as such they are subject to parliament, by no means deprives us of English liberties. Nor does it "build up absolute monarchy in the colonies." For, admitting these notions of the common and feudal law to have been in full force, and that the king was absolute in America, when it was settled; yet he had a right to enter into a contract with his subjects, and stipulate that they should enjoy all the rights and liberties of Englishmen forever, in consideration of their undertaking to clear the wilderness, propagate Christianity, pay a fifth part of ore, &c. Such a contract as this has been made with all the colonies, royal governments, as well as charter ones. For the commissions to the governors contain the plan of the government, and the contract between the king and subject in the former, as much as the charters in the latter.

Indeed, this was the reasoning, and upon these feudal and *catholic* principles, in the time of some of the predecessors of Massachusettensis. This was the meaning of Dudley, when he asked, "Do you think that English liberties will follow you to the ends of the earth?" His meaning was, that English liberties were confined to the realm, and, out of that, the king was absolute. But this was not true; for an English king had no right to be absolute over Englishmen out of the realm, any more than in it; and they were released from their allegiance, as soon as he deprived them of their liberties.

But "our charters suppose regal authority in the grantor." True, they suppose it, whether there was any or not. "If that authority be derived from the British (he should have said English) crown, it presupposes this territory to have been a part of the British (he should have said English) dominion, and as such subject to the imperial sovereign." How can this writer show this authority to be derived from the English crown, including in the idea of it lords and commons? Is there the least color for such an authority, but in the popish and feudal ideas before mentioned? And do these popish and feudal ideas include parliament? Was parliament, were lords and commons, parts of the head of the church; or was parliament, that is, lords and commons, part of the sovereign feudatory? Never. But why was this authority derived from the English, any more than the Scottish or Irish crown? It is true, the land was to be held in socage, like the manor of East Greenwich; but this was compact, and it might have been as well to hold, as they held in Glasgow or Dublin.

But, says this writer, "if that authority was vested in the person of the king in a different capacity, the British constitution and laws are out of the question, and the king must be absolute as to us, as his prerogatives have never been limited." Not the prerogatives limited in our charters, when in every one of them all the rights of Englishmen are secured to us? Are not the rights of Englishmen sufficiently known? and are not the prerogatives of the king among those rights?

As to those colonies which are destitute of charters, the commissions to their governors have ever been considered as equivalent securities, both for property, jurisdiction, and privileges, with charters; and as to the power of the crown being absolute in those colonies, it is absolute nowhere. There is no fundamental or other law that makes a king of England absolute any-where, except in conquered countries; and an attempt to assume such a power, by the fundamental laws, forfeits the prince's right even to the limited crown.

As to "the charter governments reverting to absolute monarchy, as their charters may happen to be forfeited by the grantees not fulfilling the conditions of them," I answer, if they could be forfeited, and were actually forfeited, the only consequence would be, that the king would have no power over them at all. He would not be bound to protect the people, nor, that I can see, would the people here, who were born here, be, by any principle of common law, bound even to allegiance to the king. The connection would be broken between the crown and the natives of the country.

It has been a great dispute, whether charters granted within the realm can be forfeited at all. It was a question debated with infinite learning, in the case of the charter of London. It was adjudged forfeited in an arbitrary reign; but afterwards, after the revolution, it was declared in parliament not forfeited, and by an act of parliament made incapable of forfeiture. The charter of Massachusetts was declared forfeited too. So were other American charters. The Massachusetts alone were tame enough to give it up. But no American charter will ever be decreed forfeited again; or if any should, the decree will be regarded no more than a vote of the lower house of the Robinhood society. The court of chancery has no authority without the realm; by common law, surely it has none in America. What! the privileges of millions of Americans depend on the discretion of a lord chancellor? God forbid! The passivity of this colony in receiving the present charter in lieu of the first, is, in the opinion of some, the deepest stain upon its character. There is less to be said in excuse for it than the witchcraft, or hanging the Quakers. A vast party in the province were against it at the time, and thought themselves betrayed by their agent. It has been a warning to their posterity, and one principal motive with the people never to trust any agent with power to concede away their privileges again. It may as well be pretended that the people of Great Britain can forfeit their privileges, as the people of this province. If the contract of state is broken, the people and king of England must recur to nature. It is the same in this province. We shall never more submit to decrees in chancery, or acts of parliament, annihilating charters, or abridging English liberties.

Whether Massachusettensis was born, as a politician, in the year 1764, I know not; but he often writes as if he knew nothing of that period. In his attempt to trace the denial of the supreme authority of the parliament, he commits such mistakes as a man of age at that time ought to blush at. He says, that "when the Stamp Act was made, the authority of parliament to impose external taxes, or, in other words, to lay duties upon goods and merchandise, was admitted," and that when the Tea Act was made, "a new distinction was set up, that parliament had a right to lay duties upon merchandise for the purpose of regulating trade, but not for the purpose of raising a revenue." This is a total misapprehension of the declared opinions of people at those times. The authority of parliament to lay taxes for a revenue has been always generally denied. And their right to lay duties to regulate trade has been denied by many, who have ever contended that trade should be regulated only by prohibitions.

The act of parliament of the 4th George III., passed in the year 1764, was the first act of the British parliament that even was passed, in which the design of raising a revenue was expressed. Let Massachusettensis name any statute, before that, in which the word revenue is used, or the thought of raising a revenue is expressed. This act is entitled "an act for granting certain duties in the British colonies and plantations in America," &c. The word revenue, in the preamble of this act, instantly ran through the colonies, and rang an alarm, almost as much as if the design of forging chains for the colonists had been expressed in words. I have now before me a pamphlet, written and printed in the year 1764, entitled "The Sentiments of a British American," upon this act. How the idea of a revenue, though from an ac-

knowledged external tax, was relished in that time, may be read in the frontispiece of that pamphlet.

> Ergo quid refert mea
> Cui serviam? clitellas dum portem meas.—PHAEDRUS.

The first objection to this act, which was made in that pamphlet, by its
worthy author, OXENBRIDGE THACHER, who died a martyr to that anxiety
for his country which the conduct of the junto gave him, is this:—"that a
tax is thereby laid on several commodities, to be raised and levied in the
plantations, and to be remitted home to England. This is esteemed a grievance, inasmuch as the same are laid without the consent of the representatives
of the colonists. It is esteemed an essential British right, that no person shall
be subject to any tax, but what in person, or by his representative, he hath
a voice in laying." Here is a tax, unquestionably external, in the sense in
which that word is used in the distinction that is made by some between
external and internal taxes, and unquestionably laid in part for the regulation
of trade, yet called a grievance, and a violation of an essential British right,
in the year 1764, by one who was then at the head of the popular branch of
our constitution, and as well acquainted with the sense of his constituents as
any man living. And it is indisputable, that in those words he wrote the
almost universal sense of this colony.

There are so many egregious errors in point of fact, and respecting the
opinions of the people, in this writer, which it is difficult to impute to wilful
misrepresentation, that I sometimes think he is some smart young gentleman,
come up into life since this great controversy was opened; if not, he must
have conversed wholly with the junto, and they must have deceived him
respecting their own sentiments.

This writer sneers at the distinction between a right to lay the former
duty of a shilling on the pound of tea, and the right to lay the threepence.
But is there not a real difference between laying a duty to be paid in England
upon exportation, and to be paid in America upon importation? Is there not
a difference between parliament's laying on duties within their own realm,
where they have undoubted jurisdiction, and laying them out of their realm,
nay, laying them on in our realm, where we say they have no jurisdiction?
Let them lay on what duties they please in England, we have nothing to say
against that.

"Our patriots most heroically resolved to become independent states,
and flatly denied that parliament had a right to make any laws whatever, that
should be binding upon the colonies."

Our scribbler, more heroically still, is determined to show the world, that he has courage superior to all regard to modesty, justice, or truth. Our patriots have never determined or desired to be independent states, if a voluntary cession of a right to regulate their trade can make them dependent even on parliament; though they are clear in theory that, by the common law and the English constitution, parliament has no authority over them. None of the patriots of this province, of the present age, have ever denied that parliament has a right, from our voluntary cession, to make laws which shall bind the colonies, so far as their commerce extends.

"There is no possible medium between absolute independence and subjection to the authority of parliament." If this is true, it may be depended upon, that all North America are as fully convinced of their independence, their absolute independence, as they are of their own existence; and as fully determined to defend it at all hazards, as Great Britain is to defend her independence against foreign nations. But it is not true. An absolute independence on parliament, in all internal concerns and cases of taxation, is very compatible with an absolute dependence on it, in all cases of external commerce.

"He must be blind indeed, that cannot see our dearest interest in the latter, (that is, in an absolute subjection to the authority of parliament,) notwithstanding many pant after the former," (that is, absolute independence.) The man who is capable of writing, in cool blood, that our interest lies in an absolute subjection to parliament, is capable of writing or saying any thing for the sake of his pension. A legislature that has so often discovered a want of information concerning us and our country; a legislature interested to lay burdens upon us; a legislature, two branches of which, I mean the lords and commons, neither love nor fear us! Every American of fortune and common sense, must look upon his property to be sunk downright one half of its value, the moment such an absolute subjection to parliament is established.

That there are any who pant after "independence," (meaning by this word a new plan of government over all America, unconnected with the crown of England, or meaning by it an exemption from the power of parliament to regulate trade,) is as great a slander upon the province as ever was committed to writing. The patriots of this province desire nothing new; they wish only to keep their old privileges. They were, for one hundred and fifty years, allowed to tax themselves, and govern their internal concerns as they thought best. Parliament governed their trade as they thought fit. This plan they wish may continue forever. But it is honestly confessed, rather than become subject to the absolute authority of parliament in all cases of taxation and internal polity, they will be driven to throw off that of regulating trade.

"To deny the supreme authority of the state, is a high misdemeanor; to oppose it by force, an overt act of treason." True; and therefore, Massachusettensis, who denies the king represented by his governor, his majesty's council by charter, and house of representatives, to be the supreme authority of this province, has been guilty of a high misdemeanor; and those ministers, governors, and their instruments, who have brought a military force here, and employed it against that supreme authority, are guilty of —, and ought to be punished with —. I will be more mannerly than Massachusettensis.

"The realm of England is an appropriate term for the ancient realm of England, in contradistinction to Wales and other territories that have been annexed to it."

There are so many particulars in the case of Wales analogous to the case of America, that I must beg leave to enlarge upon it.

Wales was a little portion of the island of Great Britain, which the Saxons were never able to conquer. The Britons had reserved this tract of land to themselves, and subsisted wholly by pasturage among their mountains. Their princes, however, during the Norman period, and until the reign of King Edward I., did homage to the crown of England, as their feudal sovereign, in the same manner as the prince of one independent state in Europe frequently did to the sovereign of another. This little principality of shepherds and cowherds had, however, maintained its independence through long and bloody wars against the omnipotence of England, for eight hundred years. It is needless to enumerate the causes of the war between Lewellyn and Edward I. It is sufficient to say, that the Welsh prince refused to go to England to do homage, and Edward obtained a new aid of a fifteenth from his parliament, to march with a strong force into Wales. Edward was joined by David and Roderic, two brothers of Lewellyn, who made a strong party among the Welsh themselves, to assist and second the attempts to enslave their native country. The English monarch, however, with all these advantages, was afraid to put the valor of his enemies to a trial, and trusted to the *slow effects of famine* to subdue them. Their pasturage, with such an enemy in their country, could not subsist them, and Lewellyn at last submitted, and bound himself to pay a reparation of damages, to do homage to the crown of England, and almost to surrender his independence as a prince, by permitting all the other barons of Wales, excepting four, to swear fealty to the same crown. But fresh complaints soon arose. The English grew insolent on their bloodless victory, and oppressed the inhabitants; many insults were offered, which at last raised the indignation of the Welsh, so that they determined again to take arms, rather than bear any longer the oppression of the haughty victors. The war raged some time, until Edward summoned all his military tenants, and advanced with an army too powerful for the Welsh to resist. Lewellyn was at last surprised by Edward's General, Mortimer, and fighting at a great disadvantage, was slain, with two thousand of his men. David, who succeeded in the principality, maintained the war for some time, but at last was betrayed to the enemy, sent in chains to Shrewsbury, brought to a formal trial before the peers of England, and, although a sovereign prince, ordered by Edward to be hanged, drawn, and quartered, as a traitor, for defending by arms the liberties of his native country! All the Welsh nobility submitted to the conqueror. The laws of England, sheriffs, and other ministers of justice were established in that principality.

Now Wales was always part of the dominions of England. "Wales was always feudatory to the kingdom of England." It was always held of the crown of England, or the kingdom of England: that is, whoever was King of England had a right to homage, &c. from the Prince of Wales. But yet Wales was not parcel of the realm or kingdom, nor bound by the laws of England. I mention and insist upon this, because it shows that, although the colonies are bound to the crown of England; or, in other words, owe allegiance to whosoever is King of England; yet it does not follow that the colonies are a parcel of the realm or kingdom, and bound by its laws. As this is a point of great importance, I must beg pardon, however unentertaining it may be, to produce my authorities.

"Wales was always feudatory to the kingdom of England."*

Held of the crown, but not parcel;† and, therefore, the Kings of Wales did homage and swore fealty to Henry II. and John and Henry III.

And 11 Edward I. Upon the conquest of Lewellyn, Prince or King of Wales, that principality became a part of the dominion of the realm of England. And by the statute Walliae, 12 Edward I., it was annexed and united to the crown of England, *tanquam partem corporis ejusdem,* &c. Yet, if the statute Walliae, made at Rutland, 12 Edward I., was not an act of parliament, (as it seems that it was not,) the incorporation made thereby was only a union *jure feudali, et non jure proprietatis."*

"Wales, before the union with England, was governed by its proper laws," &c.

By these authorities it appears, that Wales was subject, by the feudal law,

---

* Comyn's Digest, vol. v. p. 626.
† Per Cook. 1 Roll. 247; 2 Roll. 29.

to the crown of England before the conquest of Lewellyn, but not subject to the laws of England; and indeed, after this conquest, Edward and his nobles did not seem to think it subject to the English parliament, but to the will of the king, as a conqueror of it in war. Accordingly, that instrument which is called *Statutum Walliae,* and to be found in the appendix to the statutes, although it was made by the advice of the peers, or officers of the army more properly, yet it never was passed as an act of parliament, but as an edict of the king. It begins, not in the style of an act of parliament: "*Edwardus Dei gratia Rex Angliae, Dominus Hyberniae, et Dux Aquitaniae, omnibus fidelibus suis, &c. in Wallia. Divina Providentia, quae in sui dispositione,* says he, *non fallitur, inter alia dispensationis suae munera, quibus nos et Regnum nostrum Angliae decorare dignata est, terram Walliae, cum incolis suis prius nobis* jure feudali *subjectam, jam sui gratia,* in proprietatis nostrae dominium, *obstaculis quibuscumque cessantibus, totaliter et cum integritate convertit,* et coronae regni praedicti, tanquam partem corporis ejusdem annexuit et univit."

Here is the most certain evidence,—1. That Wales was subject to the kings of England by the feudal law before the conquest, though not bound by any laws but their own. 2. That the conquest was considered, in that day, as conferring the property, as well as jurisdiction of Wales, to the English crown. 3. The conquest was considered as annexing and uniting Wales to the English crown, both in point of property and jurisdiction, as a part of one body. Yet, notwithstanding all this, parliament was not considered as acquiring any share in the government of Wales by this conquest. If, then, it should be admitted that the colonies are all annexed and united to the crown of England, it will not follow that lords and commons have any authority over them.

This *statutum Walliae,* as well as the whole case and history of that principality, is well worthy of the attention and study of Americans, because it abounds with evidence, that a country may be subject to the crown of England, without being subject to the lords and commons of that realm, which entirely overthrows the whole argument of Governor Hutchinson and of Massachusettensis, in support of the supreme authority of parliament over all the dominions of the imperial crown. "*Nos itaque,*" &c. says King Edward I., "*volentes praedictam terram, &c. sicut et caeteras ditioni nostrae subjectas, &c. sub debito regimine gubernari, et incolas seu habitatores terrarum illarum, qui alto et basso se submiserunt voluntati nostrae, et quos sic ad nostram recepimus voluntatem, certis legibus et consuetudinibus &c. tractari, leges et consuetudines partium illarum hactenus usitatas coram nobis et proceribus regni nostri fecimus recitari, quibus diligenter auditis, et plenius intellectis, quasdam ipsarum de concilio procerum praedictorum delevimus, quasdam permisimus, et quasdam correximus, et etiam quasdam alias adjiciendas et statuendas decrevimus, et eas &c. observari volumus in forma subscripta."*

And then goes on to prescribe and establish a whole code of laws for the principality, in the style of a sole legislature, and concludes:

"*Et ideo vobis mandamus, quod praemissa de cetero in omnibus firmiter observetis. Ita tamen quod quotiescunque, et quandocunque, et ubicunque, nobis placuerit, possimus praedicta statuta et eorum partes singulas declarare, interpretari, addere sive diminuere, pro nostrae libito voluntatis, et prout securitati nostrae et terrae nostrae praedictae viderimus expedire.*"

Here is then a conquered people submitting to a system of laws framed by the mere will of the conqueror, and agreeing to be forever governed by his mere will. This absolute monarch, then, might afterwards govern this country with or without the advice of his English lords and commons.

To show that Wales was held, before the conquest of Lewellyn, of the King of England, although governed by its own laws, hear Lord Coke, in his commentary on the statute of Westminster. "At this time, namely, in 3 Edward I., Lewellyn was a Prince or King of Wales, who held the *same of the King of England as his superior lord, and owed him liege homage, and fealty;* and this is proved by our act, namely, that the King of England was *superior dominus,* that is, sovereign lord of the kingdom or principality of Wales."

Lord Coke says, "Wales was sometime a realm, or kingdom, (realm, from the French word *royaume,* and both *a regno,*) and governed *per suas regulas;*" and afterwards, "but, *jure feodali,* the kingdom of Wales was holden of the *crown of England,* and thereby, as Bracton saith, was *sub potestate regis.* And so it continued until the eleventh year of King Edward I., when he subdued the Prince of Wales, rising against him, and executed him for treason. The next year, namely, in the twelfth year of King Edward I., by authority of parliament, it is declared thus, speaking in the person of the king, (as ancient statutes were wont to do) *Divina Providentia,*" &c. as in the statute *Walliae,* before recited. But here is an inaccuracy; for the *statutum Walliae* was not an act of parliament, but made by the king, with the advice of his officers of the army, by his sole authority, as the statute itself sufficiently shows. "Note," says Lord Coke, "divers monarchs hold their kingdoms of others *jure feodali,* as the Duke of Lombardy, Cicill, Naples, and Bohemia of the empire, Granado, Leons of Aragon, Navarre, Portugal of Castile; and so others."

After this, the Welsh seem to have been fond of the English laws, and desirous of being incorporated into the realm, to be represented in parliament, and enjoy all the rights of Englishmen, as well as to be bound by the English laws. But kings were so fond of governing this principality by their discretion alone, that they never could obtain these blessings until the reign of Henry VIII., and then they only could obtain a statute which enabled the king to alter their laws at his pleasure. They did, indeed, obtain, in the 15 Edward II., a writ to call twenty-four members to the parliament at York from South Wales, and twenty-four from North Wales; and again, in the 20 Edward II., the like number of forty-eight members for Wales, at the parliament of Westminster. But Lord Coke tells us, "that this wise and warlike nation was, long after the *statutum Walliae,* not satisfied nor contented, and especially for that they truly and constantly took part with their rightful sovereign and liege lord, King Richard II.; in revenge whereof, they had many severe and invective laws made against them in the reigns of Henry IV., Henry V., &c., all which, as unjust, are repealed and abrogated. And, to say the truth, this nation was never in quiet, until King Henry VII., their own countryman, obtained the crown. And yet not so really reduced in his time as in the reign of his son, Henry VIII., in whose time, by certain just laws, made at the humble suit of the subjects of Wales, the principality and dominion of Wales was incorporated and united to the realm of England; and enacted that every one born in Wales should enjoy the liberties, rights, and laws of this realm, as any subjects naturally born within this realm should have and inherit, and that they should have knights of shires and burgesses of parliament." Yet we see they could not obtain any security for their liberties, for Lord Coke tells us, "in the act of 34 Henry VIII. it was enacted, that the king's most royal majesty should, from time to time, change, &c. all manner of things before in that act rehearsed, as to his most excellent wisdom and discretion should be thought convenient; and also to make laws and ordinances for the commonwealth of his said dominion of Wales at his majesty's pleasure. Yet for that the subjects of the dominion of Wales, &c. had lived in all dutiful subjection to the crown of England, &c., the said branch of the said statute of 34 Henry VIII. is repealed and made void, by 21 Jac. c. 10."

But if we look into the statute itself, of 27 Henry VIII. c. 26, we shall find the clearest proof, that being subject to the imperial crown of England did not entitle Welshmen to the liberties of England, nor make them subject to the laws of England. "Albeit the dominion, principality, and country of Wales *justly and righteously is, and ever hath been incorporated, annexed, united and subject to and under the imperial crown of this realm, as a very member and joint of the same,* wherefore the King's most royal majesty, of mere *droit,* and very right, is very head, king, lord, and ruler; yet notwithstanding, because that in the same country, principality and dominion, diverse *rights, usages, laws,* and customs, be far discrepant from the laws and customs of this realm, &c." Wherefore it is enacted by king, lords, and commons, "that his" (that is, the king's) "said country or dominion of Wales, shall be, stand, and continue forever from henceforth, incorporated, united, and annexed to and with this his realm of England, and that all and singular person and persons, born and to be born in the said principality, country, or dominion of Wales, shall have, enjoy, and inherit, all and singular freedoms, liberties, rights, privileges, and laws within this his realm, and other the king's dominions, as other the king's subjects naturally born within the same, have, enjoy, and inherit." Section 2 enacts that the laws of England shall be introduced and established in Wales, and that the laws, ordinances, and statutes of this realm of England forever, and none other, shall be used and practised forever thereafter, in the said dominion of Wales. The 27th section of this long statute enacts, that commissioners shall inquire into the laws and customs of Wales, and report to the king, who with his privy council are empowered to establish such of them as they should think proper. The twenty-eighth enacts that in all future parliaments *for this realm,* two knights for the shire of Monmouth, and one burgess for the town, shall be chosen, and allowed such fees as other knights and burgesses of parliament were allowed. Section twenty-nine enacts that one knight shall be elected for every shire within the country or dominion of Wales, and one burgess for every shire town, to serve in that and every future parliament to be holden for this realm. But by section thirty-six, the king is empowered to revoke, repeal, and abrogate that whole act, or any part of it, at any time within three years.

Upon this statute, let it be observed,—1. That the language of Massachusettensis, "imperial crown," is used in it; and Wales is affirmed to have *ever* been annexed and united to that imperial crown, as a very member and joint; which shows that being annexed to the imperial crown does not annex a country to the realm, or make it subject to the authority of parliament; because Wales certainly, before the conquest of Lewellyn, never was pretended to be so subject, nor afterwards ever pretended to be annexed to the realm at all, nor subject to the authority of parliament any otherwise than as the king claimed to be absolute in Wales, and therefore to make laws for it by his mere will, either with the advice of his proceres or without. 2. That Wales never was incorporated with the realm of England, until this statute was made, nor subject to any authority of English lords and commons. 3. That the king was so tenacious of his exclusive power over Wales, that he would not consent to this statute, without a clause in it to retain the power in his own hands of giving it what system of law he pleased. 4. That knights and burgesses, that is, representatives, were considered as *essential* and *fundamental* in the constitution of the new legislature which was to govern Wales. 5. That since this statute, the distinction between the realm of England and the realm of Wales has been abolished, and the realm of England, now and ever since, comprehends both; so that Massachusettensis is mistaken when he says, that the realm of England is an appropriate term for the ancient realm of England, in contradistinction from Wales, &c. 6. That this union and incorporation were made by the consent and upon the supplication of the people of Wales, as Lord Coke and many other authors inform us; so that here was an express contract between the two bodies of people. To these observations let me add a few questions:—

1. Was there ever any act of parliament, annexing, uniting, and consolidating any one of all the colonies to and with the realm of England or the kingdom of Great Britain?

2. If such an act of parliament should be made, would it, upon any principles of English laws and government, have any validity without the consent, petition, or supplication of the colonies?

3. Can such a union and incorporation ever be made, upon any principles of English laws and government, without admitting representatives for the colonies in the house of commons, and American lords into the house of peers?

4. Would not representatives in the house of commons, unless they were numerous in proportion to the numbers of people in America, be a snare rather than a blessing?

5. Would Britain ever agree to a proportionable number of American members; and if she would, could America support the expense of them?

6. Could American representatives possibly know the sense, the exigencies, &c. of their constituents, at such a distance, so perfectly as it is absolutely necessary legislators should know?

7. Could Americans ever come to the knowledge of the behavior of their members, so as to dismiss the unworthy?

8. Would Americans in general ever submit to septennial elections?

9. Have we not sufficient evidence, in the general frailty and depravity of human nature, and especially the experience we have had of Massachusettensis and the junto, that a deep, treacherous, plausible, corrupt minister would be able to seduce our members to betray us as fast as we could send them?

To return to Wales. In the statute of 34 and 35 Henry VIII. c. 26, we find a more complete system of laws and regulations for Wales. But the king is still tenacious of his absolute authority over it. It begins, "Our sovereign lord the king's majesty, of his tender zeal and affection, &c. towards his obedient subjects, &c. of Wales, &c. *hath devised and made* divers sundry good and necessary ordinances, which his majesty of his most abundant goodness *at the humble suit and petition of his said subjects of Wales,* is pleased and contented to be enacted by the assent of the lord spiritual and temporal, and the commons," &c.

Nevertheless, the king would not yet give up his unlimited power over Wales; for by the one hundred and nineteenth section of this statute, the king, &c., may at all times hereafter, from time to time, change, add, alter, order, minish, and reform, all manner of things afore rehearsed, as to his most excellent wisdom and discretion shall be thought convenient; and also to make laws and ordinances for the commonwealth and good quiet of his said dominion of Wales, and his subjects of the same, from time to time, at his majesty's pleasure.

And this last section was never repealed until the 21 Jac. 1, c. 10, s. 4.

From the conquest of Lewellyn to this statute of James, is near three hundred and fifty years, during all which time the Welsh were very fond of being incorporated, and enjoying the English laws; the English were desirous that they should be; yet the crown would never suffer it to be completely done, because it claimed an authority to rule it by discretion. It is conceived, therefore, that there cannot be a more complete and decisive proof of any thing, than this instance is that a country may be subject to the crown of England, the imperial crown, and yet not annexed to the realm, nor subject to the authority of parliament.

The word *crown,* like the word *throne,* is used in various figurative senses; sometimes it means the kingly office, the head of the commonwealth; but it does not always mean the political capacity of the king; much less does it include in the idea of it, lords and commons. It may as well be pretended that the house of commons includes or implies a king. Nay, it may as well be pretended that the mace includes the three branches of the legislature.

By the feudal law, a person or a country might be subject to a king, a feudal sovereign, three several ways.

1. It might be subject to his person; and in this case it would continue so subject, let him be where he would, in his dominions or without. 2. To his crown; and in this case subjection was due to whatsoever person or family wore that crown, and would follow it, whatever revolutions it underwent. 3. To his crown and realm of state; and in this case it was incorporated as one body with the principal kingdom; and if that was bound by a parliament, diet, or cortes, so was the other.

It is humbly conceived, that the subjection of the colonies by compact and law, is of the second sort.

Suffer me, my friends, to conclude by making my most respectful compliments to the gentlemen of the regiment of royal Welsh fusileers. In the celebration of their late festival, they discovered that they are not insensible to the feelings of a man for his native country. The most generous minds are the most exquisitely capable of this sentiment. Let me entreat them to recollect the history of their brave and intrepid countrymen, who struggled at least eleven hundred years for liberty. Let them compare the case of Wales with the case of America, and then lay their hands upon their hearts and say whether we can in justice be bound by all acts of parliament without being incorporated with the kingdom.

No. ix

MASSACHUSETTENSIS, in some of his writings, has advanced, that our allegiance is due to the political capacity of the king, and therefore involves in it obedience to the British parliament. Governor Hutchinson, in his memorable speech, laid down the same position. I have already shown, from the case of Wales, that this position is groundless, and that allegiance was due from the Welsh to the king, *jure feudali,* before the conquest of Lewellyn, and after that to the crown, until it was annexed to the realm, without being subject to acts of parliament any more than to acts of the king without parliament. I shall hereafter show from the case of Ireland, that subjection to the crown implies no obedience to parliament. But before I come to this, I must take notice of a pamphlet entitled "A Candid Examination of the Mutual Claims of Great Britain and the Colonies, with a Plan of Accommodation on Constitutional Principles." This author says,—"To him, (that is, the king,) in his representative capacity, and as supreme executor of the laws made by a joint power of him and others, the oaths of allegiance are taken;" and afterwards,—"Hence, these professions (that is, of allegiance) are not made to him either in his legislative or executive capacities; but yet, it seems, they are made to the king. And into this distinction, *which is nowhere to be found,* either in the constitution of the government, in reason, or common sense, the ignorant and thoughtless have been deluded ever since the passing of the Stamp Act; and they have rested satisfied with it, without the least examination." And, in page 9, he says,—"I do not mean to offend the inventors of this refined distinction, when I ask them, is this acknowledgment made to the king in his politic capacity as king of Great Britain? If so, it includes a promise of obedience to the British laws." There is no danger of this gentleman's giving offence to the inventors of this distinction; for they have been many centuries in their graves. This distinction is to be found everywhere,—in the case of Wales, Ireland, and elsewhere, as I shall show most abundantly before I have done. It is to be found in two of the greatest cases, and most deliberate and solemn judgments, that were ever passed. One of them is Calvin's case, which, as Lord Coke tells us, was as elaborately, substantially, and judiciously argued as he ever heard or read of any. After it had been argued in the court of king's bench by learned counsel, it was adjourned to the exchequer chamber, and there argued again, first by counsel on both sides, and then by the lord chancellor and all the twelve judges of England; and among these were the greatest men that Westminster Hall ever could boast. Ellesmere, Bacon, Hyde, Hobart, Crook, and Coke, were all among them; and the chancellor and judges were unanimous in resolving. What says the book?* "Now, seeing the king hath but one person, and several capacities, and one politic capacity for the realm of England, and another for the realm of Scotland, it is necessary to be considered to which capacity *ligeance* is due. *And it was resolved* that it was due to the *natural person* of the king, (which is ever accompanied with the politic capacity, and the politic capacity as it were appropriated to the natural capacity,) and it is not due to the politic capacity only, that is, to the crown or kingdom distinct from his natural capacity." And further on, — "But it was clearly resolved by all the judges, that presently by the descent his majesty was completely and absolutely king, &c. and that coronation was but a royal ornament. . . . In the reign of Edward II., the Spencers, to cover the treason hatched in their hearts, invented this damnable and damned opinion, that homage and oath of allegiance was more by reason of the king's crown (that is, of his politic capacity) than by reason of the person of the king, upon which opinion they inferred execrable and detestable consequences." And afterwards, — "Where divers books and acts of parliament speak of the ligeance of England, &c., all these, speaking briefly in a vulgar manner, are to be understood of the ligeance due by the people of England to the king; for no man will affirm that England itself, taking it for the continent thereof, doth owe any ligeance or faith, or that *any faith or ligeance should be due to it;* but it manifestly appeareth that the ligeance or faith of the subject is *proprium quarto modo* to the king, *omni, soli, et semper.* And oftentimes in the reports of our book cases, and in acts of parliament also, the crown or kingdom is taken for the king himself, &c. . . . Tenure *in capite* is a tenure of the crown, and is a *seigniorie in grosse,* that is, of the person of the king." And afterwards, — "For special purposes *the law makes him a body politic, immortal and invisible, whereunto our allegiance cannot appertain.*" I beg leave to observe here that these words in the foregoing adjudication, that "the natural person of the king is ever accompanied with the politic capacity, and the politic capacity

* 7 Rep. 19.

as it were appropriated to the natural capacity," neither imply nor infer allegiance or subjection to the politic capacity; because in the case of King James I. his natural person was "accompanied" with three politic capacities at least, as king of England, Scotland, and Ireland; yet the allegiance of an Englishman to him did not imply or infer subjection to his politic capacity as king of Scotland.

Another place in which this distinction is to be found is in Moore's Reports.* "The case of the union of the realm of Scotland with England." And this deliberation, I hope, was solemn enough. This distinction was agreed on by commissioners of the English lords and commons, in a conference with commissioners of the Scottish parliament, and after many arguments and consultations by the lord chancellor and all the judges, and afterwards adopted by the lords and commons of both nations. "The judges answered with one assent," says the book, "that allegiance and laws were not of equiparation, for six causes;" the sixth and last of which is, "allegiance followeth the *natural person,* not the politic. . . If the king go out of England, with a company of his servants, allegiance remaineth among his subjects and servants, although he be out of his own realm, *whereto his laws are confined,* &c.; . . . and to prove the allegiance to be tied to the body natural of the king, not to the body politic, the Lord Coke cited the phrases of divers statutes, &c. And to prove that allegiance extended further than the laws national, they (the judges) showed, that every king of diverse kingdoms, or dukedoms, is to command every people to defend any of his kingdoms, without respect of that nation where he is born; as, if the king of Spain be invaded in Portugal, he may levy for defence of Portugal armies out of Spain, Naples, Castile, Milan, Flanders, and the like; as a thing incident to the allegiance of all his subjects, to join together in defence of any one of his territories, without respect of extent of the laws of that nation where he was born; whereby it manifestly appeareth that allegiance followeth the natural person of the king, and is not tied to the body politic respectively in every kingdom." There is one observation, not immediately to the present point, but so connected with our controversy that it ought not be overlooked. "For the matter of the great seal, the judges showed, that the seal was alterable by the king at his pleasure, and he might make one seal for both kingdoms; for seals, coin, and leagues are of absolute prerogative to the king without parliament, not restrained to any assent of the people. But for further resolution of this point, how far the great seal doth command out of England, they made this distinction, that the great seal was current for remedials, which

---

* Page 790.

groweth upon complaint of the subjects, and thereupon writs are addressed under the great seal of England, which writs are limited, their precinct to be within the places of the jurisdiction of the court that must give the redress of the wrong. And therefore writs are not to go into Ireland, nor the Isles, nor Wales, nor the counties palatine, because the king's courts here have not power to hold plea of lands or things there. But the great seal hath a power preceptory to the person, which power extendeth to any place where the person may be found." Ludlow's case, &c. who "being at Rome, a commandment under the great seal was sent to him to return. So, Bertie's case in Queen Mary's time, and Inglefield's case in Queen Elizabeth's, the privy seal went to command them to return into the realm; and for not coming, their lands were seized," &c. But to return to the point: "And as to the objection," says the book, "that none can be born a natural subject of two kingdoms, they denied that absolutely; for although locally he can be born but in one, yet effectually the allegiance of the king extending to both, his birthright shall extend to both." And afterwards,—"But that his kingly power extendeth to divers nations and kingdoms, all owe him equal subjection, and are equally born to the benefit of his protection; and although he is to govern them by *their distinct laws,* yet any one of the people coming into the other, is to have the benefit of the laws, wheresoever he cometh; . . . but living in one, or for his livelihood in one, he is not to be taxed in the other; because laws ordain taxes, impositions, and charges, as a discipline of subjection particularized to every particular nation." Another place where this distinction is to be found is in Foster's Crown Law. "There have been writers who have carried the notion of natural, perpetual, unalienable allegiance much farther than the subject of this discourse will lead me. They say, very truly, that it is due to the *person* of the king, &c. . . It is undoubtedly due to the person of the king; but in that respect natural allegiance differeth nothing from that we call local. For allegiance, considered in every light, is alike due to the person of the king, and is paid, and in the nature of things must be constantly paid, to that prince who, for the time being, is in the actual and full possession of the regal dignity."

Indeed, allegiance to a sovereign lord is nothing more than fealty to a subordinate lord, and in neither case has any relation to or connection with laws or parliaments, lords or commons. There was a reciprocal confidence between the lord and vassal. The lord was to protect the vassal in the enjoyment of his land. The vassal was to be faithful to his lord, and defend him against his enemies. This obligation, on the part of the vassal, was his fealty, *fidelitas.* The oath of fealty, by the feudal law, to be taken by the vassal or tenant, is nearly in the very words of the ancient oath of allegiance. But neither fealty, allegiance, or the oath of either implied any thing about laws, parliaments, lords, or commons.

The fealty and allegiance of Americans, then, is undoubtedly due to the person of King George III., whom God long preserve and prosper. It is due to him in his natural person, as that natural person is intituled to the crown, the kingly office, the royal dignity of the realm of England. And it becomes due to his natural person because he is intituled to that office. And because, by the charters, and other express and implied contracts made between the Americans and the kings of England, they have bound themselves to fealty and allegiance to the natural person of that prince, who shall rightfully hold the kingly office in England, and no otherwise.

"With us, in England," says Blackstone, "it becoming a settled principle of tenure, that all lands in the kingdom are holden of the king, as their sovereign and lord paramount, &c. the oath of allegiance was necessarily confined to the person of the king alone. By an easy analogy, the term of allegiance was soon brought to signify all other engagements which are due from subjects, as well as those duties which were simply and merely territorial. And the oath of allegiance, as administered for upwards of six hundred years, contained a promise 'to be true and faithful to the king and his heirs, and truth and faith to bear of life and limb and terrene honor, and not to know or hear of any ill or damage intended him, without defending him therefrom.' But at the revolution, the terms of this oath being thought, perhaps, to favor too much the notion of non-resistance, the present form was introduced by the convention parliament, which is more general and indeterminate than the former, the subject only promising 'that he will be faithful, and bear true allegiance to the king,' without mentioning 'his heirs,' or specifying in the least wherein that allegiance consists."

Thus, I think that all the authorities in law coincide exactly with the observation which I have heretofore made upon the case of Wales, and show that subjection to a king of England does not necessarily imply subjection to the crown of England; and that subjection to the crown of England does not imply subjection to the parliament of England; for allegiance is due to the person of the king, and to that alone, in all three cases; that is, whether we are subject to his parliament and crown, as well as his person, as the people in England are; whether we are subject to his crown and person, without parliament, as the Welsh were after the conquest of Lewellyn and before the union; or as the Irish were after the conquest and before Poyning's law; or whether we are subject to his person alone, as the Scots were to the King of England, after the accession of James I., being not at all subject to the parliament or crown of England.

We do not admit any binding authority in the decisions and adjudications of the court of king's bench or common pleas, or the court of chancery, over America; but we quote them as the opinions of learned men. In these we find a distinction between a country conquered and a country discovered. Conquest, they say, gives the crown an absolute power; discovery only gives the subject a right to all the laws of England. They add, that all the laws of England are in force there. I confess I do not see the reason of this. There are several cases in books of law which may be properly thrown before the public. I am no more of a lawyer than Massachusettensis, but have taken his advice, and conversed with many lawyers upon our subject, some honest, some dishonest, some living, some dead, and am willing to lay before you what I have learned from all of them. In Salkeld, 411, the case of Blankard and Galdy: "In debt on a bond, the defendant prayed oyer of the condition, and pleaded the statute E. 6, against buying offices concerning the administration of justice; and averred, that this bond was given for the purchase of the office of provost-marshal in Jamaica, and that it concerned the administration of justice, and *that Jamaica is part of the revenue and possessions of the crown of England.* The plaintiff replied, that Jamaica is an island *beyond the seas,* which was conquered from the Indians and Spaniards in Queen Elizabeth's time, and the inhabitants are governed by their own laws, and not by the laws of England. The defendant rejoined, that, before such conquest, they were governed by their own laws; but since that, by the laws of England. Shower argued for the plaintiff, that, on a judgment in Jamaica, no writ of error lies here, but only an appeal to the council; *and as they are not represented in our parliament, so they are not bound by our statutes,* unless specially named.* Pemberton, contra, argued that, *by the conquest of a nation, its liberties, rights, and properties are quite lost;* that by consequence, their laws are lost too, for the law is but the rule and guard of the other; those that conquer cannot, by their victory, lose their laws and become subject to others.† That error lies here upon a judgment in Jamaica, which could not be, if they were not under the same law. Et per Holt, C. J. and Cur. 1st. In case of an uninhabited country, newly found out by English subjects, all laws in force in England are in force there; so it seemed to be agreed. 2. Jamaica being conquered, and not pleaded to be parcel of the kingdom of England, but part of the possessions and revenue of the crown of England, the laws of England did not take place there, until declared so by the conqueror or his successors. The Isle of Man and Ireland are part of the *possessions* of the crown

* And. 115.
† Vaugh. 405.

of England, yet retain their ancient laws; that, in Davis, 36, it is not pretended that the custom of tanistry was determined by the conquest of Ireland, but by the new settlement made there after the conquest; that it was impossible the laws of this nation, by mere conquest, without more, should take place in a conquered country; because, for a time, there must want officers, without which our laws can have no force; that if our law did take place, yet they, in Jamaica, having power to make new laws, our general laws may be altered by theirs in particulars; also, they held that in case of an infidel country, their laws, by conquest, do not entirely cease, but only such as are against the law of God; and that in such cases, where the laws are rejected or silent, the conquered country shall be governed according to the rule of natural equity. Judgment *pro quer'.*"

Upon this case I beg leave to make a few observations:—

1. That Shower's reasoning, that we are not bound by statutes, because not represented in parliament, is universal, and, therefore, his exception, "unless specially named," although it is taken from analogy to the case of Ireland, by Lord Coke and others, yet is not taken from the common law, but is merely arbitrary and groundless, as applied to us; because, if the want of representation could be supplied by "expressly naming" a country, the right of representation might be rendered null and nugatory. But of this, more another time.

2. That, by the opinion of Holt and the whole court, the laws of England, common and statute, are in force in a vacant country, discovered by Englishmen. But America was not a vacant country; it was full of inhabitants; our ancestors purchased the land; but, if it had been vacant, his lordship has not shown us any authority at common law, that the laws of England would have been in force there. On the contrary, by that law, it is clear they did not extend beyond seas, and therefore could not be binding there, any further than the free will of the discoverers should make them. The discoverers had a right by nature to set up those laws if they liked them, or any others that pleased them better, provided they were not inconsistent with their allegiance to the king.

3. The court held, that a country must be parcel of the kingdom of England, before the laws of England could take place there; which seems to be inconsistent with what is said before, because discovery of a vacant country does not make it parcel of the kingdom of England, which shows that the court, when they said, that all laws in *force* in England are in *force* in the discovered country, meant no more than that the discoverers had a right to all such laws, if they chose to adopt them.

4. The idea of the court, in this case, is exactly conformable to, if not

taken from, the case of Wales. They consider a conquered country as Edward I. and his successors did Wales, as by the conquest annexed to the crown, as an absolute property, possession, or revenue, and, therefore, to be disposed of at its will; not entitled to the laws of England, although bound to be governed by the king's will, in parliament or out of it, as he pleased.

5. The Isle of Man and Ireland are considered, like Wales, as conquered countries, and part of the possessions (by which they mean property or revenue) of the crown of England, yet have been allowed by the king's will to retain their ancient laws.

6. That the case of America differs totally from the case of Wales, Ireland, Man, or any other case which is known at common law or in English history. There is no one precedent in point in any English records, and, therefore, it can be determined only by eternal reason and the law of nature. But yet that the analogy of all these cases of Ireland, Wales, Man, Chester, Durham, Lancaster, &c. clearly concur with the dictates of reason and nature, that Americans are entitled to all the liberties of Englishmen, and that they are not bound by any acts of parliament whatever, by any law known in English records or history, excepting those for the regulation of trade, which they have consented to and acquiesced in.

7. To these let me add, that, as the laws of England and the authority of parliament were by common law confined to the realm and within the four seas, so was the force of the great seal of England. "The great seal of England is appropriated to England, and what is done under it has relation to England, and to no other place."* So that the king, by common law, had no authority to create peers or governments, or any thing out of the realm, by his great seal; and, therefore, our charters and commissions to governors, being under the great seal, gives us no more authority, nor binds us to any other duties, than if they had been given under the privy seal, or without any seal at all. Their binding force, both upon the crown and us, is wholly from compact and the law of nature.

There is another case in which the same sentiments are preserved.† "It was said by the master of the rolls to have been determined by the lords of the privy council, upon an appeal to the king in council from the foreign plantations; 1st. That if there be a new and uninhabited country, found out by English subjects, as the law is the birthright of every subject, so, wherever they go, they carry their laws with them, and, therefore, such new found country is to be governed by the laws of England; though after such country

---

* Salkeld, 510.

† It is in 2 P. Williams, 75, Memorandum, 9th August, 1722.

is inhabited by the English, acts of parliament made in England, without naming the foreign plantations, will not bind them; for which reason it has been determined, that the statute of frauds and perjuries, which requires three witnesses, and that these should subscribe in the testator's presence in the case of a devise of land, does not bind Barbadoes; but that, 2dly. Where the King of England conquers a country, it is a different consideration; for there the conqueror, by saving the lives of the people conquered, gains a right and property in such people! In consequence of which, he may impose upon them what laws he pleases; but, 3dly. Until such laws, given by the conquering prince, the laws and customs of the conquered country shall hold place; unless where these are contrary to our religion, or enact any thing that is *malum in se,* or are silent; for in all such cases the laws of the conquering country shall prevail."

No. x

GIVE ME LEAVE, now, to descend from these general matters to Massachusettensis. He says, "Ireland, who has perhaps the greatest possible subordinate legislature, and sends no members to the British parliament, is bound by its acts when expressly named." But if we are to consider what ought to be, as well as what is, why should Ireland have the greatest possible subordinate legislature? Is Ireland more numerous and more important to what is called the British empire than America? Subordinate as the Irish legislature is said to be, and a conquered country, as undoubtedly it is, the parliament of Great Britain, although they claim a power to bind Ireland by statutes, have never laid one farthing of tax upon it. They knew it would occasion resistance if they should. But the authority of parliament to bind Ireland at all, if it has any, is founded upon entirely a different principle from any that takes place in the case of America. It is founded on the consent and compact of the Irish by Poyning's law to be so governed, if it have any foundation at all; and this consent was given, and compact made, in consequence of a conquest.

In the reign of Henry II. of England, there were five distinct sovereignties in Ireland,—Munster, Leinster, Meath, Ulster, and Connaught, besides several small tribes. As the prince of any one of these petty states took the lead in war, he seemed to act, for the time being, as monarch of the island. About the year 1172, Roderic O'Connor, King of Connaught, was advanced to this preëminence. Henry had long cast a wishful eye upon Ireland; and now, partly to divert his subjects from the thoughts of Becket's murder, partly to appease the wrath of the pope for the same event, and partly to gratify his own ambition, he lays hold of a pretence, that the Irish had taken some natives of England and sold them for slaves, and applies to the pope for license to invade that island. Adrian III., an Englishman by birth, who was then pontiff, and very clearly convinced in his own mind of his right to dispose of kingdoms and empires, was easily persuaded, by the prospect of Peter's pence, to act as emperor of the world, and make an addition to his ghostly jurisdiction of an island which, though converted to Christianity, had never acknowledged any subjection to the see of Rome. He issued a bull, premising that Henry had ever shown an anxious care to enlarge the church, and increase the saints on earth and in heaven; that his design upon Ireland proceeded from the same pious motives; that his application to the holy see was a sure earnest of success; that it was a point incontestable, that all Christian kingdoms belonged to the patrimony of St. Peter; that it was his duty to sow among them the seeds of the gospel, which might fructify to their eternal salvation. He exhorts Henry to invade Ireland, exterminate the vices of the natives, and oblige them to pay yearly, from every house, a penny to the see of Rome; gives him full right and entire authority over the whole island; and commands all to obey him as their sovereign.

Macmorrogh, a licentious scoundrel, who was king of Leinster, and had been driven from his kingdom for his tyranny by his own subjects, in conjunction with Ororic, king of Meath, who made war upon him for committing a rape upon his queen, applied to Henry for assistance to restore him, and promised to hold his kingdom in vassalage of the crown of England. Henry accepted the offer, and engaged in the enterprise. It is unnecessary to recapitulate all the intrigues of Henry, to divide the Irish kingdoms among themselves, and set one against another, which are as curious as those of Edward I. to divide the kingdom of Wales, and play Lewellyn's brothers against him, or as those of the ministry, and our junto, to divide the American colonies, who have more sense than to be divided. It is sufficient to say, that Henry's expeditions terminated, altogether by means of those divisions among the Irish, in the total conquest of Ireland, and its annexation forever to the English crown. By the annexation of all Ireland to the English crown, I mean that all the princes and petty sovereigns of Ireland agreed to become vassals of the English crown. But what was the consequence of this? The same consequence was drawn, by the kings of England in this case, as had been drawn in the case of Wales after the conquest of Lewellyn; namely,— that Ireland was become part of the *property, possession,* or *revenue* of the English crown, and that its authority over it was absolute and without control.

That matter must be traced from step to step. The First monument we find in English records concerning Ireland, is a mere *rescriptum principis,* entitled *statutum Hiberniae de coheredibus,* 14 Hen. III. A.D. 1229. "In the old abridgment, Title, Homage, this is said not to be a statute."* Mr. Cay very properly observes, that it is not an act of parliament.† In this rescript, the king informs certain *milites,* (adventurers, probably, in the conquest of Ireland, or their descendants,) who had doubts how lands holden by knights' service, descending to copartners within age, should be divided,—what is the law and custom in England with regard to this.

But the record itself shows it to be a royal rescript only. "*Rex dilecto et fideli suo Gerardo fil' Mauricii Justic' suo Hiberniae salutem. Quia tales milites, de partibus Hiberniae nuper ad nos accedentes, nobis ostenderunt, quod, &c. Et a nobis petierunt, inde certiorari qualiter in regno nostro Angliae, in casu consimili, hactenus usitatum sit, &c.*" He then goes on, and certifies what the law in England was, and then concludes:—"*Et ideo vobis mandamus, quod praedictas consuetudines in hoc casu, quas in regno nostro Angliae habemus, ut praedictum est, in terra nostra Hiberniae proclamari et firmiter teneri, fac, &c.*"

Here again we find the king conducting himself exactly as Edward I. did in Wales, after the conquest of Wales. Ireland had now been annexed to the English crown many years, yet parliament was not allowed to have obtained any jurisdiction over it; and Henry ordained laws for it by his sole and absolute authority, as Edward I. did by the statute of Wales. Another incontestable proof that annexing a country to the crown of England does not annex it to the realm, or subject it to parliament. But we shall find innumerable proofs of this.

Another incontestable proof of this, is the *Ordinatio pro statu Hiberniae* made 17 Edward I. 1288.

This is an ordinance made by the king, by advice of his council, for the government of Ireland. "Edward, by the grace of God, King of England, Lord of Ireland, &c., to all those who shall see or hear these letters, doth send salutation." He then goes on, and ordains many regulations, among which the seventh chapter is,—"That none of our officers shall receive an original writ pleadable at the common law, but such as be sealed by the great seal of Ireland," &c. This ordinance concludes,—"In witness whereof, we have caused these our letters-patents to be made. Dated at Nottingham, 24th November, 17th year of our reign."

This law, if it was passed in parliament, was never considered to have any more binding force than if it had been made only by the king. By Poyning's law, indeed, in the reign of Henry VII., all precedent English

---

* *Vide* Ruffhead's *Statutes at Large,* v. i. 15.
† *Vide* Barrington's *Observations on the Statutes,* p. 34.

statutes are made to bind in Ireland, and this among the rest; but until Poyning's law it had no validity as an act of parliament, and was never executed but in the English pale; for, notwithstanding all that is said of the total conquest by Henry II., yet it did not extend much beyond the neighborhood of Dublin, and the conqueror could not enforce his laws and regulations much further.

"There is a note on the roll of 21 Edward I. in these words:—'*Et memorandum quod istud statutum, de verbo ad verbum, missum fuit in Hiberniam, teste rege apud Kenynton, 14 die Augusti, anno regni sui vivesimo septimo; et mandatum fuit Johanni Wogan, Justiciario Hiberniae, quod praedictum statutum per Hiberniam, in locis quibus expedire viderit, legi et publicè proclamari ac firmiter teneri faviat.*'

"This note most fully proves, that it was supposed the king, by his sole authority, could then introduce any English law; and will that authority be lessened by the concurrence of the two houses of parliament? . . . There is also an order of Charles I., in the third year of his reign, to the treasurers and chancellors of the exchequer, both of England and Ireland, by which they are directed to increase the duties upon Irish exports; which shows that it was then imagined the king could tax Ireland by his prerogative, without the intervention of parliament."*

Another instance to show, that the king, by his sole authority, whenever he pleased, made regulations for the government of Ireland, notwithstanding it was annexed and subject to the crown of England, is the *ordinatio facta pro statu terrae Hiberniae,* in the 31 Edward I., in the appendix to Ruffhead's statutes. This is an extensive code of laws, made for the government of the Irish church and state, by the king alone, without lords or commons. The kings "*volumus et firmiter praecipimus,*" governs and establishes all; and, among other things, he introduces, by the eighteenth chapter, the English laws for the regimen of persons of English extract settled in Ireland.

The next appearance of Ireland in the statutes of England is in the 34 Edward III. c. 17. This is no more than a concession of the king to his lords and commons of England, in these words: "*Item,* it is accorded, that all the merchants, as well aliens as denizens, may come into Ireland with their merchandises, and from thence freely to return with their merchandises and victuals, without fine or ransom to be taken of them, saving always to the king his ancient customs and other duties." And, by chapter 18: "*Item,* that the people of England, as well religious as other, which have their heritage and possessions in Ireland, may bring their corn, beasts, and victuals to the

* *Observations on the Statutes,* p. 127.

said land of Ireland, and from thence to re-carry their goods and merchandises into England, freely without impeachment, paying their customs and devoirs to the king."

All this is no more than an agreement between the king and his English subjects, lords, and commons, that there should be a free trade between the two islands and that one of them should be free for strangers. But it is no color of proof, that the king could not govern Ireland without his English lords and commons.

The 1 Henry V. c. 8: "All Irishmen and Irish clerks, beggars, shall depart this realm before the first day of November, except graduates, sergeants, &c." is explained by 1 Henry VI. c. 3, which shows "what sort of Irishmen only may come to dwell in England." It enacts, that all persons born in Ireland shall depart out of the realm of England, except a few; and that Irishmen shall not be principals of any hall, and that Irishmen shall bring testimonials from the lieutenant or justice of Ireland, that they are of the king's obeisance. By the 2d Henry VI. c. 8, "Irishmen resorting into the realm of England, shall put in surety for their good abearing."

Thus, I have cursorily mentioned every law made by the King of England, whether in parliament or out of it, for the government of Ireland, from the conquest of it by Henry II., in 1172, down to the reign of Henry VII., when an express contract was made between the two kingdoms, that Ireland should, for the future, be bound by English acts of parliament in which it should be specially named. This contract was made in 1495; so that, upon the whole, it appears beyond dispute, that, for more than three hundred years, though a conquered country, and annexed to the crown of England, yet, it was so far from being annexed to, or parcel of the realm, that the king's power was absolute there, and he might govern it without his English parliament, whose advice concerning it he was under no obligation to ask or pursue.

The contract I here alluded to, is what is called Poyning's law, the history of which is briefly this: Ireland revolted from England, or rather adhered to the partisans of the house of York; and Sir Edward Poyning was sent over about the year 1495, by King Henry VII., with very extensive powers *over the civil as well as military administration.* On his arrival, he made severe inquisition about the disaffected, and in particular attacked the Earls of Desmond and Kildare. The first stood upon the defensive, and eluded the power of the deputy; but Kildare was sent prisoner to England; *not to be executed, it seems, nor to be tried upon the statute of Henry VIII.,* but to be dismissed, as he actually was, to his own country, with marks of the King's esteem and favor; Henry judging that, at such a juncture, he should gain more by clemency and indulgence, than by rigor and severity. In this opinion, he sent a commissioner to Ireland with a formal amnesty in favor of Desmond and all his adherents, whom the tools of his ministers did not fail to call traitors and rebels, with as good a grace and as much benevolence, as Massachusettensis discovers.

Let me stop here and inquire, whether Lord North has more wisdom than Henry VII., or whether he took the hint from the history of Poyning, of sending General Gage, with his civil and military powers. If he did, he certainly did not imitate Henry, in his blustering menaces against certain "ringleaders and forerunners."

While Poyning resided in Ireland, he called a parliament, which is famous in history for the acts which it passed in favor of England and Englishmen settled in Ireland. By these, which are still called Poyning's laws, all the former laws of England were made to be of force in Ireland, and no bill can be introduced into the Irish parliament unless it previously receive the sanction of the English privy council; and by a construction, if not by the express words, of these laws, Ireland is still said to be bound by English statutes in which it is specially named. Here, then, let Massachusettensis pause, and observe the original of the notion, that countries might be bound by acts of parliament, if "specially named," though without the realm. Let him observe, too, that this notion is grounded entirely on the voluntary act, the free consent of the Irish nation, and an act of an Irish parliament, called Poyning's law. Let me ask him, has any colony in America ever made a Poyning's act? Have they ever consented to be bound by acts of parliament, if specially named? Have they ever acquiesced in, or implicitly consented to any acts of parliament, but such as are *bonâ fide* made for the regulation of trade? This idea of binding countries without the realm "by specially naming" them, is not an idea taken from the common law. There was no such principle, rule, or maxim, in that law. It must be by statute law, then, or none. In the case of Wales and Ireland, it was introduced by solemn compact, and established by statutes to which the Welsh and Irish were parties, and expressly consented. But in the case of America there is no such statute; and therefore Americans are bound by statutes in which they are "named," no more than by those in which they are not.

The principle upon which Ireland is bound by English statutes, in which it is named, is this, that being a conquered country, and subject to the mere will of the king, it voluntarily consented to be so bound. This appears in part already, and more fully in Blackstone, who tells us "that Ireland is a distinct, though a dependent, subordinate kingdom." But how came it dependent and subordinate? He tells us, that "King John, in the twelfth year of his reign, after the conquest, went into Ireland, carried over with him many able sages of the law; and there by his letters-patent, in right of the dominion of conquest, is said to have ordained and established that Ireland should be governed by the laws of England; which letters-patent Sir Edward Coke apprehends to have been there confirmed in parliament. . . . By the same rule, that no laws made in England between King John's time and Poyning's law were then binding in Ireland, it follows, that no acts of the English parliament, made since the tenth of Henry VII., do now bind the people of Ireland, unless specially named, or included under general words. And on the other hand, it is equally clear, that where Ireland is particularly named, or is included under general words, they are bound by such acts of parliament. For this follows from the very nature and constitution of a dependent state; dependence being very little else but an obligation to conform to the will or law of that superior person or state upon which the inferior depends. The original and true ground of this superiority in the present case, is what we usually call, though somewhat improperly, the right of conquest; a right allowed by the law of nations, if not by that of nature; but which in reason and civil policy can mean nothing more than that, in order to put an end to hostilities, a compact is either expressly or tacitly made between the conqueror and the conquered, that if they will acknowledge the victor for their master, he will treat them for the future as subjects, and not as enemies."

These are the principles upon which the dependence and subordination of Ireland are founded. Whether they are just or not is not necessary for us to inquire. The Irish nation have never been entirely convinced of their justice, have been ever discontented with them, and ripe and ready to dispute them. Their reasonings have been ever answered by the *ratio ultima* and *penultima* of the tories; and it requires, to this hour, no less than a standing army of twelve thousand men to confute them, as little as the British parliament exercises the right, which it claims, of binding them by statutes, and although it never once attempted or presumed to tax them, and although they are so greatly inferior to Britain in power, and so near in situation.

But thus much is certain, that none of these principles take place in the case of America. She never was conquered by Britain. She never consented to be a state dependent upon, or subordinate to the British parliament, excepting only in the regulation of her commerce; and therefore the reasonings of British writers upon the case of Ireland are not applicable to the case of the colonies, any more than those upon the case of Wales.

Thus have I rambled after Massachusettensis through Wales and Ireland, but have not reached my journey's end. I have yet to travel through Jersey, Guernsey, and I know not where. At present, I shall conclude with one observation. In the history of Ireland and Wales, though undoubtedly conquered countries, and under the very eye and arm of England, the extreme difficulty, the utter impracticability of governing a people who have any sense, spirit, or love of liberty, without incorporating them into the state, or allowing them in some other way equal privileges, may be clearly seen. Wales was forever revolting, for a thousand years, until it obtained that mighty blessing. Ireland has been frequently revolting, although the most essential power of a supreme legislature, that of imposing taxes, has never been exercised over them; and it cannot now be kept under but by force. And it would revolt forever if parliament should tax them. What kind of an opinion, then, must the ministry entertain of America,—when her distance is so great, her territory so extensive, her commerce so important; not a conquered country, but dearly purchased and defended; when her trade is so essential to the navy, the commerce, the revenue, the very existence of Great Britain as an independent state? They must think America inhabited by three millions of fools and cowards.

No. xi

THE CASES OF WALES AND IRELAND are not yet exhausted. They afford such irrefragable proofs, that there is a distinction between the crown and realm, and that a country may be annexed and subject to the former, and not to the latter, that they ought to be thoroughly studied and understood.

The more these cases, as well as those of Chester, Durham, Jersey, Guernsey, Calais, Gascogne, Guienne, &c. are examined, the more clearly it will appear, that there is no precedent in English records, no rule of common law, no provision in the English constitution, no policy in the English or British government, for the case of the colonies; and, therefore, that we derive our laws and government solely from our own compacts with Britain and her kings, and from the great Legislator of the universe.

We ought to be cautious of the inaccuracies of the greatest men, for these are apt to lead us astray. Lord Coke* says: "Wales was some time a kingdom, as it appeareth by 19 Henry VI. fol. 6, and by the act of parliament of 2 Henry V. cap. 6; but while it was a kingdom, the same was holden and within the fee of the King of England; and this appeareth by our books, Fleta, lib. 1, cap. 16; 1 Edward III. 14; 8 Edward III. 59; 13 Edward III., tit. Jurisdict.; 10 Henry IV. 6; Plow. Com. 368. And in this respect, in divers ancient charters, kings of old time styled themselves in several manners, as King

---

* 7 Rep. 21 b.

Edgar, Britanniae Basileus; Etheldredus, Totius Albionis Dei providentia Imperator; Edredus, magnae Britanniae Monarcha, which, among many others of like nature, I have seen. But, by the statute of 12 Edward I. Wales was united and incorporated into England, and made parcel of England in possession; and, therefore, it is ruled, in 7 Henry IV. fol. 13, that no protection doth lie, *quia moratur in Wallia,* because Wales is within the realm of England. And where it is recited, in the act of 27 Henry VIII., *that Wales was ever parcel of the realm of England,* it is true in this sense, namely,—that before 12 Edward I. it was parcel in tenure, and since, *it is parcel of the body of the realm.* And whosoever is born within the fee of the King of England, though it be in another kingdom, is a natural-born subject, and capable and inheritable of lands in England, as it appeareth in Plow. Com. 126. And, therefore, those that were born in Wales before 12 Edward I., whilst it was only holden of England, were capable and inheritable of lands in England."

Where my Lord Coke, or any other sage, shows us the ground on which his opinion stands, we can judge for ourselves, whether the ground is good and his opinion just. And, if we examine by this rule, we shall find in the foregoing words, several palpable inaccuracies of expression: 1. By the 12 E. I., (which is the *statutum Walliae* quoted by me before,) it is certain "that Wales was not united and incorporated into England, and made parcel of England." It was annexed and united to the crown of England only. It was done by the king's sole and absolute authority; not by an act of parliament, but by a mere *constitutio imperatoria,* and neither Edward I. nor any of his successors ever would relinquish the right of ruling it by mere will and discretion, until the reign of James I. 2. It is not recited in the 27 H. VIII., that Wales was ever parcel of the realm of England. The words of that statute are, "incorporated, annexed, united, and subject to, and under the imperial crown of this realm," which is a decisive proof, that a country may be annexed to the one without being united with the other. And this appears fully in Lord Coke himself:* "Ireland originally came to the kings of England by conquest; but who was the first conqueror thereof hath been a question. I have seen a charter made by King Edgar, in these words: *Ego Edgarus Anglorum Basileus, omniumque insularum oceani, quae Britanniam circumjacent, imperator et dominus, gratias ago ipsi Deo omnipotenti regi meo, qui meum imperium sic ampliavit et exaltavit super regnum patrum meorum, &c. Mihi concessit propitia divinitas, cum anglorum imperio omnia regna insularum oceani, &c., cum suis ferocissimis regibus usque Norvegiam, maximamque partem Hiberniae, cum sua nobilissima civitate de Dublina, Anglorum regno subjugare, quapropter et ego*

* 7 Rep. 22 b.

Christi gloriam et laudem in regno meo exaltare, et ejus servitium amplificare devotus disposui, &c. Yet for that it was wholly conquered in the reign of Henry II., the honor of the conquest of Ireland is attributed to him. That Ireland is a dominion separate and divided from England it is evident from our books, 20 H. VI. 8; Sir John Pilkington's case, 32 H. VI. 25; 20 Eliz.; Dyer, 360; Plow. Com. 360, and 2 R. 3, 12: *Hibernia habet parliamentum, et faciunt leges, et statuta nostra non ligant eos quia non mittunt milites ad parliamentum,* (which is to be understood, unless they be specially named,) *sed personae eorum sunt subjecti regis, sicut inhabitantes in Calesia, Gasconia, et Guyan.* Wherein it is to be observed, that the Irishman (as to his subjection) is compared to men born in Calice, Gascoin, and Guienne. Concerning their laws, *Ex rotulis petentium, de anno* 11 Regis H. III., there is a charter which that king made, beginning in these words: *Rex Baronibus, Militibus et omnibus libere tenentibus L. salutem. Satis, ut credimus vestra audivit discretio, quod quando bonae memoriae Johannes quondam rex Angliae, pater noster venit in Hiberniam, ipse duxit secum viros discretos et legis peritos, quorum communi consilio et ad instantiam Hibernensium statuit et praecepit leges Anglicanas in Hibernia, ita quod leges easdem in scripturas redactas reliquit sub sigillo suo ad saccarium Dublin.'* So, as now, the laws of England became the proper laws of Ireland; and, therefore, because they have parliaments holden there, whereat they have made diverse particular laws concerning that dominion, as it appeareth in 20 Henry VI. 8, and 20 Elizabeth, Dyer, 360, and for that they retain unto this day divers of their ancient customs, the book in 20 Henry VI. 8, holdeth that Ireland is governed by laws and customs separate and diverse from the laws of England. A voyage royal may be made into Ireland. *Vid.* 11 Henry IV. 7, and 7 Edward IV. 4, 27, which proveth it a distinct dominion. And in anno 33 Elizabeth, it was resolved by all the judges of England, in the case of O'Rurke, an Irishman, who had committed high treason in Ireland, that he, by the statute of 23 Henry VIII. c. 23, might be indicted, arraigned, and tried for the same in England, according to the purview of that statute; the words of which statute be, 'that all treasons, &c. committed by any person out of the realm of England, shall be from henceforth inquired of, &c.' And they all resolved, (as afterwards they did also in Sir John Perrot's case,) that Ireland was out of the realm of England, and that treasons committed there were to be tried within England by that statute. In the statute of 4 Henry VII. c. 24, of fines, provision is made for them that be out of this land; and it is holden in Plow. Com., in Stowell's case, 375, that he that is in Ireland is out of this land, and consequently within that proviso. Might not, then, the like plea be devised as well against any person born in Ireland as (this is against Calvin, that is, a *Postnatus*) in Scotland?

For the Irishman is born *extra ligeantiam regis, regni sui Angliae,* &c., which be *verba operativa* in the plea. But all men know that they are natural born subjects, and capable of and inheritable to lands in England."

I have been at the pains of transcribing this long passage, for the sake of a variety of important observations that may be made upon it.

1. That exuberance of proof that is in it, both that Ireland is annexed to the crown, and that it is not annexed to the realm, of England.

2. That the reasoning in the year book, that Ireland has a parliament, and makes laws, and our statutes do not bind them, because they do not send knights to parliament, is universal, and concludes against those statutes binding in which Ireland is specially named, as much as against those in which it is not; and therefore Lord Coke's parenthesis "(which is to be understood, unless they be specially named)" is wholly arbitrary and groundless, unless it goes upon the supposition that the king is absolute in Ireland, it being a conquered country, and so has power to bind it at his pleasure, by an act of parliament, or by an edict; or unless it goes upon the supposition of Blackstone, that there had been an express agreement and consent of the Irish nation to be bound by acts of the English parliament; and in either case it is not applicable even by analogy to America; because that is not a conquered country, and most certainly never consented to be bound by all acts of parliament in which it should be named.

3. That the instance, request, and consent of the Irish is stated, as a ground upon which King John, and his discreet law-sages, first established the laws of England in Ireland.

4. The resolution of the judges in the cases of O'Rurke and Perrot, is express, that Ireland was without the realm of England; and the late resolutions of both houses of parliament, and the late opinion of the judges, that Americans may be sent to England upon the same statute to be tried for treason, is also express that America is out of the realm of England. So that we see what is to become of us, my friends. When they want to get our money by taxing us, our privileges by annihilating our charters, and to screen those from punishment who shall murder us at their command, then we are told that we are within the realm; but when they want to draw, hang, and quarter us, for honestly defending those liberties which God and compact have given and secured to us,—oh! then we are clearly out of the realm.

5. In Stowell's case, it is resolved that Ireland is out of the land, that is, the land of England. The consequence is, that it was out of the reach and extent of the law of the land, that is, the common law. America surely is still further removed from that land, and therefore is without the jurisdiction of that law, which is called the law of the land in England. I think it must

appear by this time, that America is not parcel of the realm, state, kingdom, government, empire, or land of England, or Great Britain, in any sense which can make it subject universally to the supreme legislature of that island.

But for the sake of curiosity, and for the purpose of showing, that the consent even of a conquered people has always been carefully conciliated, I beg leave to look over Lord Coke's 4 Inst. p. 12. "After King Henry II." says he, "had conquered Ireland, he fitted and transcribed this *modus*," meaning the ancient treatise called *modus tenendi parliamentum,* which was rehearsed and declared before the conqueror at the time of the conquest, and by him approved for England, "into Ireland, in a parchment roll, for the holding of parliaments there, which, no doubt, H. II. did by advice of his judges, &c. This *modus,* &c. was, *anno* 6, H. IV., in the custody of Sir Christopher Preston, which roll H. IV., in the same year, *de assensu Johannis Talbot, Chevalier,* his lieutenant there, and of his council of Ireland, exemplified, &c."

Here we see the original of a parliament in Ireland, which is assigned as the cause or reason why Ireland is a distant kingdom from England; and in the same, 4 Inst. 349, we find more evidence that all this was done at the instance and request of the people in Ireland. Lord Coke says,—"H. II., the father of King John, did ordain and command at the instance of the Irish, that such laws as he had in England should be of force and observed in Ireland. Hereby Ireland, being of itself a distinct dominion, and no part of the kingdom of England, (as it directly appeareth by many authorities in Calvin's case,) was to have parliaments holden there, as England, &c." See the record, as quoted by Lord Coke in the same page, which shows that even this establishment of English laws was made *de communi omnium de Hibernia consensu.*

This whole chapter is well worth attending to; because the records quoted in it show how careful the ancients were to obtain the consent of the governed to all laws, though a conquered people, and the king absolute. Very unlike the minister of our era, who is for pulling down and building up the most sacred establishments of laws and government, without the least regard to the consent or good-will of Americans. There is one observation more of Lord Coke that deserves particular notice. "Sometimes the king of England called his nobles of Ireland to come to his parliament of England, &c.; and by special words the parliament of England may bind the subjects of Ireland;" and cites the record, 8 E. II., and subjoins "an excellent precedent to be followed whensoever any act of parliament shall be made in England concerning the state of Ireland, &c." By this, Lord Coke seems to intimate an opinion, that representatives had been, and ought to be, called from Ireland to the parliament of England, whenever it undertook to govern it by statutes in which it should be specially named.

After all, I believe there is no evidence of any express contract of the Irish nation, to be governed by the English parliament, and very little of an implied one; that the notion of binding it by acts in which it is expressly named is merely arbitrary; and that this nation, which has ever had many and great virtues, has been most grievously oppressed. And it is to this day so greatly injured and oppressed, that I wonder American committees of correspondence and congresses have not attended more to it than they have. Perhaps in some future time they may. But I am running beyond my line.

We must now turn to Burrow's Reports.* Lord Mansfield has many observations upon the case of Wales, which ought not to be overlooked. He says,—"Edward I. conceived the great design of annexing all other parts of the island of Great Britain to the realm of England. The better to effectuate his idea, as time should offer occasion, he maintained, 'that all the parts thereof not in his own hands or possession, were holden of his crown.' The consequence of this doctrine was, that by the feudal law supreme jurisdiction resulted to him, in right of his crown, as sovereign lord, in many cases which he might lay hold of; and when the said territories should come into his hands and possession, they would come back as parcel of the realm of England, from which (by fiction of law at least) they had been originally severed. This doctrine was literally true as to the counties palatine of Chester and Durham. But (no matter upon what foundation) he maintained that the principality of Wales was holden of the imperial crown of England: he treated the Prince of Wales as a rebellious vassal, subdued him, and took possession of the principality. Whereupon, on the fourth of December, in the ninth year of his reign, he issued a commission to inquire '*per quas leges, et per quas consuetudines antecessores nostri reges regere consueverant principem Walliae et barones Wallenses Walliae et pares suos et alios in priores et eorum pares, &c.*' If the principality was feudatory, the conclusion necessarily followed, that it was under the government of the king's laws, and the king's courts, in cases proper for them to interpose, though (like counties palatine) they had peculiar laws and customs, *jura regalia,* and complete jurisdiction at home." There was a writ at the same time issued to all his officers in Wales, to give information to the commissioners; and there were fourteen interrogatories, specifying the points to be inquired into. The statute of Rutland, 12 E. I., refers to this inquiry. By that statute he does not annex Wales to England, but recites it as a consequence of its coming into his hands:—"Divina pro-

* Vol. ii. 834. Rex *v.* Cowle.

videntia terram Walliae, prius nobis jure feodali subjectam, jam in proprietatis nostrae dominium convertit, et coronae regni Angliae, tanquam partem corporis ejusdem, annexuit et univit." The 27 H. VIII. c. 26, adheres to the same plan, and recites that "Wales ever hath been incorporated, annexed, united, and subject to, and under, the imperial crown of this realm, as a very member and joint of the same." Edward I., having succeeded as to Wales, maintained likewise that Scotland was holden of the crown of England. This opinion of the court was delivered by Lord Mansfield in the year 1759. In conformity to the *system* contained in these words, my Lord Mansfield and my Lord North, together with their little friends, Bernard and Hutchinson, have "conceived the great design of annexing" all North America "to the realm of England;" and "the better to effectuate this idea, they all maintain that North America is holden of the crown."

And, no matter upon what foundation, they all maintained, that America is dependent on the imperial crown and parliament of Great Britain; and they are all very eagerly desirous of treating the Americans as rebellious vassals, to subdue them, and take possession of their country. And when they do, no doubt America will come back as parcel of the realm of England, from which, by fiction of law at least, or by virtual representation, or by some other dream of a shadow of a shade, they had been originally severed.

But these noblemen and ignoblemen ought to have considered, that Americans understand the laws and the politics as well as themselves, and that there are six hundred thousand men in it, between sixteen and sixty years of age; and therefore it will be very difficult to chicane them out of their liberties by "fictions of law," and "no matter upon what foundation."

Methinks I hear his lordship, upon this occasion, in a soliloquy somewhat like this: "We are now in the midst of a war, which has been conducted with unexampled success and glory. We have conquered a great part, and shall soon complete the conquest of the French power in America. His majesty is near seventy years of age, and must soon yield to nature. The amiable, virtuous, and promising successor, educated under the care of my nearest friends, will be influenced by our advice. We must bring the war to a conclusion; for we have not the martial spirit and abilities of the great commoner; but we shall be obliged to leave upon the nation an immense debt. How shall we manage that? Why, I have seen letters from America, proposing that parliament should bring America to a closer dependence upon it, and representing that if it does not, she will fall a prey to some foreign power, or set up for herself. These hints may be improved, and a vast revenue drawn from that country and the East Indies, or at least the people here may be flattered and quieted with the hopes of it. It is the duty of a judge to declare law; but under this pretence, many, we know, have given law or made law, and none in all the records of Westminster Hall more than of late. Enough has been already made, if it is wisely improved by others, to overturn this constitution. Upon this occasion, I will accommodate my expressions to such a design upon America and Asia, and will so accommodate both law and fact, that they may hereafter be improved to admirable effect in promoting our design." This is all romance, no doubt, but it has as good a moral as most romances. For, first,—it is an utter mistake, that Edward I. conceived the great design of annexing all to England, as one state, under one legislature. He conceived the design of annexing Wales, &c. to his crown. He did not pretend that it was before subject to the crown, but to him. "*Nobis jure feodali*" are his words. And when he annexes it to his crown, he does it by an edict of his own, not an act of parliament; and he never did, in his whole life, allow that his parliament, that is, his lords and commons, had any authority over it, or that he was obliged to take or ask their advice, in any one instance, concerning the management of it, nor did any of his successors for centuries. It was not Edward I., but Henry VII., who first conceived the great design of annexing it to the realm; and by him and Henry VIII. it was done in part, but never completed until James I. There is a sense, indeed, in which annexing a territory to the crown is annexing it to the realm, as putting a crown upon a man's head is putting it on the man, but it does not make it a part of the man. Second,—his lordship mentions the statute of Rutland; but this was not an act of parliament, and therefore could not annex Wales to the realm, if the king had intended it; for it never was in the power of the king alone to annex a country to the realm. This cannot be done but by act of parliament. As to Edward's treating the Prince of Wales as a "rebellious vassal," this was arbitrary, and is spoken of by all historians as an infamous piece of tyranny.

Edward I. and Henry VIII. both considered Wales as the property and revenue of the crown, not as a part of the realm; and the expressions "*coronae regni Angliae, tanquam partem corporis ejusdem*," signified "as part of the same body," that is, of the same "crown," not "realm" or "kingdom;" and the expressions in 27 H. VIII., "under the imperial crown of this realm, as a very member and joint of the same," mean as a member and joint of the "imperial crown," not of the realm. For the whole history of the principality, the acts of kings, parliaments, and people show, that Wales never was entitled, by this annexation, to the laws of England, nor was bound to obey them. The case of Ireland is enough to prove that the crown and realm are not the same. For Ireland is certainly annexed to the crown of England, and it certainly is not annexed to the realm.

There is one paragraph in the foregoing words of Lord Mansfield, which was quoted by his admirer, Governor Hutchinson, in his dispute with the house, with a profound compliment; "He did not know a greater authority," &c. But let the authority be as great as it will, the doctrine will not bear the test.

"If the principality was feudatory, the conclusion necessarily follows, that it was under the government of the king's laws." Ireland is feudatory to the crown of England; but would not be subject to the king's English laws without its consent and compact. An estate may be feudatory to a lord, a country may be feudatory to a sovereign lord, upon all possible variety of conditions; it may be, only to render homage; it may be to render a rent; it may be to pay a tribute; if his lordship by *feudatory* means the original notion of feuds, it is true that the king, the general imperator, was absolute, and the tenant held his estate only at will, and the subject, not only his estate, but his person and life, at his will. But this notion of feuds had been relaxed in an infinite variety of degrees; in some, the estate is held at will, in others for life, in others for years, in others forever, to heirs, &c.; in some to be governed by the prince alone, in some by princes and nobles, and in some by prince, nobles, and commons, &c. So that being feudatory by no means proves that English lords and commons have any share in the government over us. As to counties palatine, these were not only holden of the king and crown, but were erected by express acts of parliament, and, therefore, were never exempted from the authority of parliament. The same parliament which erected the county palatine, and gave it its *jura regalia* and complete jurisdiction, might unmake it, and take away those regalia and jurisdiction. But American governments and constitutions were never erected by parliament; their *regalia* and jurisdiction were not given by parliament, and, therefore, parliament have no authority to take them away.

But, if the colonies are feudatory to the kings of England, and subject to the government of the king's laws, it is only to such laws as are made in their general assemblies, their provincial legislatures.

No. xii

WE NOW COME to Jersey and Guernsey, which Massachusettensis says, "are no part of the realm of England, nor are they represented in parliament, but are subject to its authority." A little knowledge of this subject will do us no harm; and, as soon as we shall acquire it, we shall be satisfied how these islands came to be subject to the authority of parliament. It is either upon the principle that the king is absolute there, and has a right to make laws for them by his mere will, and, therefore, may express his will by an act of parliament, or an edict, at his pleasure; or it is an usurpation. If it is an usurpation, it ought not to be a precedent for the colonies; but it ought to be reformed, and they ought to be incorporated into the realm by act of parliament and their own act. Their situation is no objection to this. Ours is an insurmountable obstacle.

Thus, we see, that in every instance which can be found, the observation proves to be true, that, by the common law, the laws of England, the authority of parliament, and the limits of the realm, were confined within seas. That the kings of England had frequently foreign dominions, some by conquest, some by marriage, and some by descent. But, in all those cases, the kings were either absolute in those dominions, or bound to govern them according to their own respective laws, and by their own legislative and executive councils. That the laws of England did not extend there, and the English parliament pretended no jurisdiction there, nor claimed any right to control the king in his government of those dominions. And, from this extensive survey of all the foregoing cases, there results a confirmation of what has been so often said, that there is no provision in the common law, in English precedents, in the English government or constitution, made for the case of the colonies. It is not a conquered, but a discovered country. It came not to the king by descent, but was explored by the settlers. It came not by marriage to the king, but was purchased by the settlers of the savages. It was not granted by the king of his grace, but was dearly, very dearly earned by the planters, in the labor, blood, and treasure which they expended to subdue it to cultivation. It stands upon no grounds, then, of law or policy, but what are found in the law of nature, and their express contracts in their charters, and their implied contracts in the commissions to governors and terms of settlement.

The cases of Chester and Durham, counties palatine within the realm, shall conclude this fatiguing ramble. Chester was an earldom and a county; and in the 21st year of King Richard II. A.D. 1397, it was, by an act of parliament, erected into a principality, and several castles and towns were annexed to it, saving to the king the rights of his crown. This was a county palatine, and had *jura regalia* before this erection of it into a principality. But the statute which made it a principality, was again repealed by 1 Henry IV. c. 3, and in 1399, by the 1 Henry IV. c. 18. Grievous complaints were made to the king, in parliament, of murders, manslaughters, robberies, batteries, riots, &c. done by people of the county of Chester in divers counties of England. For remedy of which it is enacted, "that if any person of the county of Chester commit any murder or felony in any place out of that county, process shall be made against him by the common law, till the exigent, in the county where such murder or felony was done; and if he flee into the county of Chester, and be outlawed and put in exigent for such murder or felony, the same outlawry or exigent shall be certified to the officers and ministers of the same county of Chester, and the same felon shall be taken, his lands and goods within that county shall be seized as forfeit into the hands of the prince, or of him that shall be lord of the same county of Chester for the time, and the king shall have the year and day, and the waste; and the other lands and goods of such felon, out of said county, shall remain wholly to the king, &c. as forfeit." And a similar provision, in case of battery or trespass, &c.

Considering the great seal of England and the process of the king's courts did not run into Chester, it was natural that malefactors should take refuge there, and escape punishment, and, therefore, a statute like this was of indispensable necessity; and, afterwards, in 1535, another statute was made, 27 Henry VIII. c. 5, for the making of justices of the peace within Chester, &c. It recites, "the king, considering the manifold robberies, murders, thefts, trespasses, riots, routs, embraceries, maintenances, oppressions, ruptures of his peace, &c., which have been daily done within his county palatine of Chester, &c., by reason that common justice hath not been indifferently ministered there, like and in such form as it is in other places of this his realm, by reason whereof the said crimes have remained unpunished; for redress whereof, and to the intent that one order of law should be had, the king is empowered to constitute justices of peace, quorum, and gaol delivery in Chester," &c.

By the 32 Henry VIII. c. 43, another act was made concerning the county palatine of Chester, for shire days.

These three acts soon excited discontent in Chester. They had enjoyed an exemption from the king's English courts, legislative and executive, and they had no representatives in the English parliament, and, therefore, they thought it a violation of their rights, to be subjected even to those three statutes, as reasonable and absolutely necessary as they appear to have been. And, accordingly, we find, in 1542, 34 and 35 Henry VIII. c. 13, a zealous petition to be represented in parliament, and an act was made for making of knights and burgesses within the county and city of Chester. It recites a part of the petition to the king, from the inhabitants of Chester, stating, "that the county palatine had been excluded from parliament, to have any knights and burgesses there; by reason whereof, the said inhabitants have hitherto sustained manifold disherisons, losses, and damages, as well in their lands, goods, and bodies, as in the good civil and politic governance and maintenance of the commonwealth of their said country; and, forasmuch as the said inhabitants have always hitherto been bound by the acts and statutes, made by your highness and progenitors in said court," (meaning when expressly named, not otherwise,) "as far forth as other counties, cities, and boroughs, which have had knights and burgesses, and yet have had neither knight nor burgess there, for the said county palatine; the said inhabitants, for lack thereof, have been oftentimes touched and grieved with acts and statutes made within the said court, as well derogatory unto the most ancient juris-dictions, liberties, and privileges of your said county palatine, as prejudicial unto the common weal, quietness, rest, and peace of your subjects, &c." For remedy whereof, two knights of the shire and two burgesses for the city are established.

I have before recited all the acts of parliament which were ever made to meddle with Chester, except the 51 Henry III. stat. 5, in 1266, which only provides that the justices of Chester and other bailiffs shall be answerable in the exchequer, for wards, escheats, and other bailiwicks; yet Chester was never severed from the crown or realm of England, nor ever expressly exempted from the authority of parliament; yet, as they had generally enjoyed an ex-emption from the exercise of the authority of parliament, we see how soon they complain of it as grievous, and claim a representation as a right; and we see how readily it was granted. America, on the contrary, is not in the realm; never was subject to the authority of parliament by any principle of law; is so far from Great Britain that she never can be represented; yet, she is to be bound in all cases whatsoever!

The first statute which appears in which Durham is named, is 27 Henry VIII. c. 24, § 21; Cuthbert, Bishop of Durham, and his successors, and their temporal chancellor of the county palatine of Durham, are made justices of the peace. The next is 31 Elizabeth, c. 9, and recites, that "Durham is, and of long time hath been, an ancient county palatine, in which the Queen's writ hath not, nor yet doth run." It enacts that a writ of proclamation upon an exigent against any person dwelling in the bishopric shall run there for the future. And § 5 confirms all the other liberties of the bishop and his officers.

And after this, we find no other mention of that bishopric in any statute until 25 Charles II. c. 9. This statute recites, "whereas, the inhabitants of the county palatine of Durham have not hitherto had the liberty and privilege of electing and sending any knights and burgesses to the high court of par-liament, although the inhabitants of the said county palatine are liable to all payments, rates, and subsidies granted by parliament, equally with the in-habitants of other counties, cities, and boroughs, in this kingdom, who have their knights and burgesses in the parliament, and are therefore concerned equally with others, the inhabitants of this kingdom, to have knights and burgesses in the said high court of parliament, of their own election, to represent the condition of their county, as the inhabitants of other counties, cities, and boroughs of this kingdom have." It enacts two knights for the county, and two burgesses for the city. Here, it should be observed, that, although they acknowledge that they had been liable to all rates, &c. granted by parliament, yet none had actually been laid upon them before this statute.

Massachusettensis then comes to the first charter of this province; and he tells us, that in it we shall find irresistible evidence, that our being a part of the empire, subject to the supreme authority of the state, bound by its laws, and subject to its protection, were the very terms and conditions by which our ancestors held their lands and settled the province. This is roundly and warmly said, but there is more zeal in it than knowledge. As to our being part of the empire, it could not be the British empire, as it is called, because that was not then in being, but was created seventy or eighty years afterwards. It must be the English empire, then; but the nation was not then polite enough to have introduced into the language of the law, or common parlance, any such phrase or idea. Rome never introduced the terms Roman empire until the tragedy of her freedom was completed. Before that, it was only the republic or the city. In the same manner, the realm, or the kingdom, or the dominions of the king, were the fashionable style in the age of the first charter. As to being subject to the supreme authority of the state, the prince who granted that charter thought it resided in himself, without any such troublesome tumults as lords and commons; and before the granting that charter, had dissolved his parliament, and determined never to call another, but to govern without. It is not very likely, then, that he intended our ancestors should be governed by parliament, or bound by its laws. As to being subject to its protection, we may guess what ideas king and parliament had of that, by the protection they actually afforded to our ancestors. Not one farthing was ever voted or given by the king or his parliament, or any one resolution taken about them. As to holding their lands, surely they did not hold their lands of lords and commons. If they agreed to hold their lands of the king, this did not subject them to English lords and commons, any more than the inhabitants of Scotland, holding their lands of the same king, subjected them. But there is not a word about the empire, the supreme authority of the state, being bound by its laws, or obliged for its protection in that whole charter. But "our charter is in the royal style." What then? Is that the parliamentary style? The style is this: "Charles, by the grace of God, King of England, Scotland, France, and Ireland, Defender of the Faith," &c. Now, in which capacity did he grant that charter; as King of France, or Ireland, or Scotland, or England? He governed England by one parliament, Scotland by another. Which parliament were we to be governed by? And Ireland by a third; and it might as well be reasoned, that America was to be governed by the Irish parliament, as by the English. But it was granted "under the great seal of England." True; but this seal runneth not out of the realm, except to mandatory writs, and when our charter was given, it was never intended to go out of the realm. The charter and the corporation were intended to abide and remain within the realm, and be like other corporations there. But this affair of the seal is a mere piece of imposition.

In Moore's Reports, in the case of the union of the realm of Scotland with England, it is resolved by the judges, that "the seal is alterable by the king at his pleasure, and he might make one seal for both kingdoms (of England and Scotland); for seals, coin, and leagues, are of absolute prerogative to the king without parliament, not restrained to any assent of the people;" and in determining how far the great seal doth command out of England, they made this distinction: "That the great seal was current for remedials, which groweth on complaint of the subject, and thereupon writs are addressed under the great seal of England; which writs are limited, their precinct to be within the places of the jurisdiction of the court that was to give the redress of the wrong. And therefore writs are not to go into Ireland, or the Isles, nor Wales, nor the counties palatine, because the king's courts here have not power to hold pleas of lands or things there. But the great seal hath a power preceptory to the person, which power extendeth to any place where the person may be found," &c. This authority plainly shows, that the great seal of England has no more authority out of the realm, except to mandatory or preceptory writs, (and surely the first charter was no preceptory writ,) than the privy seal, or the great seal of Scotland, or no seal at all. In truth, the seal and charter were intended to remain within the realm, and be of force to a corporation there; but the moment it was transferred to New England, it lost all its legal force, by the common law of England; and as this translation of it was acquiesced in by all parties, it might well be considered as good evidence of a contract between the parties, and in no other light; but not a whit the better or stronger for being under the great seal of England. But "the grants are made by the king, for his heirs and successors." What then? So the Scots held their lands of him who was then king of England, his heirs and successors, and were bound to allegiance to him, his heirs and successors; but it did not follow from thence that the Scots were subject to the English parliament. So the inhabitants of Aquitain, for ten descents, held their lands,

and were tied by allegiance to him who was king of England, his heirs and
successors, but were under no subjection to English lords and commons.

Heirs and successors of the king are supposed to be the same persons,
and are used as synonymous words in the English law. There is no positive
artificial provision made by our laws, or the British constitution, for revolutions. All our positive laws suppose that the royal office will descend to the
eldest branch of the male line, or, in default of that, to the eldest female,
&c., forever, and that the succession will not be broken. It is true that nature,
necessity, and the great principles of self-preservation, have often overruled
the succession. But this was done without any positive instruction of law.
Therefore, the grants being by the king, for his heirs and successors, and the
tenures being of the king, his heirs and successors, and the reservation being
to the king, his heirs and successors, are so far from proving that we were to
be part of an empire, as one state, subject to the supreme authority of the
English or British state, and subject to its protection, that they do not so
much as prove that we are annexed to the English crown. And all the subtilty
of the writers on the side of the ministry, has never yet proved that America
is so much as annexed to the crown, much less to the realm. "It is apparent
the king acted in his royal capacity, as king of England." This I deny. The
laws of England gave him no authority to grant any territory out of the
realm. Besides, there is no color for his thinking that he acted in that capacity,
but his using the great seal of England; but if the king is absolute in the affair
of the seal, and may make or use any seal that he pleases, his using that seal
which had been commonly used in England is no certain proof that he acted
as king of England; for it is plain he might have used the English seal in the
government of Scotland, and in that case it will not be pretended that he
would have acted in his royal capacity as king of England. But his acting as
king of England "necessarily supposes the territory granted to be a part of
the English dominions, and holden of the crown of England." Here is the
word "dominions" systematically introduced instead of the word "realm."
There was no English dominions but the realm. And I say, that America was
not any part of the English realm or dominions. And therefore, when the
king granted it, he could not act as king of England, by the laws of England.
As to the "territory being holden of the crown, there is no such thing in
nature or art." Lands are holden according to the original notices of feuds,
of the natural person of the lord. Holding lands, in feudal language, means
no more than the relation between lord and tenant. The reciprocal duties of
these are all personal. Homage, fealty, &c., and all other services, are personal
to the lord; protection, &c. is personal to the tenant. And therefore no homage, fealty, or other services, can ever be rendered to the body politic, the

political capacity, which is not corporated, but only a frame in the mind, an idea. No lands here, or in England, are held of the crown, meaning by it the political capacity; they are all held of the royal person, the natural person of the king. Holding lands, &c. of the crown, is an impropriety of expression; but it is often used; and when it is, it can have no other sensible meaning than this, that we hold lands of that person, whoever he is, who wears the crown; the law supposes he will be a right, natural heir of the present king forever.

Massachusettensis then produces a quotation from the first charter, to prove several points. It is needless to repeat the whole; but the parts chiefly relied on are italicized. It makes the company a body politic in fact and name, &c., and enables it "to sue and be sued." Then the writer asks, "whether this looks like a distinct state or independent empire?" I answer, no. And that it is plain and uncontroverted, that the first charter was intended only to erect a corporation within the realm; and the governor and company were to reside within the realm; and their general courts were to be held there. Their agents, deputies, and servants only were to come to America. And if this had taken place, nobody ever doubted but they would have been subject to parliament. But this intention was not regarded on either side; and the company came over to America, and brought their charter with them. And as soon as they arrived here, they got out of the English realm, dominions, state, empire, call it by what name you will, and out of the legal jurisdiction of parliament. The king might, by his writ or proclamation, have commanded them to return; but he did not.

Thoughts

on Government

IN LATE 1775, JOHN ADAMS ASSUMED A LEADING ROLE in the Continental Congress to encourage the thirteen colonies to begin designing and constructing new governments. The following May, Congress passed a resolution recommending to the various colonial assemblies that they establish new governments that would "best conduce to the happiness and Safety of their Constituents in particular and America in General." Considered by many as the one person who had thought most deeply about constitutional design, Adams was frequently called upon to recommend various plans of government. Just prior to the May resolution, several members of the Continental Congress approached him for advice on how to frame new constitutions for their respective states. Adams responded to their requests with his most influential writing of the Revolutionary period, *Thoughts on Government.* Adams also wrote the *Thoughts* as an antidote to the political prescriptions advanced in Thomas Paine's recently published *Common Sense.*

This short essay stands as a distillation of Adams's most advanced political thinking. The principles that he would later put forth in his great treatise, *A Defence of the Constitutions of Government of the United States of America,* are all found in *Thoughts:* republican government, frequent elections, separation of powers, bicameralism, a unitary executive armed with a strong veto power, and an independent judiciary.

The influence of *Thoughts on Government* on American constitution-makers was widespread. The historical evidence strongly suggests that *Thoughts* was used as a constitutional blueprint in North Carolina, Virginia, New Jersey, New York, and Massachusetts.

9

THOUGHTS ON GOVERNMENT:

APPLICABLE TO THE PRESENT STATE
OF THE AMERICAN COLONIES

MY DEAR SIR,—If I was equal to the task of forming a plan for the government of a colony, I should be flattered with your request, and very happy to comply with it; because, as the divine science of politics is the science of social happiness, and the blessings of society depend entirely on the constitutions of government, which are generally institutions that last for many generations, there can be no employment more agreeable to a benevolent mind than a research after the best.

Pope flattered tyrants too much when he said,

"For forms of government let fools contest,
That which is best administered is best."

Nothing can be more fallacious than this. But poets read history to collect flowers, not fruits; they attend to fanciful images, not the effects of social institutions. Nothing is more certain, from the history of nations and nature of man, than that some forms of government are better fitted for being well administered than others.

We ought to consider what is the end of government, before we determine which is the best form. Upon this point all speculative politicians will agree, that the happiness of society is the end of government, as all divines and moral philosophers will agree that the happiness of the individual is the end of man. From this principle it will follow, that the form of government which communicates ease, comfort, security, or, in one word, happiness, to the greatest number of persons, and in the greatest degree, is the best.

All sober inquirers after truth, ancient and modern, pagan and Christian, have declared that the happiness of man, as well as his dignity, consists in virtue. Confucius, Zoroaster, Socrates, Mahomet, not to mention authorities really sacred, have agreed in this.

If there is a form of government, then, whose principle and foundation is virtue, will not every sober man acknowledge it better calculated to promote the general happiness than any other form?

Fear is the foundation of most governments; but it is so sordid and brutal a passion, and renders men in whose breasts it predominates so stupid and miserable, that Americans will not be likely to approve of any political institution which is founded on it.

Honor is truly sacred, but holds a lower rank in the scale of moral excellence than virtue. Indeed, the former is but a part of the latter, and consequently has not equal pretensions to support a frame of government productive of human happiness.

The foundation of every government is some principle or passion in the minds of the people. The noblest principles and most generous affections in our nature, then, have the fairest chance to support the noblest and most generous models of government.

A man must be indifferent to the sneers of modern Englishmen, to mention in their company the names of Sidney, Harrington, Locke, Milton, Nedham, Neville, Burnet, and Hoadly. No small fortitude is necessary to confess that one has read them. The wretched condition of this country, however, for ten or fifteen years past, has frequently reminded me of their principles and reasonings. They will convince any candid mind, that there is no good government but what is republican. That the only valuable part of the British constitution is so; because the very definition of a republic is "an empire of laws, and not of men." That, as a republic is the best of governments, so that particular arrangement of the powers of society, or, in other words, that form of government which is best contrived to secure an impartial and exact execution of the laws, is the best of republics.

Of republics there is an inexhaustible variety, because the possible combinations of the powers of society are capable of innumerable variations.

As good government is an empire of laws, how shall your laws be made? In a large society, inhabiting an extensive country, it is impossible that the whole should assemble to make laws. The first necessary step, then, is to depute power from the many to a few of the most wise and good. But by what rules shall you choose your representatives? Agree upon the number and qualifications of persons who shall have the benefit of choosing, or annex this privilege to the inhabitants of a certain extent of ground.

The principal difficulty lies, and the greatest care should be employed, in constituting this representative assembly. It should be in miniature an exact portrait of the people at large. It should think, feel, reason, and act like them. That it may be the interest of this assembly to do strict justice at all times, it should be an equal representation, or, in other words, equal interests among the people should have equal interests in it. Great care should be taken to effect this, and to prevent unfair, partial, and corrupt elections. Such regulations, however, may be better made in times of greater tranquillity than the present; and they will spring up themselves naturally, when all the powers of government come to be in the hands of the people's friends. At present, it will be safest to proceed in all established modes, to which the people have been familiarized by habit.

A representation of the people in one assembly being obtained, a question arises, whether all the powers of government, legislative, executive, and judicial, shall be left in this body? I think a people cannot be long free, nor ever happy, whose government is in one assembly. My reasons for this opinion are as follow:—

1. A single assembly is liable to all the vices, follies, and frailties of an individual; subject to fits of humor, starts of passion, flights of enthusiasm, partialities, or prejudice, and consequently productive of hasty results and absurd judgments. And all these errors ought to be corrected and defects supplied by some controlling power.

2. A single assembly is apt to be avaricious, and in time will not scruple to exempt itself from burdens, which it will lay, without compunction, on its constituents.

3. A single assembly is apt to grow ambitious, and after a time will not hesitate to vote itself perpetual. This was one fault of the Long Parliament; but more remarkably of Holland, whose assembly first voted themselves from annual to septennial, then for life, and after a course of years, that all vacancies happening by death or otherwise, should be filled by themselves, without any application to constituents at all.

4. A representative assembly, although extremely well qualified, and absolutely necessary, as a branch of the legislative, is unfit to exercise the executive power, for want of two essential properties, secrecy and despatch.

5. A representative assembly is still less qualified for the judicial power, because it is too numerous, too slow, and too little skilled in the laws.

6. Because a single assembly, possessed of all the powers of government, would make arbitrary laws for their own interest, execute all laws arbitrarily for their own interest, and adjudge all controversies in their own favor.

But shall the whole power of legislation rest in one assembly? Most of the foregoing reasons apply equally to prove that the legislative power ought to be more complex; to which we may add, that if the legislative power is wholly in one assembly, and the executive in another, or in a single person, these two powers will oppose and encroach upon each other, until the contest shall end in war, and the whole power, legislative and executive, be usurped by the strongest.

The judicial power, in such case, could not mediate, or hold the balance between the two contending powers, because the legislative would undermine it. And this shows the necessity, too, of giving the executive power a negative upon the legislative, otherwise this will be continually encroaching upon that.

To avoid these dangers, let a distinct assembly be constituted, as a mediator between the two extreme branches of the legislature, that which represents the people, and that which is vested with the executive power.

Let the representative assembly then elect by ballot, from among themselves or their constituents, or both, a distinct assembly, which, for the sake of perspicuity, we will call a council. It may consist of any number you please, say twenty or thirty, and should have a free and independent exercise of its judgment, and consequently a negative voice in the legislature.

These two bodies, thus constituted, and made integral parts of the legislature, let them unite, and by joint ballot choose a governor, who, after being stripped of most of those badges of domination, called prerogatives, should have a free and independent exercise of his judgment, and be made also an integral part of the legislature. This, I know, is liable to objections; and, if you please, you may make him only president of the council, as in Connecticut. But as the governor is to be invested with the executive power, with consent of council, I think he ought to have a negative upon the legislative. If he is annually elective, as he ought to be, he will always have so much reverence and affection for the people, their representatives and counsellors, that, although you give him an independent exercise of his judgment, he will seldom use it in opposition to the two houses, except in cases the public utility of which would be conspicuous; and some such cases would happen.

In the present exigency of American affairs, when, by an act of Parliament, we are put out of the royal protection, and consequently discharged from our allegiance, and it has become necessary to assume government for our immediate security, the governor, lieutenant-governor, secretary, treasurer, commissary, attorney-general, should be chosen by joint ballot of both houses. And these and all other elections, especially of representatives and counsellors, should be annual, there not being in the whole circle of the sciences a maxim more infallible than this, "where annual elections end, there slavery begins."

These great men, in this respect, should be, once a year,

"Like bubbles on the sea of matter borne,
They rise, they break, and to that sea return."

This will teach them the great political virtues of humility, patience, and moderation, without which every man in power becomes a ravenous beast of prey.

This mode of constituting the great offices of state will answer very well for the present; but if by experiment it should be found inconvenient, the legislature may, at its leisure, devise other methods of creating them, by elections of the people at large, as in Connecticut, or it may enlarge the term for which they shall be chosen to seven years, or three years, or for life, or make any other alterations which the society shall find productive of its ease, its safety, its freedom, or, in one word, its happiness.

A rotation of all offices, as well as of representatives and counsellors, has many advocates, and is contended for with many plausible arguments. It would be attended, no doubt, with many advantages; and if the society has a sufficient number of suitable characters to supply the great number of vacancies which would be made by such a rotation, I can see no objection to it. These persons may be allowed to serve for three years, and then be excluded three years, or for any longer or shorter term.

Any seven or nine of the legislative council may be made a quorum, for doing business as a privy council, to advise the governor in the exercise of the executive branch of power, and in all acts of state.

The governor should have the command of the militia and of all your armies. The power of pardons should be with the governor and council.

Judges, justices, and all other officers, civil and military, should be nominated and appointed by the governor, with the advice and consent of council, unless you choose to have a government more popular; if you do, all officers, civil and military, may be chosen by joint ballot of both houses; or, in order to preserve the independence and importance of each house, by ballot of one house, concurred in by the other. Sheriffs should be chosen by the freeholders of counties; so should registers of deeds and clerks of counties.

All officers should have commissions, under the hand of the governor and seal of the colony.

The dignity and stability of government in all its branches, the morals of the people, and every blessing of society depend so much upon an upright and skilful administration of justice, that the judicial power ought to be distinct from both the legislative and executive, and independent upon both, that so it may be a check upon both, as both should be checks upon that. The judges, therefore, should be always men of learning and experience in

the laws, of exemplary morals, great patience, calmness, coolness, and attention. Their minds should not be distracted with jarring interests; they should
not be dependent upon any man, or body of men. To these ends, they should
hold estates for life in their offices; or, in other words, their commissions
should be during good behavior, and their salaries ascertained and established
by law. For misbehavior, the grand inquest of the colony, the house of representatives, should impeach them before the governor and council, where
they should have time and opportunity to make their defence; but, if convicted, should be removed from their offices, and subjected to such other
punishment as shall be thought proper.

A militia law, requiring all men, or with very few exceptions besides cases
of conscience, to be provided with arms and ammunition, to be trained at
certain seasons; and requiring counties, towns, or other small districts, to be
provided with public stocks of ammunition and intrenching utensils, and
with some settled plans for transporting provisions after the militia, when
marched to defend their country against sudden invasions; and requiring
certain districts to be provided with field-pieces, companies of matrosses, and
perhaps some regiments of light-horse, is always a wise institution, and, in
the present circumstances of our country, indispensable.

Laws for the liberal education of youth, especially of the lower class of
people, are so extremely wise and useful, that, to a humane and generous
mind, no expense for this purpose would be thought extravagant.

The very mention of sumptuary laws will excite a smile. Whether our
countrymen have wisdom and virtue enough to submit to them, I know not;
but the happiness of the people might be greatly promoted by them, and a
revenue saved sufficient to carry on this war forever. Frugality is a great
revenue, besides curing us of vanities, levities, and fopperies, which are real
antidotes to all great, manly, and warlike virtues.

But must not all commissions run in the name of a king? No. Why may
they not as well run thus, "The colony of   to A. B. greeting," and be
tested by the governor?

Why may not writs, instead of running in the name of the king, run
thus, "The colony of   to the sheriff," &c., and be tested by the chief
justice?

Why may not indictments conclude, "against the peace of the colony
of   and the dignity of the same?"

A constitution founded on these principles introduces knowledge among
the people, and inspires them with a conscious dignity becoming freemen; a
general emulation takes place, which causes good humor, sociability, good
manners, and good morals to be general. That elevation of sentiment inspired

by such a government, makes the common people brave and enterprising. That ambition which is inspired by it makes them sober, industrious, and frugal. You will find among them some elegance, perhaps, but more solidity; a little pleasure, but a great deal of business; some politeness, but more civility. If you compare such a country with the regions of domination, whether monarchical or aristocratical, you will fancy yourself in Arcadia or Elysium.

If the colonies should assume governments separately, they should be left entirely to their own choice of the forms; and if a continental constitution should be formed, it should be a congress, containing a fair and adequate representation of the colonies, and its authority should sacredly be confined to these cases, namely, war, trade, disputes between colony and colony, the post-office, and the unappropriated lands of the crown, as they used to be called.

These colonies, under such forms of government, and in such a union, would be unconquerable by all the monarchies of Europe.

You and I, my dear friend, have been sent into life at a time when the greatest lawgivers of antiquity would have wished to live. How few of the human race have ever enjoyed an opportunity of making an election of government, more than of air, soil, or climate, for themselves or their children! When, before the present epocha, had three millions of people full power and a fair opportunity to form and establish the wisest and happiest government that human wisdom can contrive? I hope you will avail yourself and your country of that extensive learning and indefatigable industry which you possess, to assist her in the formation of the happiest governments and the best character of a great people. For myself, I must beg you to keep my name out of sight; for this feeble attempt, if it should be known to be mine, would oblige me to apply to myself those lines of the immortal John Milton, in one of his sonnets:—

"I did but prompt the age to quit their clogs
By the known rules of ancient liberty,
When straight a barbarous noise environs me
Of owls and cuckoos, asses, apes, and dogs."

The Report of a
Constitution,
or Form of
Government,
for the
Commonwealth
of Massachusetts

JOHN ADAMS WAS ELECTED IN 1779 to a special convention to draft a constitution for Massachusetts. He was subsequently asked by the drafting committee to author a first report. The document that follows is the draft report approved and sent by the committee to the whole convention. Although a copy of Adams's original draft is not known to exist, it is generally acknowledged that the draft report sent to the convention differs from Adams's in only two respects: Article III of the Declaration of Rights, which provided tax support for religion, and Chapter VI, Section I, which protected the interests of Harvard College, were added in committee. In addition to various stylistic changes, the final document approved by the convention and ratified by the people differs from Adams's draft in just two ways: it substitutes a qualified executive veto for an absolute veto and it did not include the governor's power to appoint militia officers.

Several principles and innovations are worth noting. First, Adams's draft is remarkably democratic: the House of Representatives, Senate, and Governor were all to be elected annually. Second, with greater clarity and in greater detail than any other state constitution of that time, he organized his draft constitution around three independent and separate powers. Third, Adams provided for a true check-and-balance system. He established a tricameral legislature, with the Governor having an absolute veto.

The Massachusetts Constitution is generally regarded as the most sophisticated and influential constitution produced during the Revolutionary period. As other states began to revise their constitutions in the post-Revolutionary period, they turned to the Massachusetts model for guidance, as did the framers of the United States Constitution.

10

The Report of a Constitution, or Form of Government, for the Commonwealth of Massachusetts

Agreed upon by the Committee, — to be laid before the Convention of Delegates, assembled at Cambridge, on the first day of September, 1779; and continued by adjournment to the twenty-eighth day of October following

Preamble

THE END OF THE INSTITUTION, maintenance, and administration of government is to secure the existence of the body politic; to protect it, and to furnish the individuals who compose it with the power of enjoying, in safety and tranquillity, their natural rights and the blessings of life; and whenever these great objects are not obtained, the people have a right to alter the government, and to take measures necessary for their safety, happiness, and prosperity.

The body politic is formed by a voluntary association of individuals. It is a social compact, by which the whole people covenants with each citizen, and each citizen with the whole people, that all shall be governed by certain laws for the common good. It is the duty of the people, therefore, in framing a Constitution of Government, to provide for an equitable mode of making laws, as well as for an impartial interpretation and a faithful execution of them, that every man may, at all times, find his security in them.

We, therefore, the delegates of the people of Massachusetts, in general convention assembled, for the express and sole purpose of framing a constitution, or form of government, to be laid before our constituents, according to their instructions, acknowledging, with grateful hearts, the goodness of the great Legislator of the universe, in affording to this people, in the course of His providence, an opportunity of entering into an original, explicit, and solemn compact with each other, deliberately and peaceably, without fraud, violence, or surprise; and of forming a new constitution of civil government for themselves and their posterity; and devoutly imploring His direction in a design so interesting to them and their posterity,—do, by virtue of the authority vested in us by our constituents, agree upon the following DECLARATION OF RIGHTS, AND FRAME OF GOVERNMENT, AS THE CONSTITUTION OF THE COMMONWEALTH OF MASSACHUSETTS.

CHAPTER I

A DECLARATION OF THE RIGHTS

OF THE INHABITANTS OF THE

COMMONWEALTH OF MASSACHUSETTS

ART. I. ALL MEN ARE BORN equally free and independent, and have certain natural, essential, and unalienable rights, among which may be reckoned the right of enjoying and defending their lives and liberties; that of acquiring, possessing, and protecting their property; in fine, that of seeking and obtaining their safety and happiness.

II. It is the duty of all men in society, publicly, and at stated seasons, to worship the SUPREME BEING, the great Creator and Preserver of the universe. And no subject shall be hurt, molested, or restrained, in his person, liberty, or estate, for worshipping GOD in the manner most agreeable to the dictates of his own conscience; or, for his religious profession or sentiments; provided he doth not disturb the public peace, or obstruct others in their religious worship.

III. Good morals being necessary to the preservation of civil society; and the knowledge and belief of the being of GOD, His providential government of the world, and of a future state of rewards and punishment, being the only true foundation of morality, the legislature hath, therefore, a right, and ought to provide, at the expense of the subject, if necessary, a suitable support for the public worship of GOD, and of the teachers of religion and morals; and to enjoin upon all the subjects an attendance upon their instructions at stated times and seasons; provided there be any such teacher on whose ministry they can conscientiously and conveniently attend.

All moneys paid by the subject to the support of public worship, and of the instructors in religion and morals, shall, if he require it, be uniformly applied to the support of the teacher or teachers of his own religious denomination, if there be such whose ministry he attends upon; otherwise it may be paid to the teacher or teachers of the parish or precinct where he usually resides.

IV. The people of this commonwealth have the sole and exclusive right of governing themselves, as a free, sovereign, and independent state; and do, and forever hereafter shall, exercise and enjoy every power, jurisdiction, and right, which are not, or may not hereafter be by them expressly delegated to the United States of America, in congress assembled.

V. All power residing originally in the people, and being derived from them, the several magistrates and officers of government, vested with authority, whether legislative, executive, or judicial, are their substitutes and agents, and are at all times accountable to them.

VI. No man, nor corporation or association of men, have any other title to obtain advantages, or particular and exclusive privileges, distinct from those of the community, than what arises from the consideration of services rendered to the public; and this title, being in nature neither hereditary nor transmissible to children, or descendants, or relations by blood, the idea of a man born a magistrate, lawgiver, or judge, is absurd and unnatural.

VII. Government is instituted for the common good; for the protection, safety, prosperity, and happiness of the people; and not for the profit, honor, or private interest of any one man, family, or class of men; therefore, the people alone have an incontestable, unalienable, and indefeasible right to institute government; and to reform, alter, or totally change the same, when their protection, safety, prosperity, and happiness require it.

VIII. In order to prevent those who are vested with authority from becoming oppressors, the people have a right, at such periods and in such manner as may be delineated in their frame of government, to cause their public officers to return to private life, and to fill up vacant places by certain and regular elections.

IX. All elections ought to be free; and all the male inhabitants of this commonwealth, having sufficient qualifications, have an equal right to elect officers, and to be elected, for public employments.

X. Each individual of the society has a right to be protected by it in the enjoyment of his life, liberty, and property, according to standing laws. He is obliged, consequently, to contribute his share to the expense of this protection; and to give his personal service, or an equivalent, when necessary. But no part of the property of any individual can, with justice, be taken from him, or applied to public uses, without his own consent, or that of the representative body of the people. In fine, the people of this commonwealth are not controllable by any other laws than those to which their constitutional representative body have given their consent.

XI. Every subject of the commonwealth ought to find a certain remedy, by having recourse to the laws, for all injuries or wrongs which he may receive in his person, property, or character. He ought to obtain right and justice freely, and without being obliged to purchase it; completely, and without any denial; promptly, and without delay, conformably to the laws.

XII. No subject shall be held to answer for any crime or offence, until the same is fully and plainly, substantially and formally described to him. He cannot be compelled to accuse himself, or to furnish evidence against himself; and every subject shall have a right to be fully heard in his defence, by himself or his counsel at his election; to meet the witnesses against him face to face; to produce all proofs that may be favorable to him; to require a speedy and public trial by an impartial jury of the country, without whose unanimous consent, or his own voluntary confession, he cannot finally be declared guilty, or sentenced to loss of life, liberty, or property.

XIII. In criminal prosecutions, the verification of facts in the vicinity where they happen, is one of the greatest securities of the life, liberty, and property of the citizen.

XIV. No subject of the commonwealth shall be arrested, imprisoned, despoiled, or deprived of his property, immunities, or privileges, put out of the protection of the law, exiled, or deprived of his life, liberty, or estate, but by the judgment of his peers, or the law of the land.

XV. Every man has a right to be secure from all unreasonable searches and seizures of his person, his houses, his papers, and all his possessions. All warrants, therefore, are contrary to this right, if the cause or foundation of them be not previously supported by oath or affirmation, and if the order in the warrant to a civil officer, to make search in suspected places, or to arrest one or more suspected persons, or to seize their property, be not accompanied with a special designation of the persons or objects of search, arrest, or seizure; and no warrant ought to be issued but in cases and with the formalities prescribed by the laws.

XVI. In all controversies concerning property, and in all suits between two or more persons, the parties have a right to a trial by a jury; and this method of procedure shall be held sacred; unless in causes arising on the high seas, and such as relate to mariners' wages, the legislature shall hereafter find it necessary to alter it.

XVII. The people have a right to the freedom of speaking, writing, and publishing their sentiments. The liberty of the press, therefore, ought not to be restrained.

XVIII. The people have a right to keep and to bear arms for the common defence. And as in time of peace standing armies are dangerous to liberty, they ought not to be maintained without the consent of the legislature; and the military power shall always be held in an exact subordination to the civil authority, and be governed by it.

XIX. A frequent recurrence to the fundamental principles of the constitution, and a constant adherence to those of piety, justice, moderation, temperance, industry, and frugality, are absolutely necessary to preserve the advantages of liberty, and to maintain a free government. The people ought, consequently, to have a particular attention to all those principles, in the choice of their officers and representatives. And they have a right to require of their lawgivers and magistrates an exact and constant observance of them, in the formation and execution of the laws necessary for the good administration of the commonwealth.

XX. The people have a right, in an orderly and peaceable manner, to assemble to consult upon the common good, give instructions to their representatives, and to request of the legislative body, by the way of addresses, petitions, or remonstrances, redress of the wrongs done them, and the grievances they suffer.

XXI. The power of suspending the laws, or the execution of the laws, ought never to be exercised but by the legislature, or by authority derived from it, to be exercised in such particular cases only as the legislature shall expressly provide for; and there shall be no suspension of any law for the private interest, advantage, or emolument, of any one man, or class of men.

XXII. The freedom of deliberation, speech, and debate, in either house of the legislature, is so essential to the rights of the people, that it cannot be the foundation of any accusation or prosecution, action or complaint, in any other court or place whatsoever.

XXIII. The legislature ought frequently to assemble for the redress of grievances, for correcting, strengthening, and confirming the laws, and for making new laws as the common good may require.

XXIV. No subsidy, charge, tax, impost, or duties ought to be established, fixed, laid, or levied, under any pretext whatsoever, without the consent of the people, or their representatives in the legislature.

XXV. Laws made to punish for actions done before the existence of such laws, and which have not been declared crimes by preceding laws, are unjust, oppressive, and inconsistent with the fundamental principles of a free government.

XXVI. No man ought in any case, or in any time, to be declared guilty of treason or felony by any act of the legislature.

XXVII. No magistrate or court of law shall demand excessive bail, or sureties, impose excessive fines, or inflict cruel or unusual punishments.

XXVIII. In time of peace, no soldier ought to be quartered in any house without the consent of the owner; and in time of war, such quarters ought not to be made, but by the civil magistrate in a manner ordained by the legislature.

XXIX. No person can in any case be subjected to law martial, or to any penalties or pains by virtue of that law, except those employed in the army or navy, and except the militia in actual service, but by authority of the legislature.

XXX. It is essential to the preservation of the rights of every individual, his life, liberty, property, and character, that there be an impartial interpretation of the laws, and administration of justice. It is the right of every citizen to be tried by judges as free, impartial, and independent as the lot of humanity will admit. It is, therefore, not only the best policy, but for the security of the rights of the people and of every citizen, that the judges should hold their offices as long as they behave themselves well, and that they should have honorable salaries ascertained and established by standing laws.

XXXI. The judicial department of the state ought to be separate from, and independent of, the legislative and executive powers.

Chapter II

The Frame of Government

THE PEOPLE inhabiting the territory heretofore called the Province of Massachusetts Bay, do hereby solemnly and mutually agree with each other to form themselves into a free, sovereign, and independent body politic, or State, by the name of The Commonwealth of Massachusetts.

In the government of the Commonwealth of Massachusetts, the legislative, executive, and judicial power shall be placed in separate departments, to the end that it might be a government of laws, and not of men.

Section I

ART. I. THE DEPARTMENT of legislation shall be formed by two branches, A SENATE and HOUSE OF REPRESENTATIVES; each of which shall have a negative on the other.

They shall assemble once, on the last Wednesday in May, and at such other times as they shall judge necessary, every year, and shall be styled THE GENERAL COURT OF MASSACHUSETTS.

And the first magistrate shall have a negative upon all the laws, that he may have power to preserve the independence of the executive and judicial departments.

II. The general court shall forever have full power and authority to erect and constitute judicatories and courts of record, or other courts, to be held in the name of the commonwealth, for the hearing, trying, and determining of all manner of crimes, offences, pleas, processes, plaints, actions, matters, causes, and things, whatsoever, arising or happening within the commonwealth, or between or concerning persons inhabiting, or residing, or brought within the same; whether the same be criminal or civil, or whether the said crimes be capital or not capital, and whether the said pleas be real, personal or mixt; and for the awarding and making out of execution thereupon. To which courts and judicatories are hereby given and granted full power and authority, from time to time, to administer oaths or affirmations, for the better discovery of truth in any matter in controversy, or depending before them.

III. And further, full power and authority are hereby given and granted to the said general court, from time to time, to make, ordain, and establish all manner of wholesome and reasonable orders, laws, statutes, and ordinances, directions, and instructions, either with penalties or without; so as the same be not repugnant or contrary to this constitution, as they shall judge to be for the good and welfare of this commonwealth, and for the government and ordering thereof, and of the subjects of the same, and for the necessary support and defence of the government thereof; and to name and settle annually, or provide by fixed laws, for the naming and settling all civil officers within the said commonwealth, such officers excepted the election and constitution of whom are not hereafter in this Form of Government otherwise provided for; and to set forth the several duties, powers, and limits, of the several civil and military officers of this commonwealth, and the forms of such oaths as shall be respectively administered unto them for the execution of their several offices and places, so as the same be not repugnant or contrary to this constitution; and also to impose fines, mulcts, imprisonments, and other punishments; and to impose and levy proportional and reasonable assessments, rates, and taxes, upon the persons of all the inhabitants of, and within the said commonwealth, and upon all estates within the same, to be issued and disposed of by warrant, under the hand of the governor of this commonwealth for the time being, with the advice and consent of the council, for the public service, in the necessary defence and support of the government of the said commonwealth, and the protection and preservation of the subjects thereof, according to such acts as are or shall be in force within the same and to dispose of matters and things whereby they may be religiously, peaceably, and civilly governed, protected, and defended.

And that public assessments may be made with equality, there shall be a valuation of estates within the commonwealth taken anew once in every ten years at the least.

Section II
SENATE

I. THERE SHALL BE annually elected by the freeholders and other inhabitants of this commonwealth, qualified as in this constitution is provided, forty persons, to be counsellors and senators for the year ensuing their election, to be chosen in and by the inhabitants of the districts into which the commonwealth may from time to time be divided by the general court, for that purpose. And the general court, in assigning the numbers to be elected by the respective districts, shall govern themselves by the proportion of the public taxes paid by the said districts; and timely make known to the inhabitants of the commonwealth, the limits of each district, and the number of counsellors and senators to be chosen therein; provided that the number of such districts shall be never more than sixteen, nor less than ten.

And the several counties in this commonwealth shall, until the general court shall determine it necessary to alter said districts, be districts for the choice of counsellors and senators (except that the counties of Dukes County and Nantucket shall form one district for that purpose,) and shall elect the following number for counsellors and senators, namely,—

Suffolk	6	York	2
Essex	6	Dukes County and Nantucket	1
Middlesex	5	Worcester	5
Hampshire	4	Cumberland	1
Plymouth	3	Lincoln	1
Barnstable	1	Berkshire	2
Bristol	3		

II. The senate shall be the first branch of the legislature; and the senators shall be chosen in the following manner, namely,—There shall be a meeting on the first Monday in April, annually, forever, of the inhabitants of all the towns in the several counties of this commonwealth, to be called by the selectmen, and warned in due course of law, at least seven days before the first Monday in April, for the purpose of electing persons to be senators and counsellors. And at such meetings every male person of twenty-one years of age and upwards, resident in such towns one year next preceding the annual election of senators, having a freehold estate within the commonwealth of the annual income of three pounds, or other real or personal estate of the value of sixty pounds, shall have a right to give in his vote for the senators for the district.

The selectmen of the several towns shall preside at such meetings, and shall be under oath, as well as the town-clerk, to preside impartially, according to their best skill and judgment; and to make a just and true return.

The selectmen shall receive the votes of all the inhabitants of such towns, qualified to vote for senators, and shall sort and count them in open town meeting, and in presence of the town-clerk, who shall make a fair record, in presence of the selectmen, and in open town meeting, of the name of every person voted for, and of the number of votes against his name; and a fair copy of this record shall be attested by the selectmen and the town-clerk, and shall be sealed up, directed to the secretary of the commonwealth, for the time being, with a superscription, expressing the purport of the contents thereof, and delivered by the town-clerk of such towns to the sheriff of the county in which such town lies, thirty days at least before the last Wednesday in May, annually; or it shall be delivered into the secretary's office seventeen days at least before the said last Wednesday in May; and the sheriff of each county shall deliver all such certificates by him received into the secretary's office, seventeen days before the said last Wednesday in May.

And the inhabitants of plantations unincorporated, qualified as this constitution provides, who are or shall be empowered and required to assess taxes upon themselves toward the support of government, shall have the same privilege of voting for counsellors and senators in the plantations where they reside, as town inhabitants have in their respective towns; and the plantation meetings for that purpose shall be held annually, on the same first Monday in April, at such place in the plantations respectively, as the assessors thereof shall direct; which assessors shall have like authority for notifying the electors, collecting and returning the votes, as the selectmen and town-clerks have in their several towns by this constitution. And all other persons living in places unincorporated (qualified as aforesaid) who shall be assessed to the support of government by the assessors of an adjacent town, shall have the privilege of giving in their votes for counsellors and senators, in the town where they shall be assessed, and be notified of the place of meeting by the selectmen of the town where they shall be assessed for that purpose accordingly.

III. And that there may be a due convention of senators on the last Wednesday in May, annually, the governor, with five of the council, for the time being, shall, as soon as may be, examine the returned copies of such records; and fourteen days before the said day he shall issue his summons to such persons as shall appear to be chosen by a majority of voters, to attend on that day, and take their seats accordingly; provided, nevertheless, that, for the first year, the said returned copies shall be examined by the president and five of the council of the former constitution of government; and the said president shall, in like manner, issue his summons to the persons so elected, that they may take their seats, as aforesaid.

IV. The senate however shall be the final judge of the elections, returns, and qualifications of their own members, and shall, on the said last Wednesday in May, annually, determine and declare who are elected by each district to be senators, by a majority of votes. And, in case there shall not appear to be the full number of senators returned, elected by a majority of votes for any district, the deficiency shall be supplied in the following manner, namely:—The members of the house of representatives, and such senators as shall be declared elected, shall take the names of twice the number of senators wanting, from those who shall be found to have the highest number of votes in such district, and not elected; and out of these shall elect, by ballot, a number of senators sufficient to fill up the vacancies in such district. And in this manner all such vacancies shall be filled up in every district of the commonwealth; and in like manner all vacancies in the senate, arising by death, removal out of the state, or otherwise, shall be supplied as soon as may be after such vacancies shall happen.

V. Provided, nevertheless, that no person shall be capable of being elected as a senator, who is not of the Christian religion, and seised in his own right of a freehold within this commonwealth, of the value of three hundred pounds at least, and who has not been an inhabitant of this commonwealth for the space of seven years, three of which immediately preceding his election, and in the district for which he shall be chosen.

VI. The senate shall have power to adjourn themselves, provided such adjournments do not exceed two days at a time.

VII. The senate shall choose its own president, appoint its own officers, and determine its own rules of proceedings.

VIII. The senate shall be a court, with full authority to hear and determine all impeachments made by the house of representatives, against any officer or officers of the commonwealth, for misconduct and maladministration in their offices. But previous to the trial of every impeachment, the members of the senate shall respectively be sworn, truly and impartially to try and determine the charge in question, according to evidence. Their judgment, however, shall not extend farther than to removal from office, and disqualification to hold or enjoy any place of honor, trust, or profit under this commonwealth. But the party so convicted shall be, nevertheless, liable to indictment, trial, judgment, and punishment, according to the laws of the land.

Section III
HOUSE OF REPRESENTATIVES

I. THERE SHALL BE in the legislature of this commonwealth a representation of the people annually elected, and founded in equality.

II. And, in order to provide for a representation of the citizens of this commonwealth, founded upon the principle of equality, every corporate town, containing one hundred and fifty ratable polls, may elect one representative. Every corporate town, containing three hundred and seventy-five ratable polls, may elect two representatives. Every corporate town, containing six hundred ratable polls, may elect three representatives; and proceeding in that manner, making two hundred and twenty-five ratable polls the mean increasing number for every additional representative.

And forever, hereafter, the least number of ratable polls necessary to entitle a corporate town to elect one representative, when increased by the addition of a number equal to half the said least number, shall be the mean increasing number of ratable polls for every additional representative any corporate town may elect.

And, to prevent hereafter the house of representatives from becoming unwieldy, and incapable of debating and deliberating, by the great additions it would continually receive from the increasing settlement and population of this commonwealth, no corporate town shall, from and after the year of our Lord, one thousand seven hundred and ninety, be entitled to elect one representative, unless it shall contain two hundred ratable polls; nor to elect two representatives, unless it shall contain five hundred ratable polls; nor to elect three representatives, unless it shall contain eight hundred ratable polls; and so proceeding in that manner, making, by the aforesaid rule, three hundred ratable polls the mean increasing number for every additional representative. And every tenth year, from and after the said year of our Lord, one thousand seven hundred and ninety, and until such time as the number of representatives which may be elected for this commonwealth shall not exceed the number of two hundred, the least number of ratable polls which, at that time, any corporate town must contain to entitle it to elect one representative, shall be increased by the addition of fifty; and the least number aforesaid, thus increased by the said addition, shall be the number of ratable polls any corporate town must contain to entitle it to elect one representative; and the number of representatives any corporate town may elect shall be regulated accordingly, by the rules aforesaid.

The freeholders and other inhabitants of this commonwealth, qualified to vote for representatives, living in corporate towns, which, severally, shall contain a less number of ratable polls than is necessary to entitle them, respectively, to elect one representative, shall, nevertheless, have a right to associate with some town or towns adjoining, for the election of representatives; and, in such cases, the voters thus united, shall have a right to elect the same number of representatives as they would have done were they inhabitants of one corporate town; which representatives may be elected out of either of the associated towns, indifferently. And the legislature shall, from time to time, determine what towns shall thus associate, the manner of the association, and the method and manner of calling and conducting the meetings of the associated towns for the election of representatives.

III. The members of the house of representatives shall be chosen by written votes; and no person shall be qualified or eligible to be a member of the said house, unless he be of the Christian religion, and, for one year at least, next preceding his election, shall have been an inhabitant of, and have been seised in his own right of a freehold of the value of one hundred pounds, within the town or towns he shall be chosen to represent; and he shall cease to represent the said town or towns immediately on his ceasing to be a freeholder within the same.

IV. Every male person, being twenty-one years of age, and resident in any particular town in this commonwealth for the space of one year next preceding, having a freehold estate within the same town, of the annual income of three pounds, or other estate real or personal or mixt of the value of sixty pounds, shall have a right to vote in the choice of a representative or representatives for the said town, or for the towns united as aforesaid.

V. The members of the house of representatives shall be chosen annually in the month of May, ten days at least before the last Wednesday of that month, from among the wisest, most prudent, and virtuous of the freeholders.

VI. The house of representatives shall be the grand inquest of this commonwealth; and all impeachments made by them shall be heard and tried by the senate.

VII. All money-bills shall originate in the house of representatives; but the senate may propose or concur with amendments, as on other bills.

VIII. The house of representatives shall have power to adjourn themselves; provided such adjournment shall not exceed two days at a time.

IX. Not less than sixty members of the house of representatives shall constitute a quorum for doing business.

X. The house of representatives shall choose their own speaker, appoint their own officers, and settle the rules and orders of proceeding in their own house. They shall have authority to punish, by imprisonment, every person who shall be guilty of disrespect to the house, in its presence, by any disorderly or contemptuous behavior; or by threatening or ill-treating any of its members; or, in a word, by obstructing its deliberations; every person guilty of a breach of its privileges, in making arrests for debts, or by assaulting one of its members during his attendance at any session, or on the road, whether he be going to the house or returning home; in assaulting any one of its officers, or in disturbing him in the execution of any order or procedure of the house; in assaulting or troubling any witness or other person ordered to attend the house, in his way in going or returning, or in rescuing any person arrested by order of the house.

XI. The senate shall have the same powers in the like cases; and the governor and council shall have the same authority to punish in like cases. Provided, that no imprisonment on the warrant or order of the governor, council, senate, or house of representatives, for either of the above described offences, be for a term exceeding thirty days.

CHAPTER III

EXECUTIVE POWER

Section I
GOVERNOR

ART. I. THERE SHALL BE a supreme executive magistrate, who shall be styled, THE GOVERNOR OF THE COMMONWEALTH OF MASSACHUSETTS, and whose title shall be, HIS EXCELLENCY.

II. The governor shall be chosen annually; and no person shall be eligible to this office unless, at the time of his election, he shall have been an inhabitant of this commonwealth for seven years next preceding; and unless he shall at the same time be seised in his own right of a freehold within the commonwealth, of the value of one thousand pounds; and unless he shall be of the Christian religion.

III. Those persons who shall be qualified to vote for senators and representatives within the several towns of this commonwealth, shall, at a meeting to be called for that purpose, on the first Monday of April annually, give in their votes for a governor, to the selectmen, who shall preside at such meetings; and the town clerk, in the presence and with the assistance of the selectmen, shall in open town meeting sort and count the votes, and form a list of the persons voted for, with the number of votes for each person against his name, and shall make a fair record of the same in the town books, and a public declaration thereof in the said meeting; and shall, in the presence of the inhabitants, seal up copies of the said list, attested by him and the selectmen, and transmit the same to the sheriff of the county, thirty days at least before the last Wednesday in May; or shall cause returns of the same to be made to the office of the secretary of the commonwealth, seventeen days at least before the said day, who shall lay the same before the senate and the house of representatives, on the last Wednesday in May, to be by them examined; and, in case of an election by a majority of votes through the commonwealth, the choice shall be by them declared and published. But if no person shall have a majority of votes, the house of representatives shall, by ballot, elect two out of four persons who had the highest number of votes, if so many shall have been voted for, but if otherwise, out of the number voted for; and make return to the senate of the two persons so elected, on which the senate shall proceed, by ballot, to elect one, who shall be declared governor.

IV. The person chosen governor, and accepting the trust, shall, in the presence of the two houses, and before he proceed to execute the duties of his office, make and subscribe the following declaration, and take the following oaths, to be administered by the president of the senate, namely,—

I, A B, being declared duly elected governor of the commonwealth of Massachusetts, do now declare, that I believe and profess the Christian religion, from a firm persuasion of its truth; and that I am seised and possessed, in my own right, of the property required by law, as one qualification for that office.

I, A B, do solemnly swear, that I bear faith and true allegiance to the commonwealth of Massachusetts; that I will faithfully and impartially discharge and perform all the duties incumbent on me, as a governor of this commonwealth, according to the best of my abilities and understanding, agreeably to the rules and regulations of the constitution, and that I will not attempt or consent to a violation thereof. So help me God.

v. The governor shall have authority, from time to time, at his discretion, to assemble and call together the counsellors of this commonwealth, for the time being; and the governor, with the said counsellors, or five of them at least, shall and may, from time to time, hold and keep a council for the ordering and directing the affairs of the commonwealth according to law.

vi. The governor, with advice of council, shall have full power and authority, in the recess of the general court, to prorogue the same from time to time, not exceeding ninety days in any one recess of the said court; and during the session of the said court, to adjourn or prorogue it to any time the two houses shall desire, and to dissolve the same, at their request, or on the Wednesday next preceding the last Wednesday in May; and to call it together sooner than the time to which it may be adjourned or prorogued, if the welfare of the commonwealth shall require the same.

vii. In cases of disagreement between the two houses, with regard to the time of adjournment or prorogation, the governor, with advice of the council, shall have a right to adjourn or prorogue the general court, as he shall determine the public good shall require.

viii. The governor of this commonwealth, for the time being, shall be the commander-in-chief of the army and navy, and of all the military forces of the state by sea and land; and shall have full power, by himself or by any chief commander, or other officer or officers, to be appointed by him, from time to time to train, instruct, exercise, and govern the militia and navy; and for the special defence and safety of the commonwealth, to assemble in martial array and put in warlike posture, the inhabitants thereof; and to lead and conduct them, and with them to encounter, expulse, repel, resist, and pursue, by force of arms, as well by sea as by land, within or without the limits of this commonwealth, and also to kill, slay, destroy, and conquer, by all fitting ways, enterprises, and means whatsoever, all and every such person and persons as shall at any time hereafter, in a hostile manner, attempt or enterprise the destruction, invasion, detriment, or annoyance of this commonwealth; and to use and exercise over the army and navy, and over the militia in actual service, the law martial in time of war, invasion, or rebellion, as occasion shall necessarily require; and also from time to time to erect forts, and to fortify any place or places within the said commonwealth, and the same to furnish with all necessary ammunition, provisions, and stores of war, for offence or defence, and to commit from time to time the custody and government of the same to such person or persons as to him shall seem meet;

and in times of emergency the said forts and fortifications to demolish at his discretion; and to take and surprise, by all ways and means whatsoever, all and every such person or persons, with their ships, arms, ammunition, and other goods, as shall in a hostile manner invade, or attempt the invading, conquering, or annoying this commonwealth, and in fine that the governor be intrusted with all other powers, incident to the offices of captain-general and commander-in-chief and admiral, to be exercised agreeably to the rules and regulations of the constitution and the laws of the land.

Provided, that the said governor shall not at any time hereafter, by virtue of any power by this constitution granted, or hereafter to be granted to him by the legislature, transport any of the inhabitants of this commonwealth, or oblige them to march, out of the limits of the same, without their free and voluntary consent, or the consent of the general court, nor grant commissions for exercising the law martial upon any of the inhabitants of this commonwealth without the advice and consent of the council of the same.

IX. The power of pardoning offences, except such as persons may be convicted of before the senate by an impeachment of the house, shall be in the governor, by and with the advice of council. But no charter of pardon granted by the governor, with advice of the council, before conviction, shall avail the party pleading the same, notwithstanding any general or particular expressions contained therein, descriptive of the offence or offences intended to be pardoned.

X. All judicial officers, the attorney-general, the solicitor-general, all sheriffs, coroners, registers of probate, and registers of maritime courts, shall be nominated and appointed by the governor, by and with the advice and consent of the council; and every such nomination shall be made by the governor, and made at least seven days prior to such appointment.

XI. All officers of the militia shall be appointed by the governor, with the advice and consent of the council; he first nominating them seven days at least before the appointment.

XII. All moneys shall be issued out of the treasury of this commonwealth, and disposed of by warrant, under the hand of the governor for the time being, with the advice and consent of the council, for the necessary defence and support of the commonwealth; and for the protection and preservation of the inhabitants thereof, agreeably to the acts and resolves of the general court.

XIII. All public boards, the commissary-general, all superintending officers of public magazines and stores, belonging to this commonwealth, and all commanding officers of forts and garrisons within the same, shall, once in every three months officially, and without requisition, and at other times, when required by the governor, deliver to him an account of all goods, stores, provisions, ammunition, cannon with their appendages, and small arms with their accoutrements, and of all other public property whatever under their care respectively; distinguishing the quantity, number, quality, and kind of each, as particularly as may be; together with the condition of such forts and garrisons. And the said commanding officers shall exhibit to the governor, when required by him, true and exact plans of such forts, and of the land and sea, or harbor or harbors, adjacent.

And the said boards, and all public officers, shall communicate to the governor, as soon as may be after receiving the same, all letters, despatches, and intelligences, of a public nature, which shall be directed to them respectively.

XIV. And to prevent an undue influence in this commonwealth, which the first magistrate thereof may acquire, by the long possession of the important powers and trusts of that office; as also to stimulate others to qualify themselves for the service of the public in the highest stations, no man shall be eligible as governor of this commonwealth, more than five years in any seven years.

XV. As the public good requires that the governor should not be under the undue influence of any of the members of the general court, by a dependence on them for his support; that he should, in all cases, act with freedom for the benefit of the public; that he should not have his attention necessarily diverted from that object to his private concerns; and that he should maintain the dignity of the commonwealth, in the character of its chief magistrate, it is necessary that he should have an honorable stated salary, of a fixed and permanent value, amply sufficient for those purposes, and established by standing laws; and it shall be among the first acts of the general court, after the commencement of this constitution, to establish such salary by law accordingly.

Permanent and honorable salaries shall also be established by law for the justices of the superior court.

And if it shall be found that any of the salaries aforesaid, so established, are insufficient, they shall from time to time be enlarged, as the general court shall judge proper.

Section II

LIEUTENANT-GOVERNOR, AND THE ASCERTAINING THE VALUE OF THE MONEY MENTIONED IN THIS CONSTITUTION, AS QUALIFICATIONS TO OFFICE, &C.

I. THERE SHALL BE annually elected a lieutenant-governor of the Commonwealth of Massachusetts, whose title shall be HIS HONOR, and who shall be qualified, in point of religion, property, and residence in the commonwealth, in the same manner with the governor. He shall be chosen on the same day, in the same manner, and by the same persons. The return of the votes for this officer, and the declaration of his election shall be in the same manner. And if no one person shall be found to have a majority of votes, the vacancy shall be filled by the senate and house of representatives, in the same manner as the governor is to be elected, in case no one person has a majority of votes to be governor.

II. The lieutenant-governor shall always be, ex-officio, a member, and, in the absence of the governor, president, of the council.

III. Whenever the chair of the governor shall be vacant, by reason of his death, or absence from the commonwealth, or otherwise, the lieutenant-governor, for the time being, shall, during such vacancy, have and exercise all the powers and authorities which, by this constitution, the governor is vested with, when personally present.

IV. "The respective values assigned by the several articles of this constitution to the property necessary to qualify the subjects of this commonwealth to be electors, and also to be elected into the several offices, for the holding of which such qualifications are required, shall always be computed in silver, at the rate of six shillings and eight pence per ounce."

V. And it shall be in the power of the legislature, from time to time, to increase such qualifications, of the persons to be elected to offices, as the circumstances of the commonwealth shall require.

Section III

COUNCIL, AND THE MANNER OF SETTLING ELECTIONS BY THE LEGISLATURE; OATHS TO BE TAKEN, &C.

I. THERE SHALL BE a council for advising the governor in the executive part of government, to consist of nine persons besides the lieutenant-governor, whom the governor, for the time being, shall have full power and authority, from time to time, at his discretion, to assemble and call together. And the governor, with the said counsellors, or five of them at least, shall and may, from time to time, hold and keep a council, for the ordering and directing the affairs of the commonwealth, according to the laws of the land.

II. Nine counsellors shall out of the persons returned for counsellors and senators, be annually chosen, on the last Wednesday in May, by the joint ballot of the senators and representatives assembled in one room. The seats of the persons thus elected into the council and accepting the trust, shall be vacated in the senate, and, in this manner, the number of senators shall be reduced to thirty-one.

III. The counsellors, in the civil arrangements of the commonwealth, shall have rank next after the lieutenant-governor.

IV. Not more than two counsellors shall be chosen out of any one county of this commonwealth.

V. The resolutions and advice of the council shall be recorded in a register, and signed by the members present; and this record may be called for at any time by either house of the legislature; and any member of the council may insert his opinion contrary to the resolution of the majority.

VI. Whenever the office of the governor and lieutenant-governor shall be vacant, by reason of death, absence, or otherwise, then the council, or the major part of them, shall, during such vacancy, have full power and authority to do and execute all and every such acts, matters, and things, as the governor or the lieutenant-governor might or could, by virtue of this constitution, do or execute, if they, or either of them, were personally present.

VII. And whereas, the elections appointed to be made by this constitution, on the last Wednesday in May, annually, by the two houses of the legislature, may not be completed on that day, the said elections may be adjourned from day to day, until the same shall be completed. And the order of elections shall be as follows,—the vacancies in the senate, if any, shall first be filled up; the governor and lieutenant-governor shall then be elected, provided there should be no choice of them by the people; and afterwards the two houses shall proceed to the election of the council.

The lieutenant-governor, counsellors, senators, and members of the house of representatives shall, before they enter on the execution of their respective offices, make and subscribe the same declaration, and take the same oath, (*mutatis mutandis,*) which the governor is directed by this constitution to make, subscribe, and take.

And every person appointed to any civil or military office of this commonwealth shall, previous to his entering on the execution of his office, make and subscribe the following declaration, (*mutatis mutandis,*) namely,—

I, A B, being appointed   do now declare, that I believe and profess the Christian religion, from a firm persuasion of the truth thereof.

And he shall likewise take an oath of the form following, (*mutatis mutandis,*) namely,—

I, A B, do solemnly swear, that I will bear faith and true allegiance to the commonwealth of Massachusetts; that I will faithfully and impartially discharge and perform all the duties incumbent on me, as   according to the best of my abilities and understanding, agreeably to the rules and regulations of the constitution; and that I will not attempt or consent to a violation thereof. So help me God.

Provided, notwithstanding, that any person so appointed, who has conscientious scruples relative to taking oaths, may be admitted to make solemn affirmation, under the pains and penalties of perjury, to the truth of the matters contained in the form of the said oath, instead of taking the same.

Section IV
SECRETARY, TREASURER, COMMISSARY, &c.

I. THE SECRETARY, treasurer, and receiver-general, and the commissary-general, notaries-public, and naval officers shall be chosen annually, by joint ballot of the senators and representatives, in one room. And that the citizens of this commonwealth may be assured, from time to time, that the moneys remaining in the public treasury, upon the settlement and liquidation of the public accounts, are their property, no man shall be eligible as treasurer and receiver-general more than five years successively.

II. The records of the commonwealth shall be kept in the office of the secretary, who shall attend the governor and council, the senate, and house of representatives in person, or by his deputies, as they shall respectively require.

Chapter IV

Judiciary Power

Art. i. The tenure, that all commission officers by law hold in their offices, shall be expressed in their respective commissions. All judicial officers, duly appointed, commissioned, and sworn, shall hold their offices during good behavior provided, nevertheless, the governor, with consent of the council, may remove them upon the address of both houses of the legislature. And all other officers, appointed by the governor and council, shall hold their offices during pleasure.

ii. No justice of the superior court of judicature, court of assize, and general jail delivery, shall have a seat in the senate or house of representatives.

iii. The senate, nevertheless, as well as the governor and council, shall have authority to require the opinions of the judges upon important questions of law, and upon solemn occasions.

iv. In order that the people may not suffer from the long continuance in place of any justice of the peace, who shall fail of discharging the important duties of his office with ability or fidelity, all commissions of justices of the peace shall expire and become void, in the term of seven years from their respective dates; and, upon the expiration of any commission, the governor and council may, if necessary, renew such commissions, or appoint another person, as shall most conduce to the well-being of the commonwealth.

v. The judges of probate of wills and for granting letters of administration, shall hold their courts at such place or places, on fixed days, as the convenience of the people shall require. And the legislature shall, from time to time, hereafter, appoint such times and places; until which appointments, the said courts shall be holden at the times and places which the respective judges shall direct.

vi. All causes of marriage, divorce, and alimony, shall be determined by the senate; and all appeals from the judges of probate shall be heard and determined by the governor and council, until the legislature shall, by law, make other provision.

Chapter v

Delegates to Congress, Commissions, Writs, Indictments, &c.; Confirmation of Laws, Habeas Corpus, and enacting Style

ART. I. THE DELEGATES of this commonwealth to the Congress of the United States of America, shall, on the second Wednesday of November, if the general court be then sitting, or on the second Wednesday of the session next after, be elected annually, by the joint ballot of the senate and house of representatives, assembled together in one room. They shall have commissions under the hand of the governor, and under the great seal of the commonwealth; but may be recalled at any time within the year, and others chosen and commissioned, in the same manner in their stead.

II. All commissions shall be in the name of the commonwealth of Massachusetts, signed by the governor, and attested by the secretary or his deputy, and have the great seal of the commonwealth affixed thereto.

III. All writs issuing out of the clerk's office in any of the courts of law, shall be in the name of the commonwealth of Massachusetts. They shall be under the seal of the court from whence they issue. They shall bear test of the chief justice, or first or senior justice of the court, to which they shall be returnable, and be signed by the clerk of such court.

IV. All indictments, presentments, and informations, shall conclude, "against the peace of the Commonwealth and the dignity of the same."

V. All the statute laws of the province, colony, or state of Massachusetts Bay, the common law, and all such parts of the English or British statutes as have been adopted, used, and approved in the said province, colony, or state, and usually practised on in the courts of law, shall still remain and be in full force, until altered or repealed by the legislature; such parts only excepted as are repugnant to the rights and liberties contained in this constitution.

VI. The privilege and benefit of the writ of *habeas corpus* shall be enjoyed in this commonwealth in the most free, easy, cheap, expeditious, and ample manner; and shall not be suspended by the legislature, except upon the most urgent and pressing occasions, and for a short and limited time.

VII. The enacting style, in making and passing all acts, statutes, and laws, shall be: "Be it enacted, by his excellency the governor, the senate, and house of representatives, in general court assembled, and by the authority of the same;" or "By his honor the lieutenant-governor," &c.; or "The honorable the council," &c., as the case may be.

Chapter VI

The University at Cambridge, and Encouragement of Literature, &c.

Section I
The University

Art. I. Whereas our wise and pious ancestors, so early as the year one thousand six hundred and thirty-six, laid the foundation of Harvard College, in which university many persons of great eminence have by the blessing of God been initiated in those arts and sciences which qualified them for public employments, both in church and state. And whereas the encouragement of arts and sciences, and all good literature, tends to the honor of God, the advantage of the Christian religion, and the great benefit of this and the other United States of America,—it is declared, That the President and Fellows of Harvard College, in their corporate capacity, and their successors in that capacity, their officers and servants, shall have, hold, use, exercise, and enjoy, all the powers, authorities, rights, liberties, privileges, immunities, and franchises, which they now have, or are entitled to have, hold, use, exercise, and enjoy; and the same are hereby ratified and confirmed unto them, the said President and Fellows of Harvard College, and to their successors, and to their officers and servants, respectively, forever.

II. And whereas there have been at sundry times, by divers persons, gifts, grants, devises, of houses, lands, tenements, goods, chattels, legacies, and conveyances, heretofore made, either to Harvard College, in Cambridge, in New England, or to the President and Fellows of Harvard College, or to the said College, by some other description, under several charters successively;—It Is Declared, That all the said gifts, grants, devises, legacies, and conveyances, are hereby forever confirmed unto the President and Fellows of Harvard College, and to their successors, in the capacity aforesaid, according to the true intent and meaning of the donor or donors, grantor or grantors, devisor or devisors.

III. And whereas, by an act of the general court of the colony of Massachusetts Bay, passed in the year one thousand six hundred and forty-two, the governor and deputy governor for the time being, and all the magistrates of that jurisdiction, were, with the president, and a number of the clergy, in the said act described, constituted the overseers of Harvard College. And it being necessary, in this new constitution of government, to ascertain who shall be deemed successors to the said governor, deputy-governor, and magistrates;—IT IS DECLARED, That the Governor, Lieutenant-Governor, Council, and Senate of this Commonwealth, are, and shall be deemed, their successors; who, with the President of Harvard College for the time being, together with the Ministers of the Congregational Churches in the towns of Cambridge, Watertown, Charlestown, Boston, Roxbury, and Dorchester, mentioned in the said act, shall be and hereby are, vested with all the powers and authority belonging, or in any way appertaining to the overseers of Harvard College. PROVIDED, that nothing herein shall be construed to prevent the legislature of this commonwealth from making such alterations in the government of the said university as shall be conducive to its advantage, and the interest of the republic of letters, in as full a manner as might have been done by the legislature of the   province of the Massachusetts Bay.

Section II

THE ENCOURAGEMENT OF LITERATURE, &C.

WISDOM AND KNOWLEDGE, as well as virtue, diffused generally among the body of the people, being necessary for the preservation of their rights and liberties, and as these depend on spreading the opportunities and advantages of education in the various parts of the country, and among the different orders of the people, it shall be the duty of legislators and magistrates, in all future periods of this commonwealth, to cherish the interests of literature and the sciences, and all seminaries of them; especially the university at Cambridge, public schools and grammar schools in the towns; to encourage private societies and public institutions, rewards and immunities for the promotion of agriculture, arts, sciences, commerce, trades, manufactures, and a natural history of the country; to countenance and inculcate the principles of humanity and general benevolence, public and private charity, industry and frugality, honesty and punctuality in their dealings, sincerity, good humor, and all social affections and generous sentiments among the people.

Chapter VII and Last

Continuance of Officers, &c.

IX. To the end there may be no failure of justice, or danger arise to the commonwealth from a change of the form of government, all officers, civil and military, holding commissions under the government and people of Massachusetts Bay in New England, and all other officers of the said government and people, at the time this constitution shall take effect, shall have, hold, use, exercise, and enjoy all the powers and authority to them granted or committed, until other persons shall be appointed in their stead. And all courts of law shall proceed in the execution of the business of their respective departments; and all the executive and legislative officers, bodies, and powers, shall continue in full force, in the enjoyment and exercise of all their trusts, employments, and authority, until the general court, and the supreme and executive officers, under this constitution, are designated, and invested with their respective trusts, powers, and authority.

INDEX

Index

Richard II, 100

rights (*see also* liberty): to assemble, 133, 301; to be governed by laws one consents to, 56, 125, 126, 136, 140–41, 143, 144–45, 227; under British law, 31–32, 33; clergy's role in explaining, 185; of colonies, 31–32, 130, 136–37, 223–24, 225–27, 228–29, 240; in Constitution for Massachusetts, 298–303; under contract with king, 126, 241; defined, 22; and education, 320–21; of emigrants to establish governments, 238–39; English liberties, defined, 240; of English subjects in colonies, 121, 126–28, 237–39; and independent judiciary, 82; liberty as, 28, 33; and Magna Carta, 31, 46; of Native Americans, 121, 135; of people to revoke authority of government, 28; to petition the king, 189; property rights, 40, 55, 119, 218, 300–301; searches and seizures, 300–301; to taxation by elected representatives, 157; to trial by jury, 46, 55, 300, 301; to vote for representatives, 55, 125, 126, 140–41

Robertson, William, 218

Roman Catholic Church: as authority over the whole earth, 240–41; colonists' attitude toward, 167; controlling the population, 22; and feudal system, 134; power of, 22

Rome, 63, 223, 224–25, 281

Rousseau, Jean-Jacques, 26

Rush, Benjamin, ix, xii

Rushworth, John, 94

Sacheverell, Henry, 208

Sandys, Sir Edwin, 136

Scotland, 255, 256, 282

Scott, William, Baron Stowell, 272–73

sedition, 205–6

self-defense, 12–13, 15

self-delusion, 7–12

senate of Massachusetts, 304–8, 310

Sentiments of a British American (Thacher), 243–44

Servius Tullius, 137

Shakespeare, William, 32

Shirley, Governor William, 155–57

Sidney, Algernon, 206–7

Smollett, Tobias, 66

smuggling, 211, 226

St. John, Henry, 1st Viscount Bolingbroke, 66

Stamp Act: and authority of Parliament, 243; effects of, 34–35, 39–40; effects of expressing opinions on, 183; as excessive taxation, 179; John Adams's views on, xi; reaction of colonies, 180–81, 243–44; resistance to, 167–68; as unconstitutional, 39, 41

statesmen, motives of, 11

Stowell. *See* Scott, William, Baron Stowell

sumptuary laws, 292

Tacitus, Gaius Cornelius, 63

taxation (*see also* Stamp Act; Tea Act): authority of Parliament, 39–40, 41, 179–81, 209; and Boston Tea Party, 212; and colonial charters, 130, 228–29, 234; of colonies by Parliament, 155, 156, 158–59, 161, 210; colonies paying excessive taxes, 178; and consent of the people, 40, 46, 47, 179, 244; in Constitution for Massachusetts, 306; by England prior to Stamp Act, 177; illegal taxes, 213; import/export costs as, 156–57, 178, 244; of imports, 168, 209, 244; and the junto, 155, 157–60, 191; opinions in England, 170; power of colonial legislatures, 123, 129; power of the Crown, 123; reaction to Parliament's taxes, 168–69, 243–44; of residents of colonies, 138; uses of taxes, 161, 178–79; wars supported by, 177–78

tea, 168, 175, 204, 209–10

Tea Act, 183, 193, 243

Thacher, Oxenbridge, 244

Thayer, Ebenezer, 39

Thoughts on Government (Adams), xii

Tillotson, John, 21

Tories: committee of correspondence, 216–17; goals of, 169; on grand juries, 199;

330

The text of this book is set in 11-point Adobe Garamond, a modern adaptation of the typeface originally cut around 1540 by the French typographer and printer Claude Garamond (d. 1561). Garamond, with its small lowercase height and restrained contrast between thick and thin strokes, is a classic "old-style" face, and has been one of the most influential and widely used typefaces since its creation.

This book is printed on paper that is acid-free and meets the requirements of the American National Standard for Permanence of Paper for Printed Library Materials, z39.48-1992. ∞

Book design by Martin Lubin Graphic Design,
    Jackson Heights, New York
Typography by Impressions Book and Journal Services, Inc.,
    Madison, Wisconsin
Printed and bound by Edwards Brothers, Inc.,
    Ann Arbor, Michigan